INSIGHT GUIDES

Canada

Photography by Joe Viesti
Edited by Hilary Cunningham
Updated by Jane L. Thompson

APA
PUBLICATIONS

Canada

Second Edition (Reprint)
© 1990 APA PUBLICATIONS (HK) LTD
All Rights Reserved
Printed in Singapore by Höfer Press Pte. Ltd

ABOUT THIS BOOK

The former prime minister of Canada, Pierre Trudeau, once observed that for his country, sharing the North American continent with the United States was something like an individual sharing a bed with an elephant. While it is the second largest country in the world in area, Canada has about the same population as the state of California. The Winter Olympics of 1988 showed the world the mountainous west just as the Summer Olympics of 1976 displayed the sophistication of the east and in particular francophone Montreal. Between those parameters there is much more to Canada. For the intrepid traveler there is a vast northern landscape populated by natives whose lifestyle is shared only by other tribes around the North Pole.

Insight Guide: Canada covers this immense subject as other *Insight Guides* have explored every other continent, with a mixture of sound, well-written history, current journalism and exciting photographs. This unique formula in travel publishing was conceived by **Hans Höfer**, founder of Apa Productions. His first book, *Insight Guide: Bali*, printed in 1970, won worldwide recognition and commercial success as a new departure in the world of travel literature. Born and educated in West Germany, Höfer is a follower of the Bauhaus tradition that combines training in the disciplines of printing, production and photography that are exemplified by the *Insight Guide* series.

To assemble the best available Canadian writers and photographers, Apa designated as project editor, **Hilary Cunningham**, a native of Toronto and graduate of the University of Toronto who did her graduate studies in urban and political anthropology in the United States, finishing at Yale University. The final product of this *Insight Guide* is the coordinated effort of several photographers and a dozen writers. While the images of many photographers capture the diversity of the Canadian landscape, **Joe Viesti** is the main contributor to the guide. Viesti, who is based in New York City, has combined his profession, photography, with his love of travel and his fascination with other cultures. With his wife, **Diane Hall**, Viesti traveled Canada from one coast to the other, taking pictures while Hall wrote her impressions of the Maritime Provinces. Viesti's work has previously been in the *Insight Guides* to Florida, Southern California, the American South-east, New England, the Rockies, India, Italy, Ireland and Texas. He has shot for the National Geographic Society publications such as *Geo, Stern* and *Pacific*. In 1984 his remarkable collection was used for the UNICEF Engagement Calendar. The collection has since been exhibited at over 40 museums and galleries throughout North America. Hall has traveled to England, Guatemala, Spain, the Philippines and Melanesia. She penned the text for the 1984 UNICEF Engagement Calendar and wrote the Northern Route in *Insight Guide: Crossing America*.

Tony Byrne, a Wisconsin native assembled the Travel Tips for this book – a formidable task given the size of the nation. The University of Toronto graduate has traveled extensively in the USA, Ontario and France.

The writer of the Prairie section is **David Dunbar** whose published works include contributions to *Outdoors Canada, Atlas of Canada, Heritage of Canada* and *Walking Tours of New England*. Dunbar's travel history includes a study of archaeology in Greece and Egypt as well as trips to France, Ger-

Cunningham

Viesti

Hall

Byrne

Dunbar

many, Italy, Austria and the United States. As a writer and editor, Dunbar has worked on assignments for the Reader's Digest Book Department. Assignments took him often to Alberta, where his parents now live. Canada's Texas "never fails to surprise" him with its diversity of landscape.

A prolific writer of fiction, **Charles Foran** spent months in Québec as an anglophone. He has had his work published 'in several Canadian journals including *Waves, Canadian Fiction Magazine and Rubicon*.

The progeny of a small rural Ontario town, **Patrick Keyes** lends a unique perspective to the Canada guide. Full of compassionate understanding for Canada's often neglected and marginalized groups, Keyes contributes a sensitive account of the Inuit and Canada's two northern regions. Keyes has a degree in political economy.

Accomplishments are as natural to the young writer of the Toronto feature as the maple leaf is to Canada. **Mark Kingwell**, a reporter for Canada's most prestigious newspaper, the *Globe and Mail,* is currently pursuing Ph.D. studies at Yale.

Having already traveled throughout his native New York State and parts of the East Coast, **John Loonam** went in search of something different. He found British Columbia and "hundreds of crystal blue bodies of water scattered by the sides of old logging roads." Memories of British Columbia's beauty give Loonam moments of strength when his ninth grade English students at a New York City high school get particularly unruly. Loonam has completed a Masters degree in creative writing.

Born in Montreal, **Malcolm MacRury** finished graduate studies in philosophy at Toronto's Institute for Christian Studies. He launched *COW Magazine,* Toronto's first humor tabloid in decades and edited an anthology of early Canadian satirical writing entitled *When Canada Was Still Funny*. He has traveled throughout Canada by jet, seaplane, car, bicycle, skidoo and paddle.

When he was eight years old, **Matthew Parfitt's** family left England for Montréal on one of the last Canadian passenger liners, *The Empress of England*. Parfitt has a distinguished academic record and has traveled extensively in the Middle East and Europe. He has completed work towards a Ph.D. in English Literature at Boston College.

MacRury teamed up with **Philip Street** to write the section on Ontario. Street lived in Blyth, a village in southwestern Ontario, until he attended the University of Toronto. He participated in the thriving journalistic activity of the University of Toronto as a writer and a cartoonist. After graduating with a B.A. in English in 1982, Street traveled for six months in Europe and the Middle East. On his return he began a second academic career in classics, and became a contributing editor on *COW Magazine*. Street currently lives in Toronto where he works as freelance designer and cartoonist, and as production manager for the *Catholic New Times*.

In addition to this volume's principal photographer, those who contributed wonderful images included Pat Canova, Maxine Cass, Harry Walker, Darien Murray, Charles Shugart, Daniel Aubry, Sue Fleishman, D. Richard, Tony Stone, David Wilkins and Michel Hetier.

The editor extends special thanks to her husband, Stephen Scharper, and to Becca Cunningham, Sean Cunningham, the staff of Archives Canada, Alla Czerkasij, Fr. Brown of Maryknoll Library and Prof. Owen Lynch.

—Apa Publications

Keyes   *Kingwell*   *Loonam*   *Street*

INTRODUCTION

HISTORY AND PEOPLE

MAPS

TRAVEL TIPS

CANADA

The word calls to mind a vastness, an immensity of creation. It calls to mind a past struggle for survival, men and women pitted against the harsh, merciless elements of nature. It calls to mind a wild, untamed beauty unspoiled by the ravages of human development. Yet, Canada is also a puzzle...a nation that is home to a mere 23 million people, living in relative comfort and health in the second largest country in the world.

Just what is Canada?

It is a question that each traveler brings to this nation, and it is a question that has no single answer. Canada is a delightful labyrinth of cultures and customs, of peaceful coexistence and political squabbles, of often competing but ultimately common interests. The sibling provinces and territories that make up this land are as different from one another as the forest is from the plain. All are bound however, by an invisible yet unmistakable thread.

It is here where the hearty French established a settlement along the frothy St. Lawrence River and survived the first relentless winter. It is here that the first bewildered European immigrants wondered how they would ever be able to thrive in such an unruly land; here where the British Loyalists fled from American revolutionaries; here where provinces separated by great distances and differences joined to form one nation.

There is much to discover in this vastness. Canada's immensity is daunting but not uninviting. An encounter with Canada is to understand and appreciate the unique beauty of an ever-changing but meticulously crafted mosaic.

CANADA: A LAND IN THE MAKING

Contrary to the opening statements of many history texts, Canada begins, not with the landing of literate Europeans, but with the arrival of nomadic bands wandering from Siberia across the Bering Strait to begin a new life in the frozen wilds of northern Alaska and Yukon. Canada's first visitors probably arrived some 20 to 40 thousand years ago—their reception was not a warm one. Facing bitter temperatures and hostile winds, it is a wonder that these people survived in such an unfriendly climate. Perhaps unable to return or perhaps just robust and courageous types, the first "Canadians" stayed and developed a remarkable subsistence technology suited to the brutal environment. Today traces of their ancient culture linger in Canada and these people have come to be known as the Eskimo or the Inuit.

The Inuit peoples: The ancestors of contemporary Inuit needed both intelligence and imagination to thrive in their newly acquired continent. If a single word can describe the major theme of life in Inuit culture, it is survival.

The Arctic Inuit are often referred to as a "stone-age" culture because of the simplicity of their hunting and cooking utensils. Bows and arrows made with tips of flint, ivory or bone were the main means of catching the family dinner. Because hunting in the winter was different from summer hunting, the Inuit created special tools to accommodate the seasonal fluctuations. Archaeologists note the Inuit for their ingenious winter ice-spears. The spears have tiny feathers or hairs attached to one end—the hunter holds the hairs over a hole in the ice waiting for movement that would indicate the presence of an animal. Such a procedure often involved sitting over a hole in the freezing cold for several hours!

Food was not only a daily consumption problem for the Inuit but also a major obsession—unfortunately the diet lacked much variation. Blubber, meat and fish were staples and always eaten raw (when the most nutritious). Partially digested lichen found in a caribou's stomach was considered a delicacy and sometimes created a little diversity in a meal. When natural food supplies ran out, families would pack up and move to another area usually on sleds made of frozen fish or hides—these could be eaten if necessary.

Inuit are often associated with dome-like snow huts or igloos. Without trees (and therefore timber) the prospects of constructing even a simple hut were poor—and snow was a readily available resource. Igloos, dwelling structures that are still used by contemporary Inuit, are made of snow blocks—the result looks much like a ski toque! The house consists of one or two interconnecting rooms. Inside, a platform for sleeping or working stands across from the entrance way; an area for animal carcasses and a heating lamp completes the layout. Anthropologists who have stayed in such dwellings comment that they are quite warm and comfortable to live in.

The early Inuit had nearly 100 words for snow but no word for chief or ruler; theirs was a different understanding of power and authority. In these nomadic bands authority resided with the group—a person could assume prestige or influence but never at the expense of the community. The underlying theme to Inuit life was a principle of harmony within the group.

Existing in a harsh and rugged world, the Inuit developed a religion that reflected their feelings about their cold, hard life. Living people needed "Luck" to exist in a world full of malevolent spirits—when a person died, their "Luck" had run out. Yet today's Inuit, living almost an identical lifestyle where undisturbed by colonialism, are noted for their cheerful, fun-loving nature. As many Inuit will say: "if you knew of the dangers I live through each day, you would understand why I am so fond of laughter."

West Coast Indians: As people traveled to other parts of Canada and spread into the Plains and Woodlands, many distinct languages and cultures flourished. Wandering through Canada today, one finds evidence of a remarkably rich and varied Indian history—a history that was tragically destroyed through the process of colonization.

Preceding pages: An Arctic sled dog complacently peers out from her holding pen; Maple leaf — Canada's national symbol; Wind and water battle over Georgian Bay; Silent and snow-covered, the Canadian Rockies slumber undisturbed; Fall stealthily emerges in New Brunswick's forests; Wings extended, West Coast totem poles prepare for flight; portrait of Chief Joseph; Looking westward from the east; and Canadian Indians celebrate their heritage. Left, a Canadian reclaims his dignity.

The West Coast supported several Indian populations; among these were the Kwakiutl, Bella Coola, Nootka, Haidas, and Tlingit Indians. These groups found the Pacific coast to be extremely abundant in natural resources. The sea sported cod, halibut, salmon and edible kelp; water animals were used as furs; and the forests yielded deer, beaver and bear. Unlike the Inuit, the North West Coast Indians were able to make extensive use of timber: they are known for their huge dug-out canoes usually stretching to 66 feet (20 meters) in length and their wooden huts 270 feet (90 meters) long. The ancestral fishing grounds that still lie along the rugged Pacific coast were the sites of much activity and often a few weeks of hard work yielded enough food for the year.

sent rank, wealth and status.

The material wealth and artistic skills of the Northern Coastal cultures engendered a lively system of trade among tribes—this network was later to become very important to the fur trade in Canada. Nootkas specialized in whale products while the Haidas "mass manufactured" ceremonial canoes. Slaves were also traded. The result was a fairly sophisticated practice of interchange. Not surprisingly, the West Coast Indians show a marked preoccupation with what colonial officials considered to be private property and material wealth."

Travelers to this area of Canada will undoubtedly hear of the famous *potlatches*. These were exchange ceremonies given by a chief and his local group to another chief and

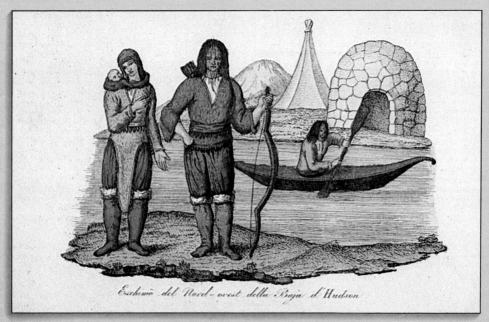

Eschimä del Nord-ovest della Baja d'Hudson

Given the bounty of food and building materials, North West Coast cultures were able to devote ample time to the creation of objects. Many of their styles and techniques remain in use today and travelers to the museums and craft reserves note the presence of one major style: the omnipresence of animals, mythical creatures with protruding canines; and strangely painted human forms. These figures are found virtually everywhere: on totem poles, houses, canoes and bowls. The beings depicted are said to be supernatural ancestors who have revealed themselves to certain artists so that they might be painted. These figure motifs, like European crests, became associated with particular lineages and came to repre-

his followers. During the ceremony huge quantities of gifts were given to each guest—the value of the gift corresponded to the status of the guest. Much feasting was followed by lengthy speeches. These celebrations usually marked a change in the status of a member of the hosting group such as the movement of an inheritor into an inheritance. Frequently if two men were eligible to inherit one position, a series of rival potlatches were held. These often involved the destruction of property by burning or demolition—sometimes the slaying of a slave (a practice quelled by the Europeans) was a part of the procedure. The potlatches continued until one contestor was "broken" financially and relinquished his claim.

Plains Indians: Inhabiting yet another area in Canada's broad geographical milieu were the Plains Indians: the Blackfoot, Sarcee and Assiniboine tribes. Each group possessed a completely distinctive language so incomprehensible to the other that sign language was used to facilitate trade. Yet each tribe was bound to the other through their dependency on the buffalo.

The buffalo was the nucleus of life for the Plains Indians. From the buffalo came *pemican* (a protein-concentrated food carried by Indians on the trail); skins that were used as blankets, clothes and tent coverings; and buffalo hair that was dried and either woven into rope or used to stuff moccasins. Before the arrival of the horse in the late 18th Century, buffalo were hunted on foot,

feet deep—2.5 meters) and broke their necks and legs. They were then shot with arrows and subsequently butchered.

Dependency on the buffalo made the Plains Peoples nomadic—they were forced to follow the wandering herds. Such mobility demanded a lightweight transportable house; it is from these circumstances that the origin of the *teepee* can be traced. A conical-shaped hut with an aperture at the tip for smoke, the teepee was not only practical for the Plains Indians but sacred. The floor of the teepee represented the earth of mortal life and the peak the sky of the gods. The roundness of the tent symbolized the sacred circle of life of which there was no beginning and no end.

Until the coming of the "White Man" and

often by stampeding the beasts into a compound. This procedure, referred to as "buffalo jumping," involved every member of the group—a herd was chased toward an enclosure erected around a pit. One person, usually the swiftest, covered himself with a buffalo hide and imitated the animal's movements in the hope of drawing the herd towards the pit. Once inside the enclosure the buffalo toppled into the pit (seven or eight

Left, 19th Century Inuit family in front of their "snow home"; and above, West Coast art: gnashing teeth and eternal ferocity.

firearms, Plains people remained fairly loosely organized and flexible—the competition created by the fur trade changed all this. Originally, however, the basic political unit of the band was a leader: when several of these bands united, a council was formed of all the leaders. During trading ventures, wars, and celebrations the council acted as a guiding and organizing body directing the affairs of the group.

One of the most famous festivals associated with the Plains Indians is their Sun Dance, then held every two or three years. During this ceremony a sacred pole was erected to the Great Spirit and offerings of food and decorated items were tied to the pole. The bands danced around the stake,

recited war deeds, and prayed for guidance in their hunt of the buffalo. Practicing their own brand of "machismo," Plains youths would frequently perform acts of self-mutilation, one of which involved piercing the chest with skewers tied to the pole with leather thongs. The youth would tug and pull at the skewers until he either fainted or pulled the thongs from the stake, the idea being that self-inflicted torture would arouse the compassion and benevolence of the Great Spirit.

Woodland Indians: Perhaps the best known (next to the Inuit) of Canada's Native Peoples are the Indians of the Eastern Woodlands. As early as 1,000 B.C. eastern Canada began to be settled by semi-nomadic tribes. It is here that one discovers the contrasting lifestyles of the peaceful Huron, the fierce Iroquios, and the entre-preneurial Algonkians.

Like the rest of the Indians of Canada, the people of this area made maximum use of their environment. The Huron of southern and central Ontario are noted for being a horticultural society. Living in longhouses within pallisaded villages, the Huron culti-vated the land and subsisted on staples of squash, beans, and maize: the "Three Sis-ters." It is the Huron who first met and baffled French missionaries to Canada. The French discovered a people who demons-trated an unusual equality between the sexes and a consensus rather than authoritarian style of government.

Walking through the woods of lower Ontario, it is easy to speculate where buried Huron and Iroquois sites might lie. These Indians chose locations for their villages on the basis of four criteria: access to water, nearness to forests for timber, nearness to rich soil for cultivation, and strategic place-ment for defense. For the amateur archaeologists these variables are the keys to locating potential Indian sites.

Life within the pallisaded compound is difficult to picture although the Jesuits and other explorers vividly describe their horror at the living conditions within the camp. Samuel de Champlain, aghast at what he perceived to be filth and disorder, wrote of the longhouses in which two or three dozen people lived. The smoke from each fire in the house, he wrote, "circulates at will, caus-ing much eye trouble, to which the natives are so subject that many become blind in their old age." For Europeans, the Indian

notions of communal sharing and sanitation offended their own individualistic sensibili-ties. It is important to note, however, that despite their lack of "proper sanitation," the Indians rarely died of disease until the im-ported European viruses decimated them.

By way of contrast to the Huron, the Iroquois were a fiercer group of people and more inclined to warfare. They were the only Indians of Canada to believe in two Great Spirits, one good and the other evil. In Iroquois religion the two deities were con-stantly at odds with one another and their myths are most frequently incidents of clashes between the good and evil gods. Be-fore the arrival of the Europeans the Iro-quois had sown the seeds of a great Empire: they had established a confederacy of sever-

al nations of tribes, they had developed a unified system of currency *(wampum)* that regulated trade, and they had organized the confederacy for warfare against enemy tribes. Perhaps if Europe had discovered North America a century later than it did, it would have encountered a highly sophisti-cated and politically unified culture of Indi-ans. But it did not. Although the history of Canada is in part a history of burgeoning European society, for the Indians of Canada it is a tragic tale of exploitation, strife and eventual extinction.

Such is the stage setting, so to speak, for the arrival of the first Europeans: a vast land inhabited by highly differentiated Indian groups, each adapted to a particular lifestyle.

Left, Chief Duck and Blackfoot family; and right, "Miss One Spot."

THE EUROPEANS

The histories of European nations usually include colorful tales of the rise of great civilizations, the construction of vast cities, and the stratagems and spoils of conquest. Canada's history, in comparison, is a humble one. And no Canadian will ever apologize for this. Canada's development is very much a story of an unmerciful wilderness, of hardship and determination, of disappointment and dreams ... the last paragraph of her turbulent history being the communities that currently cluster along the 49th parallel like beads of water on a thread.

The first visitors to encounter Canada after the crossing of the nomadic hunters were the Vikings, a group of people whose ancestors had traveled from Norway to Iceland. From Iceland, the Vikings moved westward when the much celebrated Eric the Red discovered and settled Greenland. Known as a fierce and hardy culture, the Vikings were great sailors and often took to the seas in search of food and adventure. On one such voyage a seaman, Bjarne Herjolfsen, was blown off course while journeying between Iceland and Greenland. In the midst of a heavy gale, Herjolfsen caught sight of North America and returned home with a story of an unknown land. A few years later (around 1,000 A.D.) Eric the Red's son, Lief, set out to find the new continent. The Viking sagas tell of Lief's strange adventures and his discoveries of Helluland (Baffin Island), Markland (Labrador), and Vinland. In 1961 archaeologist Helge Ingstad stumbled upon the remains of a Norse settlement in L'Anse aux Meadows and decided that Vinland was probably Newfoundland. For Lief, Vinland was a land of great marvels: the sagas recount Lief's amazement at the succulent grapes and enormous salmon.

One year after the expedition, Lief's brother Thorvald returned to North America hoping to make contact with the natives of Vinland. The legends tell of how Thorvald and his crew were attacked by "Skraelings" and shot at with bows and arrows.

In other tales the illegitimate daughter of Eric the Red, Freydis the Brave and Cruel, defends the Vikings by rushing towards the Skraelings and frightening them with her

wild eyes and gnashing teeth.

Who were the Skraelings? The Viking sagas describe them as dark-skinned people who wore their hair in a strange fashion. Historical anthropologists have speculated that the Skraelings may have been Algonkians. Whoever they were, they prevented the Vikings from establishing permanent settlements on the mainland. It is possible that the Vikings returned to northern parts of present-day Canada. The tall, blond "Copper Eskimos," so named by the explorer Vilhjalmun Stefansson in 1910, have led

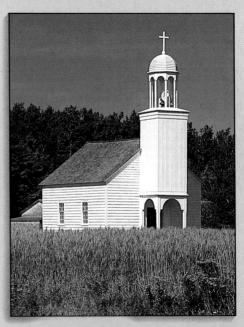

some to suggest that the Norse people interbred with the Inuit of Baffin Island.

Further Explorations of Canada: The 15th Century marked a new beginning in the consciousness of humankind, a consciousness that was to have profound significance for Canada. The dream of discovering a route across the Atlantic to the spices, jewels and silks of the Orient became the fantasy of many kings and merchants. By the early 1500s Arab and Italian traders securely controlled access to the Middle Eastern markets via the west. Frustrated, France, Spain and eventually England looked enviously at the prosperity of their neighbors. Glances were soon cast towards the "Sea of Darkness" (the Atlantic) and many began to wonder if

Left, the austere gaze of the gentry at Old Fort William; and right, a reconstructed Acadian church reflects upon two centuries of parish life.

this water route would lead to the riches of the Orient or merely to the end of the world and peril. Then, as improvements in ship building techniques occurred, the dream became a possibility. And so they set out.

Cabot and Cartier: John Cabot is the first explorer to have "officially" discovered Canada and claim it for his king. An Italian navigator, Cabot was known for his imaginative flights of fancy and adventuresome spirit. In 1496 he persuaded Henry VII to give him leave to find a route to the Indies and claim it for England. On Tuesday May 2, 1497, Cabot boarded *The Matthew* with 18 men and set sail for the Americas. After 52 weary days at sea, *The Matthew* sighted Cape Breton Island where Cabot landed on June 24th. Cabot unrolled the British flag and planting it firmly in the soil, claimed the country to be under the sovereignty of Henry VII. But where was all the gold?

Cabot soon discovered that the soil was extremely fertile and the climate warm and friendly. He was convinced that he had found the northeast coast of Asia; further investigation could only lead him to the precious silks and gems of which he had so often dreamed. Cabot found neither of these but he did report banks of teeming fish and a great abundance of timber.

Upon Cabot's return, Henry VII, who had wanted gold, was singularly unimpressed with the explorer's tales of fish and paid him £10 for his efforts. The King told Cabot to try another expedition—this was realized in 1498. This time, Cabot reached Baffin Island and Newfoundland. Cabot finally returned to England where he died at age 48.

Many explorers set out after Cabot but little came of their dangerous journeys until Jacques Cartier ventured to North America in 1534. Cartier was sent by Francis I of France; his expedition marks the origin of French and British competition for control of North America.

On his first trip, Cartier traveled inland until he found the St. Lawrence Seaway. Assured that the river was a water route to the Orient, Cartier sailed down the St. Lawrence until he came to the Iroquois villages of Hochelaga and Stadacona (the sites of modern Montréal and Québec City respectively). Here Cartier found the Indians to be so friendly and hospitable that he brought two back with him to France. Like Henry VII, Francis I was disappointed but Cartier mollified him by telling the king that he had erected a cross on Gaspé Peninsula in

Rain threatens over one of Canada's oldest forts, Calgary.

his name and had called the country New France.

The Arctic expeditions: While the early explorers devoted their time to discovering a new route to the Orient, 50 years after Cartier others became obsessed with the Northwest Passage. One such man was Martin Frobisher. With a reputation as a daredevil, Frobisher was sent by Elizabeth I to find an ice-free route to the Americas. Despite Frobisher's inability to produce anything of consequence for British history, he remains, even to this day, a cherished folk hero. No less than 300 years after Frobisher's voyages, the explorer Charles Hall discovered the relics of a structure Frobisher's crew had built. Hall wrote that in 1861, three centuries later, the native peoples spoke of Frobisher as

if he had just visited them!

Henry Hudson was another man drawn to the excitement of exploration. Hoping to open a passage to China, Hudson made several trips to North America, his last one ending tragically. In 1609 *The Discovery* froze in the ice of James Bay and the boat and its crew went into "winter quarters." After a long, tense winter aboard the vessel, Hudson quarreled with a member of his crew, John Greene, who later led his shipmates into mutiny. Hudson was set adrift in the Bay with his son and seven others loyal to him. Green was later killed in a skirmish with the Inuit and the others were thrown into prison upon reaching England. Nothing was ever heard of Henry Hudson again.

Following on Hudson's heels was Thomas James (1631)—the namesake of James Bay—who wrote vividly of his excursions in a travel account titled *The Dangerous Voyage of Captain Thomas James*. The writings of his log later became the material upon which Coleridge based his famous poem *The Rime of the Ancient Mariner*. After James, Edward Parry, a British Naval officer, pushed through the northern icebergs to reach Melville Island in 1819—he had come the farthest yet.

Perhaps the most heart-wrenching story of all the explorers is that of John Franklin, a British rear-admiral and explorer. In 1819 Franklin was put in charge of an exploration that was to mark out a route from Hudson's Bay to the Arctic Ocean. Franklin made a second trip in 1825 after the success of his first voyage and returned to North America a third time in 1845. On his last expedition, Franklin was sure he would find the Northwest Passage. He was accompanied by a Captain Crozier who had served with Edward Parry. His ships, *The Erebus* and *The Terror* were last seen on July 26th, 1845. Some years later a rescue mission discovered their skeletal remains and a diary of the last days of the journey. Franklin, only a few miles from success, had died of exhaustion and exposure. It wasn't until 1906 that Roald Amundsen finally conquered Canada's merciless north and opened up the Northwest Passage. In only a few centuries, Canada's relentless North had claimed several European "sacrificial lambs."

Travelers to the West: The West Coast of Canada was yet another site of interest for the ever curious Europeans. In 1778, Captain James Cook became the first European to step ashore the Pacific coast. Cook volunteered to find a waterway through North America originating in the west but finally had to conclude that it did not exist. George Vancouver followed him in 1791-95 and discovered the outlet of the Bella Coola River. Seven weeks later, a fiery Scotsman named Alexander Mackenzie ended up at the same spot.

The beginning of colonization: Such is the early history of Canada. For the Europeans, it yielded neither gold nor gems and was, for the most part, a disappointment from the first. With resignation the rulers of France and England began to make plans for colonizing the New World.

Left, explorer Martin Frobisher; and right, Captain James Cook, the first European to step ashore the Pacific Coast.

CANADA IN THE 17TH CENTURY

Colonizing the New World was no easy task for the rulers of Europe in the 17th Century. Cold, barren and largely unexplored, Canada held little appeal for the people of England, France and Spain. Those, however, who did venture to Canada encountered a burgeoning system of trade existing between the Europeans and the Indians and soon realized that the economic potentials of settling in Canada were very attractive.

The Fur Trade: Curious and for the most part friendly, the Indian tribes that met French and British settlers in Canada became enamored of European metalware which, for them, represented a massive technological improvement over their crude stone and wooden untensils. As a result the Indians developed a dependency on the Europeans — a dependency that was to change their lives forever.

At first the Indians had little to offer in return for the highly valued knives and axes and the Europeans complained bitterly of the relative uselessness of the handcrafted canoes and snowshoes. By the late 1500s, however, the Indians had begun to trade furs with the settlers, particularly luxury furs. When the hatmakers of Europe obtained beaver pelts from Canada they engendered a rage for beaver hats which they claimed were the warmest and most durable in the world. As a result, European fashion created an immense and ongoing market for furs in the new colony that was to last for almost 200 years. The Indians, never quite understanding the "whiteman's" infatuation with the beaver, became the main suppliers to the fur merchants and continued to receive various European-manufactured wares for their pelts. Marc Lescabot, a 17th Century French writer, noted that the Indians became awed by the beaver for, as they explained it, the little creature had mysteriously brought them kettles, axes, swords, knives and gave them food and drink without the trouble of cultivating the land. By the early 1600s the fur trade in Canada was booming and the era of competition for the monopoly of the fur market in North America had begun.

Left, trading pelts to sate the demands of European fashion (1758); and right, Samuel de Champlain, one of Canada's many progenitors.

Father of Canada: The man who was in many ways responsible for solidifying and expanding the fur trade in Canada was the French explorer Samuel de Champlain. Described in history chronicles as an idealist with a passion for exploration, Champlain is probably the most frequently cited "Father" of Canada and is often reverently honored because of his wish to found Canada upon principles of justice and compassion.

Acting on behalf of the French monarchy, in 1604 Champlain established the first French colony in North America in Acadia

(Nova Scotia). Acadia became mythologized as an idyllic French settlement where peace and prosperity reigned and her tiny villages set in the picturesque Maritimes became the subject of many folktales and poems. Champlain's Acadian village of Grand Pré was immortalized in Henry Wadsworth Longfellow's epic *Evangeline*, the tale of a town's utopian existence crumbling under the cruel administration of the British and the separation of two lovers. Of Acadia and Acadians, Longfellow wrote:

Thus dwelt together in love
*   these simple Acadian farmers...*
Neither lock had they to their doors,
*   nor bars to their windows*
But their dwellings were as open as

day and the hearts of the owners;
There the richest was poor and the
poorest lived in abundance.

After Acadia, Champlain continued his explorations into the interior of Canada and on July 3, 1608, on the site of an old Indian settlement called Stadacona, Champlain founded Québec. Although extremely momentous for the history of Canada as a whole, the founding of Québec for Samuel de Champlain was quite unextraordinary and, as he indicated in his diary, a location he chose more for convenience than historical importance:

"When I arrived there (Québec) on
July 3 I looked about for a suitable
place for our buildings, but I could not
find any more convenient or better sit-

uated than the point of Québec, so cal-
led by the savages, which is filled with
nuts and trees...near this is a pleasant
river, where formerly Jacques Cartier
passed this winter."

(The "pleasant river" turned out to be none other than the mighty St. Lawrence Seaway, which later became an important passageway for the export of furs to Europe.)

Indians and *Les Coureurs de Bois:* One year after Champlain's settlement of Québec, a group of Indians, probably the Wendots or Wyandots, came down from the northwest to trade their pelts with the French. Upon their arrival the Frenchmen were astonished by the appearance of their half-shaven heads and the tufts of hair that grew perpen-

dicularly to their scalps. Likening the Indians' hair to the bristles on the back of an enraged boar *(la hure)*, the French called them the Hurons. Thus began a long and tragic relationship.

One of the Champlain's main objectives while in Canada was to control the flourishing fur trade and to establish stricter management of the Indians. Already allied with the Hurons, Champlain failed to see that the fur trade was exacerbating already existing hostilities among Indian tribes. Animosities of a highly ritualistic nature had always existed between the Huron and the Iroquois Confederation — with the fur trade the disputes acquired a mercenary meaning and became even more bitter and brutal. When Champlain established an alliance between the French and the Huron, he immediately became the enemy of the Iroquois (the British later took advantage of this). On his famous expedition to Ticonderoga with 60 Huron warriors and three armed Frenchmen, Champlain officially initiated open warfare between the Iroquois and French. The skirmish began traditionally but Champlain's firearms soon produced 300 massacred Iroquois. The event inspired a deep and lasting hatred among the Iroquois and marked the beginning of a series of cruel and ferocious raids on French trading posts.

While Champlain was organizing settlements and repelling hostile Iroquois, other colonists, mostly men from France, began to appear. These settlers, who became known as the *coureurs de bois* or the voyagers, were men who had worked at menial occupations back at home and had looked to New France as an escape from a life of drudgery — many had exchanged prison sentences for emigration papers. The *coureurs de bois* became the backbone of Canada's trading system. Trapping animals for a living, which involved not only a precarious existence in the bush, but also fighting off unfriendly Indians, the voyagers were the intrepid entrepreneurs of Canada's early days. Described as bold, boisterous, daring fellows in French Canadian folklore, these men eventually became the employees of large European companies seeking trade monopolies in the New World. By the 1750s Canada had become an economically prosperous investment for France, and Britain began to cast a closer glance at a country she had virtually ignored for almost half a decade.

Left, a merchant displays his wares in a Thunder Bay trading post; and right, illustriously chopping wood before the noon-day heat in Farewells Trading Post, Saskatchewan.

ROUGHING IT IN THE BUSH: THE PIONEERS

When Samuel de Champlain and other explorers ventured to Canada, their plans for the settlement of the new colony, although the dreams of imaginative men, were essentially expressions of the grandiose visions of European monarchs. For them Canada was merely an addition to the ever-expanding empires of England and France. Canada was a valuable piece of property in the "Monopoly Board" the super powers of the 17th and 18th centuries ruthlessly fought to claim. But for the others who journeyed to Canada — the farmers and fishermen, the women and children, the missionaries and even the reckless *coureurs de bois* — Canada was much more than just a geographical acquisition or political concept. Canada was a very real place, empty and enormous. And at times, life was so very hard.

The missionaries: When Samuel de Champlain claimed Canada for France, his first task was to rigorously regularize the fur trade. His second task was to set about Christianizing the native population so that the continent could truly become a land made for "the glory and praise of God and France." The years 1632 to 1652 are frequently referred to as the "golden years" for the missions in Canada...a somewhat misleading phrase because, although it captures a sense of intense religious activity in Canada during this time, it fails to express low success-rates (in terms of conversions) for the missionaries.

The first missionaries brought to Canada by Champlain were four Recollects, strict Franciscans, who enthusiastically plunged into the bush in search of the "heathen savages." Believing that their vows of self-poverty would be well suited to a harsh existence in the wilderness, the Recollects patiently began to work on saving Indian souls — but with little success. Not long after, the Jesuits were invited to join the Canadian missions, and in 1625 Fathers de Brébeuf and de Noue left France to begin converting the Iroquois and Huron.

The Jesuits, like the French and most Europeans, failed to understand the Indian way of life. Communally oriented, lacking hierachical structures and methods of au-

thority, openly polytheistic and possessing different concepts of diet and sanitation, the Indians seemed to the Jesuits "barbaric" and "uncivilized" but possessing potential nevertheless. Summing up this attitude, Champlain wrote of the Indians in 1609:

"There is an evil tendency among them to be revengeful, and to be great liars, and one cannot fully rely upon them, except with caution and when one is armed...(they) do not know what it is to worship God and pray to Him, but live like beasts, but I think they would

soon be converted to Christianity if some people would settle among them and cultivate their soul, which is what most of them wish."

Converting Indians to Christianity inevitably meant converting them to *French* Christianity. As a result, in addition to monotheism, the Indians were introduced to class differentiation, corporal punishment of wives and children, the privatization of the family and the fear of eternal damnation.

Needless to say, the Jesuits were not always welcomed into Indian communities and many of them, given the name of "black robes" by the Iroquois, became symbols of evil and misfortune. Despite their ethnocentric attitudes, some of the Jesuit

Left, a Jesuit priest, Jean de Brébeuf is tortured to death by the Iroquois; and right, smallpox threatens a shipload of immigrants (1830.)

missionaries were men of great courage and endurance. Passionately hated by the Iroquois, many of them suffered horrible deaths and became the first martyrs of Canada. Such is the story of the famous Father Jean de Brébeuf, a Jesuit who worked for many years among the horticultural Huron. Brébeuf's martyrdom on March 16, 1649, was recorded by a contemporary, Christophe Regnault, in the *Jesuit Relations:*

"The Iroquois came...took our village and seized Father Brébeuf and his companion; and set fire to all the huts. They proceeded to vent their rage on these two fathers, for they took them both and stripped them naked and fastened them each to a post. They tied both their hands and feet together.

First French Canadians: In the early annals of Canadian history, there were two types of settlers who traveled to the New World. The first was the *coureur de bois,* the adventurous woodsman who, venturing into the forest regions he named *pays d'en haut,* combined fur trapping and trading. The second kind was the *habitant,* the French colonist who settled the fertile shores of the St. Lawrence Seaway and cultivated the land. From the very beginning these two lifestyles were radically different—so different that animosities soon developed. To the *habitant* the furtraders were as treacherous and vengeful as the despised Iroquois, and to the *coureur de bois* the farmer frightened away all his game and pushed him farther into the wilderness.

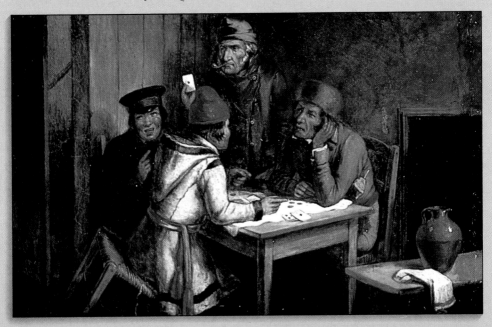

They beat them with a shower of blows from cudgels...there being no part of their body which did not endure this torment."
The unfortunate priests endured other horrific tortures, two of which were having boiling water poured over their heads in derision of baptism, and having heated collars of axe heads placed around their necks. The account states that despite his suffering, Brébeuf continued to preach to the Indians about his God until they cut off his tongue and lips. After his death, the Iroquois were so impressed by his fortitude that they removed his heart and ate it, believing that by so doing they would become as brave as Brébeuf.

Although the *coureurs de bois* are often portrayed as the more robust of the two, for different reasons life for the *habitant* was also very difficult. Clearing the tree-infested lands of the St. Lawrence shores demanded arduous, back-breaking labor, crops were often slow to start and a year's supply of food could be dashed instantly by bad weather. Women had to work long hours to fulfill domestic chores and then often went to the fields to labor there. At first the very landscape seemed threatening and alien to the *habitant:* wild beasts and hostile Indians were constant worries. One of the *habitants'* greatest concerns seems to have been the fear that one of his sons would leave the farm (where his labor was so desperately needed) to join the romantic life of the *coureurs de bois.*

Early homes in New France were wooden huts crudely built of rough logs; in the winter water for the household had to be drawn from a hole in the ice. To make life even more unbearable, there was the all-pervasive cold...a cold so nasty and ill-tempered that it seemed to freeze the marrow in one's bones. Of the icy weather in early Canada, the poet Standish O'Grady wrote:

> *Thou barren waste, unprofitable strand*
> *Where hemlocks brood on unproduc-*
> *tive land,*
> *Whose frozen air on one bleak winter's*
> *night*
> *Can metamorphose dark brown hares*
> *into white.*

available for the asking, food was bountiful, and *everyone* possessed the right to hunt and fish. By the 1630s the little settlements of Québec and Montréal had burgeoned into bustling centers of commerce and became bastions of French sovereignty. The French clergy, so unsuccessful among the Indians, had returned to the colonies and had founded schools, hospitals and even a university (Jesuit College founded in 1636, one year before Harvard). Houses for the aged and orphans were constructed and an elaborate system of courts and litigation procedures was implemented. In 1640 New France had 240 inhabitants — by 1685 the population had swelled to 10,000. Montréal and Québec had become lively colonial capitals.

The artist Cornelius Krieghoff, one of the

But then there were rewards to be reaped as well. Soon the wooden shelters gave way to houses built of stone with steep roofs and large heat-yielding fireplaces. As the forests were cleared, as settlements became towns, and as farmers prospered on their strips of land (called *seigneuries*), life changed and families of New France eventually enjoyed higher standards of living than their European counterparts. For the farmer of early Canada, tenant dues and church tithes were low, no taxes were paid, fertile land was

Left, a favorite pastime of the *habitants,* card play-was strictly forbidden by the Catholic church; and above, Cornelius Kreighoff's portrait of French Canadian life in the 19th Century.

most insightful chroniclers of early Québecois culture, portrays the French Canadians as hardworking but gay people. The winter, when fields slept under layers of snow and warehouses were fully stocked, seems to have been the time when the Québecois "played." Extremely fond of their children and tolerant of harmless mischievousness, the French Canadians socialized mainly through family gatherings, card playing, dancing, and drinking parties. (With respect to this last amusement, by 1749 drunken horse-driving had become so serious in Québec that a strict law fining inebriated drivers six livres — about six dollars — was passed.)

The only ominous presence in Québecois

life seems to have been the clergy who sternly disapproved of dancing, cards, jewelry and even hair ribbons. In 1700 the omnipotent Bishop Laval furiously chastised Québecois women for their elaborate coiffures and scandalous wardrobes, but to little avail. In early Canada the French clergy were (and continued to be) a powerful force, having the authority to excommunicate an individual on the spot. Somehow, despite the continual irreverence of their flock, the French Church remained reluctantly indulgent and avoided initiating the witch-hunts that had become so popular in New England at the time.

Settlements and skirmishes: While Jesuits continued to proselytize Catholicism in Canada and while French colonists resolute-

en-Laye. Although trade resumed and settlement seemed to proceed smoothly, France was left with some uneasiness and began to exert greater energy in solving her problem of sovereignty.

Government in New France: Bitter complaints about New France were constantly arising from the colonists — one of which was the lack of a central, authoritative government. As a result, in 1647, a council consisting of a governor, the religious superior of the Jesuits, and the Governor of Montréal was instituted. Although the council's role was to monitor economic activities in the colony, this model proved inefficient. Consequently New France was officially made a ward of the Crown (under Louis XIV) in 1663. Two men were instrumental in bring-

ly set down roots, Samuel de Champlain and other French officials were faced with the overwhelming problem of maintaining control over the new colony. Several skirmishes with other governments over territory had already occurred.

In 1627, for example, the notorious Kirke brothers, English adventurers who supported the Hugenot effort in France, managed to blockade the St. Lawrence River for three years and wrest the fur trade from France's charter: The Hundred Associates. At the same time Acadia was claimed for James VI of Scotland by Sir William Alexander. Various disputes ensued until 1632 when Canada and Acadia were restored to France under the Treaty of Saint-Germain-

ing a strong, centralized government to French Canada.

The first of these men was Jean Baptiste Colbert, an ambitious finance minister, who endeavored to recast French colonial policy by establishing a new administrative system. Colbert sought to make New France a province with a government similar to that of France; he implemented a new structure which consisted of a governor-general, an intendant and a Superior Council. The Bishop of New France was made a member of the Council and was, more often than not, engaged in bitter argument with the reigning governor.

Governor Frontenac: One of New France's more colorful governors was the Comte de

Frontenac, a man of great personal charm but the possessor of extravagant and unscrupulous tendencies. From the inception of his career, Frontenac set himself in opposition to the most influential clergymen in Canada. He wrote of the Jesuits:

"Another thing displeases me...this complete dependence of the grand vicar and seminary priests on the Jesuits, for they never do the least thing without their order..."

Frontenac complained that the Jesuits had spies everywhere, that they meddled in family affairs, and that they exerted an extraordinary and unreasonable control over all the colonists. Being a man who liked to get his own way, and also being a man who probably coveted such control himself,

Settling the St. Lawrence: Jean Colbert's reorganization of the colony gave New France a firmly centralized government that could efficiently deal with day to day problems. Jean Talon, the second man to reshape the nature of government in New France and the first intendant of Colbert's model, quickly set about reorganizing settlement and was able to bring in thousands of new colonists, many of them women. Most of the population flocked to three towns, Montréal, Québec and Trois-Rivères. Colbert and Talon hoped that settlers would establish permanency along the St. Lawrence but many became voyagers and traveled inland (these men eventually married Indian women and gave rise to the Métis, a people of half French and Indian

Frontenac often scandalized New France by his disrespectful attitude towards the Jesuits.

Governor of New France at a time when the first serious scuffles between the rival powers occurred, Frontenac (although instrumental in quelling Indian raids) overlooked the aggressive presence of the British Hudson's Bay Company in the west and underestimated its importance in the future of Canada.

Left, a habitant urges his horse to greater speed over the ice; and above, a *caleche* meanders through the frosty streets of modern Québec City.

blood). The transient nature of the population was a major obstacle in the settling of New France — Colbert, feeling that mobility was deleterious to French interests, became an adamant opponent of Western expansion. He subsequently forbade colonists to leave the central settlement and confined the fur trade to Montréal, Trois-Rivères and Tadousac. Although few followed his ordinance, Colbert's neglect of the western regions merely enabled the British to gain a firmer foothold in the New World.

Anglo-French rivalry: In the 1660s two malcontent voyagers. Médard des Groseilliers and Pierre Radisson, decided that they were going to do something about the high costs of hauling furs back to Québec (as ordered by the colonial government) and the exorbitant taxes they were paying on fur pelts. The two trappers fled to New England and were consequently escorted to Britain. In London Groseilliers and Radisson persuaded a group of London merchants to assume control over the fur trade in the middle portion of Canada by forming the Hudson's Bay Company — the company claimed exclusive trading rights in all territories draining into Hudson's Bay. As a result, New France suddenly found herself in an awkward position: to the south were the Dutch and English-supported Iroquois and to the north was the ever-expanding Hudson's Bay Company. Fearful of losing their new colony, New France's militia began to launch expeditions to throw the English out

of Hudson's Bay.

By the time the 18th Century began, hostilities had increased between the French and British, especially in the east where New England farmers began to covet Acadia. For several years New France was kept active by repelling new settlers and engaging its armies in ruthless, devastating raids that went as far south as Boston. Agreement, however, was reached in 1713 when the Peace Treaty of Utrecht was signed and North America was carved up among the European powers. The French gave much up. Acadia and Hudson's Bay was ceded to the British and Article 15 of the treaty recognized British sovereignty over the Iroquois and permitted them to trade with western

Indians in areas that had traditionally been French domains.

Years of peace: Despite France's reluctance to honor the treaty, three decades of peace reigned in the colony. As a result, Canada began to prosper — the depressed fur trade (after the Kirke fiasco) flourished; the population increased from 19,000 in 1713 to 48,000 by 1739; agriculture and fishing also blossomed, and lumbering and fishing industries began to develop. During these years, Canada's standard of living soared beyond that of almost any other European nation.

English imperialist economic aspirations, however, soon emerged and fighting broke out again in 1744. A series of small battles followed until in 1756 formal war (and what was to become a deciding war) was declared between France and Britian. France, characteristically nonchalant in her attitude towards the new colony, sent the Marquis de Montcalm with meagre reinforcements to Québec. The General was uneasy about New France's prospects — lack of soldiers and food supplies made defeat seem almost inevitable. In addition, France did not wish to risk sending her fleets to North America since it would leave the mother country in a vulnerable position. New France's frontier was lightly guarded and held widely separated points — how could Montcalm hope to defend it?

The fall of New France: Québec seemed (to both nations) to be the deciding factor in the war. In 1759 a force under the command of General James Wolfe began an advance to Québec. Montcalm, relying upon the naturally strategic position of the city (it sat atop formidable precipices) let the invaders come to him. After several unsuccessful frontal attacks,one of Wolfe's men suggested flank attack. On the night of September 12, Wolfe and his troops crossed the St. Lawrence River under the cover of darkness and stealthily gained the cliffs. Completely unprepared, the French repelled the British but panicked and hastily retreated (little did the French know that their attackers too had panicked and were on the point of retreat). Wolfe was killed in the exchange and Montcalm was mortally wounded. After the fall of Québec it was a matter of time before the rest of New France fell to the British. By 1763, under the Treaty of Paris, France lost her lands in Canada to England.

Left, a French soldier stands guard outside of Louisbourg, Nova Scotia; and right, the haughty stare of a French nobleman conveys the French disdain of the English.

CANADA UNDER BRITISH RULE

When Canada was ceded to the British, few tears were shed in France. New France, what Voltaire had called "a few acres of snow," had become a gnawing irritation for French officials and its removal from France's empire was met more with relief than regret. The political intelligentsia of the time also held the belief that colonies were a source of economic weakness rather than strength. It became ever clearer that the *habitants* who had originally settled Canada for France were to be left to their own devices.

Britain's victory in Canada began to produce major changes on the continent, one of which was the shift in control of the fur trade from French hands to British ones. Although glowing from its recent economic advancement in Canada, Britain was still faced with one serious problem: the vast majority of its newly acquired colony were people of foreign descent.

From the first Britain planned to extirpate French culture from its colony — its design was to make Québec an English settlement with English institutions, English ways and, most importantly, English inhabitants. British colonial officers hoped that American settlers would eventually move into the region and outnumber the nearly 70,000 French Canadians. For the French *habitants*, keenly aware of Britain's intention, the prospect of cultural defeat only added further to their already traumatized condition — they felt themselves abandoned by France, and although not cruelly treated by Britain, in the hands of an insensitive and arrogant administration.

Britain's attempts to anglicize Québec proved futile. Over 99 percent of the white population in Canada were French — it was blatantly unrealistic to expect a sudden transformation of Catholic *françaises* into English-speaking Anglican subjects of King George III. It soon became clear that a compromise with the French was not only necessary, but also could be advantageous.

Governor Sir Guy Carleton was one of the administrators who readily recognized the importance of securing the fidelity of the French Canadians. Acutely aware of the re-

bellious rumblings to the south, Carleton urged Britain to negotiate with the French else it might find itself faced with continental insurrection. Under Carleton's guidance, the Québec Act of 1774 which granted the Québecois cultural, political and economic protection, was passed. Under the Act, British criminal law was retained but French civil law restored; the Catholic Church retained the right to levy tithes and prosecute the recalcitrant; lastly, Franco-Catholics were no longer excluded from public office. The decree pacified most

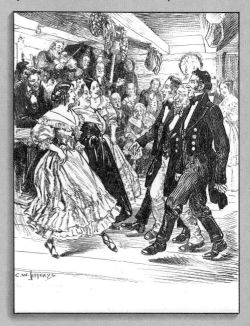

Canadiens.

The American Revolution: Sir Carleton proved to be perspicacious in his treatment of the Québecois for, as American disenchantment with Britain climaxed, it became apparent that French settlers might favor English interests. Carleton's Québec Act, however, only served to accommodate the interest of the *habitants* and consequently alienated and angered British subjects. These contradictions and tensions were brought to the surface with the advent of the American Revolution. The rebellion itself was, to some extent, engendered by the Québec Act — irritated by the extensions of French protected trapping regions (which encroached upon traditionally American

Left, a disapproving British mountie; and right, toe-tapping amusement in 1840.

lands), the American Continental Congress instituted a plot of revenge against the British in 1775. The first act of the Congress was not to declare independence from England but *to invade Canada*!

In British North America (formerly New France) sentiments about the war were mixed. The intervention of France on the American side briefly raised hopes among the Québecois. English merchants continued to sulk over what they perceived to be a betrayal of their government. Sir Frederick Haldiman, Carleton's successor, had good reason to be nervous about the loyalties of the colony. The arrival of British regulars, however, in 1776, seemed to convince French and British dissenters alike that to side with England would be the most prudent course.

The American Revolution served to cement British rule in Canada in several ways. The relative weakness and disorganization of the invaders convinced British businessmen that it was in their economic interests to support the imperial struggle — they also calmly foresaw the benefits of private and official support of Britain.

In Nova Scotia the experience of the American Revolution possessed a more distressing component. Most settlers in this region identified themselves with New England and found themselves caught between contradictory loyalties. The Americans, however, recognized the foolhardiness of dividing the colony and decided not to invade Nova Scotia — George Washington dip-

lomatically named these settlers "neutral Yankees." In the end the war strengthened ties between Britain and Nova Scotia, again primarily for economic reasons.

The Loyalists: One other significant effect of the American Revolution was the influx into Canada of 60,000 United Empire Loyalists, men and women who did not support American grievances. Most Loyalists were from upper New York State, and had fled to Nova Scotia in search of British protection — in Canada they were granted indemnity and land. The Loyalists radically altered the composition of Canada's population; their presence created a cultural dualism that contained all of the pronounced differences existing between the French and British peoples.

Upper and Lower Canada: The aftermath of the American Revolution brought with it a renewed bitterness among the British over what they perceived to be French-favored policies in the colony. The increase of the Anglo-Protestant population gave greater audibility to these complaints. The Loyalists wanted a representative government (something denied by the Québec Act). Still dependent upon British patronage, French leaders became uneasy and realized that confrontation with the Anglos was inevitable. Carleton, newly named Lord Dorchester, returned to Québec to rectify what had become "a delicate situation." As a result the Constitutional Act of 1791 was implemented. Under its directives the colony was to have an elected assembly that would exercise legislative authority in conjunction with a legislative council appointed by the king. Most importantly the Constitutional Act divided the St. Lawrence Valley into two colonies: one named Upper Canada and the other Lower Canada. The development of two distinct colonies marked a new dawn in the emergence of French-Anglo rivalries and ushered in yet another act in the drama of British North America.

After the revolution, hostilities between the British and Americans flared up again in 1812 when American rebels attempted to invade Canada for a second time. They were finally ,routed out of the new colony on October 13th during the Battle of Queenston Heights — although the British lost some of its territories to the fledgling nation, the War of 1812 formalized British North America's right to remain British.

Left, a British bell-ringer hails the hour in Halifax; and right, a sample of colonial fashions from 1863.

483.

Imp. Mariton.

L'IRIS

AIVᵉ Année.

Moniteur des Modes

de Paris. – de Leipsick. – de Vienne.

64. r. Sᵗᵉ Anne. – Postgasse 1B. Graben 618.

On s'abonne à l'Administration de L'IRIS, à Gratz. en Styrie Sporgasse 113.

THE BRITISH NORTH AMERICA ACT, 1867

Whereas the Provinces of Canada, Nova Scotia and New Brunswick have expressed their Desire to be federally united into One Dominion under the Crown of the United Kingdom of Great Britain and Ireland, with a Constitution similar in Principle to that of the United Kingdom:

And whereas such a Union would conduce to the Welfare of the Provinces and promote the Interests of the British Empire:

And whereas on the Establishment of the Union by Authority of Parliament, it is expedient, not only that the Constitution of the Legislative Authority in the Dominion be provided for, but also that the Nature of the Executive Government therein be declared:

And whereas it is expedient that Provision be made for the eventual Admission into the Union of other Parts of British North America.

CONFEDERATION CANADA FROM SEA TO SEA

The aftermath of the War of 1812 brought with it a new sense of vigor and self-determination among Canadians. As the economy flourished, Upper Canada settlers began to evaluate the political and economic role of Britain in the colonies. In Lower Canada, similar questions were being raised, although for different reasons: widespread unemployment and growing poverty engendered a bitter criticism of the British among French Canadians.

Canadian settlers were mainly disenchanted with the political structure of their colony. Although the Assembly was an elected body, a Council appointed by the king of England held executive powers and frequently overruled resolutions passed in the elected legislature. Frustrated by patronage, corruption and privilege, Canadians began to call for Responsible Government, in particular, an elected Council.

The rebellions: In Québec the Council (called the *Château Clique*) received the brunt of its criticisms from the acerbic Louis Joseph Papineau, the founder of the *Patriote Party*. The *patriotes* drew up a list of 92 resolutions and demanded, as their premier grievance, the elimination of the appointed Council. Britain flatly refused to accommodate their wishes. Eventually pushed beyond the point of polite discussion, the *patriotes* took to the streets in October of 1837 and clashed with British soldiers. After several deaths, the uprising was quelled and Papineau, whose involvement in the rebellion remained obscure, fled to the United States.

In Upper Canada the fight for Responsible Government was spearheaded by William Lyon Mackenzie, a fiery Scotsman who was the publisher/editor of a local newspaper. Mackenzie, known for his lacerating attacks against the Family Compact (the name for the Council in Upper Canada) had been elected to the Assembly in 1828 but expelled from it in 1831 for libel. In 1837 Mackenzie rallied several hundred angry protestors in Montgomery's Tavern on Toronto's Yonge Street. After a few shots of whiskey, discontent began to turn into active

dissent and the group of rebels marched down Yonge Street towards the government buildings. They were met by a group of 27 armed militiamen. When a Colonel Moodie shot at the rebel blockade, he was killed by return fire. The mishap so flustered the protestors that they fled in wild panic and disorder ... Mackenzie to the United States.

Britain adopted a rather severe stance against the rebellions although many Canadians shared the sentiments of the insurgents. When two leaders of the Upper Canada rebellion, Samuel Lount and Peter

Matthews, were hanged, vexation with the British heightened. As John Ryerson recorded of the execution:

> *Very few persons present except the military and ruf scruf of the city. The general feeling is total opposition to the execution of these men.*

The Durham report: When Britain learned of the abortive uprisings in Canada, it recognized the need to reform the colony's outmoded constitution. As a result the English Parliament established a royal commission to investigate the problems erupting in British North America. The man chosen to direct the inquiry was a politician from one of the wealthiest English families, Lord Durham, nicknamed "Radical Jack" by his

colleagues. A man of dour intensity and a violent temper, Durham was appointed Governor General of the five colonies existing in Canada.

After six short months of investigation, Durham returned to England to prepare his report on the "Canada issue." In the document, Durham complained that the colonies were stagnating and that in order to exist alongside of the dynamic and aggressive United States, Canada would have to develop a viable economy—such an economy could be realized through the unification of the colonies into a single province. Durham also believed that a union of his kind would relieve the tension existing between the English and French settlers by drawing the latter into mainstream British culture. French culture (which Durham thought was essentially "backward") the report explained, had been retarded by French colonial policies.

Despite the glaring ethnocentricism of the report, it did recommend that Canadians be granted Responsible Government. Modifying some of Durham's suggestions, Britain united Canada West and Canada East and gave each sector equal representation in a joint legislature. In 1849 the legislature formed an administration for the Province of Canada. Responsible Government had been achieved at last!

The beginnings of Confederation: The feeling that American or British domination would always threaten Canada while the colonies remained separate geographic units, pervaded political thought in the 1850s and early 1860s. Confederation, a notion that had been discussed for nearly a century suddenly reappeared as a viable possibility. Canada seemed ready for a change.

After self-government was achieved, politics became sectional in Upper and Lower Canada—for almost a decade activity in the Assembly centered around petty political bickering. Issues such as the importance of developing an intercolonial railway and the need to acquire new territories were neglected because of conflicting party interests. Governments lasted a few months, a few weeks, until in 1864 political deadlock in the Assembly emerged. With the American Civil War raging to the south, Canadians were chilled by the prospect of renewed Anglo-American conflict. Confederation seemed to be a timely way to get the colonies going again. In the same year as the deadlock, an unlikely coalition of rival parties

(the Blues led by George Etienne, the Conservatives headed by John A. Macdonald and the Liberals of the powerful newspaper magnate, George Brown) was formed. Their union was based upon a platform of Confederation.

In the Maritimes a similar discussion of uniting the coastal provinces had already surfaced. The Atlantic provinces had already called for a conference to draw up a strategy for Confederation, when the governments of Upper and Lower Canada heard of their plans. A delegation consisting of John A. Macdonald, George Brown and six other ministers decided to "crash" the conference and push for their own proposals. The *Queen Victoria* was chartered in Québec City and, loaded with $13,000 worth of champagne, set sail for Prince Edward Island. Although somewhat disconcerted by the fact that they were met by only one official in an oyster boat, the delegation was able to persuade the Maritime governments that Confederation should include Upper and Lower Canada. The rough terms of Confederation were drawn up at "the great intercolonial drunk" (as one disgusted New Brunswick editorial described it) and were ratified a few weeks later at the Québec Conference. On July 1, 1867, confederated Canada became a reality when the British North America Act divided the British Province of Canada into Ontario and Québec (formerly Upper and Lower Canada) and united them with New Brunswick and Nova Scotia. The new nation was to be called the Dominion of Canada.

The struggle for leadership: The unlikely midwife of a unified Canada was Sir John A. Macdonald, a man who had originally opposed the concept of Confederation when Alexander Galt and George Brown had proposed it, but who was to become the dominion's first Prime Minister. Born in Scotland the year of Napoleon's Waterloo, and brought to Kingston, Ontario, by his parents when still a small boy, Macdonald was perhaps the most improbable person to nurture a fledgling Canada. Although well qualified, Macdonald, a tall, gangly figure with bulbous nose and a careless but stinging sense of humor, didn't seem to fit the mold of a Canadian Prime Minister. An audacious alcoholic and a bit of a dandy, John A. Macdonald lacked the prim reserve of a British politician. But what he lacked in demeanor and appearance, Macdonald compensated for through his sharp intelligence and keen powers of insight. To Macdonald, Canada owes its tradition of witty politics. Never one to be lost for words, Macdonald

Left, the radical William Lyon Mackenzie.

introduced to Canadians a crucial qualification for a Prime Minister: articulate attack and rebuttal.

Although a successful public man, Macdonald's private life was besought, tragically, with misfortune. He had married his beloved cousin Isabella Clark whom he met on a trip to Scotland, when, shortly after their marriage, her health failed. Macdonald's first years as a politician fluctuated between attending heated arguments in the Assembly during the day and returning home at night to watch his wife die. Nine years after Isabella's death Macdonald married Susan Agnes Bernard who gave birth to a mentally handicapped daughter. Influenced by the attitudes of the times, Macdonald was scarred by the event for the rest of his life.

Despite personal hardship, Macdonald entered enthusiastically into the project of making Canada work.

The Métis Rebellion: Confederation, once approved by London, was not distinguished by a smooth transition. One of the first omens of trouble to come was the acquisition of Rupert's Land from the Hudson's Bay Company for £300,000. Unwisely, the government regarded the territory as the sole property of the Hudson's Bay Company and neglected to·take into account the indigenous population living there, namely the Métis of the Red River Colony. Trouble soon followed.

The Métis, who spoke French and practiced Catholicism, were a group of homesteaders (named "half-breeds" by the British) who had long thought of themselves as a sovereign but autonomous nation of neither European nor Indian extraction, but both. When Rupert's Land was acquired without their consultation, the Métis organized under the leadership of Louis Riel, a man of charismatic eloquence. The Métis seized Fort Garry, a British outpost, and set up a provisional government. No blood was shed during the insurrection. Supported by an American fifth.column of infantrymen, the Métis were in a strong position and the Macdonald government knew it. Negotiations had commenced when misfortune fell. All might have ended peacefully had a young upstart, Thomas Scott (who had been captured by the Métis), not tried to throttle Louis Riel. Riel snapped and had the prisoner court-martialled and shot. Much to Macdonald's dismay Scott had been a citizen of Ontario; worse still he was a Protestant murdered by a Catholic. Predictably French and English tensions mounted over the incident and the affair became politically "delicate."

The Red River incident was finally settled when the colony entered Confederation as the province of Manitoba. Riel fled to the United States.

Despite its promises, the Canadian government did not respect the integrity of the Métis community and over a decade after the first rebellion, Riel returned to begin a second one, this time in Saskatchewan. Eventually captured by British troops, Riel was put on trial for treason. Perhaps the blackest stain on Macdonald's otherwise illustrious career was his decision to have Louis Riel hanged. Responding to French cries of opposition, Macdonald remarked:

He shall hang though every dog in
Québec should bark in his favour.

Riel's death only served to entrench the old, bitter hatred between the French and the English.

The Pacific Railway Scandal: A second slight on Macdonald's political record occured through the Pacific Railway Scandal, an event that threatened to disastrously stunt the growth of the Dominion.

By the time a second election was due in Canada, Prince Edward Island, the Prairies and the Pacific Coast had been added to Confederation. The problem of connecting and maintaining links among the provinces became a major issue in the elec-

Left, the rebels march up Yonge Street; and right, Louis Riel, hung for treason.

54

Hall & Lowe

tions of 1872. A national railway stretching from coast to coast seemed to be the natural solution.

The Canadian Pacific Railway was a project proposed by Macdonald's party and was organized by Sir Hugh Allan, a prominent Montréal shipping magnate. The railway, however, was backed by large American investments and Macdonald bluntly told Allan that foreign capital must be eliminated from the project. Allan agreed to these terms but deceived Macdonald by keeping his American partners well in the background.

Six weeks before the election day, Macdonald found himself desperate for campaign funds; he asked Hugh Allan for support. Mysteriously, $60,000 appeared; another $35,000 soon followed. In a moment of fatal foolhardiness Macdonald wired Allan for a final amount:

I must have another ten thousand.
Will be the last time of calling. Do not
fail me.

Macdonald's ticket won the election and for the first time in many months Sir John A. breathed easily. At the moment of his relief, however, others were planning his demise. The offices of Sir Hugh Allan's solicitor were ransacked late one night by a confidential clerk. The plunder of the theft was sold to ministers of Macdonald's rival party, the Liberals, for a modest sum of $5,000.

Caught completely unaware, Macdonald was rudely jolted out of complacency and into alarm when the Liberals exposed the scandal: the Prime Minister had given Hugh Allan the railway project in exchange for election funds. The tell-tale telegram—"I must have another ten thousand ..."— appeared on the front pages of the newspapers the next day. Eventually forced to resign, Macdonald left office in odious disgrace. The railway was later completed but it would always lack the luster of accomplishment of which Macdonald had so often dreamed.

The close of a century: When John A. Macdonald left office, the task of shaping Canada's future was taken up by Alexander Mackenzie; Macdonald later returned as Prime Minister for over a decade and then others followed: John Abbott, J. Thompson, Mackenzie Bowell, Charles Tupper. By the time the year 1900 arrived, Canada was well on its way as a nation. Continually facing new challenges and compromising divergent interests, Canada saw the advent of the 20th Century as the beginning of a future of a golden promise.

Albertan train exhales a steamy sigh.

FRENCH AND ENGLISH IN CANADA

Five hundred miles separate Québec City from Toronto. In between lies cosmopolitan Montréal, loyalist Kingston, the edge of Ontario's prosperous "golden horseshoe" region; in between these two cultural focal points lie 300 years of Canadian history, tradition and circumstance. Québec City is archetypically French, politically resistant, insular, its visual splendor and old worldliness reminding one of Europe, of the ancient towns in Normandy or along the Rhine. Toronto is both typically English Canadian and North American. Flat, sprawling, its

streets a rigid grid pattern, the city serves as an economic center for the entire country. Everything from its skyline, waterfront, endless suburban sprawl, down to its professional baseball team locates Toronto squarely in the mode of a North American urban center. Wealthy, affluent, cultured; the city seems to embody the success of English Canada.

These two cities share in common a vast country called Canada. A 121-year-old document attests to this formal relationship. But what else do they share? What does the inner city Québec—the narrow lanes lined with cafés and bistros, the sheer cliff face edging the town up to the St. Lawrence River to Place Royale—share in common with the silver and black skyscrapers of

downtown Toronto? One city communicates in French, the other in English. One city looks to France for its cultural heritage, to the French for much of its music, film and literature. The other city combines the vestiges of British custom, an indigenous literary community, with strong leanings towards American popular culture.

The Confederation of Canada in 1867 did not in any way guarantee that these two worlds would suddenly unite. The pact was largely an exercise in economic nationalism. Indeed, economically Québec and English Canada do communicate on a regular basis. The St. Lawrence Seaway, the Trans-Canada Highway, as well as the tourist charms of Montréal and Québec City serve to maintain a steady flow of traffic between the two communities. Economic ties, along with political commitments (through the country's federal government in Ottawa), remain strong and entrenched. Canada *is* a country—a viable and functioning nation noted for its size and natural wealth. Yet a definite fragmentation exists. Once beyond economic and political considerations, the ties between the French and English grow more tenuous, more fractured and problematic. Eventually a difficult question must be asked; culturally, spiritually, what do these two worlds share in common?

The weight of history: Any understanding of French-English relations today must begin deep in North American history. There one finds the ancient animosities between England and France carried over to the New World, dividing, forcing settlers who should instinctively have united in the face of hostile environment to isolate themselves, create boundaries and borders on a continent so immense—boundless to them—that such artificial divisions should have been unnecessary. The weight of history was upon the New World from its inception. North America was a battleground for the English and French to wage imperial war on each other. In Canada the French arrivals tended to settle along the banks of the St. Lawrence, in the area now known as Québec, with the English establishing themselves

Preceding pages, two solitudes: meeting but never merging. Left, the sun-browned visage of a Québecois farmer; and right the changing of the guard in Québec: evidence of unwanted British traditions on French soil.

farther inland, initially in the Great Lakes region. By the 1750s, less than 100 years after the first influx of population, the lines were already drawn between French and English areas. With the rapid growth of the English community to the south—soon to be called the United States of America—the French were in a very real way already isolated, already defeated. The population of *la nouvelle France* was less than a tenth of that of the English colonies. From the very beginning the French in North America were a visible minority. What consolation they found derived largely from the "safety net" of mother France, watching over their interests, allowing them to imagine they were still part of the French world.

After 1759, however, this too disappeared. As usual, a war in Europe led to a conflict in the colonies. The battle on Québec City's Plains of Abraham proved decisive in the shaping of modern Canada. The English victory there, and their subsequent military possession of Québec, virtually ruled out any hope of reconciliation between the two communities. The British were the victors, the conquerors; the Québecois the defeated, French settlers were abandoned by their country and left to fend for themselves on a continent of English. The French had little choice but to accept the new authorities. For the most, returning to France was simply not a viable option. A pattern emerged in 1759 which persists to this day; a largely English-speaking government dictating to a largely French-speaking population. Tensions were, needless to say, apparent from the start.

By 1867 a fairly rigid socio-economic relationship had developed. The English in Québec were the bankers, businessmen, the power brokers; the French were the workers, farmers, the *paysans* who created and sustained a rich folk culture. In other words, the English continued to play the victors, to reap the spoils of colonial warfare.

What Confederation gave Québec was a political framework for change—the provincial government. The decentralized nature of the agreement, allotting considerable power to each province, should have provided the Québecois with a means to reassert themselves. For many reasons this did

not really happen for almost 100 years. The seeds were planted, however, the very same day the country was born.

English bosses: The first half of this century saw little overt change in the situation. English Canada expanded, solidified its borders, with Ontario coming quickly to dominate the economic scene. Naturally the markets of Montréal and Québec City were worth preserving. Statistic after statistic from this period suggests basic problems: companies located in Québec with the entire French-speaking work staff but entirely English-speaking management; blatant instances of discrimination against the natives; English-Canadian businessmen earning huge profits from the province without in any way reinvesting it back into the economy. Provincial politicians—especially the looming figure of Maurice Duplessis—found themselves supporting English hierarchies to maintain their political lives, seeking outside investment, inadvertently suppressing the aspirations of the Québecois to strengthen the province's financial status. In English Canada the French were seen as backward, remote, a society of Catholic farmers and blue-collar workers with little to offer the rest of the country except the brilliant hockey players of the Montréal Canadiens. English was simply not spoken in most parts of the province. Even in Montréal, where the Anglophone community ignored the Québecois culture around them, the majority of the inhabitants were unable to function in

necessary step to end the "solitude" in which each exists. This phrase, "two solitudes," has come to be an important part of the Canadian vocabulary. To some extent the term is as applicable today as it was 40 years ago. Yet the period between 1955 and 1980 saw a remarkable change in the fabric of both groups. In particular, the cultural and political awakening which has taken place in Québec has altered completely the dynamic of the relationship. In the last 30 years tremendous upheaval has come close to literally dissolving the Canadian experiment. It has also, as radical change often does, provided a glimmer of hope for the future.

In the late 1950s a group of artists, journalists, and political figures—Pierre Trudeau among them—began to assert the cause

the economic and political language of Canada. Ottawa and Toronto controlled the lives of most Québecois, dictated their social and economic position, yet had relatively little to do with their day-to-day existence. English Canada was a distant and foreign place.

In 1964 Montréal writer Hugh MacLennan published his novel *Two Solitudes*, a bleak if honest account of relations between the two communities, MacLennan portrayed both English and French Canada as inward looking, defensive, unwilling to take the

Left, Frontenac Hotel, Québec City; and right, Canada's parliament buildings in Ottawa: a monument to British bureaucracy.

of Québec. Known in retrospect as the *revolution tranquille*—this movement sought to create an autonomy entirely known as Québec by strengthening the cultural fabric of the society. Song writers, poets, playwrights, painters, filmmakers, historians, and even television commentators all rallied around the concept of an independent Québec. That the *revolution tranquille*, which developed into the Separatist Movement of the 1970s, had its root in cultural change is important. These artists were demanding that the Québecois take pride in their culture, their language, themselves. Québec was something quite different from the rest of Canada; they claimed that Québec was a distinct and unique culture.

As such, cast adrift in the sea of English-speaking North America, it needed to be vigilant and protective of its identity.

From the enlightened leadership of premiers Jean Lesage and Daniel Johnson, to the rise of René Lévesque and the *Parti Québecois*, the movement's political wing grew in prominence. A dark manifestation of this impulse, the terrorist group FLQ, gained much attention in the English Canadian press. While Albertans or Torontonians were oblivious to the cultural excitement in Québec, to the music of Gilles Vigneault, the writing of Hubert Aquin or Jacques Godbout, they were more than well aware of the bombings in Montréal. For them Québec's struggle for selfhood consisted of denunciations of English Canada, cries for

did any of the more positive events of the previous 20 years. For all concerned the October crisis was indeed a baptism of fire.

The proud province: The remainder of the decade saw the strengthening of the *Parti Québecois*, their assumption of power in 1976, and the referendum on sovereignty-association of 1980. By the summer of that year, Québec, while apparently unwilling to sever its ties with the rest of Canada, had emerged as a force to be reckoned with. Assertive, self-possessed, the province now had a mind of its own and, because of the nature of provincial governments, a mandate within confederation to exert considerable control over its internal affairs. In a sense the gauntlet had been thrown at the feet of English Canada.

independence, and a terrorist group running amok of authority. This distortion was disastrous to the cause of French-English relations. The assassination of Pierre Laporte in 1970—the so called "October Crisis"—proved a decisive moment in Canada's history. For a few days English Canadians witnessed with horror a brief and extremely exaggerated period of social unrest.

Suddenly news reports were filled with images of soldiers, house-to-house searches, and army checkpoints not in Northern Ireland or Chile but in *Québec*—right in Canada! These media images, the image of Pierre Trudeau declaring a state of emergency from Ottawa, did more to bring the cause of Québec's self-assertion to the surface than

During the years of the *revolution tranquille* the remainder of the country had been experiencing changes of its own, more quiet, peaceful changes, but ones sufficiently strong to demand a kind of self-examination. Emigration to urban centers, in particular Toronto and Vancouver, had altered the social make-up of the society. The "WASP" dominance of commerce in central Canada, while still unquestionable, was being flavored by new influences, new faces. Just as Montréal was no longer simply English controlled and French populated, so was Toronto no longer simply "hogtown"—city of the English money, and Anglo-Saxon temperament. Québec's growing pains greatly affected the economics of Canada. As well, they forced them to examine their priorities, their sense of self. What if Québec separated? Would Canada survive? What exactly constituted this confederation of distanced provinces? Questions like these were bandied about in the 1970s, painful questions, both uniquely private and highly public. At times speculation on the collapse of Canada was rampant; magazines would offer hypothetical maps of the country in dissolution, certain areas joining with the United States, others attempting to assert themselves as independent nations. The prospect of collapse was ludicrous, unthinkable; it was also very possible in the climate of the times. Canada lurched quietly under a weight of implications. Québec's struggle, while largely the struggle of a "solitude," nonetheless initiated a kind of collective debate on the nature of its national being.

As it stands today Québec remains a partner in confederation. Difficult economic times have relegated questions of independence to a secondary position. The issue remains important, but somehow less vital and volatile than at the turn of the decade. To some extent their point has been made; ownership of business is again largely internally (or U.S.) controlled, French is the language of commerce and politics, while the cultural life of the province continues to thrive. Relations between English Canada and Québec have suffered a further straining during the implementation of many of these policies. The exodus from Montréal of many English-language businesses offered—for the media, anyway—graphic representation of the isolation of the communities. Legislation brought in by the *Parti Québecois*, especially the controversial language bill Law 101, has left a bitter taste in the mouths of non-French speakers in Québec, along with frequent charges of discrimination against the government. Indeed many of the policies have had the effect of further entrenching the country's "two solitudes." In its bid to fortify, to strengthen from the ground up, Québec has seemingly added bricks to the considerable wall between itself and English Canada.

What then is there to be said of Canada's bilingual experiment? At first glance one might be tempted to pronounce it an outright failure. The fate of Pierre Trudeau's official bilingualism policies of the 1970s—a symbolic attempt at presenting a unified front seems indicative of the reality of the

situation. Why should *someone* in Calgary be expected to learn French? Why *should* Manitoba have its laws written in French as well as English? Québec—the "French" part of Canada—is many miles away and disinterested if not hostile towards the rest of the country. English Canada's roots lie in Britain. Many of its customs and institutions derive from there. England's queen is Canada's queen; the governor general, a representative of the throne, still offers nominal approval of all bills passed in parliament. Culturally and economically the affinities are with the United States. Québec, now that all the fuss about independence is over, remains more or less an excellent vacationing spot—exotic, foreign, yet still safely within the arms of confederation.

Québec's culture is all but ignored. English Canada has had almost no exposure to the wealth of literature, film and visual art which has emerged in the last 20 years. The death of Jacques Ferron in the spring of 1985 is only one example. A leading novelist, his passing was given scant treatment in the English press, with no apparent recognition that *Canada,* and not just Québec, had lost a major artistic figure.

One cannot overstate how much language can divide. For most people a different language suggests immediately a different culture; it suggests something strange, inaccessible, distant. To get over this reaction has proved more difficult than anyone could have imagined.

Left, a friendly chat over work in Gaspé; and right, candlelight illuminates the altar of Notre Dame, Montréal.

Yet there is room for optimism. Perhaps the most constructive way of viewing the recent events in Canada is with an understanding of their necessity in forging a genuine relationship between the two communities. English Canada can no longer patronize Québec. It can no longer view the Québecois as impoverished and backward. Likewise, French Canada can no longer complain of subjugation and inequality. No longer can they view English Canada as distant employers, selfish and indifferent to their needs. The ground has been cleared of all ancient obstacles. The communities are equal, siblings in a difficult experiment in nationhood. What better position to finally begin to talk?

Across the bridge: A visitor to Ottawa cannot help but be startled by the contrasts embodied there. The city itself is regal, stately, a miniature of an old English town. Home to the country's parliament, house of lords—to any number of British political institutions—Ottawa seems the quintessence of English Canada. From the parliament building, gazing out over the Rideau Canal and the Ottawa River, one has a fine view of the twin city on the far shore—Hull. The far shore in this instance signifies not only the Ontario-Québec border, but also the cultural borders within the country. Hull is a typical small Québecois city. Low income, working class, streets of row houses with front porches, grocery shops and cafés open until late, the town possesses a definite charm. A half dozen bridges connect it with Ottawa. In the evenings, citizens of the larger city might cross one of the bridges to take advantage of the extended bar hours in Québec. Hull is a lively night out, a night away from the pressures of working in the decision-making center of all Canada. Otherwise, the two cities have relatively little to do with each other. On these bridges languages suddenly change, perspectives alter, biases and stereotypes come to the surface. On these bridges one is confronted with the reality of Canada's "two solitudes." For the most part commerce-laden trucks comprise the largest percentage of traffic. Business is, of course, as usual. Little else is that way, however. Contact between the communities remains infrequent, tenuous, very much ill at ease. But the bridges are there. Anyone, at any time, under Canada's confederation, is free to cross over them for a visit.

Illusion or reality: building bridges between French and English culture in Canada.

THE EMERGENCE OF A NATION: CANADA IN THE 20TH CENTURY

A tentative prosperity and progress ushered Canada into the 20th Century. Under Prime Minister Laurier's government railway construction continued apace. By 1914 Canada possessed a line (the Canadian Pacific) which extended from one coast to the other. Having established a link that connected the country from each coastal terminus, Canada began to develop diplomatic relations with the rest of the world. Most international ties, however, were organized through Britain, and Canadians began to grumble about being ruled by a tiny parent island thousands of miles away. Further resentment toward Britain erupted over what came to be known as the "Alaska Boundary Fiasco."

For several years both the United States and Canada had argued over the Alaska/Yukon boundary—finally a commission consisting of three Americans, three Canadians and one British minister was formed to settle the dispute. The Americans issued a proposal that overwhelmingly favored their interests. Lord Alvertone, the British minister, voted with the Americans (much to the dismay of the Canadian team). The act was perceived as a betrayal of Canadian interests and gave further credence to suspicions of British duplicity.

Despite growing resentment of their mother country, Canadians saw a burgeoning of their nation in the early 1900s—a burgeoning that was largely due to the influx of thousands of European immigrants.

Until the arrival of Clifford Sifton (Laurier's Minister of the Interior), Canada's immigration policy favored Anglo-Saxon migrants. Travelers from the British Isles, however, were not arriving in numbers large enough to suit the Canadian government. The west, in particular, loomed large and empty. Sifton quickly altered immigration policy and initiated a widespread advertising scheme designed to attract other European settlers to the Prairies. Advertisements reading:

The Last Best West
Homes for Millions

160 Acre Farms in Western Canada
Free

were printed in a dozen different languages and distributed throughout Europe. The result was the mass migration of Ukranians, Czechs, Slovaks, Poles, Hungarians and Serbs to Alberta and Saskatchewan (provinces created in 1905). Sifton believed that Slavic immigrants, because of their farming backgrounds, were ideal settlers for Canada's west. When criticized by other members of the government for bringing "inferior breeds" to Canada, Sifton glibly replied:

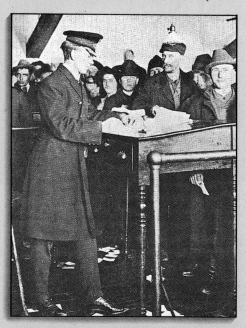

"I think a stalwart peasant in a sheepskin coat...with a stout wife and half a dozen children, *is* good quality."

For a meagre fee of 10 dollars (a registration cost) and a promise to remain on the farm for six months of the year for three consecutive years, newcomers received 160 acres of unfriendly but *gratis* prairie grass and a chance to work a farm.

Like the French *habitants*, Prairie homesteaders faced difficult beginnings. The tough prairie scrub had to be cleared to plant crops and prevent the devastating grass fires. Soil, dried for thousands of years under a blazing sun, had to be plowed using horses and oxen (one group, the Doukhobors, hitched women to their plows). For

Preceding pages, Toronto's Yonge Street, June 5, 1901. Left, Ukrainian warmth and hospitality; and right, registering immigrants, 1905.

pioneers, prairie life was both harsh and rewarding. Winters of mean blizzards and temperatures so cold they could freeze human flesh within five seconds, and torrid summers often bereft of rain, were difficulties offset only by successful harvest. As Prairie folksongs often recounted, many left the west in search of a kinder environment:

So farewell to Alberta, farewell to the west
Its backward I'll go to the girl I love best
I'll go back to the east and get me a wife
And never eat cornbread the rest of my life.

Inclement living conditions gave rise in Canada's west to a culture of strong independence mingled with a sense of mutual cooperation. Canada's unique brand of democratic socialism was born of the rugged lives of Prairie farmers struggling to survive

mittee in London. As a consequence of western outspokenness, the Senate was opened to both sexes in 1929. The first step in the battle for gender equality in Canada had been taken.

The rise of industrialism: The rugged west was not the only place where life was hard for Canadians. With the development of new businesses and industries, many Canadians experienced radical changes in their lifestyles: for the entrepreneur, commercial development meant assured affluence, but for many others it meant a life of drudgery and exploitation. In the east, the factory became the oppressive environment of the urban immigrant. Unlike Prairie farmers, however, factory workers rarely saw opportunities for advancement and truly faced an

in the early 20th Century. It is from this era that one discovers the roots of populist, radical and progressive movements in Canadian politics. One also finds the origin of a vocal women's movement in Canada—a movement headed by the efforts of Nellie McClung and Emily Murphy. Both women were involved in the famous "Persons Case" in which Canadian frontier women objected to the chauvinistic interpretation of the person's clause in the British North America Act (the Act specified that *persons* could be nominated to the Senate but Canadian parliament understood this to mean *men only*). McClung's and Murphy's petition was turned down by the Supreme Court but its decision was overruled by an executive com-

"iron cage" existence.

Early Canadian businessmen were notorious for their exploitation of migrant labor. Ten- to 12-hours days, six-day work weeks, and low wages were standard practices among factory owners. The hiring of women and children at lower rates of pay was also common. Poor working conditions and severe forms of punishment exacerbated already miserable existences. When questioned by a Labour Commission in 1910 about the appropriateness of brutally whipping six-year-old girls in his textile factory, one Montréal merchant replied that just as training a dog required strict forms of punishment, so too did the hiring of children necessitate the implementation of a rigorous discipline. In 1905 David Kissam Young, a writer for the Industrial Banner, blackly described the Canadian factory owner's shibboleth as:

> Suffer little children to come unto me
> For they pay a bigger profit than men you see.

The deterioration of working conditions and the unregulated practices of factory administrations eventually led to the rise of trade unions and labor organizations. As a result, in 1908 Ontario passed the first child-labor law in Canada—the new minimum age to work was 14 years.

The First World War: The crisis that emerged from the Balkan States in 1914 and plunged most of Europe into war had profound consequences for Canada. Still consi-

Robert Borden was Prime Minister of Canada for the duration of the World War One—his main task was to ensure that Canada found the 500,000 men it had promised to Britain. Efforts to actively support the war in Europe began to pervade Canadian society. Appeals to civic pride were made by political leaders, ministers preached of Christian duty, army officials slyly advertised the glamour of wearing complete highland regalia, and women wore badges reading "Knit or Fight." Guidelines for army admissions were stretched: the young, old, mentally or physically handicapped were admitted. As the war progressed and the need for more troops became stronger, the Canadian militia altered its ethnic policies and began to recruit Indian, Japanese and black Canadians.

dered a loyal subject of the British Empire, Canada considered it an act of duty to enter the war in support of England. The decision was not without its own advantages. When Russian wheat exports were hindered by the fighting, Canada became the main agricultural supplier of Britain and its allies. Canadian munition industries sprang up overnight and fortunes were made through the war. World War One had great economic benefits for Canada, but these were gained at' the expense of many lives.

Left, a Prairie homestead, 1918; and above, Canadian soldiers during World War I.

By 1916, however, Borden had not fulfilled his quota and his gaze slowly turned to Québec.

In Québec, French Canadians were reluctant to join the war effort. Unmoved by loyalty to either France or Britain (who had both treated the Québecois rather badly), Québec inhabitants responded cynically to the government's patriotic propaganda. In the same year conscription became a major issue in Canadian parliament—French Canadians faced forced entry into the army. Tensions in Québec eventually led to anti-conscription riots in 1918. In one skirmish, soldiers imported from Toronto opened fire on the crowds and killed four civilians. Ottawa warned that future rioters would be conscripted on the spot.

Borden's administration took an increasingly harsh attitude towards Canadians and their obligations to the war. A War Tax Measure, burdening already precariously balanced household budgets, was passed; anti-loafing legislation (which stated that any males between the ages of 16 and 60 not gainfully employed would be jailed) was issued; all "radical" unions were suppressed, and all publications printed in enemy languages were outlawed.

Then, unexpectedly, the war ended. On August 18th, 1918 Canadian and Australian troops broke through a German battalion near Amiens. The German soldiers were pushed farther back until the final day at Mons on November 11th when the German

tors experienced mild to severe harassment. In general, however, Canada's attitude towards "dissent" lacked the fanatic allegiance to "democracy" that its neighbor to the south too often displayed.

Like Americans, Canadians were thrilled by the glamorous Toronto-born Mary Pickford and flocked to see Douglas Fairbanks and Rudolph Valentino in their latest silent films: women shed several pounds of clothing, cut their hair and fought for new gender identities; Canadians politely marveled at the athletic ability of Babe Ruth ... but Canada was still a land of small towns. As such, it bolstered a small town conservative attitude—an attitude given a literary form in Stephen Leacock's *Sunshine Sketches* (1914)—subtly arrogant but at the same

army was finally defeated. By the time it was all over, Canada had lost 60,611 lives — thousands of others returned home severely mutilated, both physically and mentally.

Aftermath — the purring twenties: If the 1920s roared in the United States, they at least purred in Canada. In the States a modern equivalent of the Inquisition, the Big Red Scare, swept the country and sought to purge America of any "suspected or real communists" (including blacks, Jews and Roman Catholics). The movement never made any serious headway in Canada, much to the disappointment of the then 6 million strong American *Ku Klux Klan*. Radical parties in the Prairies, union organizers and the handful of self-avowed communist agita-

time self-remonstrating.

There were new Canadian directions to be taken as well. In the arts, the Group of Seven (really eight artists) created a stunning but scandalously different visual image of the Canadian landscape. Using techniques of the Impressionists, Ceźanne, and Art Nouveau, Lawren Harris, A.Y. Jackson, Arthur Lismer, Frederick Varley, Frank Carmichael, Frank Johnston, J.E.H. MacDonald and Tom Thomson re-explored Canada as bold iconoclasts—their works distinguished Canada internationally and had a

Left, Stephen Leacock, Canada's caustic wit; right, Tom Thomson of the Group of Seven.

lingering effect on the Canadian visual arts for many decades.

With the exception of two slumps in the agricultural market in 1923 and 1928, the 1920s seemed to be "boom years" for Canada. The insouciant manner of the times enabled Canadians to look indulgently to the future and to expect years of growth and prosperity. No one anticipated the fatal Wall Street Crash in October 1929.

The depression: The 1930s in Canada were complicated by the collapse of the world grain market—a glut of wheat on the market had made it more economical for Canada's clients to purchase supplies from Argentina, Australia or the Soviet Union. By 1929, the situation had become serious. When the depression hit Canada, it hit hard.

R.B. Bennett's Conservative government quickly rallied to address the problems of a faltering economy. Relief programs and social services (which became expert at detecting "fraud and waste") were established. Cars, telephones, pets, ornaments and jewelry were luxuries that could forfeit one's claim to relief assistance. Callous in their understanding of depression hardship, Canadian politicians claiming that "jobs were there to be found," created workcamps in British Columbia for single men. Hundreds of workers either froze to death on the trains or were murdered on their way there. Those men who made it to the camps were paid a mere 20 cents per day for their labor and barely managed to eke out an existence.

Widespread unemployment sent men and women into the streets. In Toronto a team of men would shovel snow from the driveway of a wealthy Rosedale family for seven hours, only to be paid 5 cents for their work. Women competed for the most demeaning domestic work and had to depend upon the benevolence of their employers for a decent wage.

Nowhere was destitution greater than in the Prairies. Out west it seemed as if the forces of nature had collaborated with the vagaries of the economy to make life as miserable as possible. In 1931 raging winds swept away the fertile topsoil; in 1932 a plague of grasshoppers devoured the crops, and 1933 marked the beginning of a long series of droughts, hailstorms and early frosts. Even Newfoundland, barely surviving itself, sent Prairie families dried cod cakes. (Not sure what to make of the cod, westerners soaked it in water and used it to plug up holes in their roofs.) Prairie hardship during the depression influenced the development of the Cooperative Commonwealth Federation (CCF), a farmer's labor movement

that was later to become Canada's socialist party, the NDP (New Democratic Party).

The rise of government corporations: As the depression deepened throughout Canada, radio sets became the main means of escape from a life of hopelessness. In an attempt to allay the misery of millions (so the government claimed), Bennett created the Canadian Radio Broadcasting Commission. Professional sports events, radio dramas, the lively commentaries of Gordon Sinclair, reporting of events such as the Dionne quintuplets born in Calendar, Ontario, served as diversions for many Canadians. For a few moments, an hour or an evening, families were able to forget their despair. When the depression had finally ended, millions of citizens were left scarred—a decade of hardship had produced a generation of thrifty Canadians.

World War Two: Five days before Britain declared war against Adolph Hitler and the Nazis, the front page headline of one influential Canadian paper, *The Star*, read: "WOUNDED FATHER AND SON ROUT THREE GUNMEN." No mention was made of Hitler's seizure of Slovakia, Germany's non-aggression pact with the Soviet Union, or the invasion of Poland. *The Star's* headline was indicative of the mood pervading Canadian society at the time: a blind optimism kept buoyant by the belief that the war would just go away. As Angus MacDonald, a World War One veteran remarked of Canadians before the second great war: "We all longed for peace. Everybody. Some longed so deeply that they came to believe that never again would there be a war." Even Liberal Prime Minister Mackenzie King believed that Hitler was merely a "simple peasant" with no intention of starting a skirmish with either Britain or France. But on September 3rd, 1945 Canadians had their heads pulled out of the sand. Newspaper headlines this time, read: "BRITISH EMPIRE AT WAR — HIS MAJESTY CALLS TO BRITONS AT HOME AND OVERSEAS."

Canada's involvement with the war was complicated by the fact that in 1931 the Statute of Westminister had made it an autonomous community within the British Empire, equal in status and in no way subordinate, though united by a common allegiance. Legally Canada could remain out of the war if it wished—but morally there seemed to be no alternative but to enter it on Britain's side. Aid was duly pledged.

French Canadian Opposition: In French Canada, politician Maurice Duplessis, echoing sentiments of the previous war,

challenged the government's right to speak for *all* of the people of Canada. Québec, Duplessis argued, ought to remain independent of any European struggles. Then, in the spring of 1940, the German *blitzkreig* commenced. Norway and Denmark were attacked; by June 4th Britain had been driven off the beaches at Dunkirk, and five days later France sought an armistice with Germany. Duplessis' calls for neutrality were lost amid a "total war" fervor and the scrambling of French Canadians to register for overseas service.

Prime Minister Mackenzie King maintained support for the war by promising Canadians that conscription would never be thrust upon them as long as his Liberal government remained in power. As a result, Canada plunged into a wartime economy without much complaint. Essential goods were cut down and commercial enterprises were directed to war production. Soon Canada was spending 12 million dollars a day on the war. By 1943 1.5 million Canadians were working in munition factories.

Growing U.S. ties: When Japan attacked Pearl Harbour in 1941, Canada, in recognition of the growing bonds being forged between itself and the U.S., promptly declared war on Japan. The nexus between the historically hostile nations thus acquired a stronger cooperativeness as Germany faced defeat (although the United States remained and continued to be the more aggressive partner). As the war raged brutally on, Britain began to experience severe manpower problems and the conscription issue reared its ugly visage in Canada for the second time. Under, mounting pressure, King decided to see if the Canadian people would release the government from its pledge (to fight the war on a voluntary basis) through a national plebiscite. The majority of voters agreed to release the Liberal government from its promise but the vast majority of Québecois voted against conscription. Consequently, in Québec a fierce nationalist movement rose to resist the draft; in its ranks was the young Pierre Elliot Trudeau, later to become one of Canada's most popular Prime Ministers. Fortunately for King, it was not necessary to conscript soldiers until the final months of the war.

When it was all over, Canada had lost 45,000 lives. Canadian troops had fought bravely and nobly and had played a vital role in many of the war's deciding battles. But all

was not glory and honor for Canada—like other nations, it too had amassed dark stains on its war record. The Canadian government, using the pretext that angry neighbors might do Japanese-Canadians harm, had interned 15,000 citizens in camps and had auctioned off their property. A more recent review of Canada during World War Two has indicated that under the policies of King's Minister of Justice, Ernst Lapointe, Canada refused to admit all but a few Jews fleeing Hitler's concentration camps (during and after the war). Lapointe's "none is too many" attitude received widespread support from influential anti-Semites across the country.

Postwar benefits: Canada benefited richly from the war—much to everyone's surprise. The majority of Canadians expected another depression and had prepared themselves for a decade of hopelessness and misery. Yet the war produced some unexpected results: international trade boomed, export profits skyrocketed, industrial development flourished, and the discovery of oil in the west promised great rewards for Canada. A census taken after the war showed that Canadians were living better; unlike a 1941 census which revealed that two-thirds of the population were poor, the postwar record showed only one-third to be living in poverty.

Mackenzie King attempted to reinforce growth by campaigning for increased nationwide health-and-welfare benefits and by providing minimum revenues to provinces to ensure a minimum standard of living across the country. Two wars and a depression had taught Canadians that government-run programs were important ways of averting destitution.

The 1950s: While America went through its second postwar "communist witch-hunt," Canadians settled back into readjustment. This was easier for some than for others. Women in particular who had worked actively throughout the war found themselves suffering the pangs of confusion and anger when the "feminine mystique" drove them back into their homes, and husbands patiently explained that this was their "natural" habitat. Many of the returning soldiers found the normality of everyday life burdensome to the point of mental breakdown. The 1950s, a time of rigid sex stereotypes, sought to bury the trauma of the war as quickly as possible. During the 1950s Canada began to develop a politically active and independent profile. In addition to being instrumental in the formation of the United Nations, Canada participated in the Korean War and the

Left, two hefty businessmen converse in Calgary, Alberta.

Suez crisis; it joined the North Atlantic Treaty Organization (NATO) (in which members pledged to act jointly in the event of an enemy attack); and implemented for its unpopulated northern regions, a sophisticated air defense system called NORAD. As the decade drew to a close, Canada emerged as a young and promising member of the international community.

The Cultural Revolution: The 1960s in North America call to mind laundromats, supermarkets, drive-in movies and television sets. Trademarks of prosperous families, ice-making refrigerators, dishwashers and backyard pools became ubiquitous images of the middle-class in the U.S. and Canada during the 1960s. But the 1960s was also the era of the Bay of Pigs Invasion, Martin Luther King and the civil rights movement, John F. Kennedy's assassination, the Vietnam War, "Star Trek" and "The Dick Van Dyke Show." Betty Friedan published *The Feminine Mystique* in the 60s and Timothy Leary tested the effects of LSD on undergraduates for which he was promptly fired from Harvard. The cultural revolution ignited south of the 49th parallel soon spread upward to Canada and found ferment in the minds of a people beginning to question their meaning and identity in a world overshadowed by the Cold War. A time of mediocrity, liberalism and radicalism, the 1960s shook the foundations of a historically traditional and conservative Canada. Evidence of these changes became manifest when Liberal Prime Minister Lester B. Pearson (himself the winner of the Nobel Peace Prize) announced that nuclear warheads would be included as part of Canada's NATO obligations. The announcement sparked widespread protest among Canadians and eventually became linked to criticisms of U.S. involvement in Vietnam. Peace groups emerged across the nation calling for disarmament, the abolition of nuclear warheads in Canada, and the cessation of shipments of war supplies to the United States. As often happened throughout the Western world, political issues mingled with cultural changes and "hippies" with long hair, ragged blue jeans and love beads became the new image of youth in Canada as in several other parts of the world.

In Québec different kinds of revolutionary movements surfaced. A "quiet revolution" arose in which French-Canadian artists, citizens, and politicians attempted to assert their own cultural identities against the Roman Catholic Church and vestiges of colonial dominance.

This reticent rebellion intermingled with the more violent tactics of the FLQ (*Front de Libération du Québec*). Under the leadership of Reńe Lévesque, the issue of French-Canadian nationalism erupted afresh. Québec, Lévesque passionately argued, was not a province like the others but was a homeland, a separate nation. Some of Lévesque's fanatic sympathizers resorted to terrorism to express their viewpoint: federal buildings were bombed and dynamite was placed in mailboxes of English-speaking residents. Terrorism, a seemingly European phenomenon, erupted in Canada.

Amid this turbulence, Pierre Elliot Trudeau, one of Canada's most charismatic statesmen, came to power. Flamboyant, articulate, arrogant and notorious for literally thumbing his nose at the press, Trudeau swiftly sought to introduce Canadians to the concepts of biculturalism and bilingualism. Although a firm supporter of Québec, Trudeau, himself fluent in both English and French, opposed extreme French nationalism—his solution to Québec's cries of discontent was to encourage a cooperative existence between the two cultures.

Often met with an outright stubborn rejection of multiculturalism or an only cynical enthusiasm for the idea, Trudeau was one of the first politicians to rearticulate, in a forceful

Left, reflections of Ottawa's parliament; and right, Canada's flamboyant P.M., Pierre Elliot Trudeau.

manner, the concept of Confederation for a modern Canada. Today the notion of a multicultural Canada (although the reservations still remain and the reality is far from being realized) is a main current in Canadian ideology.

Terrorism in Québec: As the 1970s approached, nationalism in French Canada adopted an increasingly aggressive stance. Riots broke out in Montréal and Québec City; the illustrious McGill University was stormed by angry students demanding that all classes be held in French. On Oct. 5th, 1970 the situation reached its climax when British Trade Commissioner in Montréal, James Cross, was kidnapped by the FLQ. Pierre Laporte, the Québec Minister of Labor was kidnapped five days later. At first

ment aid for its declining Maritime industries, and Canada as a whole was beginning to suffer from its escalating dependency upon American investment and the foreign domination of its economy.

Trudeau's hiatus: High taxes and rising inflation in 1979 brought down Trudeau's government. A relatively unknown but well-intentioned and articulate Joe Clark assumed office. Unfortunately Clark resembled in appearance (with a stretch of the imagination) Washington Irving's ill-fated Ichabod Crane. The Canadian press was quick to make that stretch and Joe Clark (familiarly called "Joe Who?" in the papers) was made the victim of vicious cartoons and attacked by hard-hitting editorials that exposed his unpolished manner, atrocious

French-Canadians applauded the actions of the FLQ—Canada would now be forced to take Québec seriously, they mused. But support quickly turned to horror two weeks later when the brutally strangled body of Laporte was found in the trunk of a car. The FLQ were no longer heroes but terrorists. On October 16th, Trudeau in a move that surprised most Canadians, invoked the War Measures Act and 10,000 soldiers swept the streets of Montréal.

While tensions gradually eased in Québec, Trudeau faced other complaints. In the west, Prairie provinces began to demand that Canada pay world market prices for its oil; Newfoundland (which had joined Confederation in 1949) wanted more govern-

French accent and indecisiveness. The Conservative government under Clark lasted less than a year and Trudeau was resoundingly returned as Prime Minister on Feb. 18th, 1980.

Pierre Trudeau's return to office was timely. In his last term as national leader, he was forced to address the one issue he had always struggled against: French separatism. As Trudeau reassumed office René Lévesque proposed that a referendum be held in which Québecois would be asked to vote "oui" or "non" for separation from Canada. On May 20th 1980, 88 percent of all Québec residents voted—41 percent cast a "yes" ballot and 50 voted "no." A crushing defeat for Lévesque and the French nationalists, the outcome was a major victory for Trudeau and the federalists. The spirit of John A. MacDonald sighed a relief.

New waves in the 1980s: After a total of three terms as Prime Minister, Pierre Trudeau decided to resign. His last legacy to the Canadian people was a new Constitution (replacing the British North America Act) which included a Bill of Rights. The new document was made law by Queen Elizabeth II in Ottawa on April 17th, 1982.

The Liberal leadership was turned over to a slick John Turner who was challenged by an even slicker Conservative, Brian Mulroney. Criticized by Ed Broadbent of the NDP as Canada's Visa and Mastercard, both Mulroney and Turner represented a new direction in Canadian politics: that of high

world's most powerful nation, Canadian society and its politics can seem at times trivial, if not a little self-conscious. Political actions that may result in a disgraceful dismissal in Canada are often considered minor offenses south of the border and elicit only casual chastisement. But Canada's talents rest (like many other countries on this planet) in its understanding of what it is like to have been a colony, and its understanding of the nature of interdependency. As a result, Canada as a nation is extremely sensitive to international issues and possesses unique abilities in the areas of compromise and negotiation. The current challenge for the Canadian leadership is to combine a confident self-assertion with a willingness to operate upon international premises.

finance and unregulated enterprise. Unimpressed by John Turner, Canadians gave Brian Mulroney a landslide victory in 1984. Mulroney's tenure as Prime Minister has been riddled with patronage scandals, environmental crises and public debates on "free trade" with the U.S. As a result, his popularity has often ebbed although recently it seems to have evened out. When Canadians elect their next Prime Minister, they will face a close race among Liberal, Conservative and NDP candidates.

A changing continuity: Sitting atop the

Without national heroes or violent revolutions, Canada has emerged in the 1980s as a hopeful nation, arising out of unique historical circumstances. In reviewing the events that led to the formation of this land, and what they signify for Canadians, one catches a glimpse of the elusive Canadian character. These flashes of insight are expanded, given form and substance through an encounter with Canada on the local level, in visiting its cities and towns, in walking across its plains or through its wilderness. History itself is constantly transformed in Canada from one region to the next—the effect of this being a sense of changing continuities and of a past being continually shaped by challenges of the future.

Left, Montréal's skyline: continual growth and expansion; and above, Canadians "go punk" in Manitoba.

SEARCHING FOR A CANADIAN IDENTITY

"All things seem to contend there (Canada) with a certain rust of antiquity ... the rust of convention and formalities. If a rust was not on the tinned roofs and spires it was on the inhabitants."
—Henry David Thoreau

There is something very old about Canada, even though in comparison with other nations it is entering *only* its adolescent years. For the native peoples, the Canadian identity stretches thousands of years into the past—their search is a struggle to retain ele-

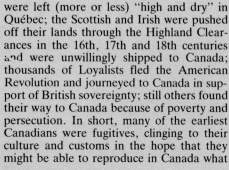

were left (more or less) "high and dry" in Québec; the Scottish and Irish were pushed off their lands through the Highland Clearances in the 16th, 17th and 18th centuries and were unwillingly shipped to Canada; thousands of Loyalists fled the American Revolution and journeyed to Canada in support of British sovereignty; still others found their way to Canada because of poverty and persecution. In short, many of the earliest Canadians were fugitives, clinging to their culture and customs in the hope that they might be able to reproduce in Canada what

ments of their ancient culture. From a colonial perspective, the traditions which surface in Canadian culture seem to be born of an earlier time, of different origins and places, of antiquated rituals and customs. Unlike the seemingly tangible character of its senior neighbor, Canada's aged-like identity is a more reclusive and subtle one, unwilling to commit itself to anything specific.

The sense of antiquity and elusiveness in Canadian culture is perhaps the product of its unusual history. As Northrop Frye, a noted Canadian intellectual, has observed, the vast majority of early Canadians (with the exception of the Indians) were people who did not wish to be in Canada. The French, abandoned by France after 1763

they had possessed at "home." In Canada one experiences echoes of different pasts, all resolutely harmonized into a uniquely Canadian score.

This is not to say that Canada has not had its own peculiar effect on its inhabitants. The cold, the hostile environment, the bounty of food, the availability of land—all have combined to make Canada both a haven and a hell for its first immigrants. Songs, poems, paintings of early Canada inevitably celebrate its compassion and callousness. Yet underlying these themes of survival is the notion, even if only in principle, of ethnic diversity or, as a Canadian would say, multiculturalism.

Multiculturalism: From coast to coast,

there is no one thing that will mark a person Canadian except perhaps for the ubiquitous "eh?" everyone seems to use without reservation (as in "It's cold outside eh?" or "The Prime Minister's not making sense eh?"). Within each region—North, East, West and Central—there are definite qualities that demarcate Prairie folks from Maritimers, Ontarians from Québeckers. The Canadian identity is an odd mixture of assertive regionalism and resigned nationalism. Summing up the constant tension between the federal and provincial aspects of the Canadian personality, Henri Bourassa, a French-Canadian statesman, once remarked: "There is an Ontario patriotism, a Québec patriotism or Western patriotism, but there is no Canadian patriotism."

da's *international* image is promoted as a "mosaic" not a "melting pot."

Canada's multifaceted identity is also reflected in its diverse political system. The strict bipartisanship of American politics is not reproduced in Canada. Although two parties dominate the Canadian political spectrum *(the Liberals and Conservatives)* their influence is mitigated by the powerful presence of Canada's democratic socialist party *(the New Democratic Party)* and to a lesser extent, by the Québecois *Social Credit Party*. Elections in Canada tend to be times of competing and compromising interests, of indentities emerging and reshaping themselves.

As a national ideology, the notion of a mosaic neatly fulfills Champlain's original

As recently as 1970 multiculturalism became an official government policy in Canada. The policy was designed to reflect one of the original principles of Confederation: that Canada become a system of coordination among different but equal parts. As a result, in Canada there is a certain toleration for ethnic and religious plurality (the growing number of Sikhs, Hindus, Buddhists, Muslims and Jews attest to this point). Cana-

Preceding pages, wisdom and patience mark the features of a Nova Scotian; and a Canadian "snow creature." From left to right, a Huron Chief in official garb; a French-Canadian laborer; two entrepreneurs from Manitoba; and a seasoned captain from P.E.I.

wishes to found Canada on principles of justice and compassion. As an implemented process, however, it falls drastically short of success. John Porter, in his classic *The Vertical Mosaic*, harshly denounced the Canadian mosaic as a highly differentiated, hierarchical structure that forced certain ethnic groups into occupational ghettos. Other critics have claimed that the cultural mosaic has only served to obscure the fact that Canada is a rigidly class-divided society. There is much truth to be found in these statements. Recent statistics maintain that the financial, political and cultural interests in Canada are controlled by a group of only 2,000 people, none of whom are women or Native Peoples. About 80 percent of this group are of British origin and 90 percent are Protestant. The elite of Canada is very much a WASP elite.

The question of a Canadian identity, then, emerges as a complex, multidimensional issue. The questions of "what is my culture?," "what is my heritage?" probably surface at one time or another in the lives of all Canadians. The endeavor to articulate a culture concept within Canada continues; it is shared by all Canadians who strive to understand their differences and celebrate them.

Native peoples: Perhaps as long ago as 40,000 years, Canada's first inhabitants crossed the Bering Strait to settle the frozen regions of the north. For many millennia Indian life flourished in Canada. This,

appreciated as improvements over a previously primitive way of life.

Visitors to Canada will frequently encounter a certain tragic pathos in the native peoples here. Reservations are often places of severe poverty and a deathly lethargy; cheap hotels and broken-down bars almost inevitably house the inner city Indian alcoholic or drug addict. Such images are used to confirm the specious argument that Canada's native people are "lazy, drunken welfare bums"— in reality they reveal the callous way in which Canada has treated its native groups. Caught between two worlds and without a place in either, the native person struggles with an alienation that no other Canadian shares.

Other images, however, abound. Across

however, was drastically altered when European explorers, greedy for the riches of the Orient, began to colonize North America. Disease, death by gunfire and forced settlement decimated most of the Canadian tribes until today, only some 550 bands remain.

Comprising less than 1 percent of the total population, Canada's native peoples (classified as Indian, Inuit and Métis) continue to struggle against policies which seek to stigmatize them as "non-people," "inferiors" or "Canada's untouchables." Communities of Indians that have been forced to live on reservations find themselves situated in semi-colonial territories where government handouts, "white" schools and running water are supposed to be accepted and

Canada colorful ceremonies and festivals attest to the fierce fighting spirit of many bands and their determination to carve out a just existence for themselves in Canada. Eloquent and powerful leaders have arisen in an attempt to synthesize divergent backgrounds and interests into a unified political entity. Increasingly, Indian groups have pressed for economically valuable land claims — some like the Dene have demanded their own nation — and have made some headway with a government whose patronage has ultimately ghettoized them. No longer submissively trusting, the Canadian native peoples have persistently emerged as a force to be reckoned with.

French Canadians: When Jacques Cartier

established a settlement along St. Lawrence at the sites of Hochelaga and Stadacona, little did he know that his fledgling community would become Canada's "black sheep of the family." Abandoned early on by France and reluctantly adopted by Britain, French Canada continues to embody a fierce ethnic pride, a distinct cultural identity and a tenacious traditionalism. Today French nationalism is alive and well in Québec and surfaces with equal ferocity when *Canadien* rights are threatened in the other French communities scattered across Canada.

A British-dominated Canada has often treated Québecois demands for cultural autonomy as the cries of a spoilt child—nothing that a few patient murmurs of biculturalism can't quell. But such is like dousing

an already well lit bonfire with gasoline. Nothing seems to irk French-Canadians more than trivializing the issue of French ethnicity in Canada.

As a result, *Canadien* attitudes towards *les anglais* (which is just about everybody else) range from a stern disapproval to outright racial hatred. Most English-speaking Canadians are capable of showing the same range. There are still some places in Québec

From left to right: a slavic smile from the Prairies; a "new wave" Canadian from Vancouver; Queen of the Calgary Stampede; and a debonaire Albertan.

where a few words in English will only get one stoney and silent stares. There are still places in Ontario where the introduction of French classes into a high school will produce hordes of angry parents threatening to transfer their children. There are, however, places where French and English attempt to understand and respect each other's differences—provided each will go at least half way.

Biculturalism overshadows the quest for a cultural mosaic in Canada. For the French-Canadians it is not just a matter of being a part of the puzzle but rather being recognized as a primary part, as a founding partner of the nation. Recently the French nationalist *Parti Quebécois* lost the political leadership of Québec to the Liberals. The rancor of separatism has, for the moment, subsided. But the quest for French integrity within Canada is far from being a settled issue—the polemic continues to pervade Canadian society at almost every level.

English, Scottish and Irish: Canada is predominantly a "British" nation. The pomp and ceremony of public events, the ubiquitous portrait of Queen Elizabeth II in hallways and antechambers, the presence of a parliamentary government—all are suggestive of an English ancestry. The history of Anglo-Saxons in Canada, however, is much more piebald in nature than British traditions might wish to admit.

In addition to authentic stock (immigrants traveling directly from England) Canada received many of its British inhabitants via the United States. Loyalist "Yankees" fleeing the American War of Independence entered Canada in droves during the 18th Century and tipped the scales in favor of an Anglo-dominated population. English immigrants were joined by Irish refugees (many of whom were victims of the Potato Famine) who had come across the Atlantic in search of food and employment. Similarly, Scottish immigrants, pushed off their lands to make room for sheep farms, ventured to Canada in one last, desperate effort to survive. The combination of Irish Catholics and Protestant Scots was rarely a compatible one and riots, usually occurring during one of the annual parades, were common events in 19th Century Canada. Not surprisingly, al-

venture onto Canadian lands. Germans came to Nova Scotia as early as 1750 and founded the town of Lunenburg in 1753. This tiny metropolis eventually became a thriving center of Maritime shipbuilding. German Loyalists also emigrated to Upper Canada and established a (still-existing) community in a town they named Berlin (later changed to Kitchener during World War One due to fear of anti-German sentiments).

Swedes, Norwegians and Finns, many escaping Czarist oppression, have also established settlements in the west, where regions most resemble the Scandinavian terrain. These areas have retained their original ethnic flavor. A group of enterprising Icelanders fostered the Prairie town of Gimli, "a hallway of heaven" and have managed

though attenuated by time, some tension continues to persist.

Today, cultural images of the Irish, English and Scottish are almost everywhere in Canada, whether it be in the opening session of parliament or in a neighborhood pub. Highland games, Irish folk festivals and political ceremonies (strangely imitative of Buckingham Palace's changing of the guard) are common sights in each of the provinces. A glance across a map of Canada will also reveal that many of the towns and cities have been named after a favorite spot in the British Isles.

Germans and Scandinavians: Next to the French and British, peoples of Germanic stock were the earliest European settlers to

to thrive on the successful commercial production of two Canadian delicacies: goldeye and whitefish.

Ukranians: The 18th Century in Canada saw the influx of thousands of Ukranians—"the people of sheepskin coats" as popular journalism of the time named them. Attracted by free farms in the west and undaunted by Prairie fields (which strongly resembled the steppes back home), Ukranians first settled Manitoba, Saskatchewan and Alberta. Their ethnic dominance in the west has been diluted but never seriously challenged by Polish, Czech, Slovak and Serbo-Croatian immigrants.

Next to French Canadians, Ukranians have perhaps the most vocal and assertive sense of a national identity. Recognition of their ethnic heritage is pursued aggressively through powerful organizations, daily and weekly Ukranian newspapers, and political groups that have spearheaded the struggle to give languages (other than French and English) official status in Canada.

The Chinese: Abandoning the exhausted goldfields of California and drawn to the mineral riches of British Columbia, the Chinese first came to Canada as miners. Through sheer endurance and a knack for frugality, the Chinese were able to set down roots in the west and eventually prospered in the face of widespread hostility and racist government policies (one of which was the imposition of a "head tax"). The 1880s in British Columbia saw the influx of Asian

ing small businesses. The relative success the Chinese experienced in developing lucrative commercial enterprises led to the Chinese Immigration Act of 1923—the legislation was sparked by the jealousy of white merchants in the area. The act effectively barred the immigration of Asians to Canada so that between the years of 1923 and 1941 only 15 Chinese were admitted.

In the 1960s immigration policies were relaxed and Asians, along with Arabs, Indians, Italians, Hispanics and Caribbean blacks, have managed to enter Canada in much larger numbers. Powerful in small commerce and increasingly visible as doctors, lawyers, university professors and engineers, Chinese-Canadians have emerged as a new voice in the debate about ethnic

"coolies"—Chinese laborers who had been recruited to work in the railway gangs that built the Canadian Pacific. Poorly paid, working under duress and in dangerous conditions, many Chinese died in the service of a country who considered them to be less than human. When the railway was completed many Chinese left Canada while others remained to eke out an existence working in factories, private homes or start-

From left to right: women from Manitoba; ethnic headgear from Canada; a Greek Canadian ready to dance; and a Scottish highlander.

identity in Canada. Summing up the feelings that most minority Canadians experience in possessing a hyphenated heritage, one Chinese-Canadian has commented:

"There is an assumption here (Canada) that there is a basic culture and add-ons. The assumption is that there is a given· culture and that there are add-on ethnic groups who are somehow second class citizens...We must encourage equality among Canadians through a mixing of experience, exposure to each other and participation in our culture. We need to establish areas where there is a similarity or a shared experience."

THE INUIT

It was just a few years ago that Canadians living south of the 60th parallel were surprised to learn that Eskimos had always called themselves Inuit or the "only people." The name is quite apt when you consider that the Inuit were the only people who had lived in the Arctic for thousands of years. The word "Eskimo" is not Inuit but Indian, meaning "eaters of raw meat." It is hardly a name that fairly describes these resilient soft-spoken people. The fact that for so long Euro-Canadians called the Inuit "Eskimo" speaks volumes of the silence that has existed between the two.

The Arctic environment over the past several thousand years has not always been static; it has undergone both warming and freezing trends with a variety of life living in the region at different periods. The north's nomadic inhabitants have had to adapt accordingly to these changes.

The first group to live in the north migrated across the Bering Strait during a relatively warm period in the earth's history. This nomadic group, known as the pre-Dorset, spread north into the Arctic Archipelago and as far east as Greenland. These people hunted seals and fished the waters of the Arctic Ocean, much like their relatives west of the Bering Strait. Around 1500 B.C. a cooling trend began in the north that forced them to move south onto the mainland. It was during this period that the pre-Dorset culture evolved into the indigenous Dorset culture. These people now stalked the caribou herds instead of hunting on the sea ice. Their cultural links with their cousins west of Bering Strait were broken.

Yet the Dorset are not the direct ancestors of the Inuit. Starting at 900 A.D. another warming trend began in the Arctic that heralded the migration of the Thule from Alaska. The Thule hunted sea mammals. With the retreat of the permanent ice pack in the mainland whales, seals and walruses swam through the Bering Strait and into the Beaufort Sea. The Thule were quick to follow.

The Thule differed from the Dorset in several respects, one was that they lived in fairly large settlements along the coastline

unlike the Dorset who lived in small family groups. Secondly, the Thule were technically more sophisticated hunters than the pre-Dorset or even the Dorset.

Ironically, about 1500 A.D., the Thule found themselves in a position similar to that of the Dorset 3,000 years earlier; yet another mini-ice age had set in. This period saw the ice pack grow so large that the number of sea mammals passing through the Bering Strait to the Arctic Ocean decreased and the migration patterns of the caribou shifted southward. The Thule adapted; they broke

into smaller groups and became more nomadic. It is these people who are called the Inuit.

The Inuit chose to make the Arctic their home, in spite of the adversity they encountered. Their history, culture and language are unlike that of the Indians, who moved south soon after crossing the Bering Strait. In that harsh unforgiving land they perfected the building of igloos and airtight kayaks; they became experts in tracking polar bear and seal on the Arctic ice. Although they suffered from time to time with famines, drownings and exposure, Inuit stayed. Forged with their innate ability for innovation was a humility that made the Inuit a tolerant, stoic society, who accepted their

Left, Arctic entertainment—a community trampoline; and right, Inuit boy shy in front of a camera.

limitations in a land where darkness reigns for six months of the year. The fact the Inuit have not just survived, but endured for centuries becomes even more remarkable when one considers that despite the technological sophistication that Euro-Canadians have brought with them to the north, they still encounter tremendous emotional upheaval in adjusting to the isolation of the north for even a few years. The Inuit do not have that sense of isolation; for them the wind, the snow, the seasons of light and darkness are simply a part of their life.

European contact: In 1576 the isolation of the Inuit from Europe ended when Martin Frobisher, an Elizabethan explorer and privateer, sailed into a large bay on Baffin Island in search of gold and the Northwest

tionally had for foreign involvement in their affairs.

Apart from Frobisher's expedition, the Inuit of the high Arctic seldom had contact with any Europeans until 1818 with the arrival of whaling vessels in the eastern Arctic Ocean. In addition to danger, these whalers risked navigating through the treacherous iceberg-laden Davis Strait in search of the bowhead whale. Many sailors were afflicted by bouts of frostbite, scurvy and a chronic mental fatigue associated with Arctic isolation. In the 1830s there were a series of whaling disasters with vessels becoming trapped and then crushed by the pressure of Arctic ice. Many questioned the feasibility of whaling in the northern clime.

A solution to these problems was to estab-

Passage to India. He was met by Inuit who circled his vessel in their kayaks. In a bid to coax the Inuit more closely to his vessel he rang a bell, the sound of which had probably never been heard in the Arctic before. One curious Inuit was close enough to Frobisher's vessel to reach for the bell. Frobisher, with both hands, pulled the man and kayak up and into the ship and stowed him away, like booty, in the hold.

After the search for gold and the passage both proved fruitless, Frobisher returned to England where the north's "ambassador" was put on display for royalty. The griefstricken man soon died in captivity of European disease. This inauspicious encounter exemplifies a reluctance the Inuit have tradi-

lish permanent whaling stations on the islands of the Arctic. In the 1840s William Penny, a typically shrewd Scottish whaling captain, began to employ local Inuit at his station on Baffin Island. He found that they were exceptional whalers, hardly surprising when you consider that the Inuit had been whaling for several centuries. Soon Penny and other astute whalers began to adopt the warm Inuit clothing, stylized harpoons and other paraphernalia of Inuit technology as their own.

Assimilation: Unfortunately, because the whaling proved so successful by the 1880s, the bowhead whale population was decimated in the Arctic Ocean. In spite of the decline in the whaling industry, the contact with the southerners, or *Kabloonat,* continued because of the growing presence throughout the Arctic of the Hudson Bay Company, Canada's largest fur-trading company. Although the Inuit maintained their semi-nomadic life, they began to rely upon trapping and trading to provide for themselves. This subtle shift away from living solely off the land provided them with guns, butter, cooking utensils and foodstuffs. For some, the Hudson Bay stores became a base or second home. However, this arrangement changed, when in the 1940s, the price of furs fell dramatically. Suddenly they could no longer purchase ammunition or other goods that had become essential. On Baffin Island, two thirds of the Hudson Bay Stores closed their doors. A long period of starvation and

1840s there were 1,000 Inuit, but in 1858 because of sickness there were but 350. One anthropologist studying at Coronation Gulf found in the 1920s that over 30 percent of the Inuit population had died from influenza over a 14-year period. Similarly in Coppermine in 1931, 19 cases of TB among a population of 100 were found.

The Canadian government intervenes: For the most part until the late 1940s the Canadian government had basically ignored the Inuit. However, after prodding from the churches, they began to take action. In 1950 medical authorities ordered 1,600 Inuit or 14 percent of their population to sanitoriums in Edmonton and Montréal. (This action though medically necessary was devastating for the Inuit, the vast majority of whom had

deprivation began. Except for missionaries who struggled to aid the Inuit, the "only people" discovered how alone they were.

At the same time, Inuit economy was collapsing, missionaries were filing reports to medical authorities that tuberculosis and influenza epidemics were annihilating the Inuit. There is evidence that long before the 1940s European viruses had been infiltrating northern communities and killing many Inuit. William Penny noted in his journals that on his arrival to Baffin Island in the

never left the North.) As well as treating TB, health authorities were startled by extremely high rates of infant mortality. In 1958 infant mortality was at 257 per 1,000 live births. By 1970 it had dropped to 100 per 1,000 and in 1981 it was 21 per 1,000.

The federal government introduced more than a medical plan for the Inuit; they coupled together policies that would rocket the Inuit into Canadian society. The central tenet of all these policies was to encourage the Inuit to abandon their nomadic life and move into government-built permanent settlements. These artificial communities provided housing, medical facilities, churches and schools. At the same time the Inuit were provided with access to universal income be-

Left, Great Whale River circa 1920; and right, spear hunting.

nefits. It is sadly ironic that Canada's original people were the last to benefit from Canada's social welfare scheme.

However well intentioned policy makers were, they failed to understand that the Arctic tundra and ocean is home for the Inuit. The Inuit were shepherded away from the land by people who knew little about Eskimo culture. Their entire way of life was undermined by southerners who failed to understand the principles through which the Inuit had been able to live in the north for so long.

The Inuit from the beginning of this resettlement period struggled to retain their identity while living in community. The first step was made in 1959; in that year the Cape Dorset Artists Co-op was formed on Baffin Island. Over the centuries the Inuit have

more than an artist's enclave. The co-op in many communities manages hunting expeditions, municipal services and trading posts. The philosophy behind the co-ops reflects the Inuit concept of community and what western thinking might call egalitarianism. In abstract terms the Inuit co-op is the resulting synthesis of a traditional social matrix being placed within a capitalist framework.

Such a configuration can bewilder outsiders. One example is a community in the arctic that has for several years run a successful polar-bear hunt for wealthy southerners. According to territorial law, dog teams must only be used for the hunt, not snow machines. One year, the man chosen for the role of hunt leader by the co-op was not a particularly adept dogsledder.

worked with ivory, stone, bones and skins to make clothing, utensils, hunting tools, toys and religious amulets. Often intricate designs were patterned onto these objects. When whalers arrived trading began to take place, with the resourceful Inuit even manufacturing ivory cribbage boards for trade. It was in the 1950s that southerners began to rediscover the Inuit's remarkable skill in carving and crafts and funding was made available to develop the craft. As a result the Inuit co-ops have flourished. Over the years the co-ops have received international recognition for their work in several mediums, including stonecut prints, stencil, sculpture and carving.

The co-op system has evolved to become

Another man in the village, who had a reputation as a skillful traditional hunter, was not considered. Consequently, after a two-week hunting expedition, the party failed to shoot a bear. The big game hunters were rather dissatisfied. The reasoning the co-op gave for hiring the poorer hunter was that he had no steady means of employment, while the best hunter already held a wage-paying position.

A sense of community: The attitude of the community was not so much that they were penalizing one individual over another but that they were maintaining a communal harmony. For the same reason Inuit town meetings tend to be excruciatingly long, and are filled with long meditative silences. Generally, the Inuit will not leave a meeting before a well thought out consensus has been forged.

A reason for the communal nature of these people is that most Inuit born into a community can expect to live out their lives in that community. Because of the relative isolation of the villages they have developed into a self-sacrificing people who are remarkably tolerant and respectful of community goals. The Inuit have learned to work and live with each other.

The importance of children in a society where the line between nuclear family, extended family and community are blurred cannot be overestimated. Traditionally, Inuit women are encouraged to have many children; many start from puberty and still bear children into their mid-forties. As a

tion procedures. Social workers were equally puzzled when they attempted to unravel whose children were whose.

Within the Inuit community there is clearly a different set of values operating from those in the south. The pursuit of personal wealth is for the most part played down. The respect one can earn in the eyes of the community is important. For men this respect has traditionally been earned through becoming a good hunter or trapper. Carving, despite its lucrative nature, is not seen as worthy an occupation as hunting and living on the land.

It is this traditional intrinsic relationship to the land that has made the Inuit, particularly the older Inuit, ambivalent towards higher education and the learning of "south-

result it is common for a nephew to be left minding his uncle. If it happens that for whatever reason the parents of a child cannot support their child, the child will quickly be adopted by the grandparents, an uncle or an aunt. Unlike the south there is less of a taboo towards illegitimacy and again that may be partly attributed to a sense of communal responsibility for children. In the 1960s the Inuit were baffled when social workers first attempted to formalize adop-

ern skills. Part of those feelings can be attributed to the early days of the federal government's intervention in the north. Mandatory school attendance was seen by the Inuit as a method of either forcing the Inuit to follow their children on to government-built communities or to separate from their children by sending them away to school. Both choices were terribly difficult for the people and caused upheaval for the community. Many Inuit questioned the relevance and importance of their children learning English, science and maths.

A chronic problem that all government agencies, including educational facilities, has is in attracting teaching staff to live in the north for more than a few years. The short

Left, Inuit women discussing their husbands; and above, taking a picture on the ice.

tenure of southerners is seen by the Inuit as only a reflection of the south's lack of commitment to the community. Schools are perceived, in many communities, not as an integral part of the community, but as a foreign body.

The federal government, however, *has* attempted to integrate the educational system into the community. A program was introduced to recruit and train Inuit to become teachers. It failed, in part because few Inuit were willing to leave their community for eight months at a time to train. It is interesting that just as many southerners feel isolated living in the north, the Inuit face an equally difficult task leaving the arctic.

Arctic baby boom: Over the past 15 years it has become apparent that the young adult

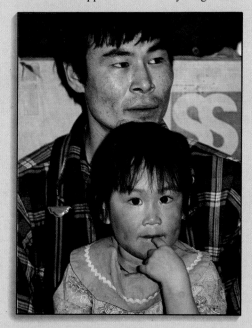

Inuit population is the most affected by the complications of living in a world with two divergent cultures. These young Inuit are the product of a "baby boom" that swept across the Arctic in the 1950s and 1960s. This boom was in part created by the lowering of infant mortality and generally improved health conditions. The question that faces this group of people is how they will support themselves in the coming years. As part of government policy many left home to attend regional high schools. That isolation had a disorienting affect upon the young. They failed to learn, as their parents had, how to live off the land. One older Inuit in an interview expressed alarm that the young did not know how to stay warm while out in the cold

or how to build an igloo. Yet, if the young are not familiar with traditional skills and their implicit philosophy, they also have not acquired the skills necessary to compete for management positions in government or in industry. The continuity in passing down the knowledge and communal values from one generation to another has been broken. The resulting problems have manifested themselves in alcoholism, vandalism and suicide.

Bringing technology: In countless interviews with older Inuit, the terrible privation suffered in the harsh environment is often recalled. There can be little doubt that technology has brought about a safer and more comfortable life for the Inuit. They ride on snowmobiles, watch TV with VCR attachments and hunt with highpower rifles. They have running water. They no longer live in snow houses. The question that many would ask is has this technology made the Inuit more or less Inuit? Yet these modern tools by themselves are not the issue. The Inuit have traditionally been eager to adopt new technology, in their environment they had to be great innovators. It is what the technology represents that bothers the Inuit. Recall the first encounter of Frobisher. It was not the bell that trapped the Inuit but the unscrupulous intentions of the bell ringer. The challenge for the Inuit is to make technology their own; then they will be rulers in their own land. In adopting this technology and making it their own Inuit must look to their knowledge of how they lived in the past if they are to avoid becoming strangers in their own land. For over 5,000 years the Inuit and their predecessors have politically, aesthetically and socially been building and rebuilding a society that has allowed them to live independently in an environment where others could not bear the physical and psychological pressure. It is their unique culture that has allowed them to make the north their home. If they are to prevail it will be by adapting the new-found technology into the culture. For generation upon generation of Inuit the Arctic has been their home. If the young are not permitted to capture that spirit, if they are overwhelmed and bullied by western society, then they will no longer be Inuit. And Canadian society will lose a fragment of its mosaic.

Left, Inuit father pauses thoughtfully over his daughter's head; and right, "read to go," an Inuit woman with her "bags packed."

C.P.R 202

PLACES

From sea to sea... such is the national motto of Canada, a land so immense and diverse that no single word, phrase, or description can adequately capture its astonishing variation. Canada stretches from one formidable coast to the other and rises upward into the mysterious regions of the unfriendly Arctic — within the journey between the seas are a myriad of moods, of changing landscapes and shifting temperaments. Canada is never predictable.

Traveling to Canada can mean encountering the windblown beaches of the Maritimes, the placid, rich valleys of the Niagara, or the seemingly endless expanse of the Prairie steppes. It can mean discovering a salty Newfoundlander whose family has existed in the same way for 15 generations, or observing the *nouveau riche* of Toronto display, somewhat selfconsciously, their mirror-and-chrome affluence. It can mean a city or a wilderness, a cultural metropolis or a conservative town. Sometimes pensive, sometimes playful, the Canadian landscape presents itself to visitors as an intriguing design, evoking Coleridge's notion of beauty: "unity in variety."

Ten provinces (Newfoundland, Nova Scotia, Prince Edward Island, New Brunswick, Québec, Ontario, Manitoba, Saskatchewan, Alberta, British Columbia) and two territories (Northwest Territories and Yukon) are the historical and geographical boundaries of Canada. The following pages divide these regions into Central, East, West and North and explore the unique character of each area by focusing on its towns and cities.

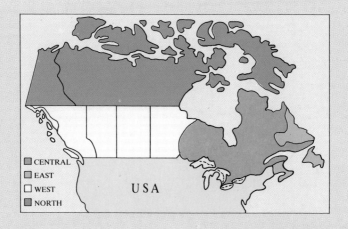

CENTRAL
EAST
WEST
NORTH

USA

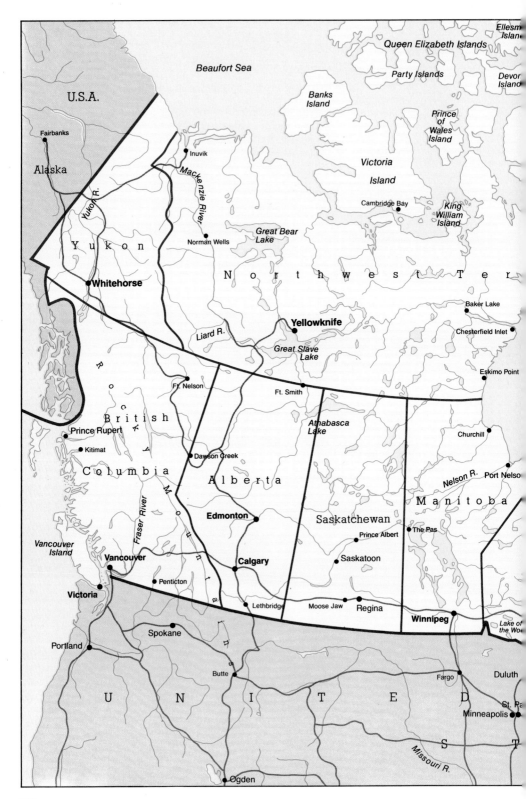

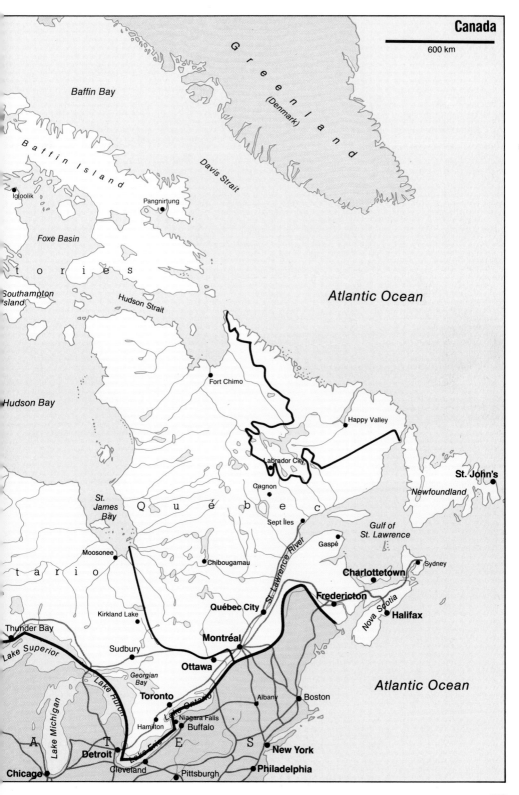

Canada

600 km

Baffin Bay

G r e e n l a n d
(Denmark)

B a f f i n   I s l a n d

Igloolik

Davis Strait

Pangnirtung

Foxe Basin

t o r i e s

Atlantic Ocean

Southampton Island

Hudson Strait

Hudson Bay

Fort Chimo

Happy Valley

Labrador City

St. John's

Cagnon

Newfoundland

St. James Bay

Q u é b e c

Sept Îles

Gulf of St. Lawrence

Moosonee

Chibougamau

Gaspé

Sydney

t a r i o

Charlottetown

St. Lawrence River

Kirkland Lake

Québec City

Fredericton

Nova Scotia

Halifax

Thunder Bay

Montréal

Lake Superior

Sudbury

Ottawa

Georgian Bay

Toronto

Lake Huron

Albany

Boston

Lake Michigan

Hamilton

Lake Ontario

Niagara Falls

Buffalo

A

T

Lake Erie

E

S

New York

Detroit

Cleveland

Pittsburgh

Philadelphia

Chicago

Atlantic Ocean

CENTRAL

Known as the right and left ventricles of Canada's heart (much to the displeasure of the other provinces), Québec and Ontario house not only Canada's most prosperous cities, but also half its population. Rich in their cultural traditions, these provinces represent the origins of colonial Canada and contain remnants of the historic tension between their British and French parents.

The Ontario section is an excursion through Canada's province of the most intense tourist activity — over 70 percent of all visitors from the United States come to Ontario and a somewhat smaller percentage of European travelers also begin here. The Ontario chapter is designed to give the reader a feel for the area by walking through its cities, towns and rural communities — each place is selected for its unique character and sights and how it fits into the Canadian mosaic. Toronto and Ottawa are highlighted as Ontario's main cities. Ontario's "smaller gems" (Stratford, Elora, Midland, Kingston, London, and so on) are also given ample coverage.

Québec is treated as the other historical center of Canada — here the emphasis is placed upon Québec's uniquely French nature, its cultural institutions, its conflict with British customs and the efforts of the province's inhabitants to retain their heritage. These themes are developed through a detailed account of Montréal's and Québec City's historical monuments, cultural activities and neighborhoods.

The author then takes the reader on a trip up the St. Lawrence River, into the countryside, and ends the Québec journey at Gaspé's peninsula.

1) ONTARIO
2) QUÉBEC

CENTRAL

ONTARIO: THE HEART OF CANADA

Preceding pages: homeward bound— Kingslanding, New Brunswick; living dangerously— a stroll along the tracks in Alberta; traversing lonely waters in Lake Louise, Alberta; skier; "all aboard"; Niagara Falls glimmers in the twilight. Left, echoes of the Victorian era— Bindretwine Festival, Kleinburg; and right, wheat harvesting on rolling hills.

Although they're far too polite to say so, Ontarians live in the most exotic land of all. It has nothing to do with palm trees or grass skirts, however, but with the province's range of cultural diversity, the variety of landscapes and seasons, and the epic conflict between civilization and wilderness.

Ontario has become Marshall McLuhan's global village, set down amongst boreal forests and glacial drumlins. The roots may be British, but every race, every tongue, every creed is here now in a patchwork of glorious particularity that spreads from subarctic James Bay to the tobacco fields along Lake Erie's shore.

Ontario is the heart of Canada. Toronto's Bay Street provides the industrial and commercial muscle, while the "mandarins" in Ottawa look after the nation's political affairs. And Ontarians are rather proud of their place in Confederation, fervently believing that the sun rises each day at the St. Lawrence River and sets in evening at the end of Lake Superior.

After all, with Lower Canada, Ontario was Canada before there was a Canada. *Bluenosers* still speak of the *Canadiens* down the road who dealt themselves such a good hand in 1867 at Confederation. Westerners, while largely descended from Upper Canada farmers, share the Maritimers' suspicions of the Yankee-slick Ontarians. Often it seems that hatred of Ontario and particularly the Toronto Argonauts football team is all that Canadians can agree on—all except the almost 9 million or 28 percent of them who live in Ontario.

It is a strange land. The most American of Canada's provinces, literally thrust down into the industrial heartland of the United States, Ontario remains profoundly suspicious of the Great Republic and ardently in love with the British monarchy. One of the most urbanized and modernized regions in the world, Ontario remains a wilderness with 90 percent of its area under forest. A vast province that dwarfs every nation in Europe and every state of the union save Alaska, its population huddles along the southern border in towns that stand like high-tech sand castles by the Great Lakes.

But it *is* a land, a country, a home. Underlying the exotic diversity of Ontario's population is a common love of place, whether that place be a Gothic revival farmhouse at Punkeydoodles Corners or a New Age zucchini plot on Toronto's Markham Street.

In 1844, J.R. Godley, a traveler from Great Britain, described Upper Canada as a place where "everybody is a foreigner and home in their mouths invariably means another country." Today Ontario is still a land of many peoples, but its residents have found their home and long for no other.

Eastern Ontario: Although home to the Canadian Indians for millennia, and corridor for the voyageur's fur trade, the living essence of modern Ontario isn't found in the longhouse or canoe portage, but in the limestone homes of the United Empire Loyalists which stretch along the St. Lawrence River.

More than any other region of Ontario, Eastern Ontario remains devoted to the Loyalist traditions of "peace, order and good government." The stolid farmhouses, regal courthouses, and

towering Anglican spires proclaim that no matter what the "democrats and levellers" in Western Ontario may do, the East will be faithful to the province's motto: "As loyal she began, so shall she ever remain."

Ontario *ou* Québec?: There's no more historically resonant place to begin a tour of Ontario than in the counties of **Prescott-Russell** and **Glengarry** wedged between the two rivers with pride of place in Canadian history: the **Ottawa** and the **St. Lawrence**.

The lower Ottawa countryside appears more *Québecois* than Upper Canadian. Barns boldly decked out in oranges and greens, silvery "ski-jump" roofs, and towns centered on massive parish churches reveal the French-Canadian character of the region.

But a closer look, or better yet, an aerial look, proves that this is Ontario not Québec. The land bears the imprint of the British system of lots and concessions rather than the long narrow strips of the *seigneuries.* Surveyed by British army engineers, all of Southern Ontario is ever so rationally divided into little blocks (lots) within big blocks (townships) dissected by concession roads,

that ever so irrationally ignore such non-Euclidian features as rocks, hills, lakes and swamps.

Glengarry forever!: Driving southwest from the Ottawa River the French placenames give way to towns named **Dunvegan, Lochiel, Maxville** and **Alexandria**, telltale signs that this is now Glengarry County.

Glengarry, known throughout the world by the works of novelist Ralph Connor, was the first of the hundreds of Scottish settlements in Ontario.

Beginning with the arrival of the loyalist Royal Highland Emigrant Regiment in 1783, the hill country north of the St. Lawrence became the destination of thousands of emigrant Scots. Entire parishes from Glengarry, Scotland emigrated for the promise of free land and the chance to escape the oppression of their landlords.

In Conner's fictional Glengarry, Presbyterian behemoths like Big Mack Cameron, Black Hugh Macdonald, or the greatest of all, Donald Bhain Macdonald, would piously turn their cheeks to the enemy − once that is − and then wade into the shantymen brawls crying, "Glengarry forever!"; thrashing the

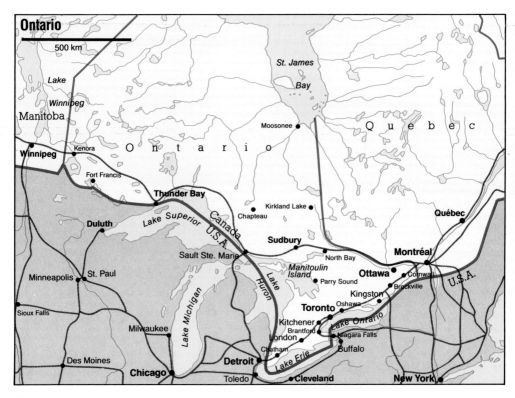

Irish Papists to within sight of Judgment Day.

The real Glengarry is still as Scottish as its fictional counterpart, though actually more Catholic than Calvinist. Perhaps a case of special pleading? For Ralph Conner was a pen name for The Reverend Charles Gordon, a minister of the Presbyterian Church.

Each year in early August former residents of the county are drawn back for the Glengarry Highland Games at **Maxville** to throw a caber or toss back a scotch. At the **Glengarry Museum** in **Dunvegan** among the many local treasures displayed is a humble cooking pot used by Bonnie Prince Charlie while hiding in the other Glengarry after his defeat at the Battle of Culloden in 1747.

River of empire: At **Cornwall**, Ontario's easternmost city, the **Robert Saunders St. Lawrence Generating Station** stretches across the river to harness the thrust of the Great Lakes as they are funnelled towards the Atlantic. Appropriately, an abstract mural by the artist Harold Town adorns the observation tower. For this is decidedly a triumph of the modern technological age over the defiant, age-old barrier of the Long Sault and International Rapids. With the opening of the **St. Lawrence Seaway** in 1959 the interior of the continent was opened to the ocean-going giants and the St. Lawrence superceded the Rhine as the world's foremost river of commerce.

It is a river of empire. French and English struggled for 150 years to determine control of the Great Lakes waterway, and when they were done the Canadians and Americans took up the cudgels.

Indeed, it is a ripe irony typical of Canada that to remain British the American Loyalists emigrated to share this river with the ancient enemy of the British Empire: *Les Canadiens*.

At **Morrisburg**, upriver from Cornwall, **Upper Canada Village** presents an historical recreation of what life for these Loyalist immigrants was like. Early log cabins are juxtaposed with spacious American classical revival houses, illustrating the changing fortunes of the first political refugees to find a Canadian haven.

Garden of the great spirit: Iroquois legend tells of two potent spirits, one good the other evil, who battled for

The *Queen City* betrays the British nature of Ontario.

control of the mighty St. Lawrence. In their titanic struggle huge boulders were tossed across the river in a tremendous cannonade, many to fall short into the narrows by **Lake Ontario**. With the triumph of the good spirit a magical blessing fell upon the land bringing rich forests of yellow birch, red and white trillium, silver maple and winged sumac to life upon the countless granite chunks scattered about the river. Today they are called the **Thousand Islands**.

Brockville, a stately Loyalist town replete with early architectural treasures along Courthouse Avenue, serves as the eastern gateway to the Islands. Cruises around the literally numberless islands leave from nearby **Rockport** and **Gananoque**, a more rambunctious resort town 38 miles (60 km) closer to Kingston. And cruising through the narrow channels and by the limestone cliffs is the only way to see the islands.

The Thousand Islands have long been a playground for the very rich, who, no matter how bad their taste in architecture, always seem to have an eye for the world's most extraordinary real estate. The most famous of the millionaire "cottages" is an unfinished one named **Boldt Castle** which broods over the island of **Hearst**. Begun in 1898 by George Boldt, King of the Waldorf Astoria, it was never completed due to his grief over his wife's death. Today it stands open to the elements and to the curious. A more lasting monument to Boldt is the Thousand Islands salad dressing that his chef concocted to honor the region.

The once and future king: Briefly the capital of the United Provinces of Canada (1841 to 1844), the city of **Kingston** has never quite recovered from Queen Victoria's folly in naming Ottawa the new capital of the Dominion of Canada in 1857. Indeed, the town burghers confidently expect Queen Victoria to reconsider her decision any day now, and to announce their elevation to the honor for which they are well-fitted.

Kingston certainly meets all the requirements of a capital city: a venerable history stretching back to 1673 and Fort Frontenac; a quiet dignity redolent in the weathered stone houses that line its streets; and a grandiose, neo-Classical **City Hall** — erected in 1843 in expectation of Kingston's greater destiny.

All that Kingston lacked as a capital

Boldt Castle broods over the island of Hearst.

city was a Berlin Wall to keep the Americans out. The martello towers strategically placed around the town's harbor and the great limestone bulwark of **Fort Henry** are testimony to the enduring fear of invasion that the War of 1812 engendered.

Apparently, the spirit of 1812 lives on at **Queen's University**, the pride of Kingston founded as a Presbyterian seminary in 1841. In 1956 the student body invaded the nearby town of Waterdown, New York, under cloak of night, replacing the "Stars and Stripes" flying at public buildings with Union Jacks.

While not quite an institution, the memory of Sir John A. Macdonald, the first prime minister of Canada, is as permanent a fixture in Kingston as any fort or college. **Bellevue House**, an Italianate villa occupied by Macdonald in the late 1840s is now a museum filled with memorabilia of the Old Chieftain.

More importantly, Macdonald's unofficial political headquarters, the **Grimason House** (now the **Royal Tavern**), is still standing and open for business in the city center. For Macdonald, the wily boozer that he was, cannot be fitted into the mythological mold of a sanitized Great Father Figure – someone who couldn't tell a lie, to take the obvious example. Once, so inebriated that he vomited in the midst of a political speech, Macdonald apologized to the crowd by claiming that his opponent always made him feel ill.

Perhaps it's just as well that Kingston never fulfilled its national ambitions. It holds a population of 55,000, a stonemason's delight, where the rival spires of **St. George's** and **St. Mary's** still dominate the city's skyline as they did 100 years before.

Just to the east of Kingston, between the harbor and Old Fort Henry, lies the southern entrance of the **Rideau Canal**. Built between 1826 and 1832 the canal follows the path of the **Rideau River** route northeast through 49 locks, numerous lakes and excavated channels until it emerges beside **Parliament Hill** on the Ottawa River.

Today the Rideau Canal region is a pleasure boat captain's delight. Sleek-lined yachts and fat-bottomed cabin cruisers play snakes and ladders with the great stone locks, many of which are still operated by hand as they were 150

Left, Scottish pipers whine their way through Kleinburg; and right, the Royal Military College in Kingston.

years ago.

But to the thousands of Irish laborers brought out to construct the canal, the route was a mosquito-ridden wilderness and their British Army taskmasters were Pharoah's satraps.

Rapids were dammed, boulders blasted and huge stone blocks hauled through roadless forests to be fitted for the locks. The cost in human life was terrific. Construction in the 18-mile-long (30-km) Cranberry marsh took 1,000 workers through yellow fever.

The purpose of the canal was military not economic. The British Army wanted a second, more secure route connecting Upper and Lower Canada in the event of an American seizure of the St. Lawrence. The military character of the canal is evident at **Merrickville**, 50 miles (80 km) southwest of Ottawa, where the largest of the 22 blockhouses built to protect the route still looms over the river.

Many of the canal's laborers stayed to settle in the region after construction was complete. A bevy of Scottish master stonemasons, lured across the water to build the canal locks, stayed on to build the town of **Perth** on the river

Tay. There in the next two decades they erected every manner of stone building imaginable. Perth today is a feast of exquisite Georgian, Adames-que-Federalist, Regency and Gothic residences — one of the most photogenic towns in Ontario.

Notorious work camp: Queen Victoria's choice of **Bytown**, then newly renamed **Ottawa**, as her capital in the Canadas was greeted with shock by her trusting subjects. The modern equivalent would be commanding all the capital's stenographers, pollsters and politicos to pack up and begin working in Tuktoyaktuk, North West Territories.

But the indignity wasn't limited to just moving to a backwater, for Bytown in the mid-1800s was also the most notorious work camp in North America. Lumber was king of the region and Bytown was its capital. Rival shantymen gangs the size of regiments set up tent and shack towns here. Worked like machines, ill-fed, isolated and divided along racial lines, the lumbermen spent their recreational hours in drunken bouts of kick fights and eye gouging. It was from these muddy, dangerous streets that the Parliament Buildings rose up in 1865, rather like the proverbial pearl in a pig sty.

The contrast between these savage shantymen and their descendants — well-ordered, hopelessly conformist civil servants — is wonderfully absurd. It's the contrast between settlement and wilderness, between convention and epic adventure that runs throughout Canadian history from the *bourgeois* and *coureurs de bois* conflict onward.

The contrast has not quite vanished from Ottawa today. In the **Gatineau Hills** that rise up behind Ottawa to the east, wolf packs still gather to howl. And at the **Royal Mint**, Canada's money-makers still churn out dollar bills and coins depicting wild birds, moose and beavers.

For Ottawa will never be a capital city in the style of Washington or Brasilia, fashioned around a grandiose design that reorders the world along geometric lines. Initiated in 1937, the Capital Region Plan of designer Jacques Greber emphasizes the area's natural beauty and molds the city around it.

Consequently, pleasure craft wend their way through the downtown center's parks in summer, while winter turns the same Rideau Canal route into an ice-skating promenade. The annual gift of thousands of tulips by the Netherlands, in gratitude for Canada's wartime hospitality to the Dutch Royal Family, makes spring a visual delight.

Because of its national stature, Ottawa has more cultural resources, museums and galleries than a population of 300,000 would normally allow. Besides **Parliament**, the **Supreme Court**, the **National Library** and the residences of prime ministers, governors-general and foreign ambassadors, Ottawa boasts the **National Gallery**, the foremost art gallery in Canada made primarily out of glass; the **National Museum of Man**; the **Canadian War Museum**; and the **National Museum of Science and Technology**.

No trip to Ottawa is complete without a visit across the river to **Hull** in the province of Québec. Because of Québec's more enlightened liquor laws, the bars in Hull stay open two hours longer than Ottawa. The comic parade starts at 1 a.m with a line-up of cars on the Ottawa side of the bridge and ends at three or four o'clock in Hull with the convoy heading back the other way. If it's a week night the Ottawans will have to hurry to exchange their leather pants for the gray-wool conformity of work.

The unknown river: Author Hugh MacLennan, in *Seven Rivers of Canada*, describes the Ottawa as the "unknown" or "forgotten" river of Canada. As the St. Lawrence superseded as the principal trade route the image of the Ottawa was dimmed and it took on the status of a short tributary linking the cities of Ottawa and Montréal.

To the voyageurs and the lumbermen of early Canada, however, the Ottawa was *la grande rivière*, the principal route to the Upper Great Lakes and the western prairies beyond.

In the **Ottawa Valley**, running north of the capital to **Pembroke** and **Deep River,** the character of the old Ottawa River comes alive. Here at **Champlain Lookout** high above the town of **Renfrew** you can see the power of the river's current as it bursts over narrows and understand why the journey either up or down the Ottawa was dreaded by the voyageurs. At Pembroke, in the valley's north, white-water rafting provides a still more vivid appreciation of the river's charms.

Parliament, Ottawa.

The Ottawa Valley is full of tall tales of the bigger-than-big lumberjacks like Joe Mufferaw, who waged war on the forest to provide the British Navy with their white pine masts. These are best heard in the Valley dialect which is a complex mix of Gaelic, Polish, French and Indian idioms stewed together by the backwood's isolation of pioneer settlement.

Central Ontario: There are no firm borders separating eastern from western Ontario, let alone the east from the middle. But when classical limestone gives way to red brick Victorian and billboards advertise the pleasures of Hotel Toronto jacuzzis over free TV and hot water in Cornwall, well, the nebulous line has been crossed. Firmly within the orbit of Toronto, whose fatted-calf suburbs gobble up rich farmland with alacrity, the hamlets and towns of the region struggle to maintain their own character and traditions.

By the sea: The town of **Cobourg** lies just far enough east of Toronto to remain relatively unscarred by bedroom dormitory blight. It, like its neighbors **Port Hope** and **Colbourne**, was once a bustling lake port in the age of Great Lake steamers. The harbors are filled with pleasure sails now, rather than commercial ones, but these small lakeside ports are still the best place to appreciate the vistas offered by Lake Ontario – with her still greater sisters, a sweet tasting ocean that rivals the Baltic Sea in stature.

The center of Cobourg is dominated by the neo-Classical **Victoria Hall**. Completed in 1856, it contains a courtroom the replica of London's Old Bailey and one of only two acoustically perfect opera houses in North America. In its time it was a marvelous statement of Canadian pretensions to cultural superiority over the rebel Yankees. Here, the colonial elite had something solid to point to in explaining why they chose to remain impoverished British North Americans while Uncle Sam boomed. The pretensions to moral superiority are still part of the Canadian character, a national defence mechanism also found among European intellectuals.

Finger lakes with bones: To the immediate north of Cobourg the long, thin **Kawartha Lakes** are strung like pegs on a clothesline tied to **Lake Simcoe** on the east. The Kawarthas have a pastoral

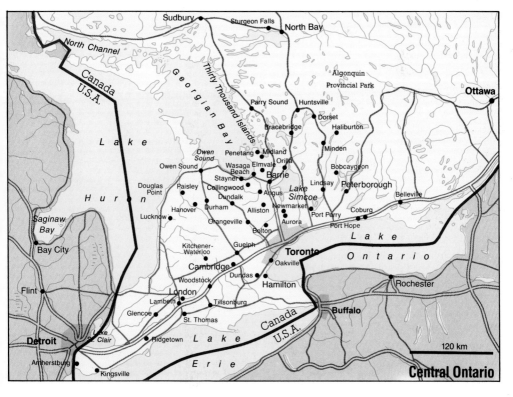

Central Ontario

120 km

appeal in contrast to the rugged beauty of the more northerly Canadian Shield lakes. **Rice Lake**, the most southerly of the lakes is especially beguiling. Framed by gently sloping drumlins bearing Holstein dairy farms on their elongated backs, Rice Lake is dotted with forested islands. Two thousand years ago, a little known Indian civilization buried their dead by these shores in 60-mile-long (38-km), snake-like ridges. **Serpent Mound Provincial Park** offers a cutaway viewing of the largest mound's bones and burial gifts.

The Kawartha Lakes form the basis of the **Trent-Severn Canal System**, which allows houseboats and cabin cruisers to sail uphill from **Trenton** on Lake Ontario to **Port Severn** on Lake Huron's Georgian Bay. By the time they reach Lake Simcoe, boaters have passed through 43 locks and ascended 598 feet (180 meters) above Lake Ontario. From Simcoe it is a drop of 262 feet (80 meters) along the route to Georgian Bay.

Peterborough, the center of the Kawarthas region, is the star attraction along the Canal. Here the **Peterborough Hydraulic Lift Lock**, the world champion boat lifter since 1904, boosts a boat up with one hand, while sinking a second vessel with the other. It is one of only eight in the world.

Settled later than the counties along Lake Ontario, the Peterborough district was reputed in the 1830s to have the "most polished and aristocratic society in Upper Canada." British army officers granted free land and younger sons of the English gentry gave the backwoods of Peterborough and **Lakefield** a tone uncommon in the earlier settlements.

Not that gentility made the hardships of pioneering any more bearable. Susanna Moodie, an early pioneer of Lakefield and of Canadian literature, described in *Roughing it in the Bush* her feelings of condemnation to a life of horror in the new world in which the only hope of escape was "through the portals of the grave." Crumbling wooden shacks, and fences made from the stumps of felled trees provide a mute testimony to the poverty and hardship of this isolated life. Today Peterborough seems to have found a middle ground between aristocracy and poverty, for it is a favorite

Friends for Life, Upper Canada Village.

testing ground for the arbiters of middle-class taste—the consumer marketing surveyors.

Sunshine sketches of every town: There isn't much of special interest in the town of **Orillia**, situated on the narrows between Lake Couchiching and Lake Simcoe — and that's what makes it so especially interesting. To be sure, there's a larger than life statue of Samuel de Champlain noting the fact that he stopped nearby on his own Great Ontario Tour of 1615, but every town has a monument to someone or other.

No, the appeal of Orillia lies in the very ordinariness of the town: canopies of shady maples over spacious side streets; wide front porches for socializing and spying — the first item to be torn down in a city home's renovation; and photographs of the local hockey heroes in the barber shop-cum-agora.

Stephen Leacock, a long-time summer resident of Orillia, caught the flavor of the place — the flavor, for example, of Mr. Golgotha Gingham, town undertaker who "instinctively assumes the professional air of hopeless melancholy" — in his comedy, *Sunshine Sketches of a Little Town.*

A work of irony (one part affection, one part castigation) *Sunshine Sketches* won Leacock praise throughout the world when it was published in 1912. Everywhere, in fact, except Orillia, where the good burghers murmured of lawsuits. Now, however, in proper small town form, Orillia has adopted the humorist as a favorite son and turned the **Stephen Leacock Home** into a literary museum.

A terrible beauty: South of Lake Simcoe, within sight of Toronto's towers, lies another shrine to Canadian artists: the **McMichael Canadian Collection** in the village of **Kleinburg**.

Started as a private gallery, the collection has grown into the finest display of the *Group of Seven's* canvases in Canada.

The Group, which included A.Y. Jackson, Lawren Harris and Tom Thomson among its members, stood the Canadian art establishment on its head in the 1920s by forging a distinctively Canadian approach to painting.

Inspired by the French Impressionists and contemporary Scandinavian artists, the seven members of *the Group* and their associates sought to portray the

Image and illusion in Toronto: left, Hydro Building; right, flat-iron building.

Canadian wilderness in all its vivid color and nordic harshness.

Human figures are rare in their landscapes, and when they appear are dwarfed by the natural environment. Their depictions of **Algonquin Park** or the Algoma Canyon in autumn were initially scorned as frauds by Toronto art dealers. So bold and dramatic were the reds and golds that patrons refused to believe that the painters were working from real scenes.

Today, *the Group of Seven* are the only Canadian painters to have achieved mass appeal throughout the nation. Their interpretations of the north's terrible beauty have shaped the Canadian imagination and identity. In Hugh MacLennan's words, "they are tolerable and beautiful, one of the chief sources of the Canadian neurosis – the stark, sombre, cold, and empty land..." The McMichael Collection, with over 30 gallery rooms, is the perfect place to feast on their labors.

Hogtown becomes Toronto: Toronto (also see pages 140 – 9) marks a kind of Great Divide in Southern Ontario, not because of any real geographical distinctions between East and West, but because both have more traffic with Toronto than with each other. Which is another way of saying that, ever since Toronto became the provincial capital, it has gotten a great deal of the gravy. The historic nickname of "Hogtown" may refer to the Toronto Stockyards, but it aptly describes how some others, elsewhere, feel about the whole place. It often seems that most of Ontario's resources, human and otherwise, go spiralling down the province's roads to that big drain on Lake Ontario.

Besides being a fortified harbor at a healthy distance from the American border, Toronto didn't have much to recommend it as the new capital way back in the 1790s. Rather, it has acquired everything since, simply by virtue of having been selected. A history or even a *list* of Toronto's attributes would be much longer than your arm. Suffice it to say that as Canada's largest city, Toronto is the country's financial powerhouse (**Bay Street** is the Canadian equivalent of Wall Street) and artistic nerve center. The theater scene here is the third largest in the English-speaking world, after London and New York. Here, too, is the home of the **Canadian**

Ready for take-off: Toronto's space-age City Hall.

Broadcasting Corporation (CBC), the wonderful institution dedicated to holding nature up to the mirror of the CBC's own face.

And the public network does a good job of providing a thoughtful alternative to commercial broadcasting. But many people − some of them at the CBC or one of the many magazines and publishing houses centered in Toronto − still spend much time gazing into their ferns and wondering about Canada's "cultural identity": Do we have one? What is it like?

An ethnic salad or melting pot?: The latest answer is in evidence out on the streets of Toronto. "Multiculturalism" is the byword in a city that has attracted so many people from everywhere, and encouraged them to maintain as much of each culture as will mesh with all the others. "We're a *salad*," they say, "not a *melting-pot*." What "multiculturalism" will ultimately mean for Toronto, and Canada, will take time to unfold. But it has already done a lot for a place that used to be called "Toronto the Good," back when the only places open on Sunday besides the churches were the drugstores, and the only things for sale there were medicines.

Torontonians take pride in the relative cleanliness and lack of crime in a city this size. They like to quote Buckminster Fuller, who in the 1970s pronounced that "Toronto *works.*" Helping it to work is the **Toronto Transit Commission's** (TTC) remarkably efficient fleet of buses, streetcars and subway trains. From the TTC's window seats you can see a lot of Toronto; and if you want to get off to take a closer look, so much the better: at the **Royal Ontario Museum**, with its mummies and Chinese tomb; at the **Ontario Science Center**, where the exhibits are *meant* to be handled; at the **Art Gallery of Ontario's** collection, the largest in the world, of Henry Moore sculptures (including the big bronze one out front for the kids to climb through); and at the **New City Hall**. The hall was built in the 1960s, from a strikingly modern design by Finnish architect Viljo Revell. **Nathan Phillips Square**, in front of the hall, is Toronto's town square.

Working its way into the background of all these vistas is the omnipresent **Canadian National (CN) Tower**. Its architectural statement seems to be a rather overly-emphatic "You are here." Nevertheless, at 1,815 feet (550 meters), it is the world's tallest free-standing structure, and from the observation decks you can sometimes make out Buffalo. And that's something.

Southern Ontario: Southern Ontario's excellent system of roads is a sign of its long-accustomed prosperity. The Macdonald-Cartier Freeway, more widely known as The 401, spans the distance between Windsor and the Québec border and is wonderful for trucks and people in a hurry. But it's no surprise that it's on the secondary highways and country roads that travelers begin to encounter Southern Ontario: the rolling fields of corn, wheat, tobacco, or grazing livestock; the majestic elms and maples that line the roads, town streets, and shady farm lanes; the graceful houses, ranging from the earliest log and stone dwellings in "American vernacular" style to stately Victorian and Edwardian homes in red and yellow brick; and the rivers. It's difficult to drive 20 miles (32 km) anywhere in Southern Ontario without crossing a creek, stream, or honest-to-God river.

West of Toronto lies some of the richest farmland anywhere. And strung

Toronto's skyline huddled against the CN Tower.

along those smooth roads are towns that sometimes seem to have forgotten how they got there. But fast-food and video rental outlets notwithstanding, the pioneer experience has made a deep impression. Almost every town and village blossoms annually with a fair or festival. Maple-syrup festivals. Apple-cider festivals. Bean festivals. Exhibitions of steam-powered tractors and threshers. And everywhere are people who are determined to remember how they got there, and what it was like before there were roads.

The green sea: With the capture of Fort Detroit in 1759, the British finally wrested complete control of the North American frontier from the French. But the settlement of the vast peninsula bounded by Lakes Ontario, Erie, and Huron, lagged behind that of the booming colonies south of the Great Lakes. It wasn't until those colonies declared their independence from Britain in 1776 that the wilderness that would one day be Ontario became inviting to settlers. These were the Loyalists, whose impact on Eastern Ontario has already been noted. Their contribution to the western part of the province is even more

fundamental. They gave up established homesteads to start all over again in the bush, simply because that bush remained under British law. Yet they were Americans, and the egalitarian sentiments and proud pioneering spirit they brought with them, helped to shape Ontario.

Once the bed of a primeval lake, southwestern Ontario was sculpted into its present shape by the heavy hand of retreating glaciers at the end of the last Ice Age. In the late 18th Century this rich soil lay under a different kind of sea: a green, rolling swell of dense forest that stretched 300 miles (480 km) from Kingston to the shores of Lake Huron. The French fur traders and their Indian guides were familiar with the elaborate river system which cut through this arboreal blanket, for these rivers were the highways of the fur trade. Though it would have strengthened their position in North America, the French had not seriously attempted to settle the land. Clearing away the giant trees and draining the swamps which lay in their shadow would have driven back the beavers whose pelts were so lucrative. For a time the British

Pioneer graves bespeckle a verdant lawn.

adopted this attitude as well. There was no hurry to settle the wilderness at the fringe of the vast British holdings.

The American War of Independence changed all this. During that war and immediately after it, thousands of settlers from the Thirteen Colonies who feared or distrusted the new regime poured across the Niagara River as their compatriots did at Kingston. John Butler, the son of a British army officer, led a group of Loyalists north to Niagara. In 1778 he recruited a band of guerrilla fighters called *Butler's Rangers,* and from this time until the end of the war the group harrassed the American communities in the area. Butler was stationed at Fort Niagara and charged with keeping the Six Nations Iroquois, whose territory was south of Lake Ontario, friendly to the British. At this he succeeded brilliantly, even persuading the Seneca and Mohawk tribes to engage in fighting the rebels.

The leader of the Mohawks was Joseph Brant, who had received an English education and was committed to the British tradition. When the former Six Nations lands were ceded to the Americans in the 1783 treaty which ended the war, Brant appealed to the British for redress. He and his followers were given the land beside the Grand River, to an extent of six miles (10 km) on either side. It's at **Elora** that the Grand River has carved a canyon that is one of the most popular rural retreats in Ontario.

In the years that followed, Brant sold much of this land to other settlers, to the consternation of the colonial government which considered the Indians to be trustees, not owners, of the tract. Nevertheless, in 1834 the Brant leases were officially confirmed – it would have been hard to revoke them – and seven years later a reserve of 50,000 acres (20,200 hectares) was set aside; this land remains Six Nations land today.

Niagara: The **Niagara Escarpment**, a rolling slope which falls away in a rocky bluff on its eastern face, is another legacy of the last Ice Age. It rises out of New York State near Rochester, follows the shore of Lake Ontario around to Hamilton, snakes overland to the Blue Mountain ridge south of Collingwood, divides Lake Huron from Georgian Bay as the Bruce Peninsula, dips

Color-coordinated grain elevators.

underwater, resurfaces as Manitoulin Island, disappears to emerge again on the western shore of Lake Michigan, and finally peters out in Wisconsin. The first farmers in the Niagara region had no idea of the extent of this formation, but they and their heirs discovered that the soil between the escarpment and the lake was very fertile. The temperate climate makes this the most hospitable place in Ontario for peaches and plums, as well as home to a growing wine industry. **The Fruit Belt** is endangered, however, due to its proximity to the heavily industrialized stretch of Lake Ontario shoreline, known as the **Golden Horseshoe**, between Hamilton and Oshawa. Every year thousands of hectares of the best agricultural land in Canada are "developed" into something else.

The **Niagara Falls**, where Lake Erie overflows into Lake Ontario at the rate of 35,000 cubic liters per second, have always been the most celebrated feature of the Escarpment. Indeed, they were a tourist attraction long before it was a settlement, and remained a must-see for all visitors to North America, including the famous. Of his pilgrimage, Charles Dickens wrote: "We went everywhere at the falls, and saw them in every aspect.... Nothing in Turners's finest water-color drawings, done in his greatest days, is so ethereal, so imaginative, so gorgeous in color as what I then beheld. I seemed to be lifted from the earth and to be looking into Heaven." Most would agree with Dickens and not with the cynical Oscar Wilde, who, noting the popularity of the Falls for honeymooners, remarked that "Niagara Falls must be the second major disappointment of American married life."

The Falls or rather the crowds that swarm around them, have attracted a host of sideshows over the years: museums devoted to The Great Houdini, Ripley's Believe It Or Not, and Madame Tussaud's wax figures. But the greatest carnival draw in the Fall's history was Blondin, the French daredevil who first crossed over the cataract on a tightrope in 1859. He repeated the stunt various ways: on stilts, turning cartwheels, pausing to cook dinner halfway, and with another man on his back. In 1901, Annie Edson Taylor became the first person to plunge over the Falls in a **Niagara Falls.**

barrel and live, but neither she nor anyone else has surpassed Blondin's reputation. In the meantime, the site has been rescued from carnival tackiness by the flower gardens and clipped lawns bordering the river.

John Butler and his Rangers founded the town of **Newark** at the mouth of the Niagara River after the American revolutionary war. In 1792, when John Graves Simcoe arrived in town, the place was called "Niagara-on-the-Lake." It was also the capital of Upper Canada, a province newly created out of the English-speaking portion of the old colony of Québec. And as the first Lieutenant-Governor of Upper Canada, Simcoe was anxious to promote the growth and security of his "Little England."

One of the first things he did was choose a new capital, for Niagara-on-the-Lake was uncomfortably close to the American border. He selected a central site at a fork of the river which he named the **Thames**. The capital would be called London (naturally), and would be linked to the western end of Lake Ontario by a road named after the British Secretary of State. But Dundas Street was no sooner hacked out of the bush than Simcoe changed his mind and moved the capital instead to Toronto — which he promptly renamed York. Mohawk Chief Joseph Brant once remarked : "General Simcoe has done a great deal for this province, he has changed the name of every place in it."

Niagara-on-the-Lake was blessed by its fall into political obscurity. It is one of the most beautiful and well-preserved colonial towns in North America. It's also home to the annual **Shaw Festival**, a major theatrical event featuring the plays of George Bernard Shaw and others.

Simcoe's instincts were good. Dundas Street, extended to Toronto, would prove valuable in settling the interior of the province. But in 1796, when Simcoe returned to England, it was barely passable, and its nickname, "The Governor's Road," became a term of derision.

The war of 1812-14: Simcoe's fears of American aggression were soon justified. In June of 1812 the United States took advantage of Britain's preoccupation with Napoleon to declare war. Many Americans thought Canada would be a pushover, a mere matter of marching. Many Canadians thought so

too. Issac Brock, the military commander and acting Lieutenant-Governor of Upper Canada, described his predicament in a letter that July: "My situation is most critical, not from anything the enemy can do, but from the disposition of the people.... What a change an additional regiment would make in this part of the province! Most of the people have lost all confidence — I however speak loud and look big." He also acted swiftly and decisively. His troops attacked and captured Fort Michilimackinac in northern Michigan and repulsed an attack at the Detroit River. These early victories won the native peoples in the area to the British cause and galvanized the settlers.

The Niagara region figured prominently in the remainder of the war. The Americans attacked **Queenston**, just down river from the Falls, in October of 1812. Brock was killed in the Battle of Queenston Heights, though the town was successfully defended. The war dragged on, but without the example of Brock's boldness the heavily outnumbered colony might not have held out at all.

In 1813, the Americans took control

of Lake Ontario and captured York. The capital was in American hands for a week and the parliament buildings were burned. The farthest the American infantry was able to penetrate was Stoney Creek, near Hamilton. Here they were repulsed in a famous battle in June of that year.

Another famous incident from that month may or may not have taken place. Legend has it Laura Secord overheard American soldiers, who had taken over her Queenston house, planning an attack on a British detachment. She set out at once, posing as a dairymaid, and walked 20 miles (32 km) through American lines to warn the British commander, Lt. FitzGibbon. Every Ontario school child has heard of Mrs. Secord's derring-do, but it is less well-known that Lt. FitzGibbon had already heard the news from his own scouts.

By 1814 the British could finally spare some more troops for their Canadian frontier. The last American advance was checked in July at the Battle of Lundy's Lane in present-day Niagara Falls. Due to the British naval presence on the Great Lakes, the quick thinking

of Issac Brock, and the generally half-hearted nature of the American effort, Upper Canada had actually managed to ward off the invader from the south. Ontarians have been annoyed ever since by Amerian history books which are not sufficiently clear on this point.

The War of 1812-14 gave Canada a stronger sense of community identity, though it didn't end the political divisions between Tories and those calling for democratic reform in the province. It also gave a signal to Britain that this colony was still too sparsely settled for its own security. The next couple of decades saw a concerted push to open up the land.

The Talbot Trail: Today the highway which hugs the northern shore of Lake Erie is designated **The Talbot Trail**. **St. Thomas**, founded in 1817 between London and Lake Erie, was also named after Colonel Thomas Talbot, who had been granted 48,500 acres (19,600 hectares) to start a settlement in 1803. But Talbot was no saint. He ruled his "principality," as he called it, with stern efficiency. He laid down stringent rules for his settlers, making sure that they cleared their lands and raised their homes as quickly as possible. Those who defaulted on the agreed conditions he evicted − a rare procedure on any frontier. And the reason why the Talbot Road was the best in Upper Canada was that farmers were responsible for clearing and maintaining some parts of the road that fronted their properties.

The Talbot Trail rolls through dairy farms and fishing villages, tobacco farms and beaches. West of St. Thomas it bends south with the lakeshore into mixed-farming country. This, the westernmost tip of Southern Ontario, is the southernmost part of Canada.

To be precise, **Point Pelee National Park**, a peninsula jutting south of **Leamington**, is the southernmost part of mainland Canada. Lying at the same latitude as Rome and northern California, Point Pelee is home to plants and animals that are rarely seen in Canada. A trail through the woods and a boardwalk over the marshlands make it a living museum of natural history.

Nearby another delight for naturalists is the **Jack Miner Bird Sanctuary** at **Kingsville**. One of the earliest, and surely the most famous waterfowl pitstop in Canada, this haven is free to migrating birds and migrating humans

A hidden retreat at Elora Ontario.

alike. Jack Miner said: "In the name of God, let us have one place on earth where no money changes hands." The sanctuary is now run by his family as a public trust.

The underground railroad: Because it extends into the heart of America, this part of Ontario played an unusual part in history: as one terminus of the so-called "Underground Railroad." In the early 1800s, runaway slaves from the American South were sheltered by sympathizers from the elements – and from slave-hunters – along several routes which led to Canada.

Reverend Josiah Henson, a self-educated slave from Maryland, made the trip with his family in 1830. He settled in **Dresden**, and subsequently devoted himself to helping other fugitives. Ironically enough, Henson was the prototype for "Uncle Tom" in Harriet Beecher Stowe's novel *Uncle Tom's Cabin*. His home in Dresden is part of **Uncle Tom's Cabin Museum** that focuses on his life and works.

Chatham was another terminus of the "railroad" – others were **Montréal**, and **St. Catherines** in the Niagara area. It was at Chatham that the abolitionist

John Brown plotted the 1859 raid on the government arsenal at Harper's Ferry, Virginia. He hoped to spark a general uprising of slaves, but he was caught, convicted of treason, and hanged.

Windsor is Canada's biggest border town, a kind of kid half-sister to Detroit. Detroit and Windsor go back a long way together, though the rather regal name of the latter indicates a parting of ways. Like Detroit, Windsor is an automobile industry town but, unlike Detroit, has a liveable downtown. Downright pleasant, in fact, with extensive parks and gardens on the riverfront.

The Windsor area was easily accessible to the Loyalists, and was quickly tamed. For the Indians who had lived here for centuries, "taming" the land was not required. But for white farmers in Upper Canada the land posed a challenge, and in the 1820s much work remained to be done.

The ambitious little city: In the 1820s the growing towns and farms along the western curve of Lake Ontario continued to nibble at the wilderness around them. **Ancaster**, **Dundas**, **Stoney Creek** and **Burlington** all eventually lost

A romantic moment at Point Pelee National Park.

their bids for supremacy at the lakehead to **Hamilton**, the "ambitious little city."

The Niagara Escarpment, referred to locally as "the mountain," divides Hamilton into split-levels. The city's steel mills and other heavy industries have given Hamilton a grim image in the minds of many. But the somewhat misleadingly-named **Royal Botanical Gardens** incorporate a wildlife sanctuary called **Coote's Paradise**, with trails winding through 1,200 acres (485 hectares) of marsh and wooded ravines. And, like everywhere else in Southern Ontario, there is history wherever you decide to look for it.

Hamilton's architectural jewel is **Dundurn Castle**. Sir Allan Napier MacNab — landholder, financier, all-round Tory, and Hamilton's first resident lawyer — had it built in 1835 as a lavish tribute to himself. The finest home west of Montréal at the time, it is now restored as a museum to reflect the 1850s when MacNab was Prime Minister of the Province of Canada.

Hello? hello?: Hamilton installed the first telephone exchange in the British Empire — the eighth in the world — in 1878, only four years after Alexander Graham Bell invented the device. That's appropriate because it was at his parents' home in nearby **Brantford** that Bell dreamed up the thing. Bell was working in Boston in those days but he customarily spent summers with his folks. After preliminary experiments, Bell built a phone on his return to Boston. He later remarked, "Brantford is justified in calling herself the telephone city.... The telephone was invented in Canada. It was made in the United States." Some of his other inventions are on display too at the **Bell Homestead**.

The telephone is not the only great idea to have been conceived in Brantford. Lately the town has been visibly proud to be the hometown of hockey superstar Wayne Gretzky.

The first thing to note about **Kitchener** and **Waterloo** is how prosperous they are. Kitchener is the fastest-growing municipality in Canada.

The second thing to note about the Twin Cities is how German they are. The original settlers in the area were members of the austere Mennonite sect transplanted from the German communities of Pennsylvania. They fol-

19th-Century affluence at **Dundurn Castle, Hamilton.**

lowed the Loyalists north in the 1780s for their own reasons: fearing that if the fledgling American republic had another war they would lose their exemption from military service; they hoped to remain exempt under British law.

Mennonite communities thrive throughout this area today. The more conservative ones still dress as they did 100 years ago, and quietly but firmly reject many aspects of modern life. They decline to use electricity or automobiles, and horse-drawn buggies and ploughs are not uncommon sights on the backroads in the fields.

The Mennonites soon had German neighbors of various creeds. The strong German character of the place, reflected in the then named town of Berlin, attracted immigrants from Germany to settle here from the 1830s onward.

This strong identity became a sore point in World War One, when the local papers were prohibited from publishing in German. To keep on good terms with the rest of Canada, Berlin chose a more British-sounding name in 1916: Kitchener, after Lord Kitchener, a British war hero who had died that year.

But Kitchener and Waterloo are as German as ever, and, as if to prove it, they host the biggest **Oktoberfest**, this side of the Rhine. "Good cheer" is spelled *Gemütlichkeit* in this part of the country.

The Canada Company: In the 1820s, the land between Lake Huron and the modern site of Kitchener was a piece of wilderness called the **Huron Tract**. The development of this, and other bits of Crown land, was the target of the Canada Company. The Company's success can be attributed to its first Superintendent of Operations, the Scottish novelist and statesman John Galt, and to his chosen lieutenant, Dr. William "Tiger" Dunlop.

Galt's first task was founding a city on the edge of the wilderness. **Guelph**, which Galt named after the ancestral name of the Royal Family, was inaugurated in April of 1827. Galt's overseers in London thought that it would have been more politically useful to name it Goderich, after the Chancellor of the Exchequer, and they told him so, but Galt stuck to his guns. Though it was clear to himself and Dunlop − and to history − that Galt was the best man

Mid-day thirst in northern Ontario.

for the job, he managed to alienate his own superiors and the colonial authorities so thoroughly that he was relieved of it in 1828.

Guelph is a striking blend of 19th Century architecture of a broad range. The Roman Catholic Church of **Our Lady of the Immaculate Conception** dominates the skyline with twin Gothic towers.

As soon as Guelph was founded, Tiger Dunlop plunged into the bush for a season of surveying. He finally emerged at the mouth of the Red River on Lake Huron, saw that the harbor would suit the needs of the Company, and began to build. Galt met him here in the summer of '27 while exploring the lakeshore by canoe. Dunlop had managed to preserve through his months of wandering a bottle of champagne, and the two celebrated the founding of a town. *This* one Galt would call **Goderich**. He would even rename the Red River the **Maitland**, after the Lieutenant-Governor, Sir Peregrine Maitland, but these accommodating gestures did not placate the powers-that-were.

The Huron road: After surveying the Huron Tract, the exuberant Dunlop had pronounced: "It is impossible to find 200 acres together which will make a bad farm." Galt wanted a road from Waterloo to Goderich so that settlement could begin in earnest from both ends. In 1828, Dunlop directed the construction of that road, through swamps, dense forest and tangled brush. It rained relentlessly that summer. Work was slow and fever plagued the work camps. For each hour road-building, Dunlop spent two doctoring. It was a stupendous achievement that is not diminished by the many improvements the road has seen since. Now Highway 8, the Huron Road became the spine of settlement in the tract.

Western Ontario: Eleven miles (18km) into the bush, the first Huron Road curved at an attractive meadow by a river. Before long the settlement that sprang up there was called **Stratford**, and the river the **Avon**. The connection to Shakespeare was strengthened in the naming of wards and streets (Romeo, Hamlet, Falstaff, etc.) while Stratford boomed in the 1850s by virtue of being the county seat and at an intersection of railway lines.

In the years after World War Two,

Almost done: Mennonite women quilting in western Ontario.

Stratford native Tom Patterson was persistent, and finally successful, in peddling his dream of a Shakespearean theater for the city. On July 13, 1953, Alec Guinness stepped onto a stage in a riverside tent as Richard the Third, and the rest, as they say, is history. The tent-like (but permanent) **Festival Theater** was opened in 1957, and its thrust stage has influenced a generation of theater-builders. The Stratford Festival now includes two other stages and the season features musical programs as well as plays.

The Festival has brought a lot of people to Stratford, whether onstage, backstage, or out in the house. The attractive meadow by the river has helped, of course. Willows hang over the banks of the Avon in a continuous park running through the city. This arrangement suits the willows, the ducks and swans, and the theater-goers just fine.

Another road which helped to open up the Huron Tract is the one north from **London**. Or south to London, if you like, because all roads in southwestern Ontario lead to London. Failing to become the capital of Upper Canada, London stayed small until it became the district seat in 1826. The "district" now under London's metaphorical shadow is most of the area between Lakes Huron and Erie (though smaller centers are permitted to cast dim shadows of their own).

British tradition and the American feeling of wide-open-spaces are in harmony here. On the street signs of London such names as Oxford and Piccadilly mix with such names from Ontario's history as Simcoe, Talbot and, of course, Dundas Street. Other names, like Wonderland Road and Storybook Gardens, may lead visitors into thinking that they have stumbled into a kind of Neverland. The impression will be reinforced by the squeaky-cleanness, and greenness, of this relentlessly cheerful city. It isn't called "the forest city" for nothing; from any vantage point above the treetops, London virtually disappears under a leafy blanket.

The aforementioned **Storybook Gardens** are in **Springbank Park**, one of the many parks along the Thames. The river also flows through the campus of the **University of Western Ontario**, a school whose presence is definitely felt in town.

Careful shopper at a farmer's market.

Bluewater country: In Ontario Ministry of Tourism language, the Lake Huron shoreline is called Bluewater Country. What that means is a lakefront dotted with cottages, beaches and a few nice places like **Bayfield**. This village, with its intact 19th Century main street, shady public beach and fine marina, is simply a gem.

A little farther north is Goderich, Tiger Dunlop's town. Not merely *planned,* Goderich was *designed;* the **County Courthouse** sits on an octagonal plot (called The Square) from which streets radiate in all directions. **The Square** is probably the world's most leisurely traffic circle (or octagon). Whether or not Goderich really is "The Prettiest Town in Canada," as the signs proclaim, this spot regularly displays some of the most spectacular sunsets on earth – and that goes for the whole lakeshore, for miles inland.

Decline and rise: When they saw how quickly the Huron Tract was being gobbled up, the British government threw open for settlement the Indian territory immediately to the north of it. The Queen's Bush, as it was called, was not as fertile as land farther south,

and some of the boom towns soon went bust. The next farming frontier, Western Canada, opened up just in time for the overflow of settlers from the Queen's Bush. Those that remained on the stony soil turned to raising beef cattle.

Several railroads snaked into Ontario between 1850 and 1900. Towns along the routes prospered, especially those where lines crossed. But as the rail lines fed city factories, industries in small towns declined and the smallest towns focused solely on the needs of the surrounding farmers.

In the 1970s there was a swell of interest in the history and architecture of Ontario's small towns. A good illustration of this is the Blyth Festival. A community hall was built in 1920 in this village northeast of Goderich. Upstairs in the hall is a fine auditorium, with a sloping floor and stage, which lay unused since the 1930s. In the mid-1970s it was "discovered" and refurbished as the home for an annual summer theatrical festival dedicated to Canadian plays: most of them new, and most of them celebrating small-town and farming experiences. That the Blyth Festival

Sailors catch a fiesty wind on Thunder Bay.

has become the darling of Canada's urban drama critics indicates both its quality and the potency of its subject-matter, namely the history and people of rural Canada.

Just south of Blyth, on the literary map lies **Clinton**, the home of writer Alice Munro. Her beautifully layered stories transcend regional interest and "local color," but there is no better introduction than her works to the life of small-town Ontario in this century.

The Bruce Peninsula: This region has always been sparsely settled; the soil is thin, and navigation on the lake hereabouts can be treacherous. But many people make the effort to reach **Tobermory**, the resort that looks like a fishing village at the peninsula's tip. They might be heading north to **Manitoulin Island**, the largest freshwater island in the world, on the giant ferry *Chicheemaun (big canoe)*. Or, they might be getting ready to hike the 450 miles (720 km) of the **Bruce Trail** along the Niagara Escarpment, through farmland and wilderness, to the Falls.

South of **Georgian Bay**, on the eastern ridge of the Escarpment, a range of large hills provides the best ski-runs in Ontario. Ontarians call these hills the **Blue Mountains**, but not too loudly in the presence of anyone from the Rockies.

Ste-Marie among the Hurons: To visit the small peninsula poking out into Georgian Bay is to step a little further back into history than most places in rural Ontario permit. This area is called **Huronia**, where 350 years ago French Jesuit missionaries traveled and preached among the Huron Indians. When the lonely fortified mission of **Sainte-Marie Among the Hurons** was established in 1639, it was the only inland settlement of Europeans north of Mexico. It prospered for 10 years; but the Huron nation was eventually destroyed in wars with their enemies, the Iroquois, who also tortured and killed the Jesuits. Ste-Marie was not attacked, but the fort was burned by retreating Jesuits to keep it out of Iroquois hands. After much research, the mission and its everyday life have been recreated on a site east of **Midland**.

Cottage country: *Friday*, July 21, 3 p.m. − leave work early to beat the weekend traffic heading north. 4 p.m. − stuck outside Toronto to beat the rush traffic jam. 10 p.m. − arrive cottage − sleep.

Saturday, July 22, 6 a.m. − woken up by the sound of dirt bike riders. 8 a.m. to 7 p.m. − chop wood, fix septic tank, drive to grocery store, run over dirt bike, relax, relax, relax. 11.30 p.m. − woken up by sound of Van Halen tape across the lake. Make note to buy neighbor's teenager a Sony Walkman.

Sunday, July 23, 3 p.m. − begin packing. 8 p.m. − leave cottage late to avoid the weekend traffic returning south. 9 p.m. − stuck on Highway 400 to wait out the rush traffic jam.

Monday, July 24, 1 a.m. − arrive home in Toronto − sleep. 9 a.m. − at work, begin planning next weekend's trip to cottage.

Although somewhat exaggerated, this portrait of an Ontario cottage weekend does describe the lengths to which the province's urbanites will go to get away from it all − or almost all of it.

The thousands of lakes in southern Ontario or in the Canadian Shield region just to the north provide a cherished escape for city dwellers. The war of extermination against the trees, which was the settler's rule, has given way to a desire to preserve the wood-

Welcoming guests to the longhouse at Ste. Marie among the Hurons.

lands and waters of the near north for recreation.

However, the **Georgian Bay, Muskoka** and **Haliburton** regions can no longer be described as forested wilds, dotted as they are by thousands and thousands of cottages. For Ontario is one of the few places in the world where seemingly everyone, rich and not so rich, has a country estate even if it's only a humble cabin.

A museum in the woods: To the north of Haliburton and the northeast of Muskoka lies the last real expanse of wild land in Southern Ontario – the 2,900-square-mile (7,511-sq-km) **Algonquin Park**. Set aside as a provincial park in 1893, Algonquin preserves the primordial, aboriginal and pioneer heritages of Ontario as a kind of natural museum.

Loons, the oldest known birds, abound in the park's 2,000 lakes or more as they did 10,000 years ago after the last Ice Age. Algonquin Indian "vision pits" can be found in the northwest corner of the park. Here, in these rock-lined holes a young Algonquin would fast for days waiting for the vision of a spiritual guardian who would draw the rite of passage to a close. And

in the park's interior, east of **Lake Opeongo**, lies the last stand of great white pines in Ontario. These few dozen ancient pines are all that are left of the huge forests cut to provide masts for the British Navy.

Algonquin should be seen by canoe. Heading north on **Canoe Lake** away from the access highway, it is only one or two portages before the motorboats and "beer with ghetto-blaster" campers are left behind. In the interior, porcupines, beaver, deer, wolves, bear and moose can all be seen by canoeists. In August, park naturalists will even organize wolf howls, where campers head out *en masse* at night to try and raise the cry of the great canines. The loons, however, need no such encouragement. Their haunting cry, which the Cree believed was the sound of a warrior refused entry to paradise, can be heard on every lake in the park.

Each season brings its own character to Algonquin. Spring is the time of wildflowers, mating calls, white water and blackflies as thick as night. Summer brings brilliant thunder storms, mosquitoes in place of blackflies, acres of blueberries, and water actually warm enough to swim in. In the fall, Algonquin turns into a *Group of Seven* canvas. The funeral for the forest's leaves is as triumphant and colorful as that of any New Orleans jazz singer. Uniform green gives way to a kaleidoscope of scarlet, auburn, yellow and mauve. While in the winter, the park falls deathly silent as it waits for the resurrection under a mantle of snow.

Algonquin's problems: Algonquin, however, is not without its problems, problems typical of an urban society unable to control its effect upon the natural environment. Not only is most of Algonquin under license to logging interests, whose long-term effect on the ecosystem cannot be gauged, but it is also being scarred by the effects of industrial pollution in the form of acid rain.

Indeed, environmentalists estimate that if acid rain continues to fall at the present rate, no loons or fish will be left in the park by the year 2000. This is already the case in **Killarney Provincial Park** to the northwest of Algonquin on the shores of Georgian Bay. Living within the shadow of **Sudbury's** smelters, Killarney's lakes are literally as clear as glass, wiped clean of all life.

Left, turnips again?! Right, moon over cottage country—an uncertain future.

TORONTO THE GOOD

In a 1971 Canadian film, *Going Down the Road*, a couple of good-natured, red-necked yahoos from the maligned eastern Canadian province of Newfoundland hurled a junky Chevrolet down the Trans-Canada Highway to the Promised Land called Toronto.

They approached the largest city in this, the second largest country in the world, in the best way possible — by car and at night. Toronto is nestled in small hills that roll down to a calm northern corner of Lake Ontario. A sheltered Great Lakes port, it boasts a magnificent downtown skyline when viewed from the highways that hug the lake shore. In the dark, the glowing office buildings and hovering Canadian National (CN) Tower (the world's tallest freestanding structure) are positively alien in their beauty.

The film was hailed by critics as a folksy paean to the misplaced hopes of backward East Coast culture — the pair found only alienation in the big city — but *Going Down The Road* has also worked into Canada's common self-perception. Everybody feels the lures of the city called *T.O.*, the political, cultural and financial juggernaut of Canadian accomplishment, with its forced claims to international stature and its unveiled urban arrogance. And, of course, everybody anywhere else in Canada wishes they were here — or so, at least, Torontonians choose to think.

Toronto's Yonge Street Strip: The alienation the two Newfoundlanders felt under the glare of depraved urban culture is prime Toronto merchandise for provincials trying to make a new life here, but it's not something the casual visitor is likely to notice. At worst, Toronto sleaze can be confined to the regulation gawking tour of Yonge Street, which is the city's main artery and reputed to be the longest street in the world (it starts at Lake Ontario and shoots straight up to Georgian Bay).

Between King and Bloor Streets, walking along the Yonge Street Strip, you can still find the fast-fading interlopers looking for action, the pimps and hookers, the shooters, foul-mouthed streetpeople and bums. The numbers are smaller than formerly, though, and the atmosphere is not so much rough

Dusk announces night over Toronto.

trade as it is circus chic – the punks and hoods often look like they're from central casting and, if you look around long enough, you'll realize the only difference between them is which bus they rode in from the suburbs.

The Strip is still worth a good look, however, even if it appears tame by some urban standards (it's nothing to Harlem, Chicago or Detroit), not least because Yonge Street restaurants and stores are often excellent. And walking is still the best way to see lower Yonge, unless you have a penchant for heavy metal and a '69 Camaro in good working order.

For the adventuresome, grittier and less stagey toughness lies on the side streets, where the kidding around gives way to hard

or 2:00 a.m. (There is one story, probably apocryphal, of a patron who leaped off one of these buses at one corner and used a phone booth to order a pizza, which was delivered hot to the bus about 15 blocks further downtown.)

Electric streetcars are a distinctive Toronto fixture on the downtown streets, revered by nostalgic patrons as fast-disappearing signs of an earlier era. The city has two kinds: dilapidated red-and-yellow heaps known as Red Rockets, with oddly slanted windows and no head room; and newer, heavier rail cars that lack the endearing shabbiness of the older ones.

Together with fleets of gas and electric buses, these streetcars will take you anywhere of interest in Toronto, including re-

sales and playing for keeps. The showy mood of the Strip belies the realities, which are a burgeoning transient population and lasting youth prostitution problems. The lures of success are sweet but ill-founded: kids from small-town Canada often end up hustling sex, drugs or both, living in cockroach-infested rooming houses or sleeping over subway grates.

Subways, buses and streetcars: Yonge Street splits the city into east and west and counts among its attributes one of Toronto's three subway lines. The subway is more often antiseptic and bloodless than anything else, however, and far more interesting are the all-night buses that charge up and down the street after the trains stop rolling at 1:30

levant subway stations for more distant locales. But walking or cycling is still preferred by most downtown inhabitants, simply because they allow a leisurely taste of a city that prides itself on the flavor of close-set variety.

Toronto islands: The one notable and obvious exception to this rule is travel to the Toronto Islands – actually one three-mile (five-km) strip of sandbar land with several names, jutting out into the city's harbor. It's a lovely haven in summer, and only about 10 minutes away by leisurely ferry. Here, too, you can transport a bike across or rent one there for some of the nicest riding in the city.

The island community is a unique aspect of Toronto, a group of fiery tenants intent on preserving their semi-primitive way of life in the middle of the city's harbor. In summer the choice land swarms with picnickers and cavorting rowdies with big radios, while the bitter winters bring winds that sweep mercilessly across Lake Ontario. Food and other supplies have to be ferried across or delivered to the tiny light plane airport at the island's west end. It's not what you'd call pleasure living.

But the natives love it, and one of the longest (and still unresolved) battles in Toronto City Hall annals is between these loyal inhabitants and a city council that wants the island exclusively for parkland.

Immigration floodgate: Toronto, like much of Canada, is the result of successive waves of immigration that washed over the wide

But if the Anglo-Saxon, pro-monarchist culture and sentiments were foremost in Toronto's history, they certainly haven't gone unchallenged. In the city proper, the chilly bun-haired matrons and their anglophile businessman spouses have been squeezed into a few hectares of prime real estate, principally in two neighborhoods — Rosedale and Forest Hill. Here you will still find a BMW or three in most garages, and the reticent, affluent people who run the financial and legal district centered on Bay Street downtown.

And, since Toronto lawyers speak for Canada (in practice if not in theory), Rosedale and Forest Hill arguably boast more power-brokers per city block than 15th-Century Florence.

western plains and sloshed into the dusty corners of the bigger cities, dampening the arrogance of "original" inhabitants — who were really just earlier immigrants anyway. Once called York, and a long-time capital of Upper Canada (the name Ontario went by before 1867's national confederation), Toronto is founded firmly on an English trading establishment that reaches back to the beaver trade and the Family Compacts of the early 1800s. Its *WASP* credentials are thus impeccable, if a little tarnished by time.

Left, Yonge Street: Toronto's den of iniquity; and above, Romanesque in miniature—Ontario's legislative buildings.

Further downtown, however, the neighborhoods begin to diversify. Italian, Greek, Chinese, Portuguese, Ukrainian, Polish, Japanese, Indian, Jamaican and Irish people all flooded through immigration sluice gates in large numbers — mostly between 1850 and 1950. Each group has managed to claim one or two city neighborhoods for its very own, carving multicultural demarcations that are well-defined and well-known.

Meeting at the market: Kensington Market is, in some ways, the place where these worlds meet on a regular basis and (unlike the artificiality of Caravan, Toronto's planned multicultural festival) it has an old-world boisterousness and scruffy charm. Here you can find frail, elderly Chinese ladies haggling vociferously with the gnarled Portuguese women who sell fruit and do incredible mental arithmetic in lieu of a cash register. Here, too, you'll encounter lethargic Rastafarian merchants hawking spicy beef patties and sharp ginger beer, or blasting reggae into streets thronged with college students hunting for used clothes, black-clad Italian widows carrying home several tonnes of fresh fruit on one arm, and chattering gangs of Chinese high school students showing off the latest fashions.

But the Market is an exception to the general rule, which is that most of these groups stick to themselves and to their own neighborhoods – the Greeks on the Danforth, the Italians and Portuguese on College Street and St. Clair Avenue, the

Chinese on Dundas Street, the East Indians mostly in the suburbs, the Jamaicans on Bathurst Street, the Eastern Europeans around Harbord Street or in Cabbagetown (Parliament and Gerrard Streets). All of this cultural diversity, more and more cherished rather than suppressed, can still mean that Toronto is a cold, tidy city to visit – almost in spite of the fact that such clean-cut bloodlessness is considered a *WASP* conceit – because of the grudging co-existence of the various groups. Neighborhoods can be closed areas; if you don't belong, you might be out of luck.

So, if Toronto seems a little brittle on top, it's because it has at least equal parts old-fashioned upscale Canadian reserve and

tight-lipped ethnic community jealousy. Together, it can mean one is in for a boring visit. What some visitors appear to miss, though, is the warmth and genuine friendliness that lies beneath. Torontonians may not be as demonstrative as say New Yorkers, but they're more of a pleasure to talk to – in whatever language.

Quiet past: Canadian history is remarkable in some ways because it lacks the violence and gun culture of many frontier developments. The West was tamed by railroads and the North West Mounted Police (now the Royal Canadian Mounted Police) and not by cowboys or outlaws. With the exception of two or three small uprisings, there has been little internal strife.

Canadians are thus reputed to have great respect for authority, and that extends to Toronto's mainstream, which is sometimes almost painfully well-behaved. The city can still become embarrassed over its 1837 reform rebellion, led by William Lyon Mackenzie, which ended peacefully anyway. Easterners in general reacted with little interest to the Manitoba Métis rebellion of Louis Riel, Gabriel Dumont and Chief Poundmaker, in 1885. Toronto was similarly distant during the 1970 October Crisis, in which the *Front du Liberation du Québec* (FLQ) kidnapped and killed cabinet minister Pierre Laporte, prompting then-Prime Minister Pierre Trudeau to invoke the War Measures Act for the first time ever during peace.

None of that matters a great deal to the visitor, though, unless he or she has a predilection for lawlessness. Jaywalking is just as popular here as anywhere else, but waiters are polite instead of bumptious–its not a bad trade-off.

Toronto's choice eateries: Speaking of waiters, Toronto is a wonderful city to eat out in, though it can be a tad expensive. Cultural mosaic often translates into good eats, and the city has terrific restaurants of every ethnic stripe. Chinese places are in dizzying abundance around Spadina and College Streets, while scattered Indian establishments and highly-prized Italian eateries will stand up to discriminating palates. Greek, French and West Indian cuisines are also well-represented. Hungarian food, the staple of many a student diet, can be found in half a dozen indistinguishable restaurants along Bloor Street near

Left, sprouting icy whiskers; and right, cornucopia in Kensington.

Bathurst Street, dishing up slabs of *weinerschnitzel* fit to sink a battleship.

In addition, solid steak and roast beef dining is always risk-free in a city raised on an English foundation of Yorkshire pudding, boiled vegetables and red meat. For those who prefer less bovine protein, Middle Eastern food – notably *falafel, taboula* and *tahini* is a healthy alternative.

Torontonians enjoy their food a great deal, as much as they cherish most leisure experiences. This is a city of studied hedonism, highly cultured but never afraid of doing things con gusto. That means, if you have the money, you are never lacking for something exciting to do. Toronto is the theater capital of the country, with a variety of spaces (and price ranges) that will do any-

closes down for the night. (Provincially regulated beer and liquor stores have even more restrictive hours, making the task of buying a bottle of *reisling* a logistic nightmare.) A few all-night dance clubs notwithstanding, nightlife doesn't go on as long as it might. Still, the live-music and dance clubs are eclectic and very good, offering jazz, rock, funk, folk or almost anything else you might be into. Toronto has a good underground of amateur bands and it's a habitual stop on most music tours, especially for European bands, which have long enjoyed popularity here. Again, prices and quality vary hugely from place to place, so it's best to do a little experimenting by consulting the ads in *Now Magazine,* a free entertainment weekly, or *T.O. Magazine,* a monthly

thing from staid Shakespeare to the latest Tom Stoppard or Sam Sheperd. It also ranks among the best cities in North America for film viewing, with some beautiful old movie palaces still standing, a good opinion and knowledge of foreign cinema, and some excellent repertory houses. The Festival of Festivals, the annual September film festival, features more than 400 screenings and galas and is now regarded in the same class as the Cannes, New York and Los Angeles events.

When night falls: In one of the more annoying Victorian carry-overs of Toronto life, bars and pubs are forced to close doors at 1 a.m., meaning that sidewalks begin to roll up around 1:40 a.m. when the subway

entertainment mag.

Multiculturalism makes some inroads into Toronto entertainment, despite the fact that leisure ads are invariably directed at young, affluent and, above all, white patrons. Caravan, while a little affected, offers good food and drink and some terrific ethnic music and dancing. Caribana, the yearly Caribbean festival, is a magnificent street-based celebration that blows away clouds of gray conservatism for at least a few days every August. And, not to be outdone, the annual Johnny Lombardi CHIN Multicultural Radio International Picnic (billed as the largest free picnic in the world) is a three-day hymn to the triumph of bad taste in any culture. Every July, Lombardi inflicts this tacky circus on the inhabitants of the city, dishing up muscle-building and bikini contests, food eating competitions, washed-up Italian heartthrobs and much else. It's an experience, that's for sure.

More sublimely, the Toronto Symphony Orchestra, the Canadian Opera Company and the National Ballet of Canada are all world-class outfits based in Toronto with extensive fall and winter seasons. Those able to meet the pecuniary demands of the Roy Thomson Hall and O'Keefe Center box offices will be suitably impressed.

The harborfront: Toronto's harborfront area, which grows more beautiful by the year as development business booms, is one of the best places to be in the summer. Since actual port traffic is scarce (most trade is

favor with their many well-earned bucks include Ontario Place (the province's spacey lakefront park), Canada's Wonderland (an amusement park that's hardly Canadian and hardly worth the trip), and the Canadian National Exhibition (an annual August fair that's been going on without fail for more than 100 years).

In sports, Toronto is wild about their pennant-class baseball team, the Blue Jays, tolerant of a decent football team, the Argonauts, and ashamed of the worst professional hockey team in North America, the Maple Leafs.

Financial capital of Canada: If Toronto's inhabitants like to play hard, it's nothing compared to what they are capable of in the workplace. The city is a highly productive,

done by train, in the hallowed Canadian way) this strip of shops, restaurants, parks and marinas is an exquisite place to spend an afternoon. Cycling and walking trails that begin at the harbor will take you eastward to The Beaches, which feature a nice boardwalk and some funky second-hand stores, or westward to High Park, the city's largest park and home to nature trails, paddle boats, outdoor theater and lots of tall, graceful trees.

Other places of leisure that Torontonians

Far left, balancing act at the Toronto Eaton Center; and left, a waiter from His Majesty's Feast dinner theater. Above, a reflective resident in one of Toronto's Italian quarters.

fast-paced place, home to most Canadian head offices, a huge stock exchange, the provincial government, two universities and five technical colleges, a bevy of law firms, three daily newspapers, dozens of publishing companies, and a good deal more. It is no idle boast to call it the center of Canadian urban life, with its solid financial and political stranglehold on the rest of the country.

And, not surprisingly, that prompts claims from some quarters that Toronto is Canada's true capital city. Ottawa, however, holds the official distinction and is located about 300 miles (500 km) northwest. That town, while bustling with bureaucratic activity and political acumen, is a little boring otherwise. In an age where politics are tied so directly to

finance, it's not unreasonable that the high power of Bay Street should have as much influence as it does on Ottawa's Parliament Hill, seat of the federal government.

Torontonians, in spite of their cool veneer, are passionately interested in politics, and especially in political economy. What they lack in the fiery commitment and streetfighter personality of Québec politicking, they make up for in sheer volume of money, influence and intellectual interest.

The two universities—University of Toronto (U of T), an English-influenced horde of buildings scattered downtown, and York University, a new suburban plot – provide a good atmosphere for the country's developing rulers (and dissidents). Ontario was for many years dominated by the Progressive Conservative Party, a strong union of big business and big agrarian interests, but they have recently relinquished power to an upstart minority government of the Liberal Party, which professes a more sophisticated urban appeal. Municipal politics are most often influenced by the New Democratic Party, which also has provincial and federal branches, and is a loose socialist mélange of young intellectuals and (less so now) farmers, who were the foundation of the budding party in the 1930s and 40s.

Historically, businesses in the city have been of two types: financial (stockbrokers, consultants, accountants) and administrative (head offices). There is very little actual manufacturing done in the city proper, though there are massive factory bases in surrounding areas. For that reason, if for no other, many of the city's residents prefer to think of it as the brain of Canada.

A world-class city: Somehow, in spite of all its pretensions (or perhaps because of them), Toronto is a world-class city, at least close to that elevated cadre that includes London, Paris, New York, Tokyo, Rome and Rio de Janeiro. It retains, with a varied population of about 2 million, some small-town aura and healthy dollops of European charm. It is also very cultured, exciting and affluent, making it something of a joy to visit. Well-groomed and tidy, like many things Canadian, Toronto seems to have just enough of whatever it is that makes a great city to climb past its own inhibitions. And those inhibitions, whatever their source, are perhaps Toronto's greatest drawback, creating the (superficial) impression that the city is boring, or haughty, or both. In fact it is neither, but makes a good show at hiding this crucial fact.

Toronto's self-conscious chrome.

QUÉBEC

In Québec, a little patience goes a long way. The foreign language and the sheer size of the province can make it appear a little forbidding, a little formidable. But what appears to be formidable turns out in most cases to be, as the French say, *formidable*—wonderful.

Don't be surprised if you sometimes encounter a protective and proud attitude towards language and culture (two great local preoccupations—obsessions with politicians). Québec is not France any more than Massachusetts is England, and the 6 million Québecois are deeply aware of being surrounded by almost 300 million anglophones whose culture seems to impinge upon their own. But language is only a seldom annoyance. One finds in Québec, in the cities as well as the countryside, a unique North American culture with a refreshing and lively approach to both work and play.

No visitor here can overlook the Québecois. French *joie de vivre* may be

a cliché, but it's real enough on Montréal's St. Denis Street or at Québec City's Winter Carnival. After all, a people who can give towns names like St. Telesphore, St. Zotique and St. Louis de Ha-Ha! must have a lively and active sense of humor.

Montréal: Always ready to celebrate something, Montréal today seems to erupt on a fairly regular basis. But there was a day many years ago when this region erupted as it has never done since. The result of this volcanic explosion was the felicitous appearance of **Mount Royal** and for posterity the park on its crest in the center of the city. And so today, from parking lots on rue Camilien Houde, to the lookout with its splendid view of the city, it's still the ideal place to begin a visit to Montréal: looking out over downtown with the hum of traffic below, watching the silent blue river with the hills in the hazy distance.

Though Montréal is no longer the largest of Canada's cities and though the political uncertainty of the late 1970s created some economic difficulty, it remains a city with extraordinary personality. Worldly but romantic, perhaps a little extravagant, more French—or rather, Québecois—than ever before, it is as earnest in its aim to enjoy life and look on the bright side as it did during Expo '67 or the 1976 Olympic Games. There have been changes in Montréal, since those events, but not decline.

Surrounded by the waters of the St. Lawrence, centering on the mountain and penetrated by a maze of subterranean shopping plazas and passages, Montréal is an unusually three-dimensional city. Everyone refers to Mount Royal as "the mountain" despite its being only 760 ft (230 m) high. The surrounding terrain is so flat, however, that the view from the summit is too good to be thought of as the view from a mere hill. In the distance lie the other mountains of the Monteregian group. On a clear day, you can see as far as the Adirondacks and the Green Mountains of Vermont.

Much closer, however, is the city that spreads out down the mountainside to the St. Lawrence. The view of the downtown core has changed rapidly over the last two decades, but the cruciform tower called **Place Ville Marie** and, to the right, the slightly taller **Bank of Commerce** building, still dominate. Be-

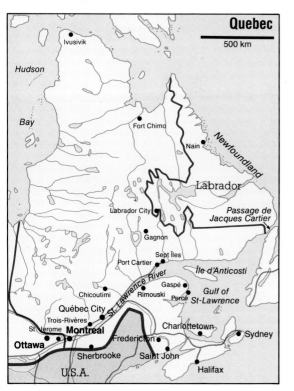

Quebec

500 km

Hudson

Bay

Ivusivik

Fort Chimo

Nain

Newfoundland

Labrador

Labrador City

Passage de Jacques Cartier

Gagnon

Sept Îles

Port Cartier

Île d'Anticosti

St. Lawrence River

Gaspé

Chicoutimi

Rimouski

Percé

Gulf of St-Lawrence

Québec City

Trois-Rivières

St. Jérome

Montréal

Charlottetown

Ottawa

Fredericton

Sydney

Sherbrooke

Saint John

U.S.A.

Halifax

tween them, rather staid and austerely Victorian, is the **Sun Life** building, once the tallest building in the British Commonwealth, and the symbol of the commercial dominance of English-speaking Montréalers.

Today, French is the language of business as confidently as it is the language of road signs and storefronts. Until the 1980s, Montréalers spoke of "two solitudes": a division of labor between English management and French employees and a division of the city between English and (usually less privileged) French quarters. After the election of the separatist Parti Québecois to the provincial government in 1976, many English-speaking Montréalers, or "anglos," left to live in other provinces, though many stayed behind to accept a new relationship with the French language and the Québecois. There was a short period of stagnancy, but now the city is vibrantly alive again. Laws have made French more obviously Montréal's first language, but visitors still find the city conveniently bilingual.

In 10 minutes, Côte des Neiges and rue Guy bring you down the mountain into the heart of the downtown shopping district. The finer grade of store and hotels such as the **Ritz Carlton** run along this section of Sherbrooke Street, being the lower limit of the "Square Mile," the old domain of the wealthiest anglos. The Montréal **Musée des Beaux-Arts,** known for its recent coups in attracting exclusive exhibitions, is here, and a few blocks east, **McGill University**, former home of Ernest Rutherford, Stephen Leacock and, many insist, Jack the Ripper.

St. Catherine's Street, two blocks south, is livelier, lined with boutiques, cafés, department stores, fast-food joints (especially croissanteries and smoked-meat delis) and arcades. Intersecting this bustling artery is Crescent Street, one of the concentrations of bistros and restaurants that give Montréal its reputation for nightlife and table-hopping. Throughout this district, there is a distinct emphasis upon terrace café-bars and fashion clothing. Here Montréalers indulge their second-favorite sport (ice-hockey is still number one): eating and drinking, seeing and being seen. Often quiet in the afternoons, the street comes vividly alive at night.

Collecting maple syrup in rural Québec.

Farther east the largest department stores and a nexus of multistory shopping centers—**Les Terrasess, 2001 and 2020**—are joined by underground passages to the Métro, Montréal's advanced subway system. Trains on rubber wheels thread their way between "designer" stations, each having its own bold architecture. Opened in 1967, the original line is just beginning to show its age, but with extensions branching out across the island and its quiet, high-speed trains, it's still the most efficient and pleasant way to get around Montréal.

Still farther east are **Complexe Desjardins**, another dramatically conceived shopping center, and **Place des Arts**, a complex of two theaters—Theater Maisonneuve and Theater Port-Royal, housed on top of one another in the step-pyramid style building—and **Salle Wilfred Pelletier**, with its elegant, sweeping curves, the home of Montréal's orchestra and opera.

L'Orchestre Symphonique de Montréal, or OSM, despite nearly disbanding in 1973, has emerged under the leadership of Charles Dutoit as one of the world's great orchestras and is often called "the world's finest French orchestra." Drawing rave reviews on recent international tours and prizes for their recordings, Place des Arts has at last become too humble a home and a new, 30-million dollar concert hall will be built for the OSM on Berri de Montigny, a few blocks east.

Place des Arts, however will soon become the home of the bizarre collection of Montréal's modern art museum, the **Musée d'Art Contemporain**. Presently located at the Cité du Havre near the port, the new facility will be completed in the next few years.

Beyond Place des Arts, there emerges an eclectic jumble of small, ardent businesses representing the ethnic communities who have made this their neighborhood: Jewish, Italian, Portuguese, Greek. Within this area lies another focus of Montréal's nightlife: **Prince Arthur Street**. Closed to motor traffic, Prince Arthur frequently fills up with hundreds of people lining up to eat at one of its popular Greek or Vietnamese restaurants. Most of Montréal's Greek restaurants, and some others, allow patrons to bring their own bottle(s) of wine, which makes an excellent

dinner easy to afford. (Every *depanneur* or corner grocery store, in Montréal sells decent table wine, while the liquor stores of the Societé des Alcools de Québec sell the complete line.) The crowds may appear daunting, but the lines move quickly, and street-artists, jugglers and acrobats usually show up to entertain.

Around the corner from the park at the east end of Prince Arthur is St. Denis Street. One stretch of road here was known for many years as the "Latin Quarter" of Montréal: bohemian, a little ramshackle, politicized. But today it surpasses Crescent Street as the hub of Montréal's night-time activity, the most completely Québecois of the bistro districts. The annual **International Jazz Festival** centers around St. Denis, and every year on June 24th, the traditional feast day of Québec's patron saint, St. Jean Baptiste, Montréalers flock down here to celebrate the Fête Nationale, to celebrate Québec. But throughout the year, St. Denis has a particularly Québecois vibrancy and charm.

Old Montréal: Although Jacques Cartier discovered an Indian settlement called Hochelaga near today's Crescent Street when he landed in 1535, Montréal was not permanently settled until a century later. The single purpose of the founders was to save the pagan "savages": by converting and/or baptizing them to Christianity, they would save their souls from eternal damnation. The project began when a secret society of wealthy Frenchmen formed a subgroup, the Societé de Notre Dame de Montréal and commissioned Paul de Chomedy, *Sieur de Maisonneuve*, to establish a settlement in this remote wilderness far from "civilization" — 70 recruits and young Jeanne Mance, a nurse, accompanied him.

The village of Québec in that year, 1642, was having a bad time defending itself against the brutal attacks of the Iroquois and they felt sure Maisonneuve's mission had almost no chance of surviving beyond a few weeks, but Maisonneuve pressed on resolutely. By chance, or perhaps, as Maisonneuve thought, by divine intervention, the Iroquois ignored the new settlement, and by the time winter came, the settlers were able to erect a few huts and a log palisade.

· **Montréal's skyline.**

The 17th Century European vogue for hats made of beaver pelt soon gave Montréal a secondary purpose, the fur trade, which became its primary purpose with greater organization and profits. The accommodation of business and religion as twin forces in Montréal's history is visible everywhere, but especially in Old Montréal.

North up rue St. Pierre and east along rue Notre Dame leads to the hub of Old Montréal, **Place d' Armes**. Banks surround the square on three sides; it was once the heart of the Canadian financial establishment, dominated by anglo-Montréalers. But on the south side stands the **Notre Dame Basilica**, the symbol *par excellence* of Québecois Roman Catholicism. Maisonneuve, standing on his pedestal in the center of the square, seems perhaps caught in a struggle between God and Mammon, between the power and the influence of the "two solitudes." But that is in the past. Today the square is busy with horse-drawn *calèches* and the inevitable tour buses.

The façade of Notre Dame is plain because stone workers were rare in Québec when the church was built around 1829. But its interior, in stark contrast, is a magnificently ornate tribute to the importance of woodworking and decoration in Québecois tradition. Everywhere there is paint laced with real gold and the reredos gleams in a vivid sky blue. Ironically, Montréal's finest church was designed by an Irish American, James O'Donnell, but the interior is the brain-child of a French Canadian, Victor Bourgeau. Neither ugly nor the epitome of subtle elegance, it is what it was meant to be: overwhelming.

Adjacent to the west wall of the basilica stands Montréal's oldest building, the **Seminary of St. Sulpice** built in 1685. The Sulpicians became the seigneurs or landlords of all Montréal when they took over missionary responsibilities from the Societé de Notre Dame in 1663. More than 300 years after its construction, the Seminary still serves its original purpose.

Across the square stands the English businessman's retort to Notre Dame's assertion of indomitable French Canadian values: the serene neo-Classical **Bank of Montreal**, built in 1847. During banking hours, the opulent main hall is

Left, street musicians; and right, one of Montréal's many artists.

open to visitors, as is a tiny and interesting museum.

Walking east past the shops and cafés on rue Notre Dame, you encounter the old Napoleonic-style **Palais de Justice**, with its white dome, on the north side, and on the south side, the less graceful "new" Palais de Justice, with its august pillars and heavy doors. The Latin inscription on the cornice "He who transgresses the law shall seek the help of the law in vain," only adds to the severity of the whole effect. Both buildings are government offices today.

Opening off the south side of rue Notre Dame lies **Place Jacques Cartier**, a center of much less serious activity than Place d'Armes. Cobblestoned, floriated, peopled and surrounded by restaurants and terrace cafés in buildings a century and a half old, it preserves the charm, the human scale, of another era. At the top of the square stands **Nelson's Column**, the city's oldest monument. Rather oddly, he faces away from the square and from the river. Naturally, nationalist Québecois have never been entirely happy with the dominance of the square by this hero of the British empire, the scourge of

Napoleon's navy, but Horatio has survived controversy as graciously as erosion. Lest the monument should be thought a rather diminutive replica of the column in Trafalgar Square, know that Montréal's predates London's by 34 years.

Facing Nelson across rue Notre Dame stands the city hall, or **Hôtel de Ville**, an elegant Second Empire style building with its slender columns and mansard roofs. Opposite, on the south side, stands the **Château de Ramezay**, looking like a sturdy farmhouse, but nevertheless the focal point of more than a century of early Canadian history.

Today, the Château is a private museum with some impressively equipped 18th-Century living quarters and some fascinating artifacts. Look out for North America's first paper money; playing cards authorized as legal tender when a cargo of coins was delayed in its passage across the Atlantic.

Yet another site to see here is the **Vieux Port**, now an entertainment area that offers summer evenings of music, dancing and beer under the stars with the city skyline as a backdrop. The port also provides the best view of the **Bonsecours Market**, which was originally the city hall (1852-78), but for almost a century the principal marketplace in Montréal. Its long, classical façade with the silver dome is the sight that greeted thousands of immigrants and travelers in the 19th Century. It now houses municipal offices.

Beside it stands **Notre Dame de Bonsecours Church**, also known as the **Sailors' Church** as sailors have traditionally come here to give thanks for being saved from a shipwreck.

Rue St. Paul on the west side of Place Jacques Cartier is mostly given over to shops and *boîtes à chanson,* those incomparable Québecois beerhalls in which packed houses sing along to old favorites, nationalist anthems, the latest hits, anything that sustains the *joie de vivre.*

Until the 1960s, religion as much as language set French Canada apart from the rest of North America. In the middle of the anglo business district Monsignor Ignace Bourget built **Mary, Queen of the World Cathedral**, a one-eighth scale replica of St. Peter's in Rome. Nowhere, however, is the importance of religion more obvious than at **St. Joseph's Oratory**, the huge church **Old Montréal.**

that rises 500 ft (152 m) above the street on the western summit of Mount Royal. It rose up out of a wave of popular devotion to St. Joseph, the patron saint of the worker, led by one humble little man, Brother André.

Alfred Bessette, Brother André, was porter and errand boy across the street at College Notre Dame when he developed a reputation as "the miracle worker" because of the many cures he performed by applying oil from a lamp of St. Joseph to the bodies of the sick. Soon, the sick were flocking to him by the thousands and continued to come for 30 years. By simply asking people to donate money or time to the construction of a monument to St. Joseph on Mount Royal, the church began to take shape in 1924 and was finally completed in 1965. Typical of Brother André's style was his answer when money ran out during the depression: he simply recommended that a statue of St. Joseph be placed in the center of the roofless church. "If he wants a roof over his head, he'll get it," he said. Two months later the money was found to keep building. Brother André's tiny living quarters still stand in the shadow

McGill University watches a soccer match.

of the oratory.

If the exterior is more remarkable for its size than its beauty (only the dome of St. Peter's in the Vatican is larger) the austere simplicity of the modern interior is more lovely. At daily recitals, the organ with its 5,811 pipes thunders through the vast church. Impressive in quite a different way is the crypt with its rows of crutches, donated by the miraculously healed, and banks of devotional candles.

St. Joseph's represents the Québec of a different era. Rules between 1936 and 1959 (except for the war years) by Maurice Duplessis, an autocratic and secretive premier known as *le Chef* or *le Patron*, Québec was conservative and backward. But the 1960s, with the death of Duplessis and an atmosphere of prosperity and change, brought the "Quiet Revolution," a deep change in the attitudes and ideas of Québecois. The buildings of the 1960s in Montréal are monuments not to the Church but to modernity: **Place Ville Marie**, perhaps the most successful creation of the famous urban architect I.M. Pei, with its cruciform tower and underground plaza, pioneered the concept of the

shopping mall in 1962. Moshe Safdie, a student at McGill University, designed **Habitat**, a sort of cubist representation of the mountain made out of 158 concrete apartment units hoisted into place by crane, for Montréal's port area in 1967. The site of **Expo '67**, an island built in the St. Lawrence, can be identified by Buckminster Fuller's 20-story geodesic dome still standing after a fire burned away its plexiglass shell.

Expo '67 became an annual exhibition called **Man and His World**, and its location on **Île Ste-Helene** and **Île Notre Dame** in the St. Lawrence still gets plenty of use. The main site today looks like the set for an ambitious sci-fi film, though it is still used in part for exhibitions, principally at the **Palais de la Civilisation**. An amusement park, **La Ronde**, is on Île Ste-Helene, including **L'aqua Parc**, a group of 20 water slides like roller coasters, ranging from the tame to the terrifying. Here also is the **Alcan Aquarium** and nearby the **Vieux Fort**, with daily reenactments of manoeuvres by the Fraser Highlanders. **Île Notre Dame** is the site of the annual **Floralies**, an international flower exhibition, and the **Canadian Grand Prix**.

But every year, indeed every month, seems to offer something different, some new international event or exhibition, and while it's always worth finding out what is happening on the islands, it's impossible to predict what that might be.

Perhaps the most impressive of Montréal's modern monuments is the **Olympic Park**, one of the world's most ambitious sports complexes, located on Sherbrooke Street East. The **Olympic Stadium** is the pride and despair of Montréalers—perhaps, to be truthful, more often the latter. Known variously as the *Big O* and the *Big Owe,* it cost taxpayers over 700 million dollars and was not fully completed until 11 years after the Olympic Games it was built to serve. The controversial stadium, with its suspended retractable roof and slanted tower, has one of the best views in the city; on clear days the view extends 50 miles (80 km) — the Laurentians can be seen to the northwest and the Monteregian Hills to the southeast. Yet, overlooking its price tag, the stadium is a magnificent piece of architecture with its 38 huge arms

Saffron brilliance from Forillon National Park.

stretching around the 60,000 seats to the central elliptical ring, forming an enormous mollusk without a single internal support. Under the base of the tower, with roofs that fan out on either side, are the Olympic swimming pools and nearby is the low, sweeping dome of the **Velodrome**, the cycling track. The main occupants today are the Montréal Expos and Montréal's new football team, the Concordes. Occasional concerts and special events also take place in the stadium.

Across the street from the Olympic Park are Montréal's **Botanical Gardens**, the world's third largest, after London and Berlin, with 180 acres (73 hectares) of flora. There are 30 gardens and nine greenhouses; the **Arid Regions** greenhouse is the best place in the city to escape from a Montréal snowstorm, but any time of year, the flowerbeds, fountains, brooks and exotic trees can carry visitors into other worlds.

The Eastern Townships: For hundreds of years, the Eastern Townships have been a place of refuge and of peace. Once predominantly English, the region is now 90 percent French (though the majority can speak both languages)

and has become known as *L'Estrie*. During the American War of Independence, many who preferred to stay loyal to the British crown settled in these parts and it has retained an English and American flavor throughout its history. It also drew benefit from the American Civil War, when southerners who felt uncomfortable in the northern states would spend holidays in one of the Townships' many fine old hotels. But no friction between the Townships and New Englanders survives today: they are the closest of neighbors. The international border runs right down the main street of Beebe-Plain and in one town straight across the counter of the general store—a problem that the owner solves by putting one cash register at each end of the counter.

Bring some quarters for the tolls of Highway 10 from Montréal, which takes you into the Townships in about one hour. **Granby,** just off the north, is known for its zoo and its collection of fountains, but head on towards **Mount Orford** (a ski resort with a chairlift to the summit year-round) and **Magog** for the most beautiful country. The gentle hills and valleys develop into the Appa-

Traversing a powdery plain.

lachian mountain range towards Vermont, and with its intricate network of lakes and streams, its country villages, diary cattle, sheep and strawberry fields, this part of Québec has a bucolic charm that is unusual in the often rugged terrain of the province. Indeed, **North Hatley** (on Rte 108 at the top of Lake Massawippi) rests in a shielded valley, warmed by sunlight reflected from the lake, giving it a "microclimate" that prolongs summer and softens winter enough to make it the home of hummingbirds and flora normally found far to the south. Equally unusual in Québec is the English-language summer theater performed at **The Piggery**.

Long, slender **Lake Memphremagog** is the largest in the area; boat cruises and a variety of water sports are available at the town of Magog on its northern tip. On its west shore, the beautiful hillside Benedictine monastery of **St.-Benoit-du-Lac** manufactures cheese and chocolate.

The Laurentians: Spring, which in Québec lasts about a day and a half, is the only season in which Montréalers avoid the Laurentians. It is the playground just beyond the backyard of the

metropolis; though its wooded lakes and hills are still lovely, the difficulty is often where to get away from it all where everyone has come to get away from it all. Winter is ski season; almost everyone in Montréal skis either cross-country or downhill. In summer, families pack up the car and head to the cottage for swimming, sailing, windsurfing and waterskiing. In fall, the leaves turn those deep shades of red and orange that draw hikers parading over the hills and valleys.

Not all the Laurentian towns are equally picturesque: prettiness tends to be in proportion to size, though **St.-Sauveur-des-Monts** and **Ste-Adèle** are worth visiting for their restaurants and exceptional character. The best bet, however, is to take Autoroute 15, or the more scenic and slow Rte 117 to **Parc Mont Tremblant**. About an hour and half from Montréal (87 miles [140 km]), Mont Tremblant offers just about all the attractions and beauty of other areas and seclusion to boot.

The Laurentians are among the oldest mountain ranges in the world, so for the most part erosion has softened peaks into gently rounded hills perhaps 1,000 ft (300 m) high. Mont Tremblant is the region's highest mountain at 3,200 ft (975 m); chairlifts operate year-round to carry visitors to the summit. There are more than 380 lakes scattered over the park, and facilities are available for windsurfing, canoeing, white-water rafting on the Rivière du Diable, fishing and, of course, swimming. The nearby village of **Mont Tremblant**, just outside the park has good hotels and golf courses; cottages with kitchenettes are available during the summer within the park. On occasional weekends, the campgrounds near the entrance to the park may suffer some congestion, but along the quiet roads that wind among the streams and lakes, there will always be plenty of lonely wilderness to make your own.

Val d'Or: Its name means Valley of Gold and it lies at the eastern extreme of the Cadillac Break, a gold-rich fault that extends west to Kirkland Lake in Ontario. Though the mines here have sustained the population ever since Stanley Siscoe struck the glittering metal in 1914, it has never been a case of scratching the soil to find big, soft nuggets: it takes about five tons of ore to yield an ounce of gold. Still, high gold

Seeking a different perspective: hotdog skiing.

prices have kept the miners working and recently the town has found another source of prosperity: its strategic location on the road from Montréal to the vast James Bay hydroelectric project.

Val d'Or got its start when the Lamaque mine opened during the depression and the mining company built a village called **Bourlamaque** exclusively for its employees. This meant that the hundreds of men who came looking for work had to pitch tents or erect shacks nearby, and it was this makeshift community that evolved into Val d'Or. Bourlamaque today is a well-preserved historic quarter that consists of 75 pinewood houses and a small museum. As for Val d'Or, its population has grown to 23,000.

Yet the town has that slightly impermanent look that mining towns so often seem to have. The residents have had to live with the knowledge that if the mines dry up or the price of gold falls, they will probably have to move elsewhere. The classic boom-bust story of Siscoe himself reflects that sobering notion: in 1955 a snowstorm forced the plane carrying him from Montréal to land on a frozen lake 32 miles (50 km) from town. After two days stranded without food, Siscoe decided to leave the pilot and try to walk to civilization. The pilot was picked up later the same day by another plane, and the next day found Siscoe spread-eagled in the snow, surrounded by the scattered paper money that he had thrown away in despair.

But a cheerful and entrepreneurial spirit prevails in modern Val d'Or. Each October, Val d'Or hosts the **Moose Festival**, during which some fortunate Valdorian beauty is crowned Moose Queen. The festival sponsors a week of events such as parades, canoe races and huntsends , with a moose-calling competition—open to both the gentlemen and the ladies.

Trois-Rivières: Trois-Rivières once produced 10 percent of the world's newsprint: 2,500 tons a day. Though still quite important commercially, today it struggles to overcome its image as a lackluster industrial town, a pit-stop halfway between Montréal and Québec City. It has prospered since 1610, but the fires that regularly swept through all Québec's communities have left little to

show from the town's first two centuries. In the rue des Ursulines, the **Manoir de Tonnancour**, the **Maison-de-la-Fresniére** (now a wine store) and the **Ursuline Convent** survive, at least in part, from the early 18th Century.

The town's attractions are modern: the **Grand Prix** race through the city streets and the **International Canoe Classic** on the St. Maurice, both in early September, the **Laviolette Bridge** that spans the St. Lawrence, and soon, a revitalized port area for entertainment and recreation.

Eight miles (13 km) east of the city, just off the Boulevard des Forges, Parks Canada recently opened **Les Forges du Saint Maurice**, a recreation of the old ironworks here. Like the other National Historic Parks in Montréal, Québec and elsewhere, the forge is a sort of hybrid between park and museum, full of "user-friendly" displays that invite you to learn through participation.

Nowhere in the vicinity draws as many visitors as the shrine, six miles (10 km) north of Trois-Rivières, called **Notre-Dame-du-Cap**. The little Notre-Dame-du-Rosaire church here was built in 1714 and drew a moderate number of pilgrims until the day in 1883 that Father Frederic Jansoone and two others saw the statue of the Virgin open her eyes.

Trois-Rivières stands at the confluence of the St. Maurice and the St. Lawrence, begging the question: where is the third river? There isn't one. If you travel up the St. Lawrence by boat, as Jacques Cartier and Samuel de Champlain did, the two delta islands at the mouth of St. Maurice give the impression that "trois rivières" end here. At least the name survives from the distant past.

Québec City: "The impression made upon the visitor by this Gibraltar of North America: its giddy heights; its citadel suspended, as it were, in the air, its picturesque streets and frowning gateways; and the splendid views which burst upon the eye at every turn: is at once unique and everlasting."

Remarkably, Charles Dicken's comment on **Québec City** is still perfectly appropriate more than a century after his visit: it retains its 18th Century ambience with narrow, winding streets and horse-drawn carriages and fine French cooking behind charming **Bitter winds scour the shores of the St. Lawrence.**

166

façades. The only dramatic change in the old town since Dickens' time is one he would have appreciated: the construction at the turn of the century of an immense castle-like hotel that perches on its promontory over the St. Lawrence river: the **Château Frontenac**.

The province's cryptic motto, *Je me souviens* (I remember), insists upon the defense of Québecois tradition, language and culture. Here in the provincial capital, reminders are everywhere that this was once performed by soldiers with guns from turrets and bastions. Today, the politicians and civil servants of Québec City have taken over the job, using the milder instruments of democracy, but hardly less ardent in their purpose.

Québec City still stands sentinel over the St. Lawrence, the only walled city on the continent north of Mexico. The views are as lovely as ever: from the **Dufferin Terrace** just in front of the Château Frontenac, one looks out at the blue Laurentian hills and Mont St. Anne, the rolling countryside and the boats passing on the shimmering St. Lawrence 200 ft (60 m) below.

Diagonally opposite **Place d'Armes**,

the former drill and parade ground, the rue du Trésor runs down to rue Buade. This lane, named after the building where colonists used to pay their dues to the Royal Treasury, is today the artist's row: hung with quite decent watercolors, etchings, silkscreens. Rue Buade winds downhill to **Montmorency Park** (usually tranquil however busy the rest of the old town becomes), opposite the grand **General Post Office** with its rather pompous monument to Bishop François de Laval-Montmorency, first bishop of Québec and founder of its largest university. Côte de la Montagne drops steeply down to the left, winding down into the lower town, following the ravine that Québec's first settlers used to climb from the Lower Town to the Upper. Just beyond the **Prescott Gate**, a recent reconstruction of the original erected here in 1797, is **L' Escalier Casse-Cou**, the "Breakneck Steps." This staircase, not quite as daunting as it sounds, leads to the narrow Petit-Champlain, lined with crafts shops and tiny galleries. From the foot of L' Escalier Casse-Cou, **Place Royale** is just around the corner. Thus one tumbles from the Château Frontenac into

Winter festivities on the river.

the cradle of French civilization in North America.

Place Royale, where the first settlement in America stood, was the business center of Québec City until about 1832. Its name derives from the bust of Louis XIV, the great Sun King of Versailles, that was erected here in 1686. Today, it is the scene of constant plays and concerts, usually recreating the culture of the 17th and 18th centuries.

Notre-Dame-des-Victoires Church, dominating the square, was built in 1688 and reconstructed after Wolfe's devastation of the lower town in 1759. The church is named for two early victories against the Anglo-Americans—or rather, one great victory and one lucky accident. A Bostonian, Sir William Phipps (knighted for discovering 32 tons of ship-wrecked bullion) sailed to Québec with 34 boats and 2,000 men in October, 1690, and demanded its surrender. Governor Frontenac promised to reply with his cannon, and during six days of fighting, his guns hammered the fleet. By land, Canadian snipers, fighting Indian style against Phipps's troops drawn up in formal battle-order, killed 150 men with only one loss to their own party. Phipps withdrew on the sixth day, unaware that the French had just run out of ammunition.

The lucky accident—or to the French, Our Lady's victory—was the storm in the Gulf of St. Lawrence that destroyed the enormous British fleet of Sir Hovendon Walker in 1711, saving Québec from almost certain defeat. Both these events are depicted in little scenes above the odd, turretted altar.

Crossing the road that runs along the waterfront, rue Dalhousie, you leave the 18th Century behind and encounter the more modern world of the port. On the right is the entrance to the government-operated ferry services to **Lévis** on the other side of the river, while straight ahead the **Louis Jolliet**, a colorful and popular cruise boat, docks. Walking north beside the river leads to the new commercial and community complex, called **le Vieux Port** despite its thoroughly contemporary design: overhead walkways of red and silver tubing and plexiglass walls connect spacious, functional pavilions. The complex surrounds the **Agora**, a 5,500-seat amphitheater set among flowerbeds, waterfalls and fountains and used for cultural events,

Two centuries draw astride.

particularly evening concerts throughout the summer.

The easiest way to get back to the Upper Town is by taking the little funicular at the head of rue Sous-le-Fort, which is worth the small charge to save wear and tear on the feet in this city-made-for-walking. It shinnies up the cliff from the house of Louis Jolliet (the explorer of the Mississippi River) to the Dufferin Terrace.

At the intersection of rue Buade and Côte de la Fabrique stands the rather heavily Baroque cathedral of Québec City, **Basilique Notre-Dame-de-Québec**. The city's principal church has been here since 1633 when Samuel de Champlain built Notre-Dame-de-la-Recouvrance in gratitude for the recovery of New France from the British. As with the later victories, the French settlers considered the rescue of New France from Protestant infidels an act of God.

Next door stands the **Seminaire de Québec** and the **Université de Laval**. The Jesuits established a college here in 1635, a year before Harvard opened, but the Seminary was officially founded only in 1663 by Bishop Laval. The university still exists, though its modern campus is now in the suburb of **Ste-Foy**, and these buildings serve their original purpose as a seminary and high school. The seminary's museum is probably the city's finest general museum, with splendid modern facilities for the displays of Baroque and Renaissance art and some of the finest of 19th Century Canadian art. There is also a gruesome unwrapped mummy from the time of Tutankhamen, an oriental collection, and some intriguing old scientific contraptions.

Across the street from the cathedral is the **Monument to Cardinal Taschereau**, looking formidable, as if quite prepared to carry out his threat to excommunicate any worker who tried to unionize. Behind him is the gray ample **City Hall**, or **Hôtel de Ville**.

Just around the corner stands the only rival to the Château Frontenac on the city's skyline, the **Price Building**. With 17 stories, it just about qualifies as the old town's only skyscraper. One is enough, and fortunately the 1937 art-deco style is not out of keeping with the neighborhood. Straight on, however, stands the **Holy Trinity Cathedral**, the

first Anglican cathedral built outside the British Isles and thoroughly English from its design (on the model of St. Martin's in the Fields in Trafalgar Square in London) to its pews made of oak imported from the Royal Windsor Forest. There is also a throne in the apse called the King's Bench, but rather ironically, though it has been graced in its 200 years by queens, princes, princesses and governors-general, but so far, no king.

Lively rue St. Louis, with its snug little restaurants and *pensiones*, slopes up from the end of rue Desjardins to the St. Louis Gate, rebuilt in a grand neo-Gothic (complete with turret and crenellated gun-ports) to replace the 17th Century original. Just in front of the gate is the lane that leads to the **Citadel**, the star-shaped bastion on the summit of **Cap Diamant**, 300 ft (90 m) over the St. Lawrence.

The Citadel, with its Changing of the Guard ceremony and its night bulwarks, appeals to childhood notions of soldierly glory and adventure. But however colorful, it continues to play a military role as the headquarters of Canada's French only 22nd Regiment, known as the "Van Doos" (a rather crude rendering of "les Vingt Deux") and visitors must join the guided tour. Built by the British in the early 1800s according to plans approved by the Duke of Wellington, with double granite walls and a magnificent position above a sheer cliff, it was considered one of the most impregnable strongholds in the Empire.

Despite its genuine military function, there is plenty of pomp and circumstance here. Besides the daily Changing of the Guard, complete with busbees and bayonets, the flag lowering ritual called "beating the retreat" is enacted four days a week and cannons are fired twice daily.

Beyond the wall's confines, the city becomes suddenly roomy, opening out onto the **Grande Allée** and the lawns of the **Hôtel du Parlement**, the seat of the National Assembly, Québec's provincial government. Though not old by the city's standards (building began in 1881), the elaborate French Renaissance design by Eugène-E. Taché does seem to embody Québec's distant roots in the court of Louis XIII. Its symbols, however, are purely Québecois: the important figures of her history are all **Midnight phantoms from the Winter Carnival.**

there, each trying to outdo the other's elegant pose in his alcove on the façade: Frontenac, Wolfe, Montcalm, Lévis, Talon .... Below, Louis-Philippe Hebert's bronze works include dignified groups of Indians, the "noble savages" of the white man's imagination.

Outside, the terraces of the Georgian houses that border the Grande Allée west from Parliament Hill are cluttered with tables where visitors and civil servants enjoy the cuisine, the wines and the serenading violins of Québec's liveliest restaurants. A block south, there is gentle peace. **National Battlefields Park**, or the **Plains of Abraham**, runs parallel to the Grande Allée with spectacular views across the St. Lawrence to the Appalachian foothills. Its two miles (3 km) of rolling lawns and broad shade trees have known far more romance than fighting, many more wine-and-cheese picnics than violent deaths, but however incongruously, it commemorates a vicious 15-minute battle in which Louis Joseph, Marquis de Montcalm, lost half of North America to the British.

It wasn't quite that simple, but the fact remains that the Indian fighting style of the Canadians had won them success after success against the British until the Marquis de Montcalm, a traditionalist and a defeatist, became head of the land troops. Always ready to retreat even after a victory, and rarely pressing an advantage, Montcalm steadily reduced the territory that he had to defend. General Wolfe, who sailed down the St. Lawrence with half as many troops as Montcalm held in the fortress of Québec City, never really hoped to succeed in taking it and so he destroyed 80 percent of the town with cannon fire. Montcalm would not emerge to fight a pitched battle, and in a last-ditch, desperate attempt, Wolfe took 4,400 men up the cliff in silence by cover of night to these heights where there was no hope of turning back. Montcalm had been expecting Wolfe at Beauport, north of the city, and he rushed back to fight on the Plains. Throwing away every advantage: time, the possession of the city stronghold, and the sniping skills of his men, Montcalm fought the kind of European-style set battle that his troops were improperly trained for. Wolfe was killed, Montcalm mortally wounded, and though the British held

The Château Frontenac looms above the deathbed of Generals Montcalm and Wolfe.

only the Plains at the battle's conclusion, Montcalm surrendered the city.

The robust little Martello tower halfway along the park was built as an outpost of the British defense system between 1804 and 1823. Its walls on the side facing the enemy are 13 ft (4 m) thick, narrowing to a mere 7 ft (2 m) on the side facing the town.

At the far end of National Battlefields Park, just beyond the now vacant jail called the **Petit Bastille**, stands the **Musée de Québec**, the imposing neo-Classical home of a large proportion of the best Québec art. Names such as Alfred Pellan, Marc-Auréle Fortin and Jean-Paul Riopelle are not quite household names throughout the world, but nevertheless the work of these modern artists, ranges from expressionistic landscapes to frenetic abstracts.

Pack your bathing suit when you head north on auto Rte. 440 to **Montmorency Falls**, which at 250 ft (83 m) are considerably higher than Niagara Falls, though less dramatic because so much narrower. Here, however, instead of looking at the falls from the top down, you approach the base, which means that the closer you get to the falls, the wetter you get in the spray. The province has thoughtfully built a large granite platform at the base of the falls so that visitors can actually stand inside the chilly cloud of spray. In winter, the spray forms a solid block which grows up from the bottom into a "sugarloaf" of ice and snow, providing a splendid slope for tobogganing.

Just a mile south of the falls, the bridge over the **Île d'Orléans** turns off the autoroute. In 1970, the provincial government declared the island a historic district to prevent the encroachment of the city and the tourist trade from destroying the milieu of one of Québec's most picturesque and historic regions. The old farmhouses and churches here are remarkable not only for their age—many date from the French regime before 1759—but for their unique architecture, a style borrowed from Normandy and Brittany and adapted to local conditions.

The exceptionally fertile soil brought prosperity early to the island. In the 1600s there were as many inhabitants here as in Montréal or Québec, but farming is still the vocation of most of the families here, many working plots

Winter solace.

172

Tadoussac Hotel makes the movies.

that have been passed down since Québec's earliest days. Few visitors can resist indulging themselves at the roadside stands that offer fat strawberries swimming in thick, fresh cream topped off with maple sugar.

The Saguenay and Lac St.-Jean: Among all Québec's uncountable lakes and waterways, perhaps none can match the splendor of the **Saguenay Fjord**, its ragged cliffs looming hundreds of feet over the broad, blue river. Vikings and Basque fishermen came and went long before Jacques Cartier named it "the Kingdom of the Saguenay" when he came seeking the orient in 1535.

Its spectacular beauty survives today, and the whales never fail to gather in the deep estuary each July, staying until December when they swim away to unknown destinations. The cruise boats that leave from the wharf at **Baie Ste-Catherine**, 95 miles (150 km) north of Québec on Rte 138, can virtually guarantee whale sightings.

A free ferry takes passengers and cars across the river to **Tadoussac**, where North America's oldest wooden church, the **Tadoussac Chapel**, has stood since 1747, and New France's first fort, built in 1600, has been reconstructed. If the **Tadoussac Hôtel** looks familiar, it may be because the movie *Hotel New Hampshire* was filmed here a few years ago.

Farther inland, the terrain levels out onto the fertile plain of the **Lac St. Jean** region. Fur-trading companies held a monopoly on the area until the mid-19th Century and it was barely settled until railroads brought pulp and paper developments after 1883 followed by large hydroelectric and aluminum smelting plants which brought to Lac St. Jean its modern prosperity. For visitors, however, the industry is relatively insignificant except in the commercial centers of Chicoutimi, Jonquière and Alma. The rich soil produces 10 million pounds (4.5 million kilos) of blueberries a year, and coupled with award-winning local cheeses, these provide the materials for an endless supply of mouth-watering, heart-stopping blueberry cheesecakes. Slightly less decadent regional specialties include various *tourtières* (spiced meat pies) and a dried-bean soup called *soup à la gourgane*. Local fish—trout, pike, dore, and plentiful freshwater salmon—complete the menu.

Beyond the commerical centers, beautiful small towns cluster around Lac St. Jean, such as **Péribonka**, the setting of Louis Hémon's novel *Maria Chapdelaine*, and **Mistassini**, the blueberry capital. **Val-Jalbert**, a ghosttown for 35 years, has re-opened, preserving its original character and buildings. The old mill stands against the 236-ft (72-m) **Ouiatchouan Falls.**

The Gaspé: Rte 132 begins and ends at Ste-Flavie, looping around the Gaspé Peninsula in a 560-mile (900-km) circle that strings together the sleepy fishing villages of the eastern coast. The Micmacs called it *Gespeg*, "the end of the earth."

Though the **Gaspé** has been settled since Shakespeare's time, it has suffered almost no industrial development. Even the roads and trains that came with the later 19th Century left the region's rural tranquility and Acadian culture largely the same as ever.

From Ste-Flavie, the road cuts southeast down the Matapédia Valley, following beside or above the "river of 222 rapids," which cascades through a deep gorge at the edge of the Chic-Choc mountains. At the village of **Matapédia**, the road turns northeast and follows the **Baie des Chaleurs.** Once known as the "Canadian Riviera," the bay is thankfully too wild and unspoiled to merit the name today. Herons and terns gather on the sandbars and the long, sandy beaches are often virtually deserted. The road weaves among coves and villages, some with English names such as New Carlisle, New Richmond and Douglastown, given to them by the Loyalists who settled here to escape the American War of Independence.

Eventually the coast vends northward and meets the red, rocky cliffs where the Chic-Chocs veer down to the sea. Rounding a curve, suddenly the Percé Rock appears, a 400-million-ton block of limestone jutting improbably out of the sea. Roughly oblong in shape, there were once as many as four arches driven by the tides through this treeless crag. Only one remains, enough to entitle it to its name "pierced rock." Nearby, the bird sanctuary on **Île Bonaventure** is home to 50,000 gannets.

The north coast of the Gaspé is more wild and rugged: the road winds along the bluffs at the edge of the highest mountains in eastern Canada. **Mt.**

Prominent features of Gaspé.

Jacques Cartier rises 4,160 ft (1,268 m) a few miles inland at the edge of the **Gaspésie Provincial Park**. This stretch along the south shore of the St. Lawrence provides perhaps the most dramatic scenery on the Gaspé: the road hugs the sheer, vertiginous cliffs that the sea washes far below. At **Mont St. Pierre** near St. Anne des Monts, a hang-gliding festival is held each July, its competitors jumping like Icarus over the St. Lawrence. An aura of danger seems to linger on this coast from the days when ships were swept against the rocks to ruin. A number of families who live along the shore are descended from Irish immigrants whose boats were destroyed on the coast. Some remember the day in 1914 when the *Empress of Ireland* collided with another boat and sank in 15 minutes, with the loss of 1,140 lives.

A gentler civilization reappears at **Métis Park** near Métis-sur-Mer where Lord George Stephen built **Reford House** in the last century with its beautiful English garden displaying 2,500 floral varieties. Both house and garden are now open to visitors.

The round trip from Québec City

covers 1,000 miles (1,600 km) — not exactly a Sunday afternoon drive, but worthwhile if you can afford a couple of Sundays, and the week between.

Anticosti Island: Looking like something coughed up out of the mouth of the St. Lawrence, **Anticosti Island** may seem a little remote. It is, and that is its principal asset. Populated by 300 people and 100,000 adorable white-tailed Virginia deer, the island became a park when the provincial government purchased it from a pulp and paper firm in 1974. Visitors must obtain a permit from the Ministry of Tourism to visit the island and another to travel or hunt. Otherwise, access is convenient: daily flights leave from Sept Îles and a ferry boat, the *Fort Mingan*, leaves from Baie Ste-Claire to carry passengers to **Port-Menier**, the only settlement on Anticosti that resembles a town.

Surrounded by steep cliffs and treacherous reefs, Anticosti was known in the days before sophisticated navigational systems as "the graveyard of the gulf." About 400 shipwrecks scatter the coast, some of them quite recently arrived. Yet despite these hazards and its isolation, the island has served various private interests since the day, in 1680, when Frontenac awarded it to Louis Jolliet, the explorer of the Mississippi. A few farmers settled there and later, English entrepreneurs tried to colonize the island, but in 1895, a wealthy French chocalatier named Henri Menier bought it, one of the world's largest parcels of real estate, for his sporting pleasure. It was he who imported the first deer, which have proliferated so impressively; the charred remains of his villa are still visible near the eponymous Port Menier, having been burned by pulp and paper firms that bought the island from Henri's son. Anticosti suddenly became a concern to Canadians when in 1937 Nazi Germany almost bought the island, ostensibly for its timber, but eventually they backed out as the deal attracted more and more public attention.

There is one hotel, the **Auberge Port Menier**, two small campgrounds and six chalets on the 140-mile (225-km) island, and though a vast area is untouched by humans, centuries of occasional inhabitation have left their marks: ghost-towns, overgrown cemeteries, an old railroad, and the 4,000 year old remains of its earliest inhabitants.

A feathered voyager drops anchor.

EAST

The recipient of Canada's first European visitors, the east coast provinces express, not surprisingly, a preoccupation with the sea. Perhaps one of the most startlingly beautiful regions of Canada, the Maritimes exude a freshness that is reminiscent of air laden with sea spray. Here one finds the achingly lonely beaches of Nova Scotia, the peculiar but charming friendliness of Newfoundlanders, the quaint, unembarrassed potato obsession of the Prince Edward Island farmers, and the graceful elegance of New Brunswick's towns.

The four Maritime provinces that constitute Canada's eastern region are all bound together by their proximity to the Atlantic Ocean, yet each possesses a charm peculiar unto itself. New Brunswick's rugged coastline begins the section and aspires to reveal the province's unusual blend of Maritime reserve in its towns with the wanton wildness of its landscape. Nova Scotia (Canada's *New Scotland*) is explored by following its circuitous coastline and stopping to examine some of its unusual cities and delightful towns. Perhaps the most quirky of all the provinces, Newfoundland's rugged beauty and remoteness serve as a backdrop to a portrait of the area's friendly inhabitants. The east section finishes off with Prince Edward Island, Canada's tiniest province. It is surrounded by miles of singing ocean and offers some of the area's most beautiful beaches amid potato fields.

1) NEW FOUNDLAND
2) NEW BRUNSWICK
3) NOVA SCOTIA
4) PRINCE EDWARD ISLAND

EAST

NEW BRUNSWICK

As the gateway to the Maritime region New Brunswick serves as a perfect beginning to experiencing the east coast lifestyle. The hustle and bustle of Toronto and Montreal can be left behind while here in New Brunswick the pace is slightly slower and the friendly people take the time to talk. The area is rich with the traditions of the two groups who settled here, the Anglo-Loyalists and the French-Acadians. Its magnificent wild forests cover 85 percent of the land, supporting a substantial pulp and paper industry. Under the tree-topped land lie lead, copper and zinc, providing a healthy mining industry. Finally, there's the mining of the sea, fishing. Most towns reflect New Brunswick's rich historical traditions and although little has changed over the years, New Brunswick has also adapted with the times.

The Acadians and Loyalists: The first people to settle in the Maritimes after the Micmac and Malecite Indians were the French in 1604. They arrived with Champlain and called the land they worked **Acadie**; it covered the Maritime provinces and Maine. The Acadians were constantly fighting battles with the British during the Anglo-French wars of the 17th Century. French rule ended in 1713 and mainland Nova Scotia was controlled by the British. In 1755 the British Governor Charles Lawrence delivered an ultimatum to the Acadians — take an oath of allegiance to the British crown, or face deportation. The Acadians did not want to take the oath for fear of being forced to fight fellow Frenchmen on behalf of Britain. The infamous Deportation Order forced 14,600 Acadians into exile. Sent to the 13 colonies, many families were separated permanently. Unfortunately they weren't welcome in the colonies and were only able to settle in Louisiana where the Cajuns survive to this day. When peace was declared between England and France in 1763 most of the Acadians returned to Nova Scotia, but they found their land occupied by new English colonists. Once again they moved on and settled in what is now New Brunswick. Today almost 34 percent of the province's population is French-speaking.

The Deportation may have had catastrophic results for the Acadians but for descendants from the British Isles it was a windfall. Many New Englanders moved, and during the American Revolution even more came — they were known as the Loyalists. With them they brought the traditions of the seafaring colonies.

Along the Saint John River: The **Saint John River** is New Brunswick's lifeblood. It was the first route traveled by Malecite and Micmac, Acadians and Loyalists, Scots and Danes. In the north-western region of the province it creates a border with Maine and from there can be traced along its winding course to Saint John at its mouth. Samuel de Champlain arrived at this point and named this the greatest of the province's estuaries. (New Brunswickers are very particular about never abbreviating Saint John, river and city, presumably to avoid confusion with St. John's Newfoundland).

New Brunswick's westernmost outcroping, a thumb-like parcel of land bordered by Québec, Maine and the Saint John River, is popularly known as the **Republic of Madawaska**. The region's inhabitants created this mythical realm in the 1800s because they were fed up with being pawns in border negotiations between Canada and the United States. With their own president (the Mayor of Edmundston) and their own flag, the Madawaskans (mostly Franco-

Preceding pages: Winding through autumnal splendor in New Brunswick, and a room with a view, Wolfe Point, New Brunswick. Below, hard work and self-satisfaction.

phones) are proud and exuberant. At no time is their spirit more in evidence than during the *Foire Brayonne* (the French in this region are known as Brayons, after a tool used in processing flax). The midsummer event features folk dancing and lumberjack competitions, the latter a long-standing tradition for it was in these forests that the legend of Paul Bunyan was conceived and nurtured. The first community along the Trans-Canada Highway in Madawaska is **Saint-Jacques**. It's the home of **Les Jardins de la République Provincial Park,** a campground that includes nature trails, an amphitheater and adventure playground.

Edmundston, an important pulp and paper center and the capital of Madawaska, is situated where the Saint John and Madawaska rivers converge. Of particular interest for travelers here is the **Church of Our Lady of Sorrows**, containing woodcarvings (The Stations of the Cross) by New Brunswick artist Claude Roussel. Nearby the beautiful and productive **Saint John River Valley** has always been a major thoroughfare. The northern segment of the Valley, from **Saint-Léonard** to **Woodstock**, is known as the "potato belt." This tuber is a major regional crop, celebrated each year at the Potato Festival in **Grand Falls**, during which flower-strewn boats are sometimes launched over the town's waterfalls. This custom harks back to the legend of Malabeam, which laments the death of a young Indian maiden who led her captors over the falls to their death. Unfortunately, the falls are not as grand as they once were, diverted as they are by a generating station that produces power for the residents of New Brunswick. The gorge, into which the water plunges, is one of the largest cataracts east of Niagara Falls.

Downstream the river is the small agricultural town of Hartland, known for its covered bridge, which majestically spans the Saint John River. This is not just any covered bridge, but the world's longest with seven spans, traversing 1,282 ft (391 m).

Just south is **Woodstock**, whose residents pride themselves on their tradition of hospitality. A landmark here is the restored **Old Courthouse**, which over the years has served not only as the seat of justice, but as a social hall, a coach stop and a political meeting house. It's only fitting that such a busy little town be the birthplace of Canada's first dial telephone system in 1900.

For a look at Loyalist life in the Valley circa 1820-1890, visit **King's Landing Historical Settlement**. This superbly re-

Morning mists caresses an awakening field.

constructed village, built on the banks of the Saint John River, depicts daily life among the Loyalists of that era. Its 60 structures include an operational sawmill; a theater featuring live entertainment; and the King's Head Inn which serves its patrons authentic 19th-Century fare.

Mactaquac, between King's Landing and Fredericton, is the site of a superb Provincial Park. Sports enthusiasts flock here year round, particularly fishermen. May brings a season-opener to this area: the **Big Bass Tournament**. (Some say New Brunswick offers the best bass fishing in North America.) The tourist area has evolved as a result of the establishment of a hydroelectric generating station. The river is used to generate power for New Brunswick.

In 1783 a committee of Loyalists exploring the Valley came upon the area and realizing its natural advantages, settled here the same year. They endured the hardship of a very severe first winter and with the spring thaw proceeded to build a town whose spirit exists to this day — **Fredericton**, "The City of Stately Elms." It is an appellation that truly befits this provincial capital.

Federicton is also the cultural center of the province, thanks in large part to the generosity of publisher and statesman Lord Beaverbrook, who never forgot New Brunswick, his boyhood home.

The **Beaverbrook Art Gallery** houses his personal collection, representing the work of Dali, Gainsborough and the Group of Seven, among others. The legislative building displays portraits by Joshua Reynolds as well as a rare copy of the *Domesday Book*. Fredericton is often referred to as the pewter capital of Canada due to the widely acclaimed pewtersmiths here. The city's most elegant structure is **Christ Church Cathedral**. Completed in 1853, it is considered one of North America's finest examples of decorated Gothic architecture. What's left of the Old Military Compound now incorporates the **York Sunbury Historical Society Museum**, which chronicles Fredericton's military and domestic past. Traces from that period can be found at the **Military Compound** where reenactments of the changing of the guard occur daily in the summer. Several buildings are open to the public including the guard house, barracks and the officers' quarters. Real military life exists however, by following the Saint John River southeast from Fredericton to **Oromocto**, home of Canada's largest military training base. Quiet, riverbank communities from **Jemseg** (south) have

Kingslanding, the center of attention.

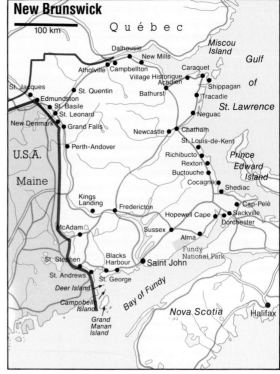

become havens for crafts-people. Numerous roadside stands offer fresh fruits and vegetables in season. Free car ferries considerately criss-cross the Saint John River at several points, enhancing the opportunity for exploration and discovery.

Saint John: Weathered **Saint John**, Canada's oldest city, sits along the Bay of Fundy at the mouth of the Saint John River. Samuel de Champlain landed here in 1604, bestowing the location with its name, but its true birth came in 1783 with the arrival of 3,000 Loyalists from New England and particularly New York.

"The Loyalist City," as it is known, celebrates its heritage each July during **Loyalist Days**. The week-long festivities include a reenactment of the Loyalists landing at Market Slip, as well as the Great Bay of Fundy Whaler Race.

Determined, energetic and ambitious, the Loyalist citizenry catapulted their new home into the forefront of the wooden ship-building industry. Unfortunately, the thriving port city declined following a disastrous fire in 1877 along with the eventual obsolescence of wooden ocean-going vessels. But recent waterfront development and urban renewal have provided Saint John with a much needed transfusion—the city has been reborn and its proud past awaits discovery around every corner. It claims the first police force in North America, the first newspaper and bank in Canada. To catch up with the city's past there are three walking tours, Prince William's Walk, A Victorian Stroll and the Loyalist Trail. One attraction the tours are bound to include is **Barbour's General Store**, a restored and fully stocked 19th-Century store. The building was located upstream and shipped down the Saint John River to this site. Thousands of artifacts, including 300 "cure-all or kill-alls," bring the past to life.

Saint John's Loyalist roots are nowhere more evident than at **King Square Area** (opposite the Loyalist Burial Ground), landscaped in the form of the Union Jack; and at **Loyalist House**, a Georgian mansion completed in 1817. Occupied for about a century and a half by Loyalist David Daniel Merritt and his descendants, it is the oldest structurally unaltered edifice in the city; indeed one of the few buildings to survive the Great Fire of 1877. With most of its original furnishings intact, Loyalist House is both the pride of the New Brunswick Historical Society, and a tribute to the fine craftsmen of 19th-Century Saint John.

Saint John's **City Market** is another sur-

World's largest covered bridge, Hartland.

vivor of the Great Fire. This institution has provided unflagging service since 1876, making it Canada's oldest market. Then as now, the market clerk rings a bell to open and close commercial proceedings. This is the place to sample dulse, a dried, deep-purple seaweed, reaped from the Bay of Fundy — a favorite of New Brunswickers, but an acquired taste for outsiders. The building itself is a pleasure to the eye, with its ship's hull roof (a revelation of the primary trade of those who built her); its big game trophies (harking back to a time when game meat was displayed and sold here); and its ornate iron gate (a masterpiece in the art of blacksmithing).

The gem of Saint John's revitalized downtown, waterfront district was officially christened **Market Square** in 1983. Its success has brought business, tourism, employment and pride back to the city. An early 19th-Century brick facade serves as an invitation to a warm and lively center for shopping, dining and otherwise communing. There is a boardwalk by the sea, a grand Food Hall and a regional library. The latter-houses a fine collection of early Canadian printed work, while providing one of the best harbor views in town.

A beacon-like clock (surely the only one of its kind in the world), stands at the entrance to Market Square, serving more as a conversation piece than a timepiece. It is a clock without hands, using a serpent's tail to indicate the hour, and making room for three realistic, seated figures at its base.

Saint John has several world-class sport complexes. It also has a national performing arts festival **Festival By The Sea**. Held for two weeks in August, it features 500 performers from all the provinces and territories of Canada, and is presented at various sites around the city.

For a panoramic view of the city and its waterfront there's **Fort Howe** and the **Carleton Martello Tower**. Perched on opposite sides of Saint John Harbor they continue to provide an excellent view as they did when they were used as sentinels against enemy attacks.

The mouth of Saint John River is also the sight of a unique phenomenon. Twice each day the tides of the Bay of Fundy reach such heights they actually force the Saint John River to flow upstream. The spectacle is known as the **Reversing Fall Rapids**.

A more serene body of water is **Lily Lake**, contained within **Rockwood Park**, the pride of local swimmers, fishers and skaters—the latter only when "...deemed

Moored in St. Johns.

safe by the Saint John Horticulture Association." Within walking distance of downtown Rockwood is one of the largest city parks in Canada. In the realm of natural science and history, Saint John boasts possession of Canada's oldest museum, the **New Brunswick Museum**. This compendium of treasures from around the world, and particularly artifacts pertaining to the history of New Brunswick, runs the gamut from a 13,000-year-old mastodon tooth (found in New Brunswick), to a gold-plated cornet, bestowed upon a member of the Saint John City Cornet Band.

The Fundy Coast: West of Saint John and east of Maine, the idiosyncratic Fundy coast is characterized by picture-perfect fishing villages. This is where United Empire Loyalists settled *en masse* in the wake of the American Revolution.

Carved out of the Bay of Fundy, between Maine and New Brunswick, is **Passamaquoddy Bay**. At its eastern edge sits **Black's Harbor**, famed for possessing the Commonwealth's largest sardine factory; it hosts the North American Sardine Packing Championship each year. On a more esoteric note, nearby **Lake Utopia** could be called the Loch Ness of New Brunswick, for those that believe it to be the domicile of a sea monster.

Rounding the bay takes you through **St. George**, where visitors can meander about one of the oldest Protestant graveyards in Canada, while nearby **Oak Bay** is the site of a lovely beachfront Provincial Park. Probably the best known community on the bay is **St. Andrews**, with its multiple personality of fishing village, resort town and marine biological research center.

Located at the tip of a small peninsula, the town is studded with 18th and 19th Century mansions. Founded by Loyalists following the American Revolution, additional families floated their homes here (one piece at a time!) when the final border with Maine was determined in 1842. That's one reason for the New England atmosphere. St. Andrews is home of the **Algonquin Hotel**, one of Canada's premier resort hotels; but perhaps its most distinctive landmark is **Greenock Church**. This pristine structure, encircled by a simple white picket fence, is embellished with a carved oak tree design, a clock and a weathervane. St. Andrews also houses the **Huntsman Marine Laboratory and Aquarium**. With live specimens, displays and audio-visual presentations it gives visitors a chance to see what exactly swims around the Bay of Fundy.

A companionable silence in St. Johns at Market Square.

St. Stephen, New Brunswick stands face to face with Calais, Maine. These border towns have traditionally been the best of friends—even during the War of 1812, when St. Stephen loaned Calais gunpowder for its Fourth of July celebration. Today, the towns get together for joint festivities each summer. The world's first chocolate bar is thought to have been invented here at the Ganongs candy factory in 1906.

A paradise for birdwatchers, whale-watchers, fishermen and other outdoor types exists where Passamaquoddy Bay widens into the Bay of Fundy—the **Fundy Islands**. Their rustic beauty and natural riches have long attracted the most illustrious of nature lovers, from James J. Audobon to Franklin Delano Roosevelt (FDR).

Grand Manan Island is the largest and farthest from the coast. It is a particular favorite of ornithologists, with about 230 species of birds identified; among them the puffin, which has become somewhat of a symbol here. For the artist there are light-houses and seascapes to paint or photograph. Grand Manan is also famous for its edible seaweed, known as dulse.

Campobello, the "beloved island" of FDR (ironically, it is also where he contracted polio), is accessible by bridge (from Lubec, Maine). It brings you to the **Roosevelt-Campobello International Park**, a natural preserve in the southern portion of the island. A visit to the park is incomplete without a visit to Roosevelt's "cottage," where he viewed so many sunrises.

Located smack on the 45th parallel (and proud of it), **Deer Island** is the most diminutive of the islands, a mere 7.5 miles (12 km) in length. It compensates for its size, however, by having the world's largest lobster pond and offshore, the world's second largest whirlpool. Everyone calls the latter the "Old Sow" because of the auditory experience it provides.

The Southeast: The southeast region of New Brunswick, traveling from Saint John to Moncton, reveals the cultural texture of the province; towns and villages gradually reflect a transition from areas primarily settled by Loyalists to those settled by Acadians. Charming and traditional pockets of civilization alternate with vignettes of wild, natural beauty.

Beyond the lovely seacoast village of St. Martins is **Fundy National Park**, a showcase for the spectacularly dramatic Fundy tides and coastal terrain. It once reverberated with the clamor of a thriving lumber industry, which along with intense trappings of the area, nearly destroyed its natural gifts for all time. By 1930 the population of **Alma**, once a roaring lumber town, was reduced to two struggling families. Thanks to Parks Canada, the region is now progressively being returned to a wilderness state, with protection of its forests and reintroduction of its wildlife, particularly salmon.

Hopewell Cape is perhaps better known than the national park, and it is also better known as home of the "Flowerpot Rocks." These peculiar rock formations are transformed from forested islands at high tide, to what look like "flowerpots" at low tide. When the tide is out, you can explore the tide pools which surround the formations.

Beyond the wilderness of the Fundy coast is **Moncton**, a railroad town, called the "hub of the Maritimes." It was originally settled by Middle Europeans, but following the era of Deportation and the influx of Acadians into what is now New Brunswick, it became known as the unofficial capital of Acadia. The **Université de Moncton** is the only French college in New Brunswick. Housed here is a collection of Acadian cultural artifacts. Moncton is also a good place to observe a Fundy tidal phenomenon—the tidal bore at the mouth of the Petitcodiac River. Another natural phenomenon that locals and tourists alike swarm to is **Magnetic Hill**. Just on the outskirts of the city, what appears to be magic is actually an optical illusion. Cars are driven to the bottom of the hill and when the brakes are released the cars appear to be coasting *up* the hill. The truth is that what appears to be an upgrade is really a downgrade.

Near Moncton, between Hillsborough and the tiny hamlet of Salem, is the **Salem and Hillsborough Railroad**. An antique steam locomotive, complete with open-air gondolas, snakes along a short course (the round trip is just over an hour) along the banks of the Petitcodiac River. This romantic excursion into the past traverses the salt water marshes, where the early Acadian settlers first harvested hay. The **Hiram Trestle**, an intricate timber bridge between two hills, is unquestionably the trip's most outstanding feature.

Sackville is a tiny southeastern town which resembles an English village. It is the home of **Sackville Harness Limited**, which has the distinction of being the only place on the continent where horse collars are still made by hand. Sackville is also a university town. The first degree given to a woman in the British Empire was handed out by the town's **Mount Allison**

University in 1875. The school is well-known for its fine arts program.

Nearby **Fort Beausejour** is where the French and English last battled in this region. Today, there is little echo of its past, but a rather magnificent panoramic view of the surrounding area.

The Acadian Coast: The coastal region of New Brunswick, north of Moncton, is popularly known as the "Acadian Coast." Washed by the warm tides of the Northumberland Strait (the warmest water north of the U.S Southern Coast), it is primarily to this region that the Acadians returned following the Deportation. Today you can discover the towns that they built, inhabited by their proud descendants.

The Northumberland beaches are an unexpected pleasure in this northern place the gentlest of the province's water in temperament and temperature. They say that **Shediac** has the warmest water on the coast, along with fine beaches. It is the lobster capital of the world and the best time to visit is in July during the **Lobster Festival.**

Tiny Acadian fishing villages are strung along the coast, **Cocagne** and **Buctonche** are particularly well-known, the latter for its oyster. The **Kouchibouguac National Park** has preserved miles of deserted but fine sand beaches.

It is a pleasant drive out to **Point Escuminac**, a place that has never forgotten its distinction as the site of the province's worst fishing disaster. A powerful monument to the men who lost their lives here in 1959, carved by New Brunswick artist Claude Roussel, stands with its back to the sea, as a constant reminder of this tragedy.

Further up the coast are **Chatham** and **Newcastle**, early lumber towns that have preserved a bit of British culture. This area is famous for its ballads and folklore, as well as for its illustrious native sons. Chatham's once busy shipyards have now been replaced by port facilities for exporting local wood products around the world. Newcastle was the boyhood home of Lord Beaverbrook, who was exceedingly generous in his bequests to this town.

Acadian flags, a French tricolor with a yellow star in the upper part of the blue stripe, become increasingly visible as you continue northward. **Shippagan** is a fairly typical fishing village, home of an exceptionally fine **Marine Center**, devoted to the world of fishing in the Gulf of St. Lawrence. Computerized maps, audiovisual presentations, and actual marine life await the visitor. (Everyone's favorite exhibit is an un-

Gateway from the ice-age: Rocks Provincial Park.

usual royal blue tinged lobster.) A free ferry can transport you away from the hustle and bustle of Shippagan to the deserted beaches of **Miscou Island**.

Caraquet, the most prosperous town on the Acadian coast, is a cultural center for the region. The **Acadian Festival** each August draws celebrants from up and down the coast and includes the traditional blessing of the fleet. It also has one of the largest commercial fishing fleets in New Brunswick, the only provincial fisheries school, boat builders and fish markets on the wharf. And if that isn't enough, Caraquet's **Village Historique Acadian** has recreated an Acadian settlement reflecting the century from 1780 to 1890, a time of reestablishment here following the Deportation. It is nestled away from modern towns and construction, near the marshland *lévees* constructed by early Acadian settlers.

Bathurst represents a successful blending of French and English cultures. Off the coast are the waters of the **Chaleur Bay**, literally "Bay of Warmth." Named by Cartier in 1534, the bay is notorious for an apparition—a phantom ship which has been sighted along the coast from Bathurst to Campbellton. Some believe it to be the ghost of a French ship which was lost in battle while others prefer a more scientific explanation.

Dalhousie and **Campbellton** were settled by Scots, Irish and Acadians and a fine-tuned ear is needed to place the accents. Campbellton rests at the foot of Sugarloaf Mountain; it is a center for salmon fishing and winter sports, and a gateway to Quécbec.

Discovering the Maritimes: New Brunswick's surrounding areas offer spectacular vistas in the region. The breathtaking views from the coastline and the beauty of New Brunswick's interior are promises of "more of the same" to come in the other Maritime provinces. In wandering through New Brunswick and in visiting its quaint Atlantic settlements, travelers will acquire a sense of the region's history and a feel for what it must have been like for Canada's first settlers to venture into the New World. Although the influence of the Acadians decreases as eastward distance is traveled, other groups, primarily New Englanders and the Scots, start to dominate. New Brunswick definitely casts a spell over its visitors and the impulse to travel on through the Maritimes, to Nova Scotia, Newfoundland and Prince Edward Islan, becomes an overwhelming one.

Below, a "loyalist" greets visitors.

NOVA SCOTIA

Nova Scotia. The name alone brings to mind a vision of craggy highlands, echoing with the sound of bagpipes. But before Scottish Highlanders fled here, there were the Micmacs, the French, the British and Loyalists from the American colonies. All have left an indelible stamp on this province. Today about 77 percent of Nova Scotians are of British descent and 10 percent are of French (Acadian) extraction. Nova Scotia also has the largest indigenous black population in Canada.

Nova Scotians are as close to the sea as they are to the past — inextricably bound to it by their very nature, by economics and by geography. Part of the province, Cape Breton, is an island; and the mainland is attached to the rest of Canada by the Isthmus of Chignecto. Appropriately, the provincial configuration resembles a lobster, with no point more than 35 miles (56 km) from the sea. Nova Scotia and its seaside resorts have been a tourist destination since the 1860s when railroads and steamships carried visitors from Upper Canada and the United States. Aside from the sea being an attraction, people are still drawn to Nova Scotia for its overwhelming friendliness. When travelers encounter Nova Scotians they are often met by the traditional Gaelic greeting *Ciad mile failte* — 100,000 welcomes.

Out of the past: The original inhabitants of Nova Scotia, the Micmacs, still walk this land and fish these waters, though their numbers are greatly reduced. It is thought possible that Norsemen visited here around 1,000 A.D. Some evidence of this has been substantiated. Centuries later, John Cabot, exploring under English flag, touched upon northern Cape Breton Island. And certainly, French and Portuguese fishermen caught and cured fish here in the 16th Century.

The French called this land *Acadie*. It encompassed what is now Nova Scotia, New Brunswick, Prince Edward Island and Maine. They settled along the Bay of Fundy and on the marshy land surrounding the Annapolis River, developing what is still the most fertile land in Nova Scotia.

A sense of Maritime pride and tradition still runs strong in Nova Scotia, but great prosperity largely abandoned the province with the advent of the 20th Century. Often central Canada looks upon the area as a liability because of the financial aid it receives from the federal government. But many Maritimers claim central Canada was desperate to include the Maritime provinces in Confederation because it had no winter ports. Without rail connections to Atlantic seaports there was no future for the new country. Consequently Maritimers believe their leaders were seduced into accepting Confederation in 1867. But history books have told another story saying Canada permitted Nova Scotia and New Brunswick to join her.

Since the creation of the St. Lawrence Seaway, the area's importance as a key transportation channel has been greatly diminished. Steam powered, steel hulled vessels rendered the wooden sailing ships obsolete, and signified the death of an all-important industry and economic base. Coal mining later supplanted shipbuilding economically, only to falter after World War Two. However, since the oil crisis in the 70s, the shipbuilding industry has undergone new revitalization.

But the province also has other natural endowments to fall back on: abundant freshwater and saltwater fishing grounds, and the rich productive land of the Annapolis Valley, once so highly prized by the Acadians. And then there is tourism, a long-

Left, a seafaring inhabitant sporting human barnacles. Right, a lonely beacon wards off stray ships at Peggy's Cove.

standing tradition here and a major economic contributor.

Twin cities: The first and second largest Nova Scotian cities respectively, **Halifax** and **Dartmouth** sit on opposite sides of one of the world's great harbors, connected by two suspension bridges. Magnificent **Halifax Harbor** is the world's second largest natural harbor, as well as being free of ice year round. The Micmacs called it *chebucto,* meaning "big harbor." It has long been a bustling international port and naval base, and continues to define life in the Halifax/Dartmouth metropolitan area.

As provincial capital, and commercial and educational center of Atlantic Canada, Halifax is unquestionably the more dominant and favored of the twins, yet Dartmouth is not without its special charms. Though known for its industry, they call it the "City of Lakes," for it is studded with 23 sparkling bodies of water. This allows Dartmouthians to enjoy freshwater fishing and canoeing all through the summer without leaving the city. Winter brings lake-top skating parties, and **Winter Carnival** (in early February), the largest such event east of Quebec City.

Dartmouth was founded in 1750 (a year after Halifax), when British troops from across the harbor came on woodcutting expeditions. The young town was periodically under siege by Micmacs.

Dartmouth was to develop largely in response to Halifax's needs, and as early as 1752 it began operating a ferry between the two settlements. The boats continue to ply the harbor, in what is the oldest saltwater ferry service in North America.

Quakes from Nantucket Island settled here between 1785 and 1792 following the American Revolution. They made Dartmouth the headquarters of a whaling company whose operations were centered at what is now the **Dartmouth Shipyards.** They also left behind a number of homes, many of which still stand. These simple structures, with their front doors placed off-center, were built to endure; a stroll down Ochterloney Street shows several of them off including the **Historic Quaker Whalers' House**, probably the oldest house in Dartmouth. On Newcastle Street is the lovely **Evergreen Historic House,** a restored Victorian home built in 1867. Folklorist Dr. Helen Creighton, author of the highly regarded *Bluenose Ghosts,* once resided here and then donated it to the city.

In recent years Dartmouth has expanded and developed to meet existing and poten-

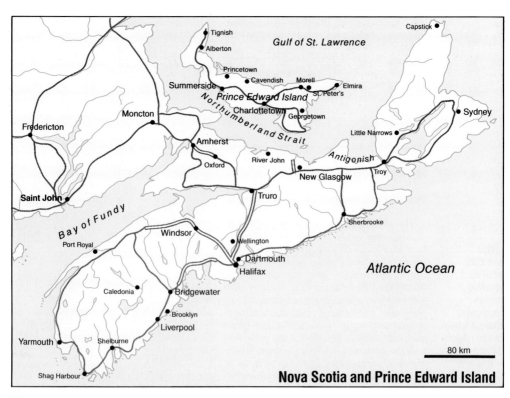

Nova Scotia and Prince Edward Island

tial industrial needs. With the addition of the second suspension harbor bridge in 1970 the **Dartmouth Industrial Park** experienced phenomenal growth. Over 750 local and national businesses are presently located in the area.

The twin waterfronts of Halifax and Dartmouth have been undergoing a significant transformation as have waterfronts across Canada. The derelict eyesores of the past have become places for people to enjoy. Halifax's restoration and redevelopment has been the most dramatic.

In the mid-1960s the people of Halifax took it upon themselves to transform their city's gray image. The waterfront area now known as **Historic Properties** was saved from demolition by the civic-minded. Now tourists can shop, dine and explore within this cobblestoned area, which externally appears as it did in the 19th Century when privateers used it to cache their goods. This superb blend of old and new comes to life especially in summer when the schooner *Bluenose II* cruises the harbor and the voice of the town crier rings out along the waterfront. The season ends on a festive note in late September with the **Joseph Howe Festival** honoring this mid-19th Century Nova Scotian leader, politician, orator and advo-

cate of the free press. It is a time for parades, revelry in the streets, and the **International Town Criers' Championship.**

Nearby, off Lower Water Street, are the more recently restored **Brewery Market** and the **Maritime Museum of the Atlantic.** Alexander Keith, the one-time mayor of Nova Scotia, built his brewery in 1820 and its courtyards and arched tunnels are filled once again with spirit. Amidst the great variety of enterprises housed here is the Halifax **City Farmers' Market**, a year round operation.

The Maritime Museum of the Atlantic not only features a magnificent view of the harbor, but a huge hydrographic ship, the *C.S.S. Acadia.* Now moored behind the museum, the *Acadia* once plied the frigid waters of the Arctic and North Atlantic while charting northern coastlines.

Just west of the waterfront is Halifax's business district. Amidst the office towers and hotels is the new **World Trade and Convention Center.** Easily spotted by its huge weathervane depicting the *Bluenose*, it hosts trade shows, conventions and live concerts.

Just north on Prince Street beside the Old Montréal Trust Building is where 14 newspapers used to be published. The eight pre-

An invisible wind stirs a friendly gathering.

Confederation buildings are presently being incorporated into a redevelopment project called **Founders Square**.

Halifax was founded in 1749 not only because of its great harbor, but as a fortress to counter the French installation at **Louisbourg**. Getting away from, but never losing sight of the waterfront, on a hill overlooking downtown Halifax, is the **Citadel**. The current star-shaped 19th-Century structure is the fourth to occupy this pedestal. It no longer serves as a military installation, but as a National Historic Park, housing the expansive collection of the **Army Museum**, while affording a spectacular view of downtown and the waterfront. This is the best vantage point from which to see the **Town Clock**, which has become the symbol of Halifax. With its four clockfaces and belfry to ring off the hours, Haligonians (residents of Halifax) need not wear wristwatches. Its construction was ordered by Prince Edward, Duke of Kent, who was said to be a stickler for punctuality and precision. He was also fond of round buildings, which led to the completion (in 1800) of **St. George's Anglican Church**, an unusual circular structure. Other churches not to be missed here are **St. Mary's Basilica**, topped by the world's tallest polished granite spire,

and **St. Paul's Church** (1750), the oldest Protestant church in Canada, located on the lovely Grand Parade. The Grand Parade also serves as an open-air venue for Maritime artists. They perform there throughout the summer. A couple of blocks away from St. Paul's is **Province House**, Canada's oldest standing legislative building. Charles Dickens referred to it as "...a gem of Georgian architecture."

At the foot of the Citadel tourists will find the resplendent **Public Gardens**, an urban oasis. Established in 1867, these are the oldest Victorian formal gardens in North America. Near the gardens on Summer Street is the **Nova Scotia Museum**, headquarters of a province-wide system incorporating 21 sites. The collection here is devoted to the natural and social history of Nova Scotia and includes a particularly fine collection of Micmac artifacts.

Waterfront sites: Going back to the waterfront, at the southern tip of the peninsula that Halifax occupies, is **Point Pleasant Park**. The federal government has retained this piece of greenery for contingency purposes, but rents it to the city for one shilling each year under the terms of a 999-year lease. **The Prince of Wales' Martello Tower** was raised here in 1796 and still

Left, Lupins on the South Shore; and right, snowshoes in their "rack."

stands, the first in a series of these circular stone sentinels to be constructed along the coastal regions of North America and the British Isles. The park, with plenty of room for joggers, hikers, swimmers, picnickers and ship-watchers, is said to be the only place on the continent where Scottish heather grows wild (from seeds shook from the mattresses of British soldiers!)

At the other end of Halifax is another park, **Fort Needham**, memorializing an infamous day on Dec. 6, 1917. What has ever since been called the **Great Halifax Explosion** occurred when a French munitions ship, the *Mont Blanc*, collided with the Belgian relief ship *Imo*, creating the largest single man-made blast prior to the bombing of Hiroshima. Thousands died, thousands more were injured, and the section of the city viewed from the park was virtually destroyed. But the city picked up the pieces and symbolically placed a sculpture containing metal from the *Mont Blanc* before the **Halifax North Memorial Library**, a monument to those who lost their lives.

The South Shore: The rugged and idiosyncratic Atlantic coastline, southwest from Halifax, is known as the **South Shore** and promoted by the tourist bureau as the "Lighthouse Route." It is an accurate appel-

lation, yet despite these sentinels of the night, this beautiful, mysterious and punishing coastline is no stranger to shipwrecks. Nor are its people strangers to the wrath and bounty of the sea.

The circuitous South Shore with all its bays, coves, inlets and islands, was a favorite of pirates and privateers. Not far from Halifax is **Shad Bay**, where **Weeping Widows Island** is found, the subject of a morbid legend connected with the notorious 17th-Century pirate, Captain Kidd. The Captain decided to bury a portion of his treasure here and engaged the services of 43 men to dig two pits. Unfortunately, he interred the men along with the treasure, thereby transforming their wives into weeping widows. Today a deep shaft on the island is evidence of the numerous treasure hunts that have taken place here.

Nearby, **Indian Harbor** and **Peggy's Cove**, lovely fishing villages nestled among and atop the granite outcroppings of this part of the coast, are treasures of a different sort. The latter has become a semi-official showcase for the province and is said to be the most photographed fishing village in the world. Yet it has not been robbed of its simplicity and authenticity. Despite a rather steady flow of visitors, the townspeople

manage to go about their business, which primarily is fishing.

The provincial government designated the community a preservation area which is one reason it retained its long-lasting rustic appeal as a fishing village.

There is some quandary over the name Peggy's Cove. Some believe it to be a diminutive of St. Margaret's Bay, while others, more romantically inclined, believe it was named for the sole survivor of a shipwreck, who subsequently married one of the local men. The late William E. De Garthe (1907-1983), a marine artist who resided here, apparently sided with the latter theory. Taking 10 years to complete, he carved the images of 32 local fishermen, their wives and children, in a 100-foot (30-meter) face of granite located behind his house. Known as the "Fisherman's Monument" De Garthe also included the image of the young woman of legend.

The **Lighthouse** is a landmark that draws many to Peggy's Cove. Visitors can wander across the deeply scarred granite expanse upon which it sits or can take care of correspondence, for this is Canada's only combination lighthouse and post office.

St. Margaret's Bay, named by Samuel de Champlain in 1631, is known for its fine sand beaches and summer cottages. It is followed by the more notorious **Mahone Bay**, with its 365 islands. This was once the realm of pirates and its name was probably derived from the French *mahonne,* a low-lying craft used by these robbers of the high seas. Other names echo that era — such as **Sacrifice Island** and **Murderer's Point**, but **Oak Island** is more intriguing than any of them. Long the site of treasure hunts, it is said that Captain Kidd buried another part of his treasure here. The island was once densely covered by large oaks and according to local legend, the mystery of the buried treasure will not be solved until all the oaks have died and seven lives have been lost. (Six persons have thus far lost their lives here and only a few trees remain standing.)

The town of **Mahone Bay**, a good place to stop for those seeking treasures in antiques and craft shops, has a legend of its own, concerning an American privateer vessel, the *Young Teazer,* torched off the coast during the War in 1812. Locals claim that a ghost of the ship can be seen in the bay each summer on the anniversary of this incendiary event.

Home of the Bluenose: "A Snug Harbor since 1753." That's what they say about **Lunenburg,** one of Canada's most impor-

Rescuing survivors engraved in granite at Peggy's Cove.

tant fishing ports. Nowhere in Canada are the traditions of the sea more palpable — carried on by sailors, fishermen and shipbuilders. The renowned championship schooner *Bluenose*, the "Queen of the North Atlantic," was built here in 1921 and sailed from this port. A symbol of pride for the people of Lunenburg (even her image is on the Canadian dime), she fell into disuse during World War Two, was subsequently sold, and ultimately lost off the coast of Haiti in 1946. The shipyards of this city later turned out the ship used in the film *Mutiny on the Bounty;* (it was sailed to Tahiti by a Nova Scotian crew). This inspired the creation of *Bluenose II*, an exact replica of the original, built by the same shipwrights. Launched in 1963, she has ever since been a floating ambassador. So many visitors walked her decks during the 1967 Montreal Expo that the boards had to be replaced.

Inland on the banks of the La Have River is **Bridgewater**, "The Hub" of the South Shore, an industrial pocket that plays host each summer to the **South Shore Exhibition**. "The Big Ex," as it is known, features the **International Ox and Horse Pull Championships**, in which the owners of these beasts of burden cajole them toward victory. Also in town is the **Wile Carding Mill Museum**, where one can see what a 19th Century wool carding mill was like, though it is no longer operational. For a comprehensive history of Lunenburg County there is the permanent display at the **DesBrisay Museum**. It's also the perfect place for a picnic.

Back to the coast, south of Bridgewater, is **Port Medway**. Quiet now, it was a major port in the late 19th Century, engaged in a brisk Caribbean trade: fish and lumber in return for rum and molasses. Things are still bustling in **Liverpool**, which is built on the banks of the Mersey River like its English counterpart. Privateering figures prominently in the city's history, and this heritage is celebrated each July during "Privateer Days." Of particular interest here is the **Simeon Perkins House**, built in 1767. Perkins kept a diary which chronicled life in colonial Liverpool and his home is a showcase for the same.

Down the coast is **Port Mouton**, a pleasant fishing village named by Sieur de Monts and his party in 1604 when one of their sheep was lost overboard here. Tiny **Port Joli** has a more notorious past. An American vessel was shipwrecked off the coast here in 1750, its crew captured by natives. The prisoners were given two choices: to

The sun sets over Lunenburg's shipyards.

stand barefoot in a fire or jump into the sea. (They all drowned.) Today it's a bird sanctuary, a favorite spot of Canadian geese in autumn and winter.

Farther down this deeply indented coast is **Shelburne**, a treasure trove of 18th-Century history. It's referred to as "The Loyalist Town," for it was settled by as many as 16,000 United Empire Loyalists from America between 1783 and 1785. It became an instant boom town — bigger than not only Halifax, but also Montreal. However, the population dropped abruptly after 1787 with the termination of government support and by the 1820s fewer than 300 people called this home.

Shelburne's **Ross Thompson House**, built in 1784, is a Loyalist home and store — thought to be the only surviving 18th-Century store in Nova Scotia. It now functions as a provincial museum, fully stocked and decorated to reflect the 1780s.

Another group of people tried to settle in Shelburne more recently. In July 1987 a boat arrived from Holland carrying 174 Sikhs. Over the past few years Canada has become a desirable destination point for people claiming refugee status. When the Sikhs landed illegally they were met by true Maritime hospitality — a local woman brought them homemade peanut butter and jelly sandwiches.

The only surviving New England style meeting house in Nova Scotia (circa 1765) is in nearby **Barrington**, along with a 19th-Century woolen mill. The town was formerly settled by the French and called *La Passage* until it was destroyed by New Englanders, its people deported to Boston. In 1760 colonists from Cape Cod and Nantucket came here making it one of the oldest outposts of settlers from New England.

Edging toward the **Bay of Fundy** brings you to **Yarmouth**. As terminus of ferry service from the States, this is the beginning of many Canadian journey. It is the province's biggest port west of Halifax, though a century ago, during the golden age of sail, it was one of the world's great ports.

Land of Evangeline: Just above Yarmouth are a number of interesting little towns. **Sandford** has the distinction of possessing the Maritimes's smallest drawbridge, **South Ohio**, a tiny lumber town, was founded by two men who wanted to move to the State of Ohio, but later had a change of heart.

The **French Shore**, home of Nova Scotia's largest Acadian population, begins past the Digby County line. It is synony-

A competitor urges his team to victory.

mous with the municipality of **Clare**, which locals are fond of saying has the largest mainstreet in the world, for it consists of 27 villages, more than half of which sit along the main thoroughfare. Many Acadians returned to this area following the expulsion to start anew, some of them on foot through the wilderness between Boston and Digby.

For unsurpassed views of St. Mary's Bay, the intrepid can embark upon an eight-mile (13-km) hiking trail which traces the cliffs between **Cape St. Mary** and **Bear Cove.** Farther north, in **Meteghan**, a short footpath takes hikers down to a secluded beach with a natural cave, purported to have been a cache for contraband rum during the days of Prohibition in the United States. One of Meteghan's oldest homes, **La Vieille Maison**, provides visitors with a glimpse into 18th-Century Acadian life. Traditional skills are alive and well, as evidenced by Atlantic Canada's largest wooden boatbuilding facility, located in Meteghan.

Most Acadian villages are dominated visually by their church and in **Church Point** *(Pointe d' Eglise)* this is particularly true. **St. Mary's Church**, built early in the 20th Century, is the tallest and largest wooden church in North America. Its 185-foot (55-meter) spire, swayed by the bay breezes, is stabilized by 40 tons (36 tonnes) of ballast. This landmark sits on the campus of the **Université Ste. Anne**, the only French university in the province. As a center for Acadian culture, the institution hosts the **Acadian Festival of Clare** each summer.

Beyond St. Mary's Bay, at the southern tip of the Annapolis Basin and overlooking Digby Gut, is **Digby**. The town has a long maritime history and was named for the commander of a ship which carried Loyalists here from New England in 1783 (among them, the great-grandfather of inventor Thomas Alva Edison). This is home of the renowned **Digby Scallop Fleet** (the world's largest), an impressive sight as its members converge at the waterfront. The town has fish processing plants and is famous for its smoked herring called Digby Chicks.

The Annapolis Basin: Champlain wrote of the Annapolis Basin: "We entered one of the most beautiful ports which I had seen on these coasts." His compatriot Marc Lescarbot considered it, "...a thing so marvelous to see I wonder how so fair a place did remain desert." Orchards and other farmlands have replaced the primeval forest along the Annapolis Basin and River, and this region, though transformed, is still beautiful to behold.

Built in the 1780s, **Old St. Edward's Loyalist Church** in **Clementsport** is situated high on a hill within an ancient cemetery. It was one of the province's earliest museums, showing off not only its own architectural integrity, but a fine collection of Loyalist artifacts. Its elevated setting also provides one of the best vantage points from which to appreciate the Annapolis Basin.

On the other side of the basin is **Port Royal,** with its reconstructed **Habitation**, the settlement built by Sieur de Monts and Samuel de Champlain in 1605. It is a place that witnessed many firsts: the first permanent North American settlement north of Florida; the first Roman Catholic mass celebrated in Canada; the first Canadian social club (Champlain introduced the Order of Good Cheer as an antidote to the prospect of another dismal winter); and the first Canadian dramatic production (*The Theater of Neptune* orchestrated by lawyer and writer Marc Lescarbot in 1606).

The Habitation was rather successful, nevertheless within a very short period, it was abandoned, reestablished and finally looted and burned by the English in 1613. Its reconstruction in 1939, after years of lobbying and painstaking research, was one of the

The end of a hard day's work.

first great successes of Canada's historic preservation movement. The buildings, authentic in appearance down to the last detail, surround a courtyard in the style of Normandy farms of that era.

The Annapolis Valley, sheltered by the North and South Mountains and extensively dyked by early Acadian settlers, is an agriculturally and scenically gifted area, known particularly for its apples. In spring the scent of apple blossoms lingers in the air, and the Annapolis Valley **Apple Blossom Festival** is celebrated throughout the valley.

Though settled primarily by Planters and Loyalists following the Deportation, the valley pays homage to Acadians — nowhere more poignantly than in **Grand Pré**, the village immortalized by Longfellow in *Evangeline*. Grand Pré was the most important Acadian settlement in Nova Scotia before the Deportation. Longfellow's 1847 *Evangeline — A Tale of Acadie* describes the separation of a young couple during the Deportation and the subsequent search by the woman for her lover. Evangeline looks all over the eastern United States until she finds him dying. At **Grande Pré National Historic Park** a simple, stone church of French design contains artifacts relating to Acadian culture and particularly the era of deportation. Outside, amidst ever-youthful gardens, stands a statue of Longfellow's tragic heroine.

Southeast of Grand Pré, where the Avon and St. Croix Rivers converge, is the town of **Windsor**. Anyone fond of expressions such as, "raining cats and dogs," "truth is stranger than fiction," "quick as a wink," and "an ounce of prevention is worth a pound of cure," should make a pilgrimage to Windsor's **Haliburton House** (circa 1839). Now a museum, it was once the home of judge, humorist and author Thomas Chandler Haliburton who created *Sam Slick*, the fictional Yankee clock peddler who spouted these and other witticisms on his travels through Nova Scotia.

High tides and warm water: The northern aspect of mainland Nova Scotia is washed by the Bay of Fundy, with the highest tides in the world; and on the other side of the Chignecto Isthmus, by the Northumberland Strait, with the warmest salt water north of the Carolinas. Whereas some bizarre natural phenomena occur only once in a lifetime, the Fundy tides put on their show twice daily, with a repertoire that varies according to the location. **Burntcoat Head,** on the **Minas Basin,** is the point at which the world's highest tides have been recorded —

Travail looms larger than life—weaving Scottish kilts.

a difference of 54 ft (17 m) between low and high tides.

Perhaps this atmosphere of extremity inspired William D. Lawrence to construct Canada's largest wooden ship in nearby **Maitland**. His namesake, a fully rigged sailing vessel, was launched in 1874 — a technical and financial success. Lawrence's stately home is now a museum containing artifacts and memorabilia relating to ships and shipbuilding, including a model of the *William D. Lawrence*.

Truro was originally settled by Acadians, (they called it Cobequid), and later by people from Northern Ireland and New Hampshire. It is a good place to observe the tidal bore, or "wall of water," in which the incoming Fundy tide rushes into the Salmon River at the rate of one foot (0.3 meter) a minute. This event attracts a crowd in summer and is usually greeted with a standing ovation. A hotline has even been set up to find out the tide times. DIAL-A-TIDE can be reached at (902) 426-5494.

Across the isthmus is a region washed by the Northumberland Strait, strung with beaches and often echoing with the sound of bagpipes. It is said that more clans are represented in Nova Scotia than in Scotland and a good number of them can be found right here. The **Gathering of the Clans** is held each year in **Pugwash**, a community where the street signs are bilingual — English and Gaelic.

Highland clearances: Pictou is the "Birthplace of New Scotland," where the first boatful of Scottish Highlanders arrived aboard the *Hector* in 1773. This fine harbor would see many subsequent waves of Scottish immigration. Today it is center for shipbuilding and fishing (especially lobster). Each July brings the **Pictou Lobster Carnival**, an annual event since 1934.

Like Pictou, **Antigonish** took its name from the Micmacs, and later became characterized by the culture of Highland Scots. The annual **Highland Games** here draw competitors from far and wide, in what is the oldest such spectacle in North America. Featuring Scottish music, dance and sports, one of the most popular features is the ancient caber toss. Contestants try to toss a telephone-pole the farthest, hoping it will land on its opposite end.

Alexander Graham Bell once wrote: " I have travelled around the globe. I have seen the Canadian and American Rockies, the Andes and the Alps and the highlands of Scotland; but for simple beauty, Cape Breton outrivals them all." Bell's words

A curious sunbeam peeps into the Fisherman's Life Museum.

have not gone unheeded; **Cape Breton Island** is the most popular tourist destination in Nova Scotia. Ironically, the island is also the most economically depressed region in a province less affluent than the rest of Canada, due in large part to the decline in coal mining.

Cape Breton has always been a place apart — occupied by the French longer than the rest of Nova Scotia (they called it *Ile Royale*) and a separate province until 1820. The **Canso Causeway,** an umbilical cord to the "Mainland," was not constructed until 1955. Perhaps because of these factors, Cape Bretoners identify more closely with their ethnic heritage, whether Scottish or Acadian, and with other Islanders, than with other Nova Scotians or Canadians.

The Cabot Trail, which is named after explorer John Cabot who sighted land here in 1497, is a 187-mile (301-km) loop which rollercoasts around the northern part of Cape Breton. It is a region greatly reminiscent of the Scottish Highlands, to the eye and to the ear. This road is popularly thought of as one of the most spectacular drives in North America, winding through lush river valleys, past (and often clinging to bluffs high above) a rugged and dramatically beautiful coastline, through dense forest lands, and up and over mountains.

It was once a series of death-defying footpaths and later, equally treacherous trails, impassable during much of the year. Northern communities were especially isolated, with **Cape Smoky** presenting the greatest barrier. By 1891, a narrow wagon trail forged its way circuitously over old Smoky, featuring a sheer rock cliff off one side and a 1,200-foot (370-meter) plunge to the sea off the other. Automobiles began taking their chances here in 1908, flagging in an era of white knuckled and ingenious motorists. One of their tricks was to tie spruce trees behind their cars to prevent running away on downhill slopes. A story is told of one foursome who traversed the trail by having one of them steer, one running ahead to spot curves, and the other two behind the car hauling rocks to place behind the wheels in the event of a problem.

Despite an increase in traffic, as late as 1920 the people who resided along the trail were responsible for its maintenance. The province later took things over and by 1932 the Cabot Trail became a "proper road." Yet it still has its hair-raising stretches and in fact, most people drive it in a clockwise direction, thereby clingling to the inside of the road. Needless to say, careful attention

Two scarecrows tanning on Cape Breton Island.

should be paid to the rules of the road.

Alexander Graham Bell, himself born in Scotland, built a summer house in **Baddeck**, the official beginning and terminus of the Cabot Trail, and spent the better part of his last 35 years here. He thought of himself as a teacher of the deaf, and as such directed Helen Keller's education and undertook research which led to the invention of, most notably, the telephone. He surely possesed one of the most fertile and brightest minds of the day, a mind that radiated in all directions. **The Alexander Graham Bell National Historic Park**, through photographs and exhibits is a monument to Bell — the teacher, inventor and humanitarian.

The Cabot Trail, traveling clockwise beyond Baddeck, traces the Margaree River, renowned for its beauty and an abundance of trout and salmon. The stretch of Gulf of St. Lawrence coastline from the **Margaree** to the beginning of Cape Breton Highlands National Park is dotted with Acadian fishing villages, inhabited by descendants of the mainland French who came here at the time of deportation. Just as the Acadian language has retained its 17th Century flavor, the culture of the people here has remained relatively undiluted. Acadian flags fly in the sea breeze, and a church steeple signifies the next community. Such is the case with **Chéticamp**, the biggest town in these parts. **Cape Breton Highlands National Park** begins in a few miles past Chéticamp, extending from the Gulf to the Atlantic and bordered on three sides by the Cabot Trail. This magnificent wilderness preserve is a paradise for hikers, swimmers, campers, golfers and other lovers of the great outdoors. Tracing the Park, the Trail reaches its northernmost point at **Cape North** and from here another road heads farther north to the beautiful fishing village of **Bay St. Lawrence**. En route, at the base of **Sugar Loaf Mountain**, is the site where Cabot is believed to have landed in 1497. A reenactment of this event is staged each June 24th on the beach.

At the eastern exit from the Park are the **Ingonishs**, a group of communities which have long been a great attraction for visitors. They comprise a year round resort area, which includes the **Keltic Lodge**, considered one of Canada's premier resorts. Just beyond Ingonish Harbor is **Cape Smoky**, its head in the clouds, rising 1,200 feet (369 meters) above the sea. Tourists can ski its slopes in winter while looking out upon the Atlantic. In summer, a ride on the chairlift to the top of Cape Smoky provides a breathtak-

Lobster traps resting near Trout River.

ing (weather permitting) view of this rugged, misty isle.

The stretch from Cape Smoky to Baddeck is known as the **Gaelic Coast**. Skirting the coast of St. Ann's Bay will take travelers to **Gaelic College**. As the only institution of its type in North America, it serves as a vibrant memorial to the Highland Scottish who settled here and has been nurtured by their descendants. The sound of bagpipes, the weaving of tartans, and the whirl of tartan-clad dancers can all be experienced in summer. In early August the clans are well represented as they gather for the annual Gaelic Mod, a seven-day festival of Celtic culture. While on campus, visit the fascinating **Highland Pioneers Museum**, with its Hall of Clans. It displays some of the effects of Angus MacAskill a 19th Century, nearly-eight-foot tall Cape Bretoner, who once worked with Tom Thumb (he held him in the palm of his hand). The museum contains memorabilia related to his life, as well as examples of his oversized apparel.

Entering coal country: Jumping off the Cabot Trail into what is called **Industrial Cape Breton**, became an introduction to a world of smokestacks and steel mills. Coal was once king in this area, and men poured in from around the world knowing only that **Sydney** or **Glace Bay** meant work. Today hiring is at a standstill but the coal industry has a future thanks to the **Cape Breton Development Corporation**. Established by the federal government in 1967, it was set up to look at the future of the coal industry. Oil had been increasing in popularity, causing mines in the area to close down. But with the oil crisis in the 70s and the problems in the Persian Gulf today, the coal industry will most likely continue for many more years. Especially now that the Nova Scotia government uses coal for 75 to 80 percent of its electrically generated stations.

Cape Breton Miner's Museum in Glace Bay has developed into one of Nova Scotia's finest museums. Artifacts and photographs chronicle the history of coal mining in this town and commemorate the men who risked their lives working in the depths; but the highlight of any visit here is the mine tour. Salty, veteran miners bring visitors down into the **Ocean Deeps Mine** (carved from under the ocean floor), and tell stories of pain, death, pride, hard work, low wages and camaraderie. Stories are told of their buddies who lost their lives, of nine year old boys working in the mines, of the Men of the Deeps Choir, of a flower garden cultivated in the midst of darkness. Listeners will emerge informed, moved and perhaps stiff from stooping under the low ceilings.

Workers have been mining coal in the vicinity of Glace Bay since the 18th Century when soldiers from nearby Louisbourg were assigned this duty. Fortress Louisbourg was the last great military, commercial and governmental stronghold of the French in the region that was once Acadia, but by 1760 it was conquered and demolished by the British. Uniquely, the site remained untouched until two centuries later when reconstruction began, in what has been termed the most painstaking, most ambitious and largest project of its kind ever undertaken in Canada.

The last French stronghold: Passing by the sentries and through the nearby gate of Louisbourg, is like stepping back in time to the summer of 1744. The people involved with the ongoing reconstruction of **Fortress of Louisbourg National Historic Park** have made this possible. From the costumed staff, trained in 18th Century deportment, to the authenticity of the structures and their furnishings, Louisbourg never fails to impress. A center for scuba diving is **Louisbourg Harbor,** and generally the waters off the southern coast of Cape Breton are known as fertile ground for "wreck-hunt-

The arched gateway of Louisbourg.

ing" — the legacy of centuries of maritime activity here, peaceful and otherwise.

Off the south shore, just before reaching mainland Nova Scotia, is **Isle Madame**, reached by a small bridge across the Lennox Passage. A scenic loop meanders around the island through lovely Acadian fishing villages. Of particular note is the **LeNoir Forge Museum in Arichat**, a restored stone blacksmith shop with working forge, in what is the oldest building on the island (1793). At Little Anse, a trail leads to **Cape Rouge** at land's end. From here travelers can look out upon **Green Island** with its lighthouse — one of the last remaining manned beacons in the province.

The Eastern shore: The eastern shore of Nova Scotia, between Cape Breton and the Twin Cities, is characterized by its unspoiled beauty, an abundance and variety of fishing opportunities, and its traditional personality. Locals maintain that things have changed little over the years. In certain communities salt cod lying on flakes in the open air can still be seen, drying just as it was done a century ago. Closer than all other mainland communities to the great Atlantic fishing banks, **Canso**, not surprisingly has developed into a center for fishing and fish processing. Its harbor has witnessed the

history of this region, from the early European fishermen and traders, to the British fleet that made its rendezvous here before the final assault on Louisbourg.

Farther down the coast, along the banks of St. Mary's River, is the village of **Sherbrooke**. A French fur-trading post in the 17th Century, the first permanent settlers came here in 1800 attracted by the tall timber and the river, then as now, filled with salmon. Sixty-one years later something happened that would change the face of this town for all time — they discovered gold. The boom, referred to as "Sherbrooke's Golden Age," lasted only 20 years.

Sherbrooke became quiet again, left alone except for seasonal visits by salmon fishermen, until the 1970s when a restoration project was established. The heart of town is now almost entirely restored, and certain streets have been closed to traffic to create **Sherbrooke Village**. It's inhabited by people in costume going about their business, so visitors can walk through 20th Century Sherbrooke and suddenly happen upon a town steeped in another era.

In use since the 1870s, **The Blacksmith Shop** produces items used in the restoration and sold in the Emporium, as does **Sherbrooke Village Pottery**. Most fascinating of all is the jail, built in 1862 and used for 100 years. Not a jail really, but an ordinary 19th-Century home once inhabited by a jailor, his family and the legal offenders.

In earlier days, the distance between Sherbrooke and Halifax was described as "...60 miles of horrible roads." Today, while the roads are excellent, there are scenes along the way reminiscent of bygone era. On the edge of town is, the reconstructed **McDonald Brothers Mill**, where the sights, smells and sounds of a 19th Century sawmill are recreated. Continuing along the coastal road brings visitors to **Tangier**, home of an enterprise known to gourmets and gourmands the world over — J. Willy Krauch and Sons. Krauch, now joined by his sons, has spent the better part of his life smoking Atlantic salmon, mackerel and eel, using the Danish method of wood-smoking. Down the coast at **Jeddore Oyster Pond** is **Fisherman's Life Museum**, intended to portray the life of a typical inshore fisherman and his family. The museum is the modest homestead of James Myers (1834-1915), restored to reflect the period after the turn of the century. The home speaks volumes on the austerity and pride which continues to characterize life along the southern shore of Nova Scotia.

NEWFOUNDLAND

Newfoundland receives about as many visitors in a year as Toronto in a weekend. Tourist facilities, while usually adequate, are rarely luxurious by international standards. There are no theme parks, there is no world-class art gallery. Newfoundland's mountains are not as high as the Rockies and are much less accessible. The weather is unpredictable in the extreme and seldom hot. While the average tourist may label these as "disadvantages" they serve as an inspiration for more adventurous travelers. Newfoundland's remoteness has probably cultivated the most individualistic part of North America. It is a difficult place to get to (most areas are only accessible by light plane, boat or helicopter) and the settlements are sparse. Imagine a land mass three times the area of New Brunswick, Nova Scotia and PEI combined, then remember that the rugged terrain is home to less than four people per square mile. A fifth of the total population live in the general area of St. John's while the rest live mainly in fishing villages along the coasts known as outports. English is the most common language spoken (99 percent) and 96 percent of the people who live in Newfoundland were born here. This is a unique trend when comparing it to the migratory tendencies of the other provinces. Jokes about Newfies can be heard across the country, but Newfoundlanders themselves have established their own brand of humor.

Even though "The Rock," as some residents call it, is the sort of place not everyone would like, it's quite hard to find anyone who has already been there and yet does not enjoy it.

John Cabot: To understand Newfoundland, one must understand some of its unique history. The **Grand Banks**, Newfoundland's greatest asset, are not in Newfoundland. They're the fishing grounds on the continental shelf southeast of Newfoundland that have been fished by European fishermen since the 15th Century. Giovanni Caboto from Venice (also known as John Cabot) sailed over the Grand Banks and into harbor on St. John's Day in 1497. He named the future capital St. John's and claimed the land for England. Henry VII gave him £10 for his trouble. Even so, the English were less interested in the land than the fish. Cabot reported that the cod were so numerous that "they would fill a basket lowered over the side." The Spanish, Portuguese and French who also fished in the area, salted their catch to preserve it for the trip home. The English, who lacked a source of cheap salt, had to dry their cod, and to do this the English fleets needed to go ashore. Until the 1930s when freezer ships came on the scene sun drying was the most common method of preserving fish in Newfoundland.

But Britain originally did not want a colony. Settlement was actively discouraged. In fact it was illegal at first for anyone to winter-over in Newfoundland. The "Masterless Men" were the first European settlers since the Vikings to come to Canada. They were indentured sailors who jumped ship, preferring a chance at a life in one of the many natural harbors along Newfoundland's rugged coastlines to virtual slavery on a fishing boat. Their independence and spirit of survival-at-all-costs is still very much a part of the Newfoundlanders' character today.

The Viking settlements of the 10th Century did not survive. Suggestions for the reasons for their demise range from a change in the climate to a vitamin deficiency causing a weakening of the bones. The Vikings called their settlement in Newfoundland "Markland." Stories of Markland have indicated that the first child born in the Americas of European origin was Snorri Thorfinnson. When Christopher Columbus visited Iceland in 1487, five years before his "discovery" of the New World, he probably would have heard the stories of the Newfoundland voyages of the Vikings. Travelers can come up to visit the site of Markland at **L'Anse-aux-Meadows** at the northern tip of the Great Northern Peninsula.

Oral Tradition: If you remember that St. John's is closer to Ireland than to Toronto, you won't be dumbfounded when you encounter what could possibly be your biggest problem in Newfoundland — the language. It is a unique blend of dialects from England's West Country and South-western Ireland brought over by the original settlers and left largely unchanged by the passing centuries. It is the closest dialect in the modern world to Shakespearean English and the only place where many words and expressions common in the 17th Century still survive in usage. Newfoundland speech can be as obscure or as beautiful as Shakespeare himself.

Another tradition transported and preserved in Newfoundland is storytelling. In Newfoundland "history" is regarded differently than in most other parts of North America.The oral traditions of handing down stories from generation to generation are still not yet gone. Times are changing but not all Newfoundlanders will change with them. It's still possible to hear Guglielmo Marconi talked of as an "irrepressible dandy" although he hasn't been in Newfoundland since 1901 when he came to receive the first wireless transatlantic message. The "old days" are described as the times when "most people could neither read nor write, but my, how they could talk!" Modern times differ only in that people can now read and write as well.

Reluctance to join Canada: Confederation with Canada was (and sometimes still is) one of the liveliest topics for discussion in Newfoundland. It did not take place until 1949, making Newfoundland Canada's most recent province. It was a hard-won victory for the federalists. An old Newfoundland song sings of the island:

Her face to Britain, her back to the Gulf,
Come near at your peril Canadian wolf.

(In some Newfoundland dialects "Gulf" rhymes with "wolf".)

During the Confederation period there was a referendum with three choices offered to Newfoundlanders: a commission government indirectly responsible to Britain; colonial status; or Confederation (meaning union with Canada). No option received an outright majority on the first round so a second ballot was issued from which the Canada Option won by only 7,000 votes. It is generally accepted that the promises of social programs, particularly the "baby bonus," tipped the balance in Canada's favor.

The sea: Until well into this century the vast majority of Newfoundlanders lived along the coasts making an extremely modest and difficult living from the sea. Cod is the most plentiful fish but there are also commercial stocks of sole, flounder, redfish and turbot on the Grand Banks. Migrating salmon are caught at sea and in the larger rivers, along the south coast, crab and lobster are trapped. As long as there has been human habitation on the island there has been a seal hunt off Newfoundland in the spring. In 1983 animal rights groups from outside the province persuaded foreign governments to ban the import of seal pelts on humanitarian grounds. This protest polarized Newfoundland fishermen who were proud of their humane methods of

killing and adherence to quotas. Now, there are problems resulting from overpopulation of seal herds.

In the last 50 years mining and forest industries have taken a larger place in Newfoundland economics. Although the fishing industries are still the largest employers, the province no longer depends upon them exclusively for its livelihood. In recent years an abundance of gas and oil reserves off the coast of the island and off Labrador have been discovered. Exploration of the reserves has been slow due to the interference of drifting icebergs, but the federal government has given the go-ahead to a $5.2 billion project known as the **Hibernia Oil Fields**. Just off the east coast of St. John's the project is expected to generate several thousand jobs.

Tourism is a relatively recent phenomenon in Newfoundland and Newfoundlanders seem determined to avoid the mistakes made elsewhere. The prevailing attitude is still that the visitors should "take us as they find us" rather than expect special treatment. Facilities are improving and increasing in number every year but the best are still the most traditional. In the "Hospitality Home Program" tourists can sleep and eat in Newfoundland homes and avoid the hotel-

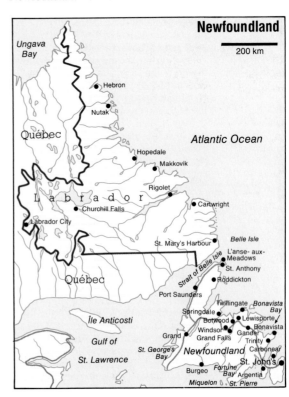

motel circuit. This is a good way for visitors to meet the locals and it usually becomes a source of entertainment for both.

Screech, found in many households and neighborhood taverns, is the drink Newfoundland is famous for. Originally it was the washings and dregs from casks of rum. It was drunk by sailors when there was nothing else available. It's now bottled under government supervision and, although safer than in earlier days, it is still like the Newfoundland character — more interesting than it is refined. If visitors are interested in trying this local drink, one of the best ways is to attend a "screeching-in" ceremony. Usually held in someone's home or a town hall, first-time visitors are treated to the drink followed by swallowing some raw fish. Once officially screeched-in, they receive from the master of ceremony a scroll as proof of their passage.

For the seafood lover Newfoundland homes are the ideal venue. Fish is served as often and in as much variety as one could wish: halibut, crab, Atlantic salmon, lobster and much more. But be aware that the word "fish" on a menu, without a more specific reference, means "cod." Never "boring old cod," it could be poached, baked, fried, cod tongues, or in chowder, in casseroles, in cakes, in a stew with hardtack called brewis, or in any one of the thousands of recipes. Newfoundlanders have spent the last few hundred years perfecting.

Getting around: The best way for the independent traveler to get around is still by private car. There are bus services to virtually all locations but the farther off the beaten path, that is to say the more interesting your destination, the more infrequent the service. Tours are available and are sometimes the best way to go. There are still many locations that are best reached or only accessible by boat. The main road in Newfoundland is the **Trans-Canada Highway** which runs through Newfoundland on an indirect path between **Port-aux-Basques** in the west to St. John's in the east. It's 576 miles (925 km) long and is the lifeline of the province.

The National Parks in Newfoundland are a source of pride for the Newfoundlanders and a source of delight to the visitor. On the west coast, north of Corner Brook, is mountainous **Gros Morne National Park.** Its fjords are best seen by boat from **Western Brook**; here you have the best chance of seeing such wildlife as whales, seals, caribou and moose. It is even rumored that there are polar bears which have swum ashore

St. John's Harbour.

from passing icebergs.

Terra Nova National Park on the east coast is a bit of typical Newfoundland fishing coast. Here, there is boating, fishing and moonlight cruises on beautiful **Clode Sound.** Inland in the park there is good camping and hiking, and it is one of the few places in the province where the water in the lakes is warm enough to swim. The park at the site of the Viking settlement at **L'Anse-aux-Meadows** is well worth a visit, but being at the most northerly tip of the island, it is more than a little off the beaten path. But then the route along the coast will show how much fun getting there can be.

Cape Spear National Historic Park is the most easterly point of Newfoundland. Take a boat tour there to see and listen to the school of whales. In fact, you can put all of North America behind you because Cape Spear is also the most easterly point of the continent.

On even the shortest boat ride off Newfoundland's coast you will be reminded of the power of the sea. Though Newfoundlanders rarely speak of it, the sea is often thought of and never taken for granted. With rough seas and drifting icebergs floating around the island disasters can't always be avoided. One of the world's most infamous sinkings happened just off the coast of Newfoundland on April 15, 1912. The luxury liner *Titanic* sank after hitting an iceberg, taking the lives of 1,513 people. Locals tend to paint their houses in bright colors, especially if they are visible on top of a hill, to ensure they can be spotted by fishermen at sea.

For opportunities to enjoy unspoiled nature, Newfoundland cannot be surpassed anywhere in Canada, and of course that means it is not surpassed anywhere in the world. For sport fishermen the fishing spots are as many and as varied as the Newfoundland coastline and all the rivers and lakes inland. Fishing lakes are known as "ponds." Atlantic salmon, Arctic char, Northern pike and giant bluefin tuna are among the sport fishing species that draw fishermen to the "ponds" and coasts. Even a Newfoundlander would find the appeal to anglers difficult to exaggerate. Quite simply Newfoundland is the sort of place of which fishermen dream.

Although the trend to urbanization is as apparent in Newfoundland as it is in the rest of the country, open spaces, small towns and wilderness are still the visitors' idea of what constitutes Canada. Canadian cities are usually said to be great places to live, but

A Maritime specialty: lobster with a dash of lemon.

only good places to visit. In this regard Newfoundland is typically Canadian. It is unlikely that a visitor would choose to spend all their time in Newfoundland in St. John's. On the other hand it is hard to avoid spending a few days there. It is the biggest village you will ever see.

St. John's: The first thing to remember about St. John's is that it is not Saint John. The latter is in New Brunswick and although it was named for the same saint it is a relative newcomer in the area, not having been founded until 1630. The "Saint" in Saint John, New Brunswick, is always spelled out in full; the "St." in St. John's, Newfoundland, never is. By this convention it is not possible to confuse the former with the latter — except perhaps for someone from the mainland.

The aimless streets of **St. John's** were originally cowpaths wandering up from the harbor. The statue of Peter Pan in a downtown park is polished only by the bodies of the children who climb over it. **Government House** was built with a moat to keep out snakes, although there are none in the province. **Signal Hill Park** is a must-see: more events of historical importance have taken place on this site than in most other provinces.

Signal Hill was the site in 1762 of one of the final battles of the Seven Years' War. Visitors to this site can still see fortifications ranging from the Napoleonic Wars to World War Two.

The best way to get a sense of St. John's is to walk the main street. It is called — can you guess? — Water Street, the oldest street on the continent. When Newfoundland joined Canada in 1949 most of the province lived in poverty, but nevertheless Newfoundland had more millionaires (they were known as "Water Street Men") per capita than elsewhere in North America.

When you visit an outport don't expect just poverty and cod. No one will be rich and visitors will get lots of fish and see a way of life most people think had vanished in the 19th Century. It is a way of life that represents the soul not only of Newfoundland but also of Canada. The policemen of St. John's still do not carry guns. Doors are seldom locked, visitors don't go unnoticed and no one goes by without being spoken to. Newfoundlanders generally don't like pushy or aggressive people. They will enjoy a loud person much less than they will enjoy putting a shy person at ease.

St. Pierre and Miquelon: Not only is Newfoundland closer to Ireland than

A solitary Maritime church.

Toronto but it is also closer to France than it is Nova Scotia. At least it's closer to a part of France. Just off the end of the Burin Peninsula on Newfoundland's southern coast are the islands of **St. Pierre and Miquelon.** They are the remnants of France's once great empire in North America. It too has been a haven for fishermen. The islands can be reached by ferry or by air and a passport is usually required. It truly is a taste of Europe with narrow streets and European cars. But it is essentially a fishing village. With a population of about 6,000 St. Pierre and Miquelon manage to send a député to French Parliament and a member to the Senate.

Something in a name: In Newfoundland, even Shakespeare might agree that there is something in a name. Come by Chance, Run by Guess, Blow me Down, Gripe's Point, Famish Gut, Empty Basket, Heart's Delight, Heart's Desire, and Heart's Content are names of outport towns that were definitely not chosen by a committee. You can actually go on the "Gynecologists Tour" to Placentia, Virgin's Arm, Dildo, Bare Need and Conception Bay. There is also another odd-name place called Joe Batt's Arm. A prize at a Miss Goofy Newfy contest was presented to a young lady dressed up as Joe Batt's Other Arm.

There is a story told in Newfoundland about a bragging Texan who came up and told a Newfoundland "I can get on my horse and ride all day, and by the end of the day I'm still not at the edge of my property." The Newfoundlander was unimpressed and merely responded: "Yep, I feel for you. I once had a horse like that."

Humor as a way of life: In Canada Newfoundlanders are more famous for their sense of humor than for their fish. Generations of Canadians have been brought up on Newfy jokes — jokes which are apparently at the expense of Newfoundlanders but are most often and best told by Newfoundlanders themselves.

Newfoundland's first day as a Canadian province was April 1, 1949. The First of April is traditionally April Fool's Day, the day when practical jokes, especially ones involving tall stories, may be played with impunity. Humor is such a part of the Newfoundland way of speech and life that it is often hard to know when there is a joke being played. It is not true for example, that those icebergs you may see off St. John's in the winter are styrofoam structures towed out for the sake of decorations by the Chamber of Commerce — although if your informant recognizes you as a mainlander he may manage to assure you to that effect with a very straight face.

The time is now: The time to see Newfoundland is now. In the last 30 years the changes have been profound and show no sign of slowing down their pace. The consolidation of the outports, a program for moving inhabitants of isolated outports into major centers has been compared to the clearances of the Scottish Highlands. The importance of the fishing industries is diminishing and will have even less prominence if the Hibernia Oil Fields live up to their expected potential. These rich offshore oil reserves could bring with them the single thing most likely to cause irreparable change to the fabric of Newfoundland society — industrial prosperity.

In many ways Newfoundland is the most unusual Canadian province, in many other ways it is the most typical. It is a land of beauty and of hardships, a place of hospitality and isolation. It is not the place for everyone, but it is a place where even the short-term visitor may gain memories to last a lifetime. The sweetest memory would be the sound of a Newfoundlander bidding you farewell by saying "And don't be a stranger!"

Left, satisfied with a day's catch; and right, far from the maddening crowd: Newfoundland Coast.

PRINCE EDWARD ISLAND

Prince Edward Island (PEI) is the tiniest province in this land of vast horizons. It rests in the Gulf of St. Lawrence, cut off from the mainland by the Northumberland Strait. Less rugged than its fellow Atlantic Provinces, PEI's quaintness seems untouched by the modern world — its past is still the present. Agriculturally, the land is well-groomed and cultivated. Some have gone so far as to describe the Island as two beaches divided by potato fields.

The importance of potatoes cannot be overestimated; they are the preeminent crop in a province heavily dependent on agriculture. Tourism is second in economic importance and the season is compressed into the summer months. (Few Island attractions are open for business off-season.) There are 128,000 inhabitants on the island, and befitting the cultural makeup of Canada most of them are descendants of early French, Scottish, English and Irish settlers. But despite the ties that bind, these quirky islanders tend to refer to everyone who isn't from the island as "from away."

PEI begs to be explored. An excellent road system provides access virtually every corner of the island and the distances are remarkably short. Fortunately, tourism has not spoiled this truly lovely rural province — a tribute to its people, as hardworking and traditional as they are warm and hospitable.

Abegweit: According to Micmac legend, the Great Spirit molded brick-red clay into "the most beautiful place on earth" and gently placed it in the Gulf of St. Lawrence. He presented it to his people and they came here in summer to camp and to fish nearly 2,000 years ago. They called it *Abegweit*, "land cradled on the waves." Today the Micmacs account for less than one percent of the PEI population.

The first European to covet the island was Jacques Cartier, who claimed it for France in 1534. He considered it "...the fairest land 'tis possible to see...!"; yet **Ile-St-Jean,** as the French affectionately named it, had no permanent settlement until rather late in 1719 (at **Port La Joye**). It became the breadbasket for the French stronghold of **Louisbourg** and the island still serves a similar function for the region as the "Garden of the Gulf."

The west: PEI is geographically sepa-rated into three parts roughly identified by the county lines: traveling from west to east — **Prince, Queens** and **Kings**. The westernmost region is less developed than the other two in terms of tourism, but it is no less attractive.

Lady Slipper Drive (named for the delicate, pink orchid which is the provincial flower) is the official tourist route for this area. It meanders around a deeply indented coastline; past sand-stone cliffs and sun-bleached dunes; and through tiny villages, many of them ringing with the sounds of Acadian French. (Five percent of PEI's population is French-speaking.)

The route officially begins and ends in **Summerside**, the biggest town in this province with the exception of only one city (Charlottetown). Located on **Bedeque Bay**, the town was presumably named for being on the warmer or "sunny-side" of PEI. Once a center for shipbuilding, the waterfront is now crowded with vessels loading up with potatoes. The highlight of Summerside's calendar comes in mid-July with eight days of gustatory merriment known as the **Lobster Carnival**.

The spires of **St. John the Baptist Church**, one of the Island's loveliest (and probably also the most photographed)

Left, a "Father Time" from Prince Edward Island; and right, a timid Canadian poised for flight.

churches, announce one's arrival in **Miscouche**. It was in this town that the National Acadian Convention decided to adopt the Acadian flag in 1884. Today this banner can be seen throughout French-speaking regions of Atlantic Canada, waving proudly in the sea breeze.

Miscouche is also home of **Le Musée Acadien**, whose collection of antique tools, household items, religious artifacts, photographs and documents, preserves the culture of these early settlers. The museum also houses a genealogical department with records available to researchers upon special request.

North of Miscouche is **Malpeque Bay**, where the world-renowned Malpeque oysters (now harvested around the Island) were first discovered. The **Tyne Valley Oyster Festival** celebrates these bivalves annually in August. Aside from oysters, the Malpeque Bay area is known for its fine sand beaches and for having been a great center for shipbuilding in the 19th Century, a part of the Island heritage commemorated at **Green Park Provincial Park** in **Port Hill**.

Green Park is the former estate of shipbuilding magnate James Yeo, Jr., which today includes his restored circa-1865 home, a shipbuilding museum and a recreated 19th-Century shipyard. The yard is home of a partially completed brigantine schooner, the sight of which gives the impression that time has stood still.

Beyond Port Hill is a causeway leading to **Lennox Island**, a reservation inhabited by approximately 50 Micmac families. The Micmacs are known for their skill at basketry and several practitioners of the art can be found here. David Bernard, a fourth generation basket maker, laments the reality that few young people seem interested in carrying on the tradition, while reminiscing on how he learned to make baskets at his mother's knee. Lennox Island's Indian Arts and Crafts specializes in the sale of beaded and silver jewelry, clay pottery, wood carvings, woven baskets and ceremonial head-dresses made by Indians from many different nations.

The **Cape Kildare** area, beyond **Alberton Harbor**, is where Jacques Cartier dropped anchor in 1534, thereby "discovering" the Island. A provincial park honors the great explorer, stretching along the dune-lined coast for three miles (five km). Campers will find this a very pleasant spot to pitch their tents.

Inland and to the north is **Tignish**, a town founded in 1799 by a group of Acadians who were later joined by two Irishmen. (Tignish ranks among the world's top producer-exporters of canned lobster meat.) Both cultures are still well-represented and, typically, the church is the focal point of the community. The **Church of St. Simon and St. Jude** is the proud repository of a rare Tracker organ, built in 1882 by the first in a line of French Canadian organ builders, and one of the finest and most melodious instruments of its kind.

The northernmost tip of PEI is named, unimaginatively, **North Cape**. This continually eroding point, (so much so that the lighthouse and the road that encircles it have been moved inland several times), is where the tides of the Gulf of St. Lawrence and Northumberland Strait meet. Its strategic location prompted development of the **Atlantic Wind Test Site**, a national facility for the testing and evaluation of wind generator, where visitors are welcome to watch at any time of the year.

Along the Northumberland shore tourists are likely to see Irish moss drying by the road or perhaps, following a storm, being gathered and hauled by horse-drawn carriages and pickup trucks along the beach. The area around Miminegash is particularly known for the harvesting of this commer-

Sanctuary in the woods.

cially viable seaweed.

Sightings of a "ghost ship," full-rigged and aflame, are frequently reported along the Northumberland shore, most often between **Campbellton** and **Burton**. Legends abound here; from the Micmac explanation for the red-stained rocks at **Cape Wolfe** (the god Thunder, betrayed in love by a young maiden, wrathfully threw her to earth), to tales of Captain Kidd's buried treasure at **West Point**, and tall-tales told by fishermen up and down the coast.

Inland is the town of **O'Leary**, smack in the center of one of PEI's richest and largest potato-producing areas. Perhaps the most potato-obsessed community in a province where this tuber is all-important, it is home of the **Potato Museum** (part of the **O'Leary Museum**) and host to the annual **Potato Blossom Festival** (held each July).

Tracing **Egmont Bay**, approaching the Summerside area, is the *Région Acadienne* — punctuated by the villages **Abram-Village**, **Cap-Egmont** and **Mont-Carmel**. There is no better place to experience Acadian culture and *joie de vivre* than in the first of these, host to the Egmont Bay and Mont-Carmel Exhibition in late August which overlaps with **Le Festival Acadien de la région Evangéline**. They include ag-

ricultural competitions, step-dancing, fiddling, lobster suppers, the Blessing of the Fleet and more. Abram-Village is also a center for crafts (particularly quilts and rugs), which are demonstrated and sold at the local Handicrafts Cooperative. As for the lively arts, tradition is very much alive and stepping at Club 50's Saturday night square dances. Just tune in, grab a partner and take the floor.

The lovely seaside community of Cap-Egmont has a rather unusual attraction — **The Bottle Houses**. A recycling project (undertaken in retirement) of the first magnitude, Edouard T. Arsenault built his glass houses and chapel from bottles (the first called for 12,000 of them). After a "...long winter cleaning bottles," the former fisherman and carpenter began work in 1980, obsessively and lovingly laboring over the project until his death four years later. Arsenault's typically Acadian spirit, a mixture of creative energy and humor, shines through the walls of these curious structures.

The Island's city: Not the least of **Charlottetown's** considerable charms is that it is still predominantly wooden (structurally, but decidedly not in demeanor). It is the center of all things for PEI — government,

Glass
menagerie—
the Bottle
House at
Cap-Egmont.

commerce and culture; and it is the province's only city, though it seems more like an intimate, elegant small town, complete with a town crier, gaslights and Canada's oldest drug store (**Huges Drug Store**).

Historically, Charlottetown is best known for being the "Cradle of the Confederation." The 1864 meeting, which led to the formation of the Dominion of Canada three years later, was held in **Province House**, the province's first public building. Ironically in 1864 PEI was somewhat hesitant to join Canada, and it did not in fact enter Confederation until 1873. This neo-classical stone structure is now a National Historic Site (the chamber where the Fathers of Confederation met has been restored), though it continues to house the legislature.

Just next door is the **Confederation Center** (of the Arts), established to commemorate the centennial of the main event. Each province contributed 15 cents for each of its citizens to help finance construction. It includes gallery and theater spaces and is host each summer to the **Charlottetown Festival**. Running from late June to mid-October, it is Canada's best-known music and theater festival.

The most popular production each summer is the musical version of *Anne of Green Gables*, the venerated (nowhere more than in PEI) children's classic, penned by Island author Lucy Maud Montgomery. This beloved children's book about a young orphan girl (Mark Twain called it "the sweetest creation of child life ever written") was first published in 1908 and has subsequently been translated into more than 30 languages.

One of the loveliest parts of town is **Rockford Square**, shaded by 110 trees, the legacy of Arbor Day 1884. Adjacent to the square is **St. Peter's Anglican Church** (1869) with a notable attachment, **All Souls' Chapel.** This tiny sanctuary was actually created in 1888 as a memorial to one of the Cathedral's first clergymen. It was a labor of love from William Harris, who designed it, and for his brother Robert, who executed a number of luminous paintings for its walls. Harris specified that Island materials be used, from the rich, red sandstone exterior to the wood and stone used for interior carvings. This High Victorian Gothic-style shrine is a testament to the spirit of both brothers, as well as to the skill of Island craftspeople who did most of the work. A place apart, it is very close to perfection.

Lobster and L.M. Montgomery: The

Left, a precious bundle; and right, potato farming.

central region of PEI is traced by the route known as **Blue Heron Drive**, which comes full circle at Charlottetown. It is distinguished by fine beaches — white sand along the Gulf shore and red sand along the Northumberland shore — colorful fishing villages, *Anne of Green Gables* related attractions (an Island sub-industry in and of itself) and community lobster suppers. Every summer night throughout PEI's small towns and districts, amazing feasts are organized and prepared by local women. Held either in churches or big halls, as many as 400 to 500 people are fed. For a reasonable price travelers can experience, and expect to enjoy, some of the best homemade food and lobster dishes they've ever had in a long time.

Most of **Queens County's Gulf** coast belongs to **PEI National Park** (one of the nation's most popular), with some of the finest beaches in eastern Canada. The mansion of Dalvey-By-the-Sea, now a popular tourist resort which stands at the entrance to the Park, was built in 1896 by Alexander Macdonald.

Rustico Island, part of the National park, is the summer home of a protected colony of Great Blue herons, the possessors of six-foot (two-meter) wing spans; while **North**

Rustico is a nuts-and-bolts fishing village, whose inhabitants appear and sound as if they were sent here by Central Casting. You can purchase seafood practically off the boats here, or pass the time talking with locals (who tend to be as jocular as they are friendly) — at dockside or out at sea on a tuna charter.

Green Gables House: Still within PEI National Park west of the Rusticos, is **Cavendish**, the center of *Anne of Green Gables* country. Visitors come from far and wide to see the settings described by L.M. Montgomery in *Anne* and other works of fiction, as well as to explore landmarks in the author's life.

The lovely **Green Gables House** on Highway 6 is one of the Island's most popular attractions. The **L.M. Montgomery Birthplace** can be found in nearby **New London**. Bordering on the cultic, a brochure sets the stage with this comment: "As you walk through the rooms of the Birthplace, you will thrill to the realization, that it was in this house that Lucy Maud first saw the light of day."

Victoria (its residents like to call it Victoria By-the-Sea) is a picturesque, English-flavored town, drenched in the past. It was once a major Island seaport and today its

A surviving relic of colonialism.

resident schooner, the *Mirana*, carries visitors off on sailing excursions. Landlubbers need not shrug the town off, for it is also a haven for antiques and fine crafts, as well as theater at the restored **Victoria Playhouse**. Or perhaps you and the gang could bring a picnic basket to the local Provincial Park, edged by red sand.

The east: The easternmost piece of PEI, most of it corresponding to Kings County, is encircled by the **Kings Byway**. This is the longest of the three routes.

East of Charlottetown, in the vicinity of **Hillsborough Bay**, travelers find themselves in prime strawberry country. Many local farms have "U-Pick" operations beginning in July when the luscious fruit ripens. Farming has long been a way of life on the Island. In **Orwell**, the **Orwell Corner Rural Life Museum** has recreated the atmosphere of a late 19th Century rural crossroads community. Most of the early settlers here were Scottish and in summer the traditional sounds of the Highlands can be enjoyed at weekly *ceilidhs* (pronounced kay-lee).

In 1803 a Scotsman by the name of Lord Selkirk, financed the immigration of three shiploads of Highlanders to PEI. The "Selkirk Pioneers" settled in **Eldon** and today a restoration and reconstruction, the **Lord Selkirk Pioneer Settlement**, provides insight into their existence (at times subsistence) on this side of the Atlantic. It is one of the largest collections of authentic log buildings in Canada. Carrying on tradition, the clans gather in Eldon every year in early August for the Highland Games.

Farther east in the community of **Flat River**, you'll come upon the **Flat River Studio**, featuring the pottery of Robert Wilby and the batik of his sister Roslynn. (A life-size nude sculpture beckons visitors to come in and browse.) As with many other Island crafts studios, the artists welcome spectators of their works in progress.

Beyond **Woods Island** (a boarding point for the Nova Scotia ferry), is **Murray River**. This lovely town was once an activity center for shipbuilding, but today wood is worked on a much smaller scale at **A.W. Shumate's Toy Factory**. Specializing in wooden toys and ornaments, the workshop, whose proprietor bears an uncanny resemblance to a certain Mr. Claus, is a delight to behold.

Murray Bay is the home of a large natural seal colony. These sleek creatures can be best observed from the **Seal Cove Campground** in **Murray Harbor North**, cavort-

Watching the day go by, Cavendish.

ing in the sun on their offshore sandbar. The surrounding area is replete with a seemingly endless variety of wildlife — indigenous and otherwise.

Nearby **Montague** is a commercial center for this part of the Island. The **Garden of the Gulf Museum** here interprets local history through a display of Indian artifacts and primitive weapons, while the annual **Garden of the Gulf Fiddle and Step-dancing Festival** in July revives local traditions.

Approaching the easternmost tip of PEI is the **Bay Fortune Area**, washed by a string of legends throughout its history. There is talk of the early 19th Century murder by a tenant of landlord Edward Abell at **Abells Cape**, of buried treasures along the sandstone cliffs, and of actor Charles Flockton, who in the late 19th Century bought the Cape and spent each summer here with his comedy company. American playwright Elmer Harris once spent summer in the vicinity and was inspired to feature nearby **Souris** as the setting for his book *Johnny Belinda* (based on the local legend of a young deaf and dumb girl). Today Souris serves as the seasonal embarkation point for passengers heading for the nearby Magdalen Islands.

Basin Head, east of Souris, is home of the **Fisheries Museum**. August brings the **Harvest of the Sea Feastival** where time-tested Island recipes can be sampled. The Museum is located beside a particularly beautiful stretch of dunes (all the way to East Point), where the sand "sings" as you walk along it.

Rounding **East Point**, (called *Kespemenagek*, "the end of the Island," by the Micmacs), where the tides of the Strait and the Gulf converge, lands one in **North Lake**, the "Tuna Fishing Capital of the World." Tourists from all over the continent flock here in pursuit of the giant bluefin tuna — the ultimate in sportfishing. Any good catch is often an unexpected one.

Heading back to Charlottetown one realizes that in 2,000 years much hasn't changed. The Micmacs were right in calling PEI *Abegweit*. The island is indeed a land cradled by waves. The Gulf Coast provides endless water activities for travelers, from fishing and boating to swimming and digging a clam dinner out of the brick-red, sand beaches. Inland the flat, quaint terrain provides a perfect route for adventurous trekkers and cyclists. In the end one discovers that the people with the potato obsession aren't "crazy" at all.

Bicycle touring the island.

WEST

Smoldering from the off-handed treatment it has historically received from Ontario and Québec, the West has recently emerged as a powerful presence in Canada. Rich in minerals, oil and natural gas, Manitoba, Saskatchewan and Alberta have become forces to be reckoned with.

Sometimes referred to as Canada's "Garden of Eden," British Columbia, the final western region that flanks the Pacific, is the West's warmest province. British Columbia encompasses not only the irascible Rocky Mountains, but also a gentle coastline.

The west section opens with an exploration of British Columbia, beginning with a description of Indian life and the arrival of European explorers. Modern B.C. is encountered first in Victoria, the province's capital city ... after a stroll through its streets, readers are taken up the coastline and into the area's awesome wilderness. Civilization reappears in the final pages as the author describes Vancouver.

Following B.C. are Canada's Prairie provinces: Alberta, Saskatchewan and Manitoba. Although markedly different from B.C., these three provinces constitute the remainder of Canada's "official" west. Alberta begins the search for the "Prairie existence" and demonstrates the unexpected diversity of the region by journeying up into Canada's vast playground: the Rocky Mountains. Banff's isolated beauty is contrasted with the exciting city-life of Edmonton and Calgary. Saskatchewan is explored through its rich history and its proud and prolific cultural features. Manitoba, concluding the section, provides an experience of the Prairie itself: wide open spaces and land, no longer shaded by forests, rolling, on to a distant horizon.

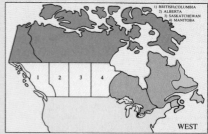

1) BRITISH COLUMBIA
2) ALBERTA
3) SASKATCHEWAN
4) MANITOBA

WEST

BRITISH COLUMBIA

Almost half the people who live in British Columbia were born somewhere else. This statistic doesn't seem all that odd when you consider what British Columbia has to offer. People are drawn to its overwhelming natural beauty: its rocky coastline and thick forests, its teeming mountains and its mild temperatures. Things on the west coast are more "laid back" compared to central Canada and people in B.C. take the time to appreciate their surroundings: it's clean living. At the same time all is not calm beneath this peaceful surface; it can be a land of extremes. Aside from health enthusiasts, the area has also attracted die-hard hippies and vegetarians, monarchists and trade unionists and profit-oriented business people. With such diverse interests and great beauty the 2.6 million residents of British Columbia can't be wrong about B.C.'s attractiveness. Nor can the millions of tourists that come to explore the province each year.

Indians of the West: It is the natural beauty of the land that attracted the Haida people to the coast of Canada. The Indians of the coast have always lived quietly and harmoniously here, even after they were "discovered" by the famous Captain Cook in 1793.

It was a Scotsman, Simon Fraser (1776-1862), who having adopted Canada as his home, dedicated his life to exploring and developing the richness of British Columbia. Fraser traveled up the smaller of the region's two important rivers, named it the Fraser River, and established it as a major fur-trading route.

Fur trading in the 19th Century was big business, and the competition for control of this new market marks the early history of the British Columbia. The Northwest Company was chartered by the British Government specifically to develop the resources of the northwest. The company had to fight for trade routes and profits with the Hudson Bay Company, an older "eastern" company that already had a monopoly on Canadian trade with Europe.

The Nor'west, as the company was affectionately called, established an inland trading post Fort George, which is now the city of Prince George. The Hudson Bay Company, being the larger company and seeing the value of the fur trade as well as the future of lumber and mining, finally bought out Nor'west in 1820 and maintained virtual monopoly control over the area until 1858.

In the 19th Century, economic competition became increasingly motivated by nationalistic impulses. The rich fur trade along the Columbia River was carried out largely by Americans, many having come north from the tiny settlements in California. They saw themselves as part of the Manifest Destiny of the United States to control the entire continent and their loyalty to Washington had an almost religious zeal. The trade along the Fraser River, just to the north of the Columbia, however, was clearly oriented towards Great Britain. It was worked by men who had followed Simon Fraser and who shared his loyalty to the Empire.

The American population grew faster than the British community, and accusations of stolen furs and territorial encroachment were a constant problem. The Americans' desires to control the trade of both rivers were becoming increasingly clear. The American battle cry "Fifty-Four-Forty or Fight!", referring to the latitude that marked the northern boundary of the territory, finally prompted the British to build Fort Victoria in 1843.

Complicated negotiations, which even-

British Columbia

500 km

Yukon

Altin

Juneau

Radium Hot Springs

Muncho Lake Park

Stone Mountain Park

Fort Nelson

Kwadacha Wilderness Park

Tatlatui Park

U.S.A.

Fort St. John

Alberta

Hazelton

Dawson Creek

Smithers

Carp Lake Park

Prince Rupert

Terrace

Vanderhoof

Kitimat

Burns Lake

Prince George

Queen Charlotte Is.

Tweedsmuir Park

Bowron Lake Park

Bella Coola

Quesnel

Wells Gray Park

Williams Lake

Kamloops

Revelstoke

Port Hardy

Cache Creek

Salmon Arm

Kelsey Bay

Kelowna

Vernon

Campbell River

Lytton

Kimberley

Fernie

Courtenay

Vancouver

Peniction

Nelson

Vancouver Island

Naniamo

Hope

Trail

Cranbrook

Port Alberni

Chilliwack

Creston

Duncan

U.S.A.

Pacific Ocean

Victoria

Seattle

Spokan

tually involved Spain, Russia, France and Germany, divided the territory in two at the 49th parallel. This handed most of the Columbia River, and the best fur-trading territory over to the United States. The British Loyalists now needed to find an "all British route" inland to the fur trapping territory. The only solution, development of the Fraser River, created a need for strong leadership, and a more organized government.

As a result, in 1856 Governor James Douglas, a bear-like man with the political skill to negotiate with the British Parliament, the personal magnetism to appeal to the woodsmen and fur-trappers, and the physical stamina to tackle the region's awesome physical barriers, called for Vancouver Island's 774 whites (half of whom were under the age of 20) to elect their first legislature. The group met in Bachelor's Hall in Victoria in 1856, with no way of knowing into what they were getting themselves.

In April of that year a group of Indians discovered gold in the North Thompson River, just above Kamloops. Governor Douglas sent a team to survey the entire area, and in October reported that all the tributaries of the Fraser would produce gold. Douglas was aware of what a gold rush had done to San Francisco in 1848, and he knew that he would need to take stern measures to protect the area's wealth, and to handle the boom that was about to hit Victoria.

Becoming a gold miner meant leaving home and traveling thousands of miles to work unbearably long hours at dirty, dangerous, back-breaking labor; the miner had to be willing to risk everything for a slim chance at striking it rich. However, for most people staying at home meant living in a dirty, dangerous city, working arduously in a factory for long hours with no chance of making more than $1 a day. Since the first miners to get to a goldfield stood the best chance of striking it rich, an announcement like Douglas's invariably caused a gold rush.

Becoming independent: The mainland quickly achieved economic independence from Vancouver Island, and the British wanted to make it a separate colony. But what should this new colony be called? The area, between the Rocky Mountains and the coast, had long gone by the name Simon Fraser had given it: New Caledonia. But that was the name of a French colony in the South Pacific. Queen Victoria favored the name "Columbia," but that was the name of a South American country, and the Columbia River was south of the 49th parallel, in the United States. Finally, the Queen, after some deliberation, came up with the variation "British Columbia," and on Nov. 19, 1858, James Douglas was inaugurated first governor of British Columbia (he remained governor of the separate colony of Vancouver Island until the two were united in 1866).

As the mainland developed, the city of Victoria suffered from an economic hangover. Its glory days were over, and the bust that followed the gold rush made Vancouver Island an economic parasite living off the bright future of the rest of the colony. New industry was needed to diversify the island's economy and to provide jobs for the men that didn't make their fortunes in the Cariboo (the Indian name for the upper Fraser River), where the best goldfields were found.

Remember, gold was not the first wealth offered by the rich land, it had simply replaced furs. The whites of Vancouver Island looked at the vast forests and saw the future in lumber. The Alberni Sawmill, the first sawmill west of the Rockies in Canada, was built on the west coast of Vancouver Island, on land stolen from Indians. This not only

Hell's Gate Atrium over the Fraser River.

228

created tensions between whites and Indians, but the sawmill created a hierarchy of labor as whites were paid 25 cents an hour to log and work the mill, while Asians and Indians were paid a mere 15 cents.

This was not the glorious future imagined by the gold-rushers of '58. The river beds had been panned out, and working in a sawmill or a gold mine was similar to the factory work back east: low-paying wage labor that was difficult to get. The independent spirit of the colony had to face the economic reality of its need for the outside world. A final attempt to get the colony to defect to the United States was defeated by the offer to build a Canadian-Pacific Railroad, which would link the young city of Vancouver with the rest of Canada. British Columbia became a Canadian Province in 1871. Today British Columbia continues to survive by exploiting its natural resources. It produces about a quarter of the marketable timber in North America (it provides the *world* with chopsticks), making forestry the province's number one industry. Mining is still important as is fishing.

Modern British Columbia: Just as the history of British Columbia begins in **Victoria**, the capital is still the "first" city in the province for many. **The Parliament Build-** ings make an excellent place to begin a tour of this province. During the day two of the province's political parties — the New Democrats (NDP) and the Social Credit — use the forum of the Legislative Assembly to haggle with the Premier over public policy. This is probably the best introduction to British Columbia because you'll notice just how different it is politically from the other provinces. The two mainstream parties in Canada, the Liberals and the Conservatives, haven't held a seat in the provincial legislature since the 1970s. The reason is based on the history of the people who live here. Due to harsh confrontations between owners and workers in the small mines and logging camps of the 19th Century, the socialist movement gained a strong foothold in the body of the NDP. The Social Credit, the ruling party for years, is traditionally the party of small-town businessmen. Ironically the Social Credit usually win because the moderate left in B.C. find the NDP too radical; the left end up voting right. With intense debating going on within these walls instant relief can be found by joining people who still celebrate the British monarchy at the **Empress Hotel**. High tea is served daily reminding people that this was a former British colony.

Victoria's Parliament Buildings.

Another introduction to the various sides of **Vancouver Island** can be had by visiting the city's museums. **The British Columbia Provincial Museum** covers the history of the Province. Its Main Street Exhibit, for example, shows what life was like in 19th Century Victoria. There are also many interesting exhibits covering the natural history of the coast, the culture of its native inhabitants, and an excellent introduction to the explorers that brought Europe to this remote wilderness.

The city has several fine art collections—notably **The Art Gallery of Greater Victoria**, on Moss Street, and the **Maltwood Art Museum** on the campus of the **University of Victoria**. Both have collections of modern paintings and sculpture, as well as an important collection of oriental art: Tang and Ming Dynasty rugs at the Maltwood, and Japanese prints at the Art Gallery of Greater Victoria. There's also the **Emily Carr Gallery** which features one of Canada's most original painters. Her specialties include west coast landscapes and Indian villages.

Even though the sun only shines about half the days of the year in this part of the world, tourists would miss the greatest of the islands' offerings if too much time were spent indoors. To begin with, the whole province is a vast fisherman's paradise—saltwater and freshwater, game fishing and just plain good eating. All along the coast, but especially on Vancouver Island, the talk every summer will be of the salmon which flood the rivers on their way to spawn in the inland streams in which they were born. Many fishermen have traveled thousands of miles for a shot at the *Tyee*, or king salmon, monsters that grow to over four feet (over one meter), weigh more than 80 pounds (36 kilos), and, if one is hooked, can take hours to bring ashore. There are also trout and steelhead in freshwater, and saltwater offers tuna and cod, as well as crabs, clams, oysters and shrimp.

It is essential for everyone planning on fishing to get the proper licenses and to follow all regulations. The Canadian Ministry of Environment is quite serious about wildlife preservation, and enforces the regulations thoroughly.

Saltwater fishing literally surrounds travelers to the region but a trip to **Barkley Sound** on the west coast offers topnotch fishing, and the scenery of the **Pacific Rim National Park**. Here is an excellent view of the Pacific coast: rocky islands, sea lions playing in the crashing surf, harbor seals

The Empress Hotel.

hiding in the coves, and sea birds hovering above it all with ministerial grace.

The area also holds a wealth of backpacking opportunities. The **Broken Group Islands**, off the southwest coast of Vancouver Island, are accessible by boat, and the gorgeous Long Beach, has hiking trails and sunsets into the endless Pacific.

There's much to see on the **Gulf Islands**. Situated between Vancouver Island and Vancouver, there's a ferry that lets people get off and explore the area. The islands share the same climate as Victoria and artists and writers tend to make the area their home. Hardier backpackers have the opportunity to hike the "Life-Saving" Trail, from **Bamfield** to **Thrasher Cove**. The 50-mile (84-km) trail got its nickname when it was built to help shipwrecked victims find their way back to civilization through the densely forested shoreline. The trail offers views of gray whales, sea lions, seals, rock formations, two lighthouses, and good spots for surf-casting. This trail is a serious backpacker's dream–full of steep hills, narrow muddy trails, nearly impenetrable forests, and stretches along the beach that can only be traversed at low tide. More civilized backpacking is available in any of British Columbia's Provincial Park. They offer great views, invigorating exercise, and a closeness to nature that can make each tree seem like a unique experience in color. The best way to see the coast in all its glory is to take the trip on the **Prince Rupert Ferry**. Once the only way to get from Victoria to Prince Rupert or Alaska, it still makes the trip, leaving from **Port Hardy**, at the northern tip of Vancouver Island. On the way to Port Hardy stop at **Port McNeill** and take the short ferry to **Alert Bay** for an education into what is the most important art form in the Northwest: Indian wooden carvings, known to non-Indians as totem poles. Alert Bay is a Kwakiutl village, and the best place to see carvings is at their **U'mista Cultural Center**.

The carvings, in particular the poles, are statements of family identity, serving a purpose roughly similar to family crests in European culture. There is a great deal of status associated with the number of animals depicted, status that reflects on the person commissioning the carving (perhaps the leader's replacement). Poles stretching 30 feet (nine meters) into the air, blend from one animal to another, in shapes and characterizations that remind one of modern art. These animals influenced Picasso and other modern artists, a generation after the Indi-

A patriotic riverboat tours B.C.'s coastline.

ans carved them.

It is rare to find pre-20th Century sculptures still in Native ownership, but that is what one will see here, as well as recent sculptures in the new styles developed in the revival of carving that has taken place since the 1950s.

On a trip up the coast to **Prince Rupert** it is possible to visit a number of other sites where carving is practiced: more Kwakiutl sculpture at **Bella Bella** and **Kitimat**, Nishga work at **Kincolith**, north of Prince Rupert, and Tsimshian carvings in the area around **Kitwancool Lake**, northeast of Prince Rupert. Another ferry to the **Queen Charlotte Islands** will take travelers to see the work of the Haida at **Skidegate** and the beaches at **Sandspit**, where Indian legend says the ravern *Ne-kil-stlas* landed and began the propagation of the race.

Heading back inland from Prince Rupert the amount of open land becomes overwhelming to the eyes. Being surrounded on all sides by miles of unspoiled beauty might make it difficult to choose a direction.The choices are limited by the shortage of roads. Aside from the main East/West Highway (16), most of the roads are unpaved and no more than one and a half lanes wide (they were designed more for logging than for tourism). One of the longest and most beautiful of these heads north from **Terrace** and goes clear to the Alaska Highway near **Watson Lake**, Yukon, and offers side trips to **Mount Ediza Provincial Park** and the town of **Stewart**. From Stewart one can cross over to **Hyder**, Alaska. The road to Stewart passes through the Cambria snowfield and offers spectacular views of **Bear Glacier**.

There are literally thousands of lakes in Central B.C., and countless rivers and streams connecting them. Everything from moose and caribou to the bald eagle and the white Kermode bear can be seen here. The fishing offers both quantity and variety. The lakes to the south have rainbow-, lake- and brooke-trout, and the delicious Dolly Varden—a large salmon-like fish not as heavy as salmon, but meatier than trout. Farther north in the **Peace River Area** the fishing action turns to the Arctic grayling and the northern pike.

One wonderful stop in the northeast corner of the Province is the **Liard River Hot Springs Park** at Mile 493 of the Highway. The springs are naturally heated, slightly sulfurous pools of water, surrounded by orchids and tropical vines as thick as the northern forests just a few yards away. The

Female Dall sheep seen in northwest B.C. mountains.

232

water is over 110°F(42°C) and is so relaxing it is literally difficult to get up the steps out of the water. The pools are a favorite with the truckers that travel the Highway, and they recommend that one takes a nap before driving: the heat of the water can often make a motorist sleepy enough to drive off the road.

South of the Alaska Highway, around **Quesnel** and **Bowron Lake Provincial Park** travelers will find the history of the Cariboo Gold Rush. The streams and lakes along the Fraser River had been either played out or claimed by 1860, and the miners had driven farther north to Quesnel, discovering even richer finds around 1860. With the completion of the Cariboo Wagon Road in 1865, the area was made relatively accessible for wagons carrying supplies and new miners. The **Cariboo Highway** now follows roughly the same route as the old Cariboo Wagon Road. Ironically the completion of the road, as well as the exhaustion of easily panned gold, helped end the frontier phase of the gold rush and made way for more organized shaft-mining operations. While gold continued to be mined in quantity until the 1870s the romance was gone. Canadian and American miners were soon replaced by immigrant Chinese, and this

accounts for the Oriental flavor found along much of the coast of Canada.

The fact that the rush is over should not discourage tourists from trying their hand at panning for wealth. **Bowron Lake Park** is largely dedicated to educating tourists about that history, while allowing some modern-day prospecting on a small level. If spending several hours kneeling on rocks with hands in ice cold water, swishing mud around in a broken tin plate is someone's idea of a good time, there are many locals willing to offer advice and sell supplies. Two days panning should enable one to collect enough "dust" to buy a newspaper back in Vancouver. Tourists may find it more enjoyable to hike along the streams that have beds of raw jade stone, although the green stone might not be as impressive as the gold.

Organized camping is possible in the many Provincial Parks in this area. One of the largest is the **Wells Gray Provincial Park**. It has all the beauty that the rest of B.C. has shown, but is also a place where one can search for old homesteads abandoned by families that did not survive the 19th Century frontier days, or extinct volcanoes that are considerably older.

This is also British Columbia's cowboy

The majestic Rocky Mountains.

country, where most of the region's cattle industry is located. Here travelers are able to see the actual work of modern-day cowboys, in addition to helping the area celebrate the old glories with rodeos and horseback riding. The hub of much of this summer activity is **100 Mile House**. **Williams Lake** puts on one of the biggest rodeos in Canada; it's a show second only to the Calgary Stampede.

Continuing south and west, all roads begin to lead to **Vancouver**, but there is still plenty to see in the areas that border the U.S. For example, while Banff and Jasper in Alberta are more famous, there is no denying the beauty of the **British Columbia Rockies**, and the parks that capture it are well worth visiting: **Mount Robson Provincial Park** contains the highest point in the Canadian Rockies, while **Yoho** and **Glacier National Parks** have camping, skiing and gorgeous views of snowfields. Another favorite spot for skiing is the **Whistlers**. Canadians flock here year-round to race down their sides.

The towns near here, notably **Nelson**, grew up as supply routes to the gold miners and many original buildings are preserved. That's probably one reason why Nelson has served as a backdrop to a handful of feature films, among them Steve Martin's *Roxanne*. There are beautiful routes just to take a drive along. Highway 3, the "Crow's Nest Road," offers views of the Rockies and a few surviving gold mines.

As any traveler knows, highway travel has a way of lulling drivers and then shocking them awake with some incredible vista. Along these roads one will see an endless sea of forest suddenly give way to a snow-peaked mountain, or a broad sweep of valley. Highway 1 north from **Hope** to **Cache Creek** travels along the Fraser and Thompson rivers. Built by the Royal Engineers in the 1860s, the old Cariboo Wagon Road is now a modern highway, but it still goes through the **Fraser Canyon** and will give tourists some idea of the challenges facing the miners, as well as those that still face the salmon.

The more adventurous types, traveling in the summer, can try what was then a short cut: a route that bypassed the treacherous Fraser Canyon. The **Lillooet Shortcut** takes one around **Garibaldi Provincial Park**, along a logging road to Lillooet. Since no canoe could be counted on to survive the current of the Fraser River, this was the best way to get to the interior in the days before the Cariboo Road.

Nestled against the Rockies, Vancouver awakens.

Returning to civilization: Travelers will know that they are re-entering civilization when the subject of sports stops producing obscure lessons in fly tying, and begins producing curses against the New York Islanders (native hockey team of Long Island) and praise for the Vancouver Canucks.

The sporting life is as central to Vancouver as it is to the rest of British Columbia, but it has a different flavor. During the hockey season the sporting life centers around the **Forum**, home of the Vancouver Canucks of the National Hockey League. The beautiful bubble dome of the **British Columbia Place Stadium** is the home of the B.C. Lions of the Canadian Football League.

For many visitors and local residents, Vancouver's most important resource is the magnificent **Stanley Park**. The park has a six-mile (10-km) perimeter drive that offers a panoramic view of the sea, as well as the thousands of recreational boats and 256 cruise vessels that are docked regularly in the harbors. Vancouver is not only Canada's premier port, but it's also the most important port on the North American west coast. It is here that grain from the Prairies, and lumber, coal and sulphur from the interior of B.C., are shipped to Japan and elsewhere in the Pacific.

One of the highlights of the park is the **Aquarium**, located in the southeast corner of the park. This is more than a place to see a killer whale kiss a pretty volunteer on the nose, it is a serious center for the study of the sea. Watching the otters and seals play and cavort is glorious, whether seen in an aquarium or in nature, but seeing, a moment later, a great white shark devouring a huge piece of meat in the blink of an eye, gives an excellent view of the power and variety of the water life that covers three quarters of this planet.

In addition to the flesh and blood attractions of the Aquarium, Vancouver is filled with museums of history and fine art. Leading these is the **U.B.C. Museum of Anthropology**, which contains the greatest collection of Indian wood carvings in the world, including examples of totem poles created before the arrival of whites to the region, as well as contemporary work by living Indian sculptors. In a similar vein is the **Centennial Museum**, which traces back the history of the native peoples to the Stone Age, and includes exhibits on the history of white settlers and the modern history of the Province. The **Vancouver Art Gallery** has an impressive collection of the works of a famous Canadian artist, Emily Carr. There

are also many commercial galleries featuring the work of living local artists.

The theater season runs from September to June and offers every kind of performance. Traditional theater can be found at the **Queen Elizabeth Theater and Playhouse**, which houses two stages and several restaurants. The two Universities in the area feature modern theater by members of their drama departments, and amateur theater for the city has been collectivized under the **Metro Theatre**, where some 17 groups perform. Avant-garde theater is performed at the **Arts Club**, and outdoor theater is shown in Stanley Park's **Malkin Bowl** during the summer.

The real strength of the city, like any great city, is in its neighborhoods. These are the places where people and buildings are not just anonymous cogs in some swirling commercial mass, but where they take on a character of their own, and live out a culture unique to their block or avenue. Vancouver has several distinctive neighborhoods that give it this kind of life.

One of the most famous of these is **Gastown**, named after "Gassy" Jack Deighton, the area's premier barkeep. The area, which sprung up around a sawmill, and had little to do with gas but much to do with

A tourist at Liard Springs.

poverty, has now undergone a transformation similar to that of Cabbagetown in Toronto, or Greenwich Village in New York. The neighborhood gets its flavor more from craft and antique dealers than skid-row bars, and is a haven for all types of creativity: pottery, leatherwork, linens, a variety of crafts, and working artists. The **Robsonstrasse** district is another tale of a neighborhood's transformation. This time the new flavor was supplied by German immigrants who settled along Robson Street in the 1950s, but it took a more high-rise direction, as the West End of the city became a center of boutiques, restaurants and specialty stores. If tourists are interested in some old-world cooking, or in purchasing items from all over the world that may not be available in one place anywhere else, this is the place to go and browse on a warm afternoon.

Eaters will not want to miss the **Granville Island Public Market**, where food is the main ingredient in the restoration of an abandoned warehouse section. It is now something of a phenomenon for cities to turn sections where industry once thrived into giant restaurant centers (such permanent food festivals can be found in New York, Boston, Philadelphia, San Francisco,

Baltimore and Seattle). Aside from restaurants there are art galleries, boutiques, theaters and hotels.

The king of neighborhoods in this much varied city is **Chinatown**, home for many of the 45,000 Asians in Vancouver. It's the second largest Chinatown in North America, falling just behind San Francisco. While it offers a diversity of shopping for everything from cooking supplies to artworks, the main attraction is the food. In most of the restaurants the food is served *dim sum* style, which involves waiters and waitresses taking around trays of small dainty dishes, which one can select from or pass up. The bill for the meal is based on the number of dishes on a table when diners call for the check. This is a bit more expensive than the more communal atmosphere to which some people may be accustomed to (where the entire table orders and shares from central plates), but it does provide an unlimited variety of tastes.

There is yet another side to the Asian community: Chinese immigrants helped keep the gold rush going when white frontiersmen had lost interest and left for home, and their contribution to the construction of the Canadian Pacific Railroad is something for which they can be justly proud. Another

Taking advantage of the sun on English Bay.

chapter of the experience of Asians in Canada can be seen in the Japanese fishing village of **Steveston**, just south of Vancouver. In 1887 a single Japanese fisherman came to this tiny town for the annual salmon season. The abundance of his catch was such that 40 years later there were 3,000 Japanese in the village. These were mostly fishermen supporting families back in Japan, though more and more women were arriving to work in canneries. The Canadian government feared that this new community would displace the white fishing industry, and began placing quotas on the number of fishing permits allowed to Japanese immigrants.

This subculture was dealt its most severe blow when the Canadian Government began forcibly evacuating Japanese families from coastal areas during World War Two. Virtually the entire village of Steveston was evacuated, and all their boats and fishing equipment confiscated. Many people were moved inland, some of them 2,000 miles to Northern Ontario. After the war they were freed, and many did return to Steveston to again try to make a living without going to work for white men.

Continuing southeast from Vancouver, the geography begins to change slightly.

The rainfall is less frequent, there are arid hills and even sagebrush. Believe it or not this is Canada's best known fruit belt — the **Okanagan Valley**. Lake water is used for irrigation but when that is combined with huge amounts of sunshine it creates a lush garden. Apples, peaches, plums, grapes, cherries, apricots and pears, are all grown here in abundance. The area is also known for its wine-making, sandy beaches and lakes. In other words, it's a popular resort area. Some favorite spots for travelers are **Penticton** between Lake Okanagan and Lake Skaha, and **Kelowna**. Kelowna is the marketing center for the Okanagan and is famous for its **International Regatta** held in August.

British Columbia does seem to be a virtual Garden of Eden, a paradise for people attracted to a more leisurely lifestyle. Mountain climbing, hiking, skiing and boating can be done almost anywhere throughout the province that has countless mountains, parks and lakes. The area has also attracted a diverse group of cultures: the Haida, Nishga, Tsimshian and Kwakiutl Indians; the Japanese and Chinese; and the Irish and Scots. All of these groups and countless others have combined to create the human landscape of British Columbia.

Left, handcarved house posts from Comox; and right, starting a new trend in Vancouver's Chinatown.

ALBERTA

If a province could walk, Alberta would swagger just a bit, chest out, chin up, eyes fixed firmly on the future. And why not? It has the best of the West: fertile farmland; oil, gas and coal in abundance; exciting cities like Calgary and Edmonton; and the incomparable blue Canadian Rockies for a playground.

Albertans exuberantly inform the rest of the country about the virtues of their province, and their pride sounds to some Canadians like flat-out American bragging. The petroleum industry, which fueled Alberta's tremendous economic growth in the 1970s, was founded mostly by American oilmen. Their can-do spirit, essential in a business that rewards risktakers, seems to have rubbed off on everyone else.

Oil rich Alberta: Rancher John Lineham didn't risk much when he sank a well in 1920 among the oil seepage pools along **Cameron Creek** in the southwest corner of the province. Kutenai Indians had been using the oil for centuries as a balm to heal wounds. Lineham's well, the first in Western Canada, produced 300 barrels a day until the flow ebbed after four years. The site of **Discovery Well** is marked with a cairn in **Waterton Lakes National Park**.

The park's landscape changes abruptly from rolling grasslands to snowcapped peaks chiseled by Ice Age glaciers. Boat tours on the Lakes pass many of the park's outstanding glacier-carved formations, including hanging valleys high up mountain walls. A hiking trail winds through **Red Rock Canyon**, streaked with the red, purple, green, and yellow of mineral deposits; another path leads to **Cameron Lake**, a blue gem set in a bowl-shaped valley. Retreating glaciers also left a flat-topped site now occupied by the **Prince of Wales Hotel**, a 100-room chalet-style resort that looks down the broad valley of Waterton Lakes.

Canada's only Mormon temple, a white marble edifice built in 1913, gleams in the Prairie sun at **Cardston**, founded by Charles Ora Card, a son-in-law of Brigham Young. It is currently undergoing renovation. When it reopens visitors can tour the grounds

and Card's 1887 cabin. An information center explains more about this group, which emigrated from Utah in 1897. The Mormons developed Canada's first major irrigation project soon after their arrival. They dug 60 miles (96 km) of canals out from the St. Mary's River, and grew bumper crops of sugar beets, corn, potatoes and other vegetables.

Less desirable American immigrants were the traders who came up from Montana in the 1870s to swap furs and buffalo hides with the Indians for a shot of rot-gut whiskey. **Fort Macleod** was built in 1874 and manned with Mounties who halted the degrading trade. The fort museum tells about daily life around the post; interpretive guides dressed in 1870s Mountie uniforms parade on horseback.

Japanese memorials: Fort Whoop-up was the first and most notorious of the whiskey forts the Mounties put out of business. A reconstruction stands in **Indian Battle Park** near **Lethbridge**, a prosperous city set in a coulee of the Oldman River. Local boosters claim Lethbridge gets 4,000 hours of sunshine a year, more than any other Canadian city. The town's role in a dark chapter

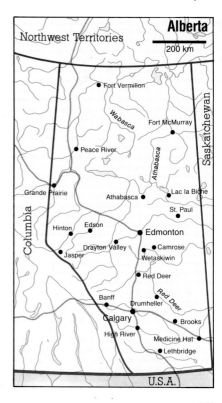

of the country's history is brightened somewhat by the **Nikka Yuko Centennial Garden**, a serene oasis of water, rocks and willows. The garden was built by the city in 1967 to remember the 6,000 Japanese-Canadians who were interned here during World War Two.

The **Alberta Badlands**, once part of a subtropical swamp that sheltered a vast array of prehistoric life, contain one of the world's finest respositories of dinosaur fossils. The most spectacular badlands are preserved along the Red Deer River in **Dinosaur Provincial Park**, selected as one of UNESCO's World Heritage Sites. From a lookout near the park entrance, visitors can survey 7,000 acres (2,830 hectares) of this gnarled sandstone landscape with its weirdly eroded formations. A circular three-mile drive with sidetrips on foot leads to dinosaur bones preserved where they were found. Other areas of the park are accessible on organized bus tours and hikes.

Farther north, the town of **Drumheller** lies deep within the badlands, which drop abruptly here below the lip of the prairie. The sheer unexpectedness of the scene shocks the eye and delights the imagination. A 32-mile (50-km) circular drive called the **Dinosaur Trail** takes motorists from the impressive new **William Tyrrell Museum of Paleontology** (one of the best collections of dinosaur fossils in the world) up to the rim of the mile-wide valley. Highlights of the trip are the lookout at **Horsethief Canyon** and the **Bleriot Ferry**, one of the province's last cable ferries.

In the late 1970s, Pierre Trudeau reputedly remarked that Calgary looked like it had been unpacked just before you arrived. The Prime Minister's comment still applies to this young Prairie metropolis, the most dynamic city in the newly rich Canadian West. The glittering downtown canyons deepen monthly with new skyscrapers, suburbs continue to sprawl in all directions, and the city keeps boosting civic pride with public structures like the $75-million performing arts center, home of the Calgary Philharmonic, and the 17,000-seat **Saddledome**, where the hockey and skating competitions of the 1988 Winter Olympics took place.

Part of the price for this rapid growth is downtown congestion. Fortunately the city created a three-block pedestrian

The graveyard of the earth's ancient inhabitants: Dinosaur Park.

mall along Stephen Avenue, a civilized thoroughfare of two-story buildings and street-level shops, benches and wandering musicians.

Elevated promenades will further ease foot traffic. Nearly half the downtown core is connected by *Plus 15s* — skyways 15 feet (five meters) over the traffic that link new high-rises, shopping complexes and hotels. At an elevated indoor park called **Devonian Gardens**, office workers on their lunch break brown-bag it on benches scattered amid waterfalls, ponds and 130 species of greenery.

Rodeo days in Calgary: The slicker the city gets, the more it seems to revel in the down-home fun of the Calgary Stampede, the world's largest rodeo. For 10 days in early July residents of Canada's number-one cowtown don stetsons and cowboy boots and let loose at free flapjack breakfasts, square dancing and parades. The liveliest event on the **Exhibition Grounds** is chuck-wagon racing, not surprising since $290,000 in prize money is up for grabs.

Pioneer days are also relived at **Heritage Park**, a first-rate collection of reconstructed buildings and authentic structures gathered from all over the province. A vintage steam train tours the site, and a replica paddlewheeler plies the **Glenmore Reservoir**. Delve further into the past at the **Glenbow Museum**, which displays the best collections of Plains Indian artifacts in the world.

If Calgary's hectic pace becomes overwhelming, escape to **St. George's Island** in the Bow River, where picnickers and nature lovers share the woods with life-size reproductions of dinosaurs. The zoo itself contains more than 1,000 animal species.

Travelers heading for the mountains can get a taste of alpine adventure to come by ascending the 626-foot-high (190-meters) **Calgary Tower**. Below is the city, all 162 sq miles (420 sq km) of it, and to the west, the serrated ridge of the **Rockies,** much of it protected by national and provincial parks.

Kananaskis Provincial Park contains foothills, mountains, ice caps and sparkling lakes. Dirt-bike trails thread its forests, fishermen try their luck in dozens of prime trout streams, and downhill skiers challenge the slopes at **Fortress Mountain**, site of skiing events

"Hangin' in there" at the rodeo.

for the 1988 Winter Olympics. One of the best ways to enjoy the Kananaskis is to stay at a guest ranch like **Rafter Six** or the **McKenny Homeplace Ranch**, where greenhorns work up mountain-size appetites on trail rides, hiking trips and then satisfy them with filling home-cooked fare.

Jewel of the Rockies: Crown jewel of the Rockies, **Banff National Park** has some of the continent's finest mountain scenery within its confines along the eastern flank of the continental divide. The park was founded a century ago as Canada's first national preserve to protect hot springs just outside the present-day town of **Banff.** The **Cave and Basin Hot Springs Centennial Center**, opened in time for the park's 100th anniversary, lures visitors to its mineral-rich waters, reputedly good for gout and rheumatism. Bathers can rent old-fashioned tank suits for dips in a swimming pool fed by the hot springs. The 1887 bathhouse has been reconstructed and a tea house serves refreshments.

A gondola ride up **Sulphur Mountain** ends at a summit tea-house where mountain sheep are often seen snuffling for snacks. A ski tow up **Mount Nor-**

quay also affords panoramas of Banff's encircling peaks. Jutting above the trees are the granite spires of the **Banff Springs Hotel**, a 600-room Scottish baronial castle, complete with kilted pipers and a hinth-floor ghost. Sunday brunch here has long been a popular outing.

The summer sidewalks of Banff are crowded. Strollers browse in the dozens of gift shops or munch on delights from **Ye Olde Fudgery.** Mexican food seems to suit mountain appetites at inexpensive eateries like the **Magpie and Stump.**

To escape the crowds, wander the grounds of the **Banff Center,** an advanced conservatory of fine arts, music and drama. In this Salzburg of the Rockies a summerlong Festival of the Arts showcases opera, dance, musical theater and jazz.

Lake Louise, a jade gem set against the backdrop of Victoria Glacier, is one of the Rockies' most famous beauty spots. A Scottish piper wanders among the flower beds and the pines on the grounds of **Chateau Lake Louise**; the echo of his skirling resounds from surrounding peaks. Romantics rent canoes

The tranquil Rockies peer into Morraine Lake in Banff.

and swoon and sigh as they stroke about the lake. Athletic types hike the two-mile (three-km) trail to **Lake Agnes** to yet another tea house, this one perched near the top of a waterfall.

The junction of the Trans-Canada Highway and State 93 is the starting point of the **Icefields Parkway**, one of the world's great mountain drives. The beauty of Lake Louise is challenged within 25 miles (40 km) by **Peyto Lake**, set in the **Mistaya River Valley**. A platform at the end of a half-mile trail off the parking lot affords unobstructed views of the lake, 800 feet (240 meters) below.

Mother of three rivers: The Parkway continues north in the valley of the Mistaya (Cree for "grizzly"), then follows the braided channels of the North Saskatchewan River to the Rockies' apex: the **Columbia Icefield**, at 126 sq miles (326 sq km) the biggest ice cap in the range. This "mother of rivers" feeds three great systems, the Columbia, the Athabasca and the Saskatchewan. **Athabasca Glacier**, one of dozens that flow from Columbia's bowl of ice, extends almost to the parkway. A rubber-tired *Sno-coach* takes visitors out on this great expanse of ice, past pressure ridges, meltwater channels and blue-walled crevasses.

Farther north, the Parkway enters **Jasper National Park**, largest in the Rockies. Take the scenic alternate route, State 93A, along the west bank of the Athabasca River to Athabasca Falls, which thunder over a 100-foot-high (30-meters) ledge and hurtle through a narrow canyon. A self-guiding trail along the gorge provides close-ups of the violent beauty of the powerful cataract. Nearby **Mount Edith Cavell**, a snow-covered dome of rock rising sheer from **Angel Glacier** is another "must-see" in the park. A hiking trail climbs into alpine meadows spangled with wildflowers; another path wanders across the boulder-strewn outwash of the glacier.

The town of **Jasper**, smaller and quieter than Banff, is the starting point for dozens of scenic hiking trails, bicycle routes and driving tours. A sky tram whisks sightseers to the stony summit of **The Whistlers**, an 8,000-foot (2,400-meter) peak. From its summit, you can glimpse on clear days the solitary tip of the highest peak in the Rockies, Mount Robson, 48 miles (77 km) northwest in British Columbia.

Jasper's answer to the Banff Springs Hotel is the more rustic **Jasper Park Lodge**, a cluster of 50 chalets along the shores of **Lac Beauvert**. Room service comes on a bicycle, bears have been known to commandeer the lawns, and a moose once took over a water hazard on the golf course for two months. And yes, there is a piper. He performs at a sunset flag-lowering ceremony that has been held every summer since 1826.

En route to Edmonton, take a side-trip to the **Miette Hot Springs**, hottest in the Rockies. The waters are cooled to 102 degrees Fahrenheit (39 Celsius) before being fed into a huge swimming pool. Guest ranches scattered through this region include the renowned **Black Cat Guest Ranch** off State 40.

Travelers reluctantly leave the Rockies behind as they head east through the parklands and forests of northern Alberta. Hearty fare like Russian borscht and Ukrainian cabbage rolls from the Homesteader's Kitchen at the **Stony Plain Multicultural Center** may take the edge off the disappointment. On Saturdays, don't miss the farmers' market for a sample of other

At the top of the world, Whistler Mountain.

regional food.

Edmonton: The provincial capital and Canada's most northerly metropolis, Edmonton is a world-class city with all the superlatives to back it up: the **West Edmonton Mall**, largest in North America, with an astounding 800 stores, 110 restaurants and the world's largest indoor amusement park; the **Citadel Theater,** Canada's largest; the **Space Sciences Center**, home of the nation's largest planetarium and the western world's largest Zeiss-Jenastar projector. And don't forget the **Brick Warehouse**, which sells more furniture than any other store in the world.

Oil deals are made at the head offices in Calgary; the actual work of turning black gold into more useful commodities, like gasoline and diesel, occurs in Edmonton. The city flexes its industrial muscle along **Refinery Row**, a glittering galaxy of lights, tubing, giant storage tanks and gas flares that light up the night sky like a scene from a science fiction movie. The Row produces 10 percent of the nation's petrochemical products.

But Edmonton is no blue-collar town. In fact, it seems more sophisticated in some ways than its southern rival, where the backyard mountains attract lots of outdoorsy types more interested in backpacking than Bach. Seat of provincial government and home of the **University of Alberta**, Edmonton has opera and classical ballet companies, a symphony orchestra and several professional theater groups. Why, crystal chandeliers even adorn a couple of subway stations!

Klondike days: All this refinement disappears for 10 days in July beneath sourdough stubble, battered hats and checked shirts as the city gets grizzled during Klondike Days, a 10-day revival of the tempestuous 1890s Klondike Gold Rush. False storefronts sprout in the city center, roulette tables spin at the Silver Slipper Saloon on the Exhibition Grounds, a flotilla of bathtubs, barrels and home-made houseboats float downstream on the North Saskatchewan River during the Sourdough Raft Race, and downtown streets become pedestrian malls so Edmontonians can stroll about in their Klondike finery during the Sunday Promenade. Contests ranging from rock lifting to log chopping are held to determine the

Rising from the plains: the city of Edmonton.

King of the Klondike.

An outdoor museum beside the river, **Fort Edmonton Park** is perhaps a clearer window on the past. Thirty-five buildings along three small-town streets recapture the flavor of three separate eras: 1885, 1905 and 1920. Old Strathcona, the city's original commercial district, preserves along its narrow streets early Edmonton structures like the **Old Firehall**, the **Strathcona Hotel** and the **Klondike Cinema**. The **Old Strathcona Foundation** distributes free walking-tour maps of the neighborhood, which is also the site of the colorful Fringe Theater Event in August. This nine-day festival attracts performers from all over North America and Europe. The streets echo with mime music, puppet shows and plays. The Foundation also conducts a murder mystery tour.

Canada's largest urban greenbelt preserves 10 miles (16 km) of riverbank along the North Saskatchewan River, where you can hike, cycle, picnic and ride horseback. Guides at a nature center near Fort Edmonton conduct walks in all seasons. Four glass pyramids nestled in the valley house the **Muttart Conservatory**, a showcase of plants from the tropics to the deserts of the world.

The valley is also the site of a manmade wonder that expresses Alberta's exuberant spirit. As his contribution to the province's 75th anniversary celebrations in 1980, artist Peter Lewis installed a series of water pipes along the top of the **High Level Bridge**. Now, on civic holidays in summer, a tap is turned somewhere, and presto! water flows through the pipes, and the bridge becomes a waterfall.

Did the beautiful North Saskatchewan River Valley really need improvement? No, but maybe Lewis thought the hometown of the world's largest shopping mall could use a world-class waterfall. Or maybe it's just that when the Prairie dynamo known as Alberta starts to hum, it kicks off sparks that fire the imaginations of native and visitor alike.

Relations with the east: The Prairies once seemed like a land apart, cut off from the Pacific Coast by the mountains of British Columbia, isolated from the industrial heartland of Ontario and Québec by the Canadian Shield. But the region has come into its own econo-mically in the last 20 years, and now it wants its political day in the sun.

The West has long felt alienated from Eastern Canada, where most of the population – and, therefore, political power – resides. During the last government of Pierre Trudeau, the disaffected West elected only one member of parliament to the ruling Liberal Party. There were confrontations between the provinces and Ottawa over freight rates and farm support, creeping socialism, taxes and over-regulation of the oil industry. Talk of secession flared up again.

Separatist sentiment has cooled recently. The Prairies have weathered the recession that ended the economic boom of the 1970s, and are ready to grow again. The Conservative Party is in power in Ottawa with a full slate of Western members to voice the concerns of the region in national debate. People in Manitoba, Saskatchewan and Alberta feel confident, and why not. After all, they've only got oil and gas and coal, beef and grain and timber, money and optimism and courage. This is no longer Next Year Country; next year is now.

SASKATCHEWAN

A hush falls over the crowd as the solemn jurors return to the courtroom with their verdict. They pass the dock where the defendant Louis Riel kneels in prayer, clutching his ball and chain. Riel has been charged with high treason for leading the Métis people in rebellion against the Crown. Dressed all in black, moccasins on his feet, Riel rises to meet his fate.

The clerk of the court asks the foreman if the jury members are agreed upon their verdict. The foreman rises and bows. "They are."

"How say you: Is the prisoner guilty or not guilty?"

"Guilty."

The foreman asks the judge for leniency but the judge passes his sentence: Riel will hang.

This scene from *The Trial of Louis Riel,* a play by John Coulter, is re-enacted three times a week in summer in the ornate ballroom of **Regina's Government House**, once the official residence of the Lieutenant Governor of Saskatchewan. Three times a week the jury finds Riel guilty beyond a reasonable shadow of doubt. But a century after his trail, many people in Saskatchewan still aren't sure what to make of the evangelical-like Louis Riel.

Riel and the Métis: Traitor to some, hero to others, the charismatic Métis twice tried to defend the rights of his people, the mixed-blood offspring of Indian mothers and French fur-trading fathers. In 1869 he established a provisional Métis government in Manitoba, an ill-fated experiment in self-determination that ended when the Canadian militia marched West and put down the insurrection. Riel fled to Montana, where he lived quietly for a decade teaching school.

Then in 1884 federal agents began surveying traditional Métis lands in the Saskatchewan River Valley in preparation for the coming of white settlers. Métis leaders again called on Riel, who returned to Canada to lead a ragtag army against the Canadian militia. The Métis' brief uprising ended in defeat at Batoche in June, 1885. Riel was tried in July in Regina, and was hanged in November. Transcripts from his trial

form the basis of Coulter's play.

Saskatchewan has a hard time with heroes, especially a fiery, French-speaking Catholic who once called himself "Prophet, Infallible Pontiff and Priest King." That sort of talk delayed his acceptance as an authentic folk hero for about 80 years; this province demands humility even from its hockey stars.

Saskatchewan's longtime indifference to Riel and his botched uprising has been due in part to another tragedy that looms larger in Prairie hearts and minds: 10 lost years called the Depression, when a generation saw its dreams blown away with the topsoil. This land, so rich with its promise, so fickle with its bounty, became Next Year Country, and nurtured a cautious people equally skeptical about the pronouncements of politicians and the fiery rhetoric of a Métis mystic like Riel.

The thirties will color provincial perceptions as long as anyone who lived through the era is alive, maybe even longer. But in addition to a bitter crop of pessimism, that experience also produced sturdy self-reliance. Take **Regina**, for example, provincial capital

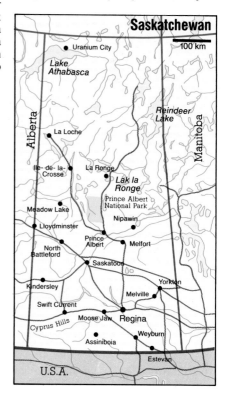

Left, Cypress Hills cowboy, Saskatchewan.

and Queen City of the Plains. Its less-than-regal setting prompted Sir John A. Macdonald, Canada's first Prime Minister, to remark in 1886: "If you had a little more wood, and a little more water, I think the prospect would be improved."

Landscaping Regina: When Regina was named capital of the newly formed province of Saskatchewan in 1905, city leaders took Macdonald's suggestion of "more wood" to heart. They dammed muddy Wascana Creek to create a small lake, erected the Legislative Building nearby, planted trees, laid out formal gardens, and splashed it all with fountains, including one from London's Trafalgar Square.

The result was **Wascana Center**, still an oasis of woods and water. A ride through the 2,300-acre (930-hectare) park on a double-decker bus is a fine way to see the sights. Cyclists and joggers circle the lake, picnickers ride a 50-cent ferry out to shady **Willow Island**, and bird-lovers feed the Canada geese at the waterfowl sanctuary. You can also admire the Egyptian sculpture in the **University of Regina**'s art gallery, or listen to orators pontificate at **Speaker's Corner**.

In late July, Wascana Center is the scene of a Sunday picnic that kicks off a week of horse racing, rodeo riding and entertainment known as Buffalo Days. Regina saloons like **Shooter's** on Broad Street haul out the stetsons and the wagon wheels to get patrons in a festive, pioneer and uniquely "western" spirit.

Once headquarters for the **Royal Canadian Mounted Police** (1882-1920), Regina is still home of Depot Division, a training center where all recruits endure a combination of boot camp and police academy. Visitors can watch rookies march smartly across the parade square at 1 p.m. daily. Displays in the museum here recound legendary Mountie exploits like the Lost Patrol and villains like the Mad Trapper of Rat River. Prized artifacts include handcuffs worn by Riel and the Crucifix he carried to his execution (the site of the gallows is just outside the museum).

Regina's **Museum of Natural History**, one of the finest in Canada, provides an excellent introduction to the province's flora and fauna. Dioramas show stampeding bison, frisking Prairie

Original jury that condemned Louis Riel to death.

dogs, bugling wapiti, as well as ducks, geese and pelicans, all in recreated natural settings.

Wide and open prairies: To the northwest of Regina the **Qu'Appelle River Valley** is a welcome change from the Queen City in topography and tempo. Carved by glacial meltwaters, this verdant furrow in the brown prairie divides the flat and open plains to the south and rolling parkland to the north.

The valley is best appreciated from State 56 where it flanks the **Fishing Lakes** – four broadenings in the Qu'Appelle River. **Echo Valley** and **Katepwa** provincial parks offer camping, fishing, swimming and nature trails that wind through wooded ravines. Other diversions in the area include tours of the **Hansen-Ross Pottery Studio** and a visit to the **Sacred Heart Church**, set high on a hillside. Weekend concerts at the summer art school in **Fort San** are open to the public.

Unfortunately, Hiway 56 doesn't continue through the valley east of the Fishing Lakes. Motorists must jog south to the Trans-Canada, head east to 47, then re-enter the valley on 247. Here, the Qu'Appelle is even more secluded,

and steep enough for a ski run at **Last Oak Park.** A roadside interpretive display describes a 1,000 year-old burial mound commanding a lovely view of **Crooked** and **Round** lakes; the setting is as peaceful today as it was a millennium ago.

Eastern spires crown many churches northeast of the Qu'Appelle, testifying to the predominance of Ukrainian settlers. In **Yorkton,** a stroll through the **Western Development Museum** reveals household scenes of early settlers. A colorful Ukrainian pioneer kitchen, brightened with ceramic tiles and embroideries, contrasts with an austere English parlor. In August the museum sponsors the Threshermen's Show, with wagon rides, threshing competitions and square dancing.

British eccentricity: Eccentricity is an old Saskatchewan tradition, and no flakes were more flamboyant than the English aristocrats who tried to recreate a corner of their sceptered isle on the bald-headed Prairie at **Cannington Manor,** now an historic park. Here, in 1882, Captain Edward Pierce established a manorial village, where blue bloods bred racehorses, baited badgers

Embracing a lawn of flowers, Regina's legislative buildings.

with bull terriers, played rugby and cricket, and hired immigrants to do the farming.

When the railroad bypassed Cannington, the settlement became a ghost town. Still standing are the **Maltby** and **Hewlett** houses, a carpenter's shop, and **All Saints Church** (its chalice was once used as a racing trophy). Beside the log church, beneath the cottonwoods, is the grave of Pierce, far from his beloved England.

Despite its name, nearby **Moose Mountain Provincial Park** is a favorite with bird-watchers who scan the skies for turkey vultures, teal, ducks and dozens of other species. There's also horseback riding through forested uplands, fishing and camping.

The Badlands: At the turn of the century, the **Big Muddy Badlands** south of Regina sheltered a loosely knit community every bit as strange as Cannington Manor. Outlaws like Bloody Knife and the Pigeon Toed Kid hid out in caves between cattle rustling raids on Montana ranchers, just a gallop away across the U.S. border. On two weekends in July, guided auto tours start in the town of **Big Beaver** and wind through the badlands, past outlaw hideouts and a 1902 Mountie post.

After a while, the pancake-flat Prairie produces a yearning for anything higher than just a gopher mound. **St. Victor Petroglyphs Park** satisfies that need with a weirdly eroded sandstone outcrop, where prehistoric Indians carved dozens of designs in the soft rock. The outcrop also affords a panorama of chessboard crops, alkali lakes, escarpments and brightly painted grain elevators, those "cathedrals of the plains" which give prairie towns their distinctive (and only) skylines.

South-central Saskatchewan is the province's predominantly French-speaking region, so don't be surprised to overhear conversations *en français* in the **St. Victor** beer parlor. Nearby **Willow Bunch**, an attractive town nestled in the flank of Wood Mountain, was the birthplace of Edouard Beaupré, an eight-foot (2.4-meter) giant who won renown with P.T. Barnum's circus. A museum displays his oversize bed and clothing. (For picnics in the shade, try the regional park, set in a well-treed coulee southwest of town.)

From west of **Gravelbourg** to the

Left, bidding visitors adieu at Farewell's Trading Post. Right, Mountie barracks at Fort Walsh.

Alberta border, the plains begin to buckle into uplands. **Wood Mountain** briefly became a refuge to Sitting Bull and his band of Sioux after the Battle of Little Big Horn in 1876. The barracks and mess hall of a Mountie post established to watch over the Sioux have been recreated in the **Wood Mountain Historic Park**.

The **Cypress Hills** are one of the few parts of Western Canada left uncovered by Ice Age glaciers. The hills rise like a long, green wedge near **Eastend** and extend 60 miles (96 km) west into Alberta. This oasis of coniferous forests, cool valleys and rounded buttes has long been a refuge for travelers on the hot and dusty plains. Roads in the park wind through forests of aspen and lodgepole pine and pastures rippling with fescue grass. Campgrounds, cabins, tennis, golf and skiing are all available at **Loch Leven**.

There is history here too, at **Fort Walsh**, built by the North West Mounted Police in 1875 to eradicate the illicit whiskey trade to Plains Indians, who swapped buffalo hides for swigs of a vile concoction that was one part alcohol and three parts water, colored with tobacco juice and spiced with Jamaica ginger. The recreated fort shelters the officers' quarters, commissioner's residence and other buildings. A few miles away, **Farewell's Trading Post** is staffed with guides in 1870s dress, and stocked with whiskey kegs and patent medicine.

North of Cypress Hills the "Old Cow Town" of **Maple Creek** drowses beneath its canopy of cottonwoods. Capital of bone-dry ranchland, Maple Creek is about as Old West as Saskatchewan gets. The lobby of the hotel on the main drag looks like a set from a western movie. The **Old Timers' Museum**, with its Indian artifacts and 1890 fire engine is worth a visit.

Moose Jaw's raucous past: Sheltered in a broad valley, **Moose Jaw** is a quiet town with a raucous past. In the 1920s, bootleggers and brothels flourished along **River Street**, and Chicago gangsters on the lam cooled their heels here until the heat died down back home. Most of the excitement today comes in May when the Kinsmen Band Competition attracts 5,000 musicians from across the continent. In June, the Canadian Forces, Snowbirds host an air show

Indications of the transcendent over the Prairies.

at their base. Moose Jaw's branch of the **Western Development Museum** emphasizes early transportation with biplanes, antique autos and a steam locomotive.

Temperance in Saskatoon: Bootleggers never darkened the streets of **Saskatoon**, founded in 1884 as a temperance colony, a legacy that endures only in the sign for **Temperance Avenue**. The city's best feature is the **South Saskatchewan River**, which flows between high, wooded banks protected from development by parks. The summer cruise boat *Northcote* passes riverside landmarks like the turreted **Bessborough Hotel**, the **Mendel Art Gallery and Conservatory** and the graystone buildings of the **University of Saskatchewan**.

The university gives Saskatoon a cultural and cosmopolitan cachet. Five theater groups and a symphony orchestra perform here, and restaurants that border on the bohemian by Saskatchewan standards — **Mad Mary's**, **Cousin Nik's**, the **St. Tropez Bistro** — are popular with those who think young.

The city commemorates Louis Riel in its own peculiar way with the Louis Riel Relay Race, in which about 30 teams canoe, run and ride horseback to a finish line on the riverbank. The contest initiates the city's July exhibition **Pioneer Days**, a weeklong potpourri of rodeo events, tractor pulls, even a demolition derby with combines. Fairgoers can ride to the nearby **Western Development Museum** in a covered wagon. The museum's centerpiece is **Boomtown 1910**, a complete indoor prairie community with 22 buildings and staff in pioneer costume.

North of Saskatoon, on a high bluff commanding a mighty bend of the South Saskatchewan River, the Métis made their last stand during the Northwest Rebellion of 1885. The only remains of the Métis "capital" at **Batoche** are a simple white church which served as Louis Riel's headquarters and a bullet-scarred rectory. Look for holes above the door, reputedly the work of a Gatling gun fired by a U.S. Army captain who had received permission from Canadian officials to test the new weapon on the Métis. Panels beside the remains of trenches dug by Canadian militia high on the riverbank explain the Battle of Batoche; Métis rifle pits can still be seen, despite years of ploughing.

Fortress on the plains.

A few miles west stands palisaded **Fort Carlton**, once the most important fur-trade depot between the Red River and the Rockies. Torched during the Métis uprising, the restored fort is stocked with fur-trade items and memorabilia from the rebellion.

Fifty miles (80 km) northeast of this battle-scarred valley is **Prince Albert,** gateway to the province's northlands, famous among fishermen for pristine lakes and record-size trout. Prince Albert is also home to **Lund's Wildlife Exhibit,** where hundreds of Canadian animals and birds are mounted in recreations of their natural habitats. The **Heritage Museum** details the city's development; while there, visit the tearoom, where you can munch home-baked cakes on a sun deck and watch the **North Saskatchewan** glide by.

Parks and forts: Straddling a transition zone between parkland and boreal forest is **Prince Albert National Park.** Pines scent the air of **Waskesiu Lake**, park headquarters, attractive year-round resort town and home port of the popular paddlewheeler *Neo-Watin*. This excursion boat makes hour-long cruises around the lake; sailboats and

fishing boats are also available at the townsite. The nature center introduces visitors to the park's flora and fauna. The most popular hikes here are the **Mud Creek** and **Boundary Bog** trails (both take about an hour to walk) and the **Tree Beard Trail**, which passes a stand of 150-year-old trees − veritable Methuselahs in this fire-prone forest.

Southwest of the park, the twin cities of **North Battleford** and **Battleford** flank the North Saskatchewan. Battleford, former capital of the Northwest Territories, occupies a wooded setting far superior to that of its successor, Regina. The **Battleford National Historic Park**, a Mountie post where Canada's last public execution took place in 1885, contains officers' quarters and residences, and other restored buildings.

But the fort's most poignant artifact again recalls Riel, whose ghost seems to haunt every corner of the province. For there in the interpretive center stands the Gatling gun used in the Battle of Batoche. The weapon's brass gleams, as polished and shiny as it was a century ago, when the dreams of a Métis nation died on a high bluff above South Saskatchewan River.

MANITOBA

After driving endless miles through the forests of northern Ontario, a traveler coming from Eastern Canada is likely to find Manitoba bursting upon the senses with space and light and color. The land, no longer bound by a corridor of ragged trees, rolls on and on to a distant horizon. The sky, once confined to a gray strip above the highway, expands into a dome of deep blue. Ah, thinks the traveler, the Prairie at last.

Well, yes and no. The boreal forest is close by, blanketing the northern two-thirds of Manitoba with a lake-dotted wilderness that remains virtually unpopulated. And the sunny south refutes the old equation of Prairie equals flat. West of Whiteshell Provincial Park, the land rises in stone and gravel ridges, flattens around Winnipeg, turns marshy south of Lake Manitoba, dips into the wide valleys of the Pembina and Assiniboine rivers, then rises again in a series of western uplands.

The towns and cities are as varied as the land, and herein lies Manitoba's special appeal, the thing that makes it so different from, say, neighboring Saskatchewan. Settlers from Europe and Eastern Canada established towns with character, not just supply centers for surrounding farmers, and proudly added their ethnic flavor: French-Canadians at Ste. Anne, Icelanders at Gimli, Russians at Tolstoi.

Winnipeg: The vigor of these communities is remarkable considering the overwhelming presence of **Winnipeg**, provincial capital and home to 600,000 people, more than half of Manitoba's population. No other province is so dominated by one city.

Winnipeg looks similar to other Western Canadian cities, although there's no mistaking the junction of Portage and Main, reputedly the widest, windiest, coldest street corner in Canada. But downtown avenues curve with the Assiniboine and Red rivers, giving some buildings delightfully quirky angles and avoiding the West's usual rigid street grid. Leafy residential areas, originally separate towns, are much more distinctive than the tract-housing communities that homogenize much of the suburban West. They also contain

outstanding greenswards like **Assiniboine Park**, with its excellent zoo and tropical conservatory, and **Kildonan Park**, designed by Frederick Law Olmsted, architect of New York's Central Park. Kildonan is home to the 2,300-seat **Rainbow Stage**, where musicals and plays are presented outdoors.

Old city in a young land: Winnipeg is also an old city in a young land. The first Europeans to build on this site were French fur traders who constructed Fort Rouge in 1738 near the flood-prone confluence of the Red and the Assiniboine rivers, silt-laden waterways which eventually gave the city its Cree name of *Winni-nipi* (muddy water).

After the French came those fierce fur-trade rivals, the London-based Hudson's Bay Company and the North West Company of Montréal. During the late 18th and early 19th centuries, the two companies built a series of palisaded forts within shooting distance near the Assiniboine and the Red.

Then in 1812, Scottish crofters who had been turned out of their homes by the Highland Clearances, arrived on the scene with a few farming implements

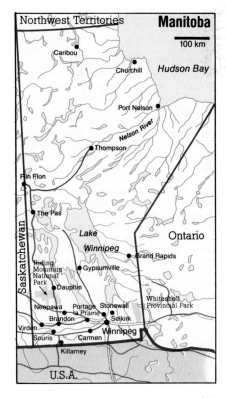

and a bull and a cow named Adam and Eve. The trip, tools and livestock were courtesy of Scottish humanitarian Lord Selkirk, who established farming colonies throughout North America for homeless Highlanders.

But like cattle ranchers and sheep farmers, fur traders and settlers don't mix. The conflict between the two ways of life erupted on June 19, 1816, when Métis (half-breed) employees of the North West Company slaughtered 20 settlers in what became known as the Seven Oaks Massacre.

Lord Selkirk heard the bad news in Montréal, and promptly marched West with a private army of veterans from the War of 1812. He arrested the fur traders and their Métis employees, then reestablished his settlement, which eventually prospered despite floods, Prairie fires and grasshopper plagues.

There are several reminders of the fur-trade era in Winnipeg, in addition to the ubiquitous historic plaques. **Grant's Old Mill** is a working replica of the settlement's first gristmill, built in 1829 by Cuthbert Grant, leader of the Métis at the massacre. (Visitors to the mill can buy freshly ground wholewheat flour.)

The **Seven Oaks House** and the **Ross House**, both built in the 1850s by fur traders, are museums worth visiting, as is the **Manitoba Museum of Man and Nature**. Its most impressive fur-trade display is a full-size replica of the *Nonsuch,* a Hudson's Bay Company vessel that in 1669 brought the first cargo of furs from Canada to England.

But the most evocative relic of this exciting era is the lone remaining gate of **Upper Fort Garry**, built by the Hudson's Bay Company in 1835, and now preserved in a quiet park in the shadow of the turreted **Hotel Fort Garry**. This was once the center of the settlement's social life. Dr. John Blum wrote in the 1840s, "To describe the balls would be a task beyond the weakness of human nature. There were cards for the infirm and lazy, brandy for the thirsty, and unremitting hospitality. All became hiccups and happiness."

Canadian Pacific Railway: The city's economic good times arrived with the Canadian Pacific Railway in 1881 and the hundreds of thousands of immigrants who followed the ribbon of steel: Europeans fleeing persecution, British city dwellers hungry for land,

A mischievious trio from Anishabe Days, Winnipeg.

Americans who saw their own West filling up. Almost all of them came through Winnipeg, and enough stayed on to swell the city's population.

Each year for two weeks in August, Winnipeg remembers its rich ethnic mosaic with Folklorama, a festival held in some 40 informal pavilions scattered throughout the city. In the evening, church basements and school auditoriums are filled with the aromas of Polish sausage and Ukrainian cabbage rolls and the strains of German polkas and Greek *sirtakis,* as each group celebrates its heritage with food, song and dance. A passport to this round-the-world review buys entrance to the pavilions and transportation on the city's transit system.

The Ukrainians: Ukrainian-Canadians are particularly prominent in Winnipeg. The pear-shaped domes of half a dozen major churches grace the skyline, and the **Ukrainian Cultural and Educational Center** contains a museum displaying such treasures as 17th-Century church vestments, as well as a series of rooms decorated with the hand-carved furniture and hand-painted ceramics typically found in village homes. The **Ukrainian Museum of Canada**, **Manitoba Branch** displays folk arts like tapestries *(kylymy)* and Easter eggs *(pysanky)*.

Across the Red River is **St. Boniface**, the bastion of French culture in the West, where streets are *rues,* and domes yield to the belfries of **St. Boniface Basilica**, built in 1908 and partially destroyed by fire in 1968. Here once rang the bells of St. Boniface, celebrated by John Greenleaf Whittier in the *Red River Voyageur:*

The voyageur smiles as he listens
To the sound that grows apace:
Well he knows the vesper ringing
Of the bells of St. Boniface.

In the shadow of the basilica, a stark granite monument marks the grave of Louis Riel, the most colorful figure in the Canadian West. This self-styled messiah twice tried to form an independent Métis nation on the Prairies, and was hanged for his efforts in 1885. A nearby museum in a former convent contains Riel's bridle and stirrups and the coffin that bore his body here from Regina, where he was tried and hanged.

For years, Winnipeg was a lone cultural beacon shining across the

Weekend entertainment—Dog Sled Races.

Prairies. Since then other cities have come into their own, but Winnipeg still offers the greatest cultural diversity in the West. Vacationers here between September and May can enjoy the Manitoba Opera Company, the Winnipeg Symphony Orchestra, mainstream plays at the Manitoba Theater Centre and experimental works at the Manitoba Warehouse Theater. **Stage West** on Kennedy Street and the **International Inn** on Wellington Avenue offer dinner theater year round, and the former Esso station in **Osborne Village** is now home of the **Gas Station Theater**, which also showcases jazz and classical music at an outdoor terrace in summer. And if you're really lucky, the celebrated and peripatetic Royal Winnipeg Ballet will be in town during your visit.

Once considered something of a dowager by younger, upstart Prairie communities like Calgary and Edmonton, Winnipeg is turning its age into an asset with a flurry of sandblasting, wood stripping and brass polishing. This fling with the past is centered on the **Old Market Square Heritage District**, a 15-block area bounded by Main and Princess streets and William and Notre Dame avenues. Here, the largest concentration of commercial turn-of-the-century architecture in the West has been given a new lease on life as shops, restaurants, nightclubs and galleries. Hot spots include **Cibo's** for fresh seafood and pasta, **Al's** for inexpensive deli lunches with artistes, and great Polish fare can be found on the terraces of **Chopin.** If food and a place to dance are the preferred combination there's the hottest spot in town, the **Rorie Street Marble Club** in the **Exchange District.**

Vacationers who want more tranquil pursuits can board the *Paddlewheel Princess* or *Lady Winnipeg,* and cruise downstream (north) on the Red River to **Lower Fort Garry National Historic Park**, North America's last intact stone fur-trade fort and the most impressive historic site on the Prairies.

Impressive and ludicrous. Stone walls seven feet high and round bastions seem like overkill for a commercial enterprise. In fact, no shots were ever fired in anger from this Hudson's Bay Company outpost, restored to the 1850s era. The beautifully landscaped grounds and the riverside setting are almost as compelling as the costumed attendants

The endless Prairie.

demonstrating how old-timers made candles and pressed beaver pelts into 90-pound bales.

Larger than Lake Ontario, vast **Lake Winnipeg** stretches north into the wilderness. Cottage communities ring its southern end: **Grand Beach, Winnipeg Beach, Victoria Beach**, all slightly tacky and crowded but blessed with long stretches of white sand where it's still possible to find seclusion.

Farther north on the western shore, the Icelandic community of **Gimli** remembers its past with a fiberglass statue of a Viking and an historical museum which explains the fishing economy established on Lake Winnipeg by the town's forebears. **Hecla Island**, once a self-governing Icelandic republic, is now part of a provincial park. Tennis courts, a fine golf course and sunrise bird-watching safaris attract guests to the stylish **Gull Harbor Resort Hotel**.

The good earth: South of Winnipeg stretches flat farmland with rich black gumbo soil of silt and clay. This land was described by 18th-Century fur trader Alexander Henry as "a kind of mortar that adheres to the foot like tar." In the midst of this good earth stands **Steinbach**, whose tidy streets and freshly painted houses reflect the enduring values of the town's industrious Mennonite founders. The **Mennonite Village Museum** recalls the old ways with reconstructed thatched-roof cabins, a blacksmith's shop and a wind-driven gristmill. Costumed guides in bonnets and long, high-necked dresses draw water from a well, churn butter, and serve up excellent borscht and spicy sausages at the museum restaurant.

West of the Red River and south to the American border lies the **Pembina Triangle**, one of the most fertile farming areas on the continent. Sheltered by the gentle Pembina Hills, the region has Manitoba's longest growing season and its widest variety of crops: beets, corn, potatoes, sunflowers and the only apple orchards between the Niagara Peninsula and the Okanagan Valley.

Sunflowers, onions and carrots: It may just be that people here like to celebrate, but seemingly every town in the region advertises the local agricultural specialty with theme fairs. Fields of sunflowers nodding in hot prairie breezes around the Mennonite community of Altona inspired the Manitoba

Corn husking contest in Modern.

Sunflower Festival, held the last weekend in July.

Nearby **Winkler**, also settled by Mennonites, has every right to throw an Onion and Carrot Festival but instead celebrates farming every third weekend in August with Old Time Value Days. Locals man booths stocked with local wares, as Main Street becomes an outdoor mall. Almost 50,000 people are drawn during the week, all of them taking advantage of the discounts and a chance to see new farm equipment.

The **Pembina Valley**, which yields a variety of secluded spots and private vistas as it angles across southwestern Manitoba, is particularly appealing in a land where wheatfields seem to stretch into the next time zone. Steep enough at **La Rivière** for a downhill ski run, the valley was carved by the willow-fringed Pembina River, which broadens into a chain of sparkling lakes — **Pelican, Lorne, Louise** and **Rock** — popular for camping, canoeing and fishing.

The attractive town of **Killarney** has a small lake at its feet and a hill wooded with maple and oak at its back. This setting, said to be reminiscent of Kerry, Ireland, has produced Killarney's Celtic touches: a green fire engine and Erin Park, with its replica of the Blarney Stone and shamrock-shaped fountain containing a statue of a leprechaun astride a turtle. (The park also has a good beach and campsites.)

The **International Peace Garden** straddles the North Dakota-Manitoba border, near the geographical center of the continent. Dr. Henry Moore, an ardent gardener from Toronto, tabled a modest proposal for a joint peace park in 1929 at a meeting of the Gardeners Association of North America. Three years later, his dream became a reality. Today, the 2,300-acre (930-hectare) garden soothes the senses and the soul with fountains, sunken pools, ornamental shrubs, flower-bordered walkways and a brook flowing along the international boundary.

Sandhills and wilderness: If all this cultivation creates a craving for wilderness, visit the **Carberry Sand Hills** in **Spruce Woods Provincial Park**, a scruffy mixture of evergreen stands, grassy plains and barren sand dunes along the sinuous Assiniboine River ("more elbows than a roomful of schoolboys," according to an old saying). The sand-

A misty shroud over Portage La Prairie.

hills were formed about 12,000 years ago when a mile-wide glacial river deposited a vast delta of sand, silt and gravel.

Ernest Thompson Seton, a naturalist-author who homesteaded near Carberry in the 1880s, loved to roam the sandhills, and made them the setting for his book, *The Trail of the Sandhill Stag*. He spent every spare moment in what came to be known as "Seton's Kingdom" observing grouse, foxes, deer and wolves in the most important natural region in Manitoba. Be sure to try the self-guiding **Spirit Hills Trail**, which winds through barren sand dunes inhabited by rare creatures like hognose snakes, spadefoot toads and northern prairie skinks.

Due west in the broad valley of the Assiniboine River lies **Brandon**, Manitoba's second city, noted for handsome public buildings and gracious private homes dating from the early 1900s. A walking tour brochure distributed by the Chamber of Commerce directs you to the most notable structures. The **Brandon Allied Arts Center**, which contains an art gallery and craft shop, is housed in just such a stately turn-of-the-century home.

State 10 leads north past fields of wheat and rye interspersed with pothole lakes that attract millions of ducks and geese during spring and fall migrations, and on into the evergreen forests of **Riding Mountain National Park**. Approaching the park from this direction, the usual reaction is: *Where's the mountain?* since the change in elevation is so gradual. Patience, however, will be rewarded.

First, enjoy the resort town of **Wasagaming**, with its tennis courts, golf course and riding stables. Then make a sidetrip to **Lake Audy**, where a small herd of bison roam a vast paddock. Naturalists lead intrepid visitors on wolf-howl expeditions through remote areas of the park.

Now for that alpine view. Continue north on State 10 to the edge of the park, where the "mountain" rises abruptly from farmland. The reward is a superb panorama 1,500 feet (450 meters) above a colorful patchwork of crops: yellow rapeseed, brown squares of oats and barley, and green and gold wheatfields. Ah, thinks the traveler, again the endless Prairie.

Left, railroad rises above a wheatfield; and right, going to the city—a country farmer seeks the urban life.

NORTH

Home to the body of myths many foreigners hold of Canada, the North is the nation's most sparsely populated region. Here it *is* bitterly cold almost 365 days a year, here some people *do* live in snow huts, and here dog-sled racing across the frozen tundra *is* a popular form of entertainment.

Despite its formidable geography, the North is the natural habitat of the "first Canadians," the Inuit, who have thrived here successfully for thousands of years. To some extent the last uncharted frontier in Canada, the Northwest Territories and Yukon are regions of delicately balanced ecosystems and unparalleled glacial beauty.

While Canada's northern hinterland may not be the vacation spot for everyone, for those intrigued by unusual habitats, landscapes and wildlife the north presents an exciting adventure. Yukon is the first of Canada's two northern regions to be explored in the following pages. Here, readers discover the significance of the goldrush for Canada's neglected north and are provided with a vivid description of Yukon's geography, climate and spectacular vistas. The section also provides information about the province's sights and the kinds of vacations that are suitable to the area. The Northwest Territories are treated in much the same fashion, although with greater emphasis on geological formations and wildlife. The two articles together present a comprehensive picture of the radically different world looming over Canada's other 10 provinces.

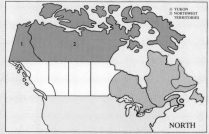

1) YUKON
2) NORTHWEST TERRITORIES

NORTH

YUKON

Before 1896 the northwest corner of Canada was a mountainous wilderness where few outsiders, besides the occasional whaler and fur-trader, ever ventured. Other than the Dene Indians who had lived there for perhaps 60,000 years this was land unknown to most. But in 1896 this land that the Canadian government had forgotten was suddenly overrun by every type of man and beast imaginable. Gold, and lots of it, had been discovered in the Klondike.

The young Dominion of Canada, like any new heir, soon had the headaches that accompany sudden wealth. These migraines were brought about by a gold-feverish breed clamoring for a stake in the rivers of the Klondike. Driven by the same base desire, this remarkably diverse group gladly gambled with their own lives for a stake in the North. Their loyalty, however, to the Queen, her government and the Commonwealth was questionable. In the early days the challenge for the government was to bring order (or at least a civilizing influence) to the North. If it could not it might lose millions in gold tax revenues. Therefore the Queen's ministers, in recognition of the sudden prominence of a land most knew little about, decided to redraw the map of Canada. They roped off the northwest corner of the Northwest Territories and created Yukon territory.

What the federal officials lassoed in their haste to reassert Canadian sovereignty is a territory larger than the New England States, double the landmass of the British Isles, and two and one half times the size of Texas. It is roughly drawn in the shape of a triangle. Contained within Yukon's borders are some of the largest mountains in North America, as well as magnificent glaciers, plateaus and tremendous river valleys. This is a land whose wild beauty could easily outstrip the pecuniary ambitions of its new "citizens."

Mountain country: Collectively the Yukon region is known as part of the Western Highlands and within this region there are a series of mountains. Along the eastern border of the territory there lie the **Mackenzie Mountains** that pass over into the NWT and gently roll up to the foot of the **Mackenzie River**. Within this range there are rivers carved into the rock by ancient glaciers. One such river, the **Nahanni**, contains Virgina Falls. Unlike Ontario's great Niagara, no one has ever attempted to go over these falls in a barrel. Mountains are an omnipresent sight in Yukon. The **Selwyn Mountain Range** lies to the east of the MacKenzie range and to the north are the very ancient **Ogilvie Mountains.** The best known peaks are **St. Elias** and **Mount Logan.** Standing at 19,520 feet (5,950 meters), Mount Logan is second only to Mount McKinley in Alaska as the highest mountain in North America. Many peaks in the St. Elias Range must push through glaciers, glaciers that are in part sustained by the "chill factor" associated with great heights. The St. Elias range, besides offering some of the most spectacular sights in the world, also acts to block much of the moisture coming off the Pacific Ocean. It is because of this that most of the interior of Yukon receives little precipitation. In fact much of Yukon receives less precipitation than Cairo, Egypt. Anywhere from nine to 17 inches (23 to 43 cm) is the average amount of rain. Yet Yukon does receive more precipitation than the NWT and because of the relatively cold temperatures and high altitudes, whatever snow does fall in winter will not evaporate until spring. This snow helps provide excellent cross-country trails for Yukoners.

Between the mountain ranges are plateaus, the **Peel**, the **Porcupine** and the **Yukon**. Each plateau is named after the river that flows through it. The Yukon Plateau is the largest of the three, with the Yukon River passing through it.

Although glaciers remain in Yukon Territory, curiously much of the Yukon Plateau was untouched by the last glacial era and for this reason is unique among geological areas in North America. Thus the Yukon River, unlike the other northern rivers that felt the effects of glaciation, flows gently through the plateau and is devoid of rapids, falls and other such unpleasantries that can make canoe trips an unholy excursion. An ice-free millennia has allowed the Yukon River to find its own path.

Within the plateau one finds mountains that have dome-like summits rising to heights of 6,000 feet (1,800 meters).

Preceding pages, layers of existence at Jasper National Park; and vestiges in the snow. Left, an inquisitive sled dog.

These domes were formed by a million years of sediment accumulating on top of the mountains. Unlike the neighboring mountains, such as the Mackenzie or St. Elias that have been scoured by glaciers and left with whittled down pencil-shaped peaks, the mountains of Yukon Plateau have few rocky outcroppings. This plateau is a relic of another age, one apart from the geological violence of the last Ice Age. For that reason ancient mastodon and mammoth species survived far longer in this area than in any other. Likewise, the plateau offered shelter for Asians who entered North America by way of the Bering Strait perhaps tens of thousands of years ago.

Because of the rich soil deposits in Yukon there is a tremendous abundance and variety of flora and fauna. Except for its barren northern tip much of Yukon is covered in forest and heavy underbrush that can support a sizable local logging industry. Because of the plentitude of vegetation there is an excellent food supply to support many species of animals. These species include moose, caribou, dale sheep, mountain goats, cougars, grizzly and black bears. Within the rivers of Yukon one finds large runs of salmon, salmon that has traveled thousands of miles from the Pacific Ocean to enter the Yukon River and from there down its many tributaries.

Golden days: But there also was a time when not only thousands of salmon swam through the Yukon River but thousands of men waded into her. Unlike the salmon, these men came not to spawn, but to seek out the placer gold that laid buried deep in the sediment of river beds.

In contrast to the manner in which it is extracted, placer gold is created by an eternally slow process of erosion. Gradually the river flows over a rock face wearing down the quartz bearing gold until it breaks off into pieces varying anywhere from that of a tennis ball to microscopic specks.

This irridescent mineral lay complacently in Yukon river beds for thousands of years, quite unaware of the lust men held for it. Finally on August 17, 1896, a day that is now a territorial holiday, three men, Skookum Jim, Tagish Charlie (two Yukon Indians), and George Washington Carmack (an American) became the founding fathers of the gold rush. They struck gold at **Rabbit Creek** and the love affair with the Klondike began. Eventually, close to 80,000 men would scurry northward to seek their fortune, with the gold stories of Randolph Hearst's hyperbolic newspapers rattling in their heads.

The routes some miners chose to take were rather bizarre. A group of Edmonton businessmen advertised a trail through the rugged interior of Alberta and British Columbia. Little did those who took this passage know 'that Dawson City, the center of the goldrush, lay a few thousand miles away and that this "trail" was a hoax. Of the thousands who attempted this route many lost their lives and only a handful managed to straggle on into Yukon.

Soapy Smith and Sam Steele: A more conventional route to take was to travel by steamer to Skagway, Alaska, and then onwards through either the White Pass or Chilfort Pass into Yukon. Although these trails were better than the Edmonton trail, they posed many dangers: not the least of which was your fellow miner. In Skagway a n'er do well named "Soapy" Smith managed to gather around him a rather unscrupu-

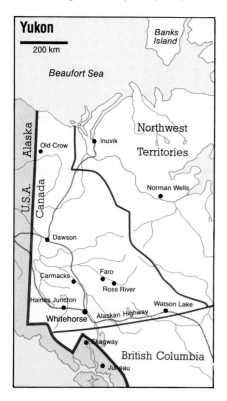

Yukon

200 km

Beaufort Sea

Banks Island

Alaska

U.S.A.

Canada

Old Crow

Inuvik

Northwest

Territories

Norman Wells

Dawson

Carmacks

Faro

Ross River

Haines Junction

Watson Lake

Whitehorse

Alaskan Highway

Skagway

British Columbia

Juneau

lous flock who fleeced many a would-be prospector of his stake long before he got to Dawson. The wild west made quite a revival in northern Skagway. Soapy's denouement came when a group of armed townspeople drew Soapy and his boys out. The gang quickly scattered, Soapy held his ground and for that was shot dead, but not until he managed to mortally wound the vigilante who shot him.

The Canadian authorities looked upon both the outlaw activity and the vigilantism with disdain. As a response to the gold-feverish hordes pouring into Yukon, the Canadian cabinet ordered that 300 Northwest Mounted Police be sent to Yukon. They were headed by a man whose name almost stereotypically symbolized not only his own character but the character of his police force. His name was Sam Steele.

Steele was charged with several tasks, the first of which was to enforce and impress upon the prospectors Canadian sovereignty. Over 90 percent of those entering Yukon were Americans. (Then as now Canadian investment was small in its own resources.)

Another of Steele's responsibilities was to ensure that every man and woman entering Yukon had enough supplies to last an entire year. Steele stationed mounties at all mountain passes and ordered that all would-be Yukoners with less than one thousand pounds of equipment and food be turned back. This was a sensible order: you could hope for, but not depend, on charity in Yukon.

However, carrying the requisite equipment through mountain passes 3,800 feet (1,160 meters) or more in height was a herculean and dangerous task. In April of 1898, with spring well on its way in Yukon, 63 people were smothered to death in an avalanche at Chilkoot Pass. Within a day the pass was reopened and people continued their grim ascent.

During the early years of the gold-rush in **Dawson City** inflation was an endemic problem: an orange sold for 50¢ a piece and pint of champagne cost 40 dollars. The amount of gold pouring out of Yukon was remarkable. In 1896 300,000 dollars worth of gold was produced; the following year 2.5 million dollars worth was mined; in 1898 10 million dollars in gold was ex-

tracted; and by 1900, the peak year, 22,275,000 dollars worth of gold was taken from Yukon.

Rivers run dry: Yet every boom has a bust and Yukon's halcyon days began to abate in 1902. The most obvious reason was that there was simply less gold to be had. In addition, large companies began filing claims on many "used" claims and then reworked them. In this way corporations consolidated the gold industry and consequently displaced the traditional small-time operators. With the exodus of the original "sourdoughs" there followed the closing of the dancehalls, gambling parlors and drinking establishments. The freewheeling and freespirited days were over. At the height of the Gold Rush, Dawson City had a population of 30,000, by 1910 there were 1,000 inhabitants. Today, a shadow of itself, about 600 people live there, and few of those are prospectors.

There has been speculation that both Yukon and Canada missed a great opportunity to develop an indigenous industry. If the small-time operator had been encouraged to stay, perhaps a tertiary industry could have sustained the remarkable culture. Interestingly,

there still remains roughly 200 one- or two-man placer gold outfits working the rivers of Yukon, long after the large gold companies have left.

Mining has always been the backbone of Yukon's economy. When the gold production began to slow, large zinc, lead and silver deposits were discovered and mined in Yukon. However, with the world mineral markets in a state of depression there has been a corresponding depression in Yukon. The permanent closing of Cyprus Anvil's gates in Faro has been a major blow to the economy of Yukon.

With the mining industry in a slump, one part of Yukon's Gross National Product (GNP) that is growing is tourism. Naturally Klondike nostalgia is used as a major theme to promote tourism. So even if the gold boom broke 80 years ago, today its legacy is still paying a modest dividend. In Dawson City, the former capital of Yukon and hub of the goldrush, there stands Canada's only legalized casino. In the summer months this little gambling establishment, along with a Klondike-style dance revue, is a reminder that Yukon was founded by hustlers, gold diggers and dreamers, not fishermen or farmers.

Yukon today: There are tours that will take travelers down the same rivers that paddlewheelers sailed and prospectors worked. Along the riverbanks and hiking trials are the remains of prospectors' old camps and abandoned towns; tourists to Yukon can relive the "golden days" of Yukon's Klondike. Ironically, many in the tourist industry now wish to restrict and eliminate activity of the modern placer-gold prospectors. Placer-gold extraction has done and can do tremendous environmental damage to riverbeds.

There is more to Yukon than a land of faded "glory days." It is interesting that if you ask people who are vaguely familiar with Canada for a sketch of the country they will invariably mention mounties, mountains, snow and ice. What they are describing is Yukon. The portrait they often describe is a little like saying that Mona Lisa is a sketch of a smiling lady. This peaceful wilderness with its rivers, meadows mountains and glaciers existed long before fortune hunters from the south noisily made their way into the interior. Yukon remains a silent beauty long since those men have left.

Left, autumn gold against the Klondike Highway. Right, gold nugget, Dawson City.

NORTHWEST TERRITORIES

The Northwest Territories, NWT to most Canadians and non-Canadians alike, is a land of the unknown. Many would simply picture it as a flat, perennially icy slab stretching from the 60th parallel towards the North Pole with only the occasional polar bear or Inuit igloo to give some relief to this monotonous landscape. Yet if you look farther than a sterotypical picture, you find not one land but many lands, lands that are foreign to most people, and yet so mystical that each person who visits there is not so much a tourist as an explorer. There is within this wilderness a force that can evoke something undiscovered within oneself.

The Northwest Territories cover an area of 1.3 million square miles (3.3 million sq km). Its southern border begins at the 60th parallel and stretches 2,110 miles (3,400 km) to the North Pole and runs 2,645 miles (4,260 km) east to west. This means the total landmass of the NWT is close to half that of the contiguous United States, yet it has a population of only 40,000. If the NWT seems short on cultural history it is certainly very long on geophysical history.

Scars of the last Ice Age: It was only 10,000 years ago that the last Ice Age finally retreated from much of the area. That Ice Age, the Pleistocene, began somewhere between 2 to 4 million years ago and left behind moraines, dry gravel beds and drumlins. Venturing north above the tree line into the tundra where it is too cold for lush vegetation and forests to survive, the scars of thousands of centuries of geological history stand before the eyes.

One legacy of this recent Ice Age are the literally thousands upon thousands of rivers and lakes that cover more than half of the NWT's landmass. Many of these lakes and rivers, particularly in the Mackenzie Delta, were formed by glaciers creating indentations in the earth and leaving behind melted glacial ice. In the eastern mountainous region, however, when the weight of the glacier finally dissipated, the earth heaved upwards and many inlets suddenly became lakes. This phenomenon can be seen on Baffin Island where lakes are located close to 600 feet (180 meters) above sea level.

One interesting environmental fact about the NWT is that much of the territory is classified by geographers as desert. The typical picture of the Canadian North being smothered in yards of snow is not accurate. The mean annual precipitation for both the eastern and western Arctic is only 12 inches (30 cm) or the equivalent of a single Montréal snowstorm. However, during the long arctic winters the sun may only appear for a few brief hours if at all, so whatever snow does fall will not melt until spring. Ironically the Territories would be devoid of its abundant fresh water if the frigid temperatures did not prevent evaporation.

Indeed, the temperatures can be frigid. The record plunging temperatures in the region are legendary. In the community of **Hay River**, in the MacKenzie Delta, the average January temperature is -13 degrees Fahrenheit (-25 Celsius). In **Eureka**, the temperature has sometimes dropped to a frosty -33 degrees Fahrenheit (-36 Celsius). Generally the farther one moves north and toward the center of the Arctic Ocean the cooler it becomes.

Yet a traveler should not be misled by these freezing temperatures. When summer arrives and there is sunlight for 20 hours a day the temperatures rise in the Mackenzie Delta to the high 60 and mid-70 degrees Fahrenheit (16 to 24 Celsius), ideal for hiking or camping. In fact the summer in this region is remarkably similar to that in the rest of Canada, except of course there is more sunshine in the north.

Breeding grounds for the birds: While the NWT receives relatively few human visitors, it is estimated that 12 percent of North America's bird population breeds in here during the spring and summer months. Almost all of the estimated 80 species of birds in the NWT are migratory. Biologists claim that these birds are attracted to the North primarily because of the lack of natural predators. Many species of birds live below the tree line in the taiga, where there are coniferous trees, dense brush and an abundant source of food. Birds such as chickadees, jays, woodpeckers and crossbills are just a few of the species found in the taiga.

Birds are certainly not the only animals in the North. Below the tree line, where the weather is less harsh and the

Left, transformed by contact: a modern-day Inuit.

trees offer protection from the elements, there are moose, beaver, marten, muskrat, red fox, timber wolf and black bear, as well as huge herds of caribou and bison. Above the tree line are arctic wolves with white coats, as well as arctic fox, lemmings in the east, and of course in the summer and fall, caribou. Along the coastline and on the islands polar bears, seals and walrus can be seen. **Melville Island** is inhabited by the exotic hirsute musk ox.

Life in the tundra: Perhaps one of the most remarkable facts about survival on the tundra is the dependency of all life on soil frozen to a depth of from 100 feet to 1,000 feet (30 to 300 meters). This ground is appropriately called *permafrost*. In the summer the sun's rays are able to melt topsoil here to a depth of perhaps 80 feet (24 meters). It is within this slender layer of soil that small organisms, such as lichen, can grow. Lichen and low-lying vegetation are a main source of food for the mammals of the tundra.

In summer seasons that are too short in length for plant life to grow, all species (including humans) lose members from their population. Over many seasons decimated species eventually recover; the natural order is maintained, but it is a precarious one. Any external force can disrupt this fragile ecosystem. It is for this reason that the intrusion of southern development is seen by native peoples and environmentalists as a dangerous threat.

Early explorations for gold: For southern intruders (or outsiders), the North has always held a sense of mystery. Many believed there were untold fortunes to be made there. The first recorded European exploration of the Arctic was undertaken by the Elizabethan, Martin Frobisher, who searched for gold and the elusive Northwest Passage in 1576. Frobisher found neither gold nor the Passage on his first or many subsequent journeys. He did manage to bring back to England seven hundred tons of "fools" gold from Baffin Island, however.

Henry Hudson was another intrepid English explorer who set out to find the Passage. Hudson traveled extensively in the north for several years. Not only did he fail to find the Northwest Passage but his long suffering crew mutinied. Hudson, his son and 10 ailing seamen

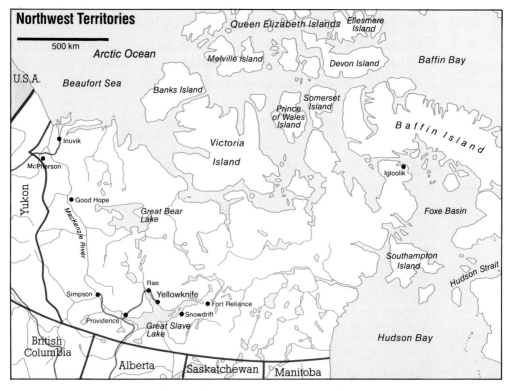

Northwest Territories

500 km

Arctic Ocean

Queen Elizabeth Islands Ellesmere Island

Melville Island

Devon Island

Baffin Bay

U.S.A.

Beaufort Sea

Banks Island

Somerset Island

Prince of Wales Island

Baffin Island

Inuvik

Victoria Island

McPherson

Igloolik

Good Hope

Great Bear Lake

Foxe Basin

Yukon

Mackenzie River

Southampton Island

Hudson Strait

Rae

Simpson Yellowknife

Fort Reliance

Snowdrift

Providence

Great Slave Lake

Hudson Bay

British Columbia

Alberta Saskatchewan Manitoba

were set adrift in a barque in the bay that now carries his name. They were never seen again. Due to the discouraging results of expeditions undertaken by Frobisher, Hudson and others of the era, the British Crown and other financial backers abandoned the search for a northerly route to the Orient and India.

Within Canada, fur traders were searching for routes leading from the interior of Canada to markets in Europe. One such entrepreneur was Alexander Mackenzie, who in 1789 followed the Mackenzie River for its entire length 2,560 miles (4,120 km) in the hope it would lead to the Pacific Ocean. Instead it led to the Arctic Ocean. Little did Mackenzie realize in the 18th Century that he had reached an opening to a sea that covered vast oil deposits.

Even though this area had proven to have little commercial value in the 17th and 18th centuries there were those in England during the 19th Century who looked towards the Arctic region with a mixture of wide-eyed romanticism and genuine scientific curiosity. This era in Arctic exploration was similar to the period of space exploration embarked upon by the U.S. space program of the 1960s and 1970s. Prizes were put up by British Parliament for any person who would find the Northwest Passage and/or discover the North Pole.

William Parry was one who managed to collect a purse of five thousand pounds for his excursion to the far western Arctic Islands (1819-1821). John Franklin was another who, in typical British Bulldog manner, risked his life many times on his journeys mapping the Arctic coastline. On his final journey in 1848, Franklin left England with a crew of 129 men aboard two ships; their objective was to find the Northwest Passage. Unfortunately they became locked in the ice for two years at Victoria Strait. In 1850 search parties were sent out, and eventually over the next eight years articles of clothing, logbooks and mementos were found strewn across the chilly coastline. Of the 129 men on the Franklin expedition not one survivor was found. All perished.

Traveling in the North today: Today travel for "outsiders" to the Arctic is far less hazardous than in Franklin's day. There are two reasons for that. The first is that after the Franklin debacle, "out-

Black bear races across the highway.

siders" began to pay attention to the ways of the Inuit, a people who had survived in the North for so many centuries. Secondly, technology improved; particularly communications, and of course with the arrival of the airplane in the early 1920s the NWT became far more accessible to the outside world.

Airflight is now both routine and safe in the Territories. To reach many communities, particularly in the Eastern NWT where there are no highways, air routes have become the "real" highways for the North. The NWT is served by six scheduled airlines with flights originating from major cities in Canada to all large communities in the Territories. Once in the NWT there are over 40 scheduled and chartered services between cities and remote camps.

Of course the NWT contains conventional highways too. The highways of the NWT connect most of the large communities in the Western region such as **Yellowknife**, **Hay River**, **Fort Smith**, **Inuvik** and **Tuktoyaktuk** with the outside. These highways are all hard-packed gravel, not paved, so some adjustment to your driving style may be necessary. Because of a lack of vehicu-

lar traffic travel can be relaxing. Drivers are more likely to have their trip interrupted by wildlife such as moose or caribou crossing the road than by meeting another vehicle. In fact the **Dempster Highway** has restrictions on travel in fall and spring while herds of caribou numbering in the thousands make their annual migration.

NWT's accommodation options: As far as accommodations go, there are relatively modern hotels in most major centers such as Inuvik or Yellowknife. An added attraction in Yellowknife is the NWT's only golf course. In general though the North does not often provide ordinary luxuries; its camps and hotels provide the opportunity to view the last genuine wilderness in the world.

In the western Arctic, that is all of the territory west of **Great Slave** and **Great Bear Lake** up toward Inuvik, there are numerous outfitters operating out of the major communities. Below the tree line, canoe trips take place from late May to mid-September. In the tundra area most trips take place from mid-June to mid-August. Recently cross-country ski trips have been set up in the spring so tourists can witness the migra- **Alpine flowers.**

tion of caribou herds. On this tour participants are flown into a base camp and from there glide onto frozen lakes and rivers to observe the caribou migration.

For the sake of the bison: In the western NWT there are two spectacular national parks. **Wood Buffalo National Park** is located on either side of the Alberta — NWT border and was established in 1922 to preserve the bison. This objective has been a success and one can attend a "Bison Creep" to view these creatures.

The second national park in the west is located on the Yukon border. At **Nahanni National Park** tourists can see impressive river gorges, underground caves and hot springs. Those who enjoy water travel can journey down the meandering South Nahanni River until arriving at **Virginia Falls**, a falls that plunges 300 feet (90 meters), more than twice that of Niagara Falls.

If traveling to Yellowknife, a stop at the new **Yellowknife Cultural Center** where drama and music are regularly performed is recommended. Also in Yellowknife is the **Prince of Wales Northern Heritage Center** which houses excellent histories and artifacts of the Inuit, Dene and Métis Indians.

The Eastern Arctic: The Eastern Arctic, the area that includes much of the Archipelago and the terrain east of Great Slave Lake, had been a hidden world until the age of the airplane. It is a unique world with its barren ground, plateaus, mountains and unique Inuit communities. An ideal place to visit in the Eastern Arctic is **Baffin Island**, home of roughly a quarter of the Canadian Inuit population. Baffin Island contains some of the oldest northerly communities in the world; **Frobisher Bay** is the largest of these. There the Inuit have created extensive walking trails that pass by ancient cairns first built centuries before to act as landmarks. Some of these trails overlook cliffs from which the ocean, harped seals, and even the occasional beluga whale can be seen.

Cape Dorset is another Baffin Island Community, that, like Frobisher Bay, is rich in the Inuit heritage. It is the home of modern Inuit art which first developed in the 1950s. Inuit art has an understated simplicity that expresses the harmonic Inuit vision of Arctic life. The **West Baffin Eskimo Co-op** now displays and sells local artwork. In addition, Cape Dorset has hiking and cross-country skiing tours. From these trails the source of the Inuit artists' inspiration can be appreciated.

Another source of inspiration for anyone who has viewed them are the glaciers on Baffin Island. The **Penny Ice Cap** is 2,200 square miles (5,700 sq km) of ice and snow: to view this glacier high up in the mountains is to revisit the Ice Age. Similar monuments from the Ice Age are the cliffs and fjords. On sections of Baffin Island's east coast, cliffs rise out of the ocean to a height of 7,000 feet (2,100 meters) higher than the walls of the Grand Canyon.

The Northwest Territories is a land so very different from any place on the globe because so much of it is completely untouched by civilization. When visiting the NWT the traveler realizes that it is a land containing a history in which humankind has played a minuscule role. For that reason it is a humbling experience to see its mountains, its barren grounds, its stunted forests, its overarching skies, its thousands of freshwater lakes and rivers, and to consider the physic that built this vast land.

Right, the Arctic midnight sun. Following page, a Canadian goose cools off.

TRAVEL TIPS

How To Use Travel Tips

Travel Tips is divided into three sections taking travelers from the general to the specific. It informs visitors in Canada about the area and land they're visiting. The guide takes people from the moment they cross a border or enter an airport in Canada, right through to when they leave.

The first section outlines information on a national basis touching on modes of transportation, postal services, business hours and holidays, climate, types of accommodation, and the national media in brief.

The second section is the **Foreign Supplement**. This has a more specific approach to Canada, and details things that a foreign visitor may not be aware of. It covers the government and economy, tables for exchange rates and weights and measures, time zones, clothes and language. It also touches on embassies and consulates.

The third and final part is the **Directory**. It lists addresses and phone numbers on a *provincial* and *city* basis for things to do and see while traveling. The provinces are featured alphabetically, covering transportation, accommodation, restaurants and attractions. A national list of contacts for general information leads off the section.

Getting There

By Air: Many people choose to fly into Canada, then continue their trip by bus, train, rented car or plane. Nearly all the major international airlines serve Toronto and Montréal, while Vancouver has become an important connection to the Far East.

Air Canada and CP Air fly to numerous destinations overseas, but visitors also come in on Air France, Alitalia, British Airways, El Al, KLM, Lufthansa, Scandinavian Airlines, and Swissair jets. And nearly a dozen U.S. airlines offer flights into Canada originating from major U.S. hubs.

It is possible to fly a private plane into Canada, though you are still expected to pass immigration and customs inquiries. A log book, certificate of registration, and valid pilot's license are required. For more details write Canada Transport listed in the **Directory.**

By Sea and Lake: Car ferries chug between Maine and Nova Scotia, and from Seattle, Washington to British Columbia. Some prefer to sail in on a private yacht or boat, but in the summertime dock space can be tight.

Check ahead with marine officials and/or the relevant provincial travel office, and remember that you are still required to pass immigration and customs. The Hydrographic Canadian Service provides nautical charts, see Directory. Happy Sailing!

By Land: From the U.S., visiting Canada by *car* is simply a matter of driving to the border, then passing customs and immigration queries (see below). From overseas, automobiles must of course be shipped–usually a prohibitively expensive proposition.

The major bus company with routes into Canada is Greyhound. Some routes end at a city just over the border, where you can transfer to a Canadian carrier, but there are also special packages from certain U.S. cities (like Boston, New York, Chicago, San Francisco) to Vancouver, Winnipeg, Toronto, Montreal, and other destinations in Canada. Inquire at the nearest Greyhound office for schedules and prices.

Amtrak offers three direct passenger train

routes into Canada: Seattle to Vancouver, New York to Toronto (via Buffalo), and New York to Montréal. It is also possible to take a train to the border, then hook up with the Canadian passenger service, VIA Rail. For instance, one can ride Amtrak to Detroit, then take a bus across to the Windsor train station. Addresses for Greyhound and Amtrak are listed in the **Directory**.

Getting Acquainted

One of the smartest things to do once in Canada is to go to the nearest tourist information center. Each city has one staffed with informative, friendly personnel. Aside from being able to answer questions, they provide travel brochures on areas of interest as well as free maps. Each province also has a toll-free number for tourism information. These are listed in the **Directory**. For general information on traveling in Canada write to the Canadian Government Office of Tourism. Canadian consulates in foreign countries also provide travel information. Some of the consulates are listed in the **Foreign Supplement.**

Local Transportation

For people who know where they want to travel in Canada, a number of transportation venues are open. Domestic air travel is preferable for going from one end of the country to another, or if remote areas are on the itinerary. Buses are good for shorter distances or for getting to small towns that aren't serviced by railways or airplaines (they are also very cheap). The railway is good for both long and short distances. Via Rail, Canada's only train service, offers package discounts and travel passes as do Greyhound and Voyageur buslines.

If adventure and exploring are on the agenda, cars can be rented easily here. Speed Limits, seat-belt regulations, and other laws offer differ from province to province. Foreign driver's licenses are valid in Canada. The Canadian Automobile Association is a good source of information and maps. Gasoline prices range between 45 cents to 55 cents per liter (there are 3.8 liters in a U.S. gallon, 4.5 liters in a Canadian Imperial gallon), falling somewhat in Alberta.

Addresses and phone numbers for all these services are listed in the **Directory**.

Climate

It is difficult to generalize about the Canadian climate. Most visitors come during the summer, when temperatures average in the mid-70s (mid-20s°C). During July and August, however, the mercury can climb into the 90s on the prairies and in southern Ontario. In northern Canada, summer temperatures stay at 65° (15°C) during the day, but will often drop near freezing at night.

Canadian winters have been slightly exaggerated in popular lore. Winter temperatures average between 10-25° (-5 to 10°C) from the Maritimes through southern Ontario. It gets colder and windier from northern Québec through the Rockies, with temperatures ranging from 0-10°(-18 to -5°C). In Yukon and Northwest Territories, the mercury can drop to -40°C. On the balmy southern coast of B.C., however, warm Pacific currents generally keep the temperature above freezing throughout the winter.

The snowfall is consistently heavy throughout Canada, with the exception of Nova Scotia and parts of southern Ontario. Skiers take to the slopes and trails by late November, and the snow lasts generally until April, or even May in the mountains.

Postal Services

Stamps can be purchased at post offices (open daily during business hours and often on Saturday mornings) or sometimes at your hotel desk. Postal rates for letters and post cards, the first ounce:

Within Canada 37 cents
To the U.S. 43 cents
Overseas Airmail 74 cents

Privately owned, overnight express and courier outfits have mushroomed across the continent. Canada Post can send electronic facsimiles from coast-to -coast or overseas.

Telephone/Telecommunication

The telephone system in Canada is similar to that in the United States. Pay phones cost 25 cents. For collect, operator-assisted, or overseas calls, dial "0," then the number you wish to reach. Note that an "800" exchange indicates a toll-free number: simply dial a "l" first, and there is no charge.

The first several pages in public phone books explain everything you may need to know, including emergency numbers and long-distance country codes.

Canada's telex network encompasses over 50,000 units throughout the nation and handles over 3 million messages per year. CNCP Telecommunications dispatches telegrams and cablegrams.

Business Hours

Standard business hours are 9 a.m to 5 p.m., but the trend is toward greater flexibility. Most stores open on Saturdays and offer weekday evening hours. Drug and convenience stores generally close at ll p.m., and may stay open on Sundays. Banking hours are from l0 a.m. to 3 p.m., Monday through Thursday; l0 a.m. to 6 p.m, Friday; with some Saturday morning hours.

Banks, schools, government offices, beer and liquor stores all close on national holidays. Hotels, restaurants, and most retail outlets stay open. See the **Diary** sections for listings of provincial holidays.

Public Holidays

New Year's Day
 January 1
Good Friday
Easter Monday
Victoria Day (Queen's Birthday)
 Monday preceding May 25
Canada (Dominion) Day
 July l
Labour Day
 First Monday in September
Thanksgiving Day
 Second Monday in October

Remembrance Day
 November 11
Christmas Day
 December 25
Boxing Day (except Québec)
 December 26

Hospital and Emergency Services

Visitors are urged to obtain health insurance before leaving their own country. If taking prescription medicine bring an adequate supply as well as copy of the prescription in case it needs to be renewed. If travelers require medical attention they needn't worry. Canadian hospitals are known for their high medical standards.

If caught in an emergency requiring the police, an ambulance or firemen, immediate action can be had in Canada's major cities by dialing 9ll. Emergency telephone numbers are listed in the front of all local telephone directories. If caught in a legal bind, foreign visitors can contact their consulates. A listing of consulates and cities follows in the **Foreign Supplement.**

Accommodations

Canadian accommodations are similar to those in the United States in the range of choices available, but you will find most lodgings in Canada more personalized and service-orientated.

Reservations are a must during the busy summer months. Hotels generally will hold a room until 6 p.m., but if you plan to arrive later, notify the establishment in advance. If you do not have reservations, begin looking for accommodations early in the afternoon, particularly during the summer, when most establishments (especially those along highways) fill up quickly.

Almost all hotels, motels and resorts accept major credit cards, but it's a good idea to check in advance, especially if you travel in remote areas.

Bed and Breakfast and Hostels are becoming increasingly popular alternatives to hotels. Generally cheaper and more friendly, they are located throughout the country. Another practical and fun place to stay is in one of Canada's 2,000 campgrounds. Addresses for accommodation are in the **Directory** listed on a city and province basis.

Food and Drink

Each Canadian region is known for its unique dishes and style of cooking. Newfoundland for its "brewis" (cod) and flipper pie, the Maritimes for seafood, and Québec for its "habitant" cooking and French cuisine. The prairies feature grain-fed beef, while in B.C. it's salmon and king crab. The northern territories dish up sumptuous Arctic grayling and char.

Dining out in Canada also reflects the country's multicultural heritage. Ukrainian, German, Japanese, French, Chinese, Hungarian, Italian, Vietnamese, and Middle Eastern cuisine are well represented in the restaurants of Canada's cities.

Canadian beer is tastier and more alcoholic than the American variety; it comes in lagers, pilsners, ales or becks. English and Australian brew, by the pint or draught, is increasingly popular.

Liquor laws vary from province to province, although 19 is emerging as the legal age of choice. Most provinces regulate heavily the marketing of alcohol, sometimes restricting its sale to special stores (check the "yellow pages" phone book for the nearest carry-out location). Most restaurants are licensed to serve liquor, though it pays to check first. Specific details about provincial liquor and restaurants to visit are given in the **Directory.**

Spectator Sports

Hockey is of course Canada's favorite sport. Children start playing it as soon as they can skate, so the country is filled with organized leagues. Canadians avidly follow their National Hockey League teams: the Vancouver Canucks, Calgary Flames, Winnipeg Jets, Stanley Cup Champion Edmonton Oilers, Toronto Maple Leafs, Montréal Canadians and Québec Nordiques. The season lasts from October to April. Inquire with a provincial travel bureau on how to go about obtaining tickets, a difficult but not impossible task.

If you miss the hockey season, don't fret: Professional Baseball has taken Canada by storm. The Montréal Expos have been long-time contenders, and now the Toronto Blue Jays have assembled a World Series-calibre club. Games in both towns can be exciting events. Vancouver hosts a "Triple A" farm club, while currently wooing a major league franchise.

Other sports are popular too. Canada's national sport is Lacrosse, a hard hitting Native American game. For another glimpse of Canadiana, try curling (sort like bowling on ice), where only the rocks are hard hitting. Basketball and volleyball draw more interest yearly. Rugby, the grueling popular-English sport, is played vigorously on university quadrangles throughout Canada. During the summer, Alberta becomes a rodeo country.

Recreation

Canada's vast outdoors is perhaps its finest attraction. Consult the individual **Sports, Recreation and Parks** sections in the **Directory** for more details about the activities listed below.

Hiking: All over Canada, particularly on provincial and national park trails.

Rafting and Canoeing: Every province, especially Ontario, B.C., Yukon and Northwest Territories.

Sailing: Throughout Canada, especially on the coasts and Great Lakes.

Diving: Nova Scotia and Georgian Bay, Ontario.

Golf: Every province, especially southern B.C. and Ontario.

Tennis: All of Canada, but resort areas are popular.

Fishing and Hunting: Throughout Canada, but regulations, licensing, and seasons differ from province to province. There is no hunting in National Parks.

Mountain Climbing: Alberta, B.C., Yukon, Northwest Territories.

Alpine Skiing: Alberta, B.C., Québec, Ontario.

Cross-country Skiing: Throughout Canada, particularly in the provincial and national parks.

Snowmobiling ("skidooing"): All over Canada, especially in Ontario, Yukon, Northwest Territories.

Other possible recreation activities include skating, snow-shoeing, ice-fishing, hang gliding, windsurfing, sky diving, horseback riding, nature study and photography.

Parks

Provincial parks tend to be very people oriented, and are often the best bet for a good campsite. Some are small rest stops along the highway, while others stretch for hundreds of miles, offering hiking, canoeing, fishing, etcetera. Provincial government travel offices provide comprehensive information about these parks.

In an effort to preserve representative portions of the Canadian wilderness, the federal government has set aside 28 National Parks. For a \$10 annual fee, people can visit to swim, canoe, hike camp, ski, fish, take photographs and so on. A description of some of the parks is given in the **Sports, Recreation and Parks** sections of the Directory.

National Media

Television

The Canadian Broadcasting Company (CBC), a Crown Corporation, operates two nationwide networks (French and English), while CTV broadcasts a third. Other regional and provincial networks, along with independents and U.S. broadcasting, account for the remainder. There's also a new 24-hour music channel called *Much Music* . It's Canada's answer to MTV. Three quarters of Canada has access to U.S. network telecasts, and this number grows yearly with the advent of cable. The major cities usually boast at least one multilingual, or ethnic channel.

Canadian-based broadcasts feature excellent sports programs, documentaries, and performing arts, with top-notch news coverage. The same, alas, cannot be said for much of the indigenous entertainment, which most viewers shun in favor of U.S. or British fare.

Radio

CBC operates the sole national networks, both AM and FM, in English and French. There are hundreds of private stations that fill the airwaves with news and radio plays, as well as pop and funk.

Newspaper

A respected business journal, the *Financial Post*, and the Canadian edition of Toronto's *Globe* and *Mail* are distributed nationally. *La Presse* is the ranking Québec daily. News stores sell major American, British, and French newspapers.

Magazines

Canada's major news magazine, *Maclean's*, is published weekly. The monthly *Saturday Night* is popular among pro-Canada intellectuals. Other magazines from all over the world are widely available, including the *Economist, Time,* and *Newsweek* .

Foreign Supplement

For foreign visitors traveling in Canada this section serves as a brief introduction to what they can expect upon arrival here. Basic things about Canada are discussed all with the foreign visitor in mind. Areas covered are: Immigration and Customs, Government and Economy, Exchange Rates, Weights and Measurements, Time Zones, Clothing, and Consulates and Embassies.

There may be some surprises. For example, if people from France are expecting smooth sailing in Québec because they share the same mother tongue, they should be prepared for the linguistic idiosyncrasies of the Québecois.

Immigration

Crossing the Canada-U.S. border is relatively simple American passengers will be asked where they were born, where they live, and the purpose and length of their stay.

Some form of identification is required. Residents of Great Britain, Australia and New Zealand enter in a similar manner.

Those coming from elsewhere in the Commonwealth, the Americas, or Western Europe may need a visa if they plan to spend more than three months in Canada. For more details contact the Department of Employment and Immigration listed in **Directory.**

Customs

The same officer will often serve as a customs inspector. British and American visitors may bring their cars duty-free, for up to six months. If you have rented a vehicle, be sure to bring the contract. Boats, trailers, cameras, sports equipment, radios, etc, may be brought in without paying a duty, though Customs Canada may require a refundable deposit on some items, to ensure that they are not sold for profit.

Other items are regulated closely. You may bring in a hunting rifle or shotgun (with 200 rounds of ammunition), but handguns or automatic weapons are absolutely prohibited. Tobacco and alcohol are limited. All pets (save cats) require a veterinarian's certificate proving the absence of communicable diseases. Plants must be examined at the border, to ensure that they are not carrying destructive insects. For further details, write Revenue Canada, Customs and Excise, listed in the **Directory.**

On Departure

Citizens of Great Britain may bring home, duty free: 200 cigarettes or fifty cigars, 4 liters of wine, one liter of alcohol, 50 grams of perfume, and additional goods totalling no more than £28.

Each American citizen who spends more than 48 hours in Canada may return with $400 worth of goods, duty-free. Some airports and border points feature duty-free shops, offering liquor and other goodies at bargain prices. Americans should direct their questions to the U.S. Customs Service, P.O. Box 7407, Washington, D.C. 20044, or any Customs office.

Travelers from other countries should contact the customs office in their own country for information about what they can bring back.

Government

As a constitutional monarchy, the Queen of England is the titular head of government acting through her appointed Governor General in Canada. However, both the Queen and Governor General are figureheads, as actual power rests with the Prime Minister in Ottawa, Canada's capital.

The Canadian Parliament is a bicameral legislature, with a 282-member elected House of Commons, and a 104-member appointed Senate. The Senate remains largely a deliberative body, with little putative power. In the House of Commons, there are three parties, the Conservatives, the Liberals and the social democratic New Democrats. The Conservatives presently hold a majority with Prime Minister Brian Mulroney.

Canada is a federal state, with shared powers between the national and provincial governments. The federal government in Ottawa oversees National defense, trade and foreign affairs, banking, commerce, criminal law, fisheries, etc. The national and provincial governments concurrently assume responsibility for unemployment insurance and agriculture.

Provincial governments are also parliamentary, although their legislatures have no upper house. With jurisdiction over health, education, natural resources, and highways, the provinces enjoy a good degree of power, certainly more than a U.S. State. Consequently laws differ significantly from province to province—witness the various speed limits and tax codes. Canada is a diverse country in which provincial governments have emerged as the principal purveyors of regional interests.

Economy

Canada is a trading nation with a mixed economy. The majority of Canadian trade and investment transactions are with the United States, followed distantly by the British Commonwealth, Japan, and the U.S.S.R. Although the current Conservative government in Ottawa takes a somewhat free market approach to the economy, national and provincial governments have largely followed interventionist philosophies over the past four decades, State-owned (Crown) corporations have proliferated, particularly in the natural resource sector. The current trend, however, has been toward cautious deregulation.

Traditionally, Canada's economic strength lies in its natural resources. Forestry accounts for 10 percent of Canadian employment, newsprint and lumber being the premier products. Minerals and energy are important exports, as Canada is a leading producer of uranium, potash, asbestos, nickel, silver and gold, coal, oil and gas, and hydroelectricity. Farming remains important throughout Canada, and is virtually a way of life on the eastern prairies. Commercial fishing has suffered a prolonged slump, but continues to exert a profound influence on coastal Canada.

Canada's manufacturing base, though less renowned, is equally as important. Petroleum refining, its largest industry, and food processing (third largest) are tied directly to Canada's resource sector. However the automobile (second) and machine and equipment industries (fourth) have become significant employers, especially in Ontario and Québec, where two-thirds of all Canadians reside. Electronic and computer companies now have a firm toe-hold, as evidenced by the space shuttle Columbia's "Canadarm."

Banking, insurance, and real estate are some of the thriving business sectors, and they have already made significant inroads into U.S. markets. Also of note, is tourism, which makes up over 5 percent of the GNP while employing one Canadian in ten. This eagerness to attract foreign visitors helps to explain why Canada is such a delightful country in which to travel.

Money

There is no limit to the amount of money visitors may bring to, or exchange in, Canada. To get the best rate, exchange your money back home just before leaving for Canada. Canadian banks and the usual foreign exchange outfits will convert funds, but only after taking a percentage for themselves. The same goes for department stores, hotels, and restaurants, which will usually accept payment in U.S. dollars, but at a percentage premium somewhat lower than the going rate.

Exchange Rates

Approximate exchange rates of major currencies to the Canadian dollar, as of August, 1988:

	$1 Cdn obtains	Cdn $ exch. rate
Australia/Dollar	.98	1.02
Britain/Pound	.53	2.118
France/Franc	4.80	.205
Italy/Lira	1125	.0009
Japan/Yen	105	.0095
Netherlands/Guilder	1.60	.596
W.Germany/Mark	1.48	.675
United States/Dollar	.81	1.23

Credit Cards/Traveler's Checks

Major credit cards are widely accepted in Canada. Most American gasoline credit cards are accepted at one or another Canadian company-simply check the back of the card. Credit card companies automatically figure in the exchange rate. Nonetheless, interest charges present a hidden cost.

Traveler's checks offer a safe, convenient way to carry funds. Simply countersign show proper identification, and they will be accepted as cash. Buying checks denominated in Canadian funds saves the hassle and expense of exchanging upon arrival. American Express, Thomas Cook and Visa traveler's checks are widely accepted.

Weights and Measures

Canada has converted to the metric system. Well, sort of. Official weights and measures (like speed limits) are given in metric, but the federal government has hesitated to stamp out the last bastions of Standard Imperial usage (like most liquor bottles). Indeed, most Canadian think and speak in the old imperial. This conversion table, then, should come in handy:

Length
 1 cm = .4 in
 2.5 cm = 1 in

 1 m = 3.38 ft
 .3 m = 1 ft

 1 km = .6 mi
 1.6 km = 1 mi

Capacity
11 = 35 oz (33.8 US)
11 = .22 gal (.26 US)

Temperature
$9/5°C + 32 = °F$
$°C = 5/9°F - 32$

Area
1 ha = 2.5 acres
.4 ha = 1 acre

$1 \text{ km}^2 = .4 \text{ mi}^2$
$2.5 \text{ km}^2 = 1 \text{ mi}^2$

Weight
1 kg = 2.2 lbs.
.45 kg = 1 lb.

Time Zones

From Yukon to Newfoundland, Canada straddles six time zones. Daylight savings last from the final Sunday in April to the final Sunday in October, but is not observed in Saskatchewan. Newfoundland is a half-hour ahead of Atlantic Time.

Pacific Standard Time:
Yukon and most of B.C., Alaska is two hours behind Yukon.
Mountain Standard Time:
Alberta, Northeastern B.C., Saskatechewan, the Mackenzie district of N.W.T.
Central Standard Time:
Manitoba, the Keewatin district of N.W.T., Ontario west of Lake Superior.
Eastern Standard Time:
The rest of Ontario, Québec, the Franklin District of N.W.T.
Atlantic Standard Times:
Nova Scotia, New Brunswick, Labrador (Newfoundland), Prince Edward Island.
Newfoundland Standard Time(half hour ahead):
Newfoundland (except Labrador).

Clothes

If visitors plan an outdoors-oriented vacation (e.g. canoeing), they should bring warm, water-proof clothing, as summer storms can develop quickly. Insect repellent is also in order, since mosquitoes and black flies are a nuisance.

Remember that high winds can significantly reduce the "dead air" temperature, raising the specter of frostbite. If tourists plan to ski, snowmobile, hike, or otherwise spend time outdoors in the winter, bring very warm clothing and be prepared to cover exposed skin. Canadians resist the cold by wearing lightweight, non-synthetic clothing, in layers, to retain heat.

French Canadians.

Language

English: Though officially bilingual, English is the language of choice throughout most of Canada. Canadians speak with their own distinct accent, but written Canadian English is very similar to that of Great Britain. Americans will note the British spellings: in such words as "labour," "centre," and "civilised," and usage: such as "return," rather than "round trip," and "airlines," instead of "airways."

Newfoundland English: Newfoundlanders speak a dialect all their own. The thick accent is vaguely Irish, but the idioms and expressions are truly unique:

"Go to the law with the devil and hold court in hell"	the odds are against you
"to have a noggin to scrape"	an extremely difficult task
"Pigs may fly but they are very unlikely birds"	a vain hope
"in a hobble"	not worrying
"he is moidering my brains"	he is disturbing me

289

"Long may your big good good luck jib draw"

French: As a general rule, travelers who attempt to speak the native language are received more warmly than those who do not. French-speaking, or "francophone" regions of Canada are no exception to this. French as a mother tongue is fading outside of Québec, and although francophone communities still survive in the Maritimes, northern Manitoba and Ontario, the language in some areas has become strongly infused with English words and syntax, resulting in an interesting, if unintelligible, melange known as "franglais."

Nevertheless, an ability to speak and understand French adds tremendous bonus to any visit to Québec, especially since the former Parti Québecois government passed legislation making it the official language of the province. Montréal and Hull are home to sizable English-speaking ("anglophone") minorities and most inhabitants are bilingual, but if you travel further east in the province-to Québec City, for example-you may encounter Québeckers who speak very little English, and then perhaps reluctantly. The language they do speak is "Québecois," a hybrid evolved so thoroughly away from French that it is no longer considered a dialect, but rather a tongue unto itself.

Québecois French: Speakers of Standard French may have trouble understanding Québecois, which began as an archaic dialect and has become imbued with a heavy admixture of anglicisms.

The marked differences between the two languages are most evident in "joual," the jargon of urban Québecois. Joual employs non-standard grammar, missing or added syllables, English words and syntax, and a very nasal, elongated pronunciation. Hence, "je ne suis pas capable" is "shway," while "frére" is pronounced "friar". The fewer verbs and tenses, the better.

Quebeckers love to swear: "saint cibonne" and "maudit tabernac" are favorite expletives, too strong for polite company (like most Québecois profanity, they take aim at the Catholic Church). Other joual expressions:

avoir l'air anglais to look odd
ben gros very much

je pare la traite the drinks are on me
fifi, catiche male homosexual
aller a la peau to frequent prostitutes
piastre dollar
bidous cents

French speakers should also be wary of "false friends:" French words which Quebeckers use in their English, rather than French meaning. Here are just a few to start with:

English	Québecois	French
accommodations	accomodations	logement
to marry	marier	epouser
to affect	affecter	influencer
change	change	monnaie
ignore	ignorer	négliger
opportunity	ooportunité	occasion
appointment	appointement	rendez-vous

Tourist Information

Travelers who want to plan ahead for their trip to Canada can do so by writing the Canadian embassy or consulate in their own country for information. Listed below are Canadian embassies and consulates. The countries represent the people who most often visit Canada.

France
First Secretary of Tourism
Canadian Embassy, Commercial Division
37 ave. Montaigne
Paris 75008

Germany
Tourism Canada
Biebergasse 6-l0
D6000 Frankfurt/Main

Italy
Consul and Trade Commissioner
Canadian Consulate General
Via Vittor Pisani, l9
20l24 Milan

Japan
Counsellor of Tourism
Yamakastu Building, 5th Floor

5-31 Akaska-ku
8-CHOM Minato-ku
Tokyo l07

United States
Canadian Embassy
l2ll Connecticut Ave., Suite 300
Washington, D.C
20036

(Note:There are Canadian consulates in
every major American city.)

Foreign Consulates

While foreign visitors are traveling in
Canada they may need to contact their own
country in case of an emergency. Consulates
can be most helpful if a passport is stolen or
if a message needs to be relayed quickly
back home. Listed below are consulates
located across Canada, in Edmonton, Vancouver, Winnipeg, Toronto and Montréal.

Edmonton

Britain
10025 Jasper Ave.,
Suite 1404
403/428-0325

Federal Republic of Germany
2500 CN Tower
1004-104 Ave.
403/422-6175

Italy
1020-10405 Jasper Ave
403/423-5151

Japan
2480 Manulife Place
10180-101 St.
403/422-3752

Vancouver

Australia
Oceanic Plaza, 1066 W. Hastings St.,
Suite 800 604/684-ll77

Britain
111 Melville St.,
Suite 800
604/683-442l

Federal Republic of Germany
50l-325 Howe St.
604/684-8377

France
The Vancouver Block
736 Granville St.,
Suite 1201
604/684-8377

Italy
1200 Burrard St.,
Suite 505
604/684-7288

Japan
177 W. Hastings St.,
Suite 900
6904/684-5868

The Netherlands
Crown Trust Building,
475 Howe St.,
Suite 821
604/684-6448

United States
1075 West Georgia St,
604/685-4311

Winnipeg

Italy
283 Portage Ave.,
Suite 381
204/943-7637

Japan
730-215 Garry St.,
204/943-5554

Toronto

Australia
25 King St W.,
Commerce Court North
416/367-0783

Britain
Colledge Park
777 Bay St., Suite 1910
416/593-1290

Federal Republic of Germany
77 Admiral Rd

416/363-7038

France
130 Bloor St. W.,
Suite 400
925-8029

Italy
136 Beverly St.
416/977-1566

Japan
2705 Toronto Dominion Centre
416/363-7038

The Netherlands
One Dundas St. W.,
Suite 2106
416/598-2520

United States
360 University Ave
416/595-1700

Montréal

Britain
1155 University St.,
Suite 901
514/866-5863

France
Place Bonaventure,
2 Elysée
514/878-4381

Italy
3489 Drummond St.
514/849-8351

Federal Republic of Germany
3455 Mountain St.
514/286-1820

Japan
600 rue de la Gauchetiére
Suite 1785
514/866-3429

The Netherlands
Edifice Standard Life,
1245 Sherbrooke St. West,
Suite 1500
514/849-4247

United States
P.O. Box 65
Postal Station Desjardins
514/281-1886

Halifax

Britain
1959 Upper Water St.,
Suite 1501
902/429-4230

Italy
9 Downsview Dr.,
Dartmouth
463-3371

United States
Scotia Square,
Cogswell Tower
Suite 910
902/429-2480

Directory

In General

On travel in Canada write: Canadian Government office of Tourism, Dept., of Industry, Trade and Commerce, 235 Queen St., Ottawa, Ontario KIA OH5.
On Parks write: Parks Canada, Dept of the Environment, Ottawa, Ontario KIA OH3.
For nautical maps write: Dominion Hydrographer, Canadian Hydrographic Servec, Dept of Fisheries and Oceans, Ottawa, Ontario KIA OE6.
If flying a private plane, for a valid pilot's license write: Transport Canada, SLPP, Ottawa, Ontario KIA ON5.
On customs and what you can bring home write: Revenue Canada, Customs and Excise, Public Relations Branch, Ottawa, Ontario KIA OL5.
On visas and staying over three months write: Dept.of Employment and Immigration, Ottawa, Ontario KIA OJ9.

Getting Around

For road maps write: Canadian Automobile Association, 1775 Courtwood Cr., Ottawa, Ontario K2C 3J2.

Busing It: Greyhound offers a 7-day, 15-day or 30 day "Ameripass," good throughout North America Voyageur features similar package discounts. These options are often honored by Canada's 60+ regional and provincial bus lines. For more details, write:

-Greyhound Lines of Canada Ltd., 877 Greyhound Way SW, Calgary, Alberta T3C 3V8, or your nearest Greyhound office.

-Greyhound Inc., 901 Main St., Suite 2500, Dallas, TX 75202.

-Voyageur Colonial Ltd., 265 Catherine St., Ottawa ON K1R7S5; 613/238-5900, or any Voyageur office.

Railways: VIA Rail offers group, family, and senior citizen's discounts, as well as flat-rate "Canrail" passes. First class and coach accommodations are available, both with access to dining cars.

For more information, call the nearest train station, or contact: VIA Rail Canada Inc., 2 Place Ville Marie, Montréal, PQ, H3B 2G6. In the United States, Amtrak handles VIA Rail inquiries.

Write Amtrak at 400 N. Capital St. N.W. Washington, D.C. 20001. Or call toll-free in the U.S. at 800/USA-RAIL, in Canada call 800/426-8725.

Car Rentals: Several car rental companies have offices throughout Canada. They can be called, toll-free, for information and reservations:

Avis
In the U.S. : 800/331-2112 (domestic reservations);
800/331-1084 (international reservations)
In Canada: 800/268-2310

Hertz
In the U.S.: 800/654-3131
In Canada: 800/263-0600

Tilden (Associated with National Rent-a-Car in the U.S.)
In the U.S.: 800/328-4567
Canada: 800/268-7133 (Ontario)
800/387-4747 (Alta., B.C., Man, NFLD, NWT, Sask.)
800/361-5334 (N.B, N.S., PEI, Que)

Budget U.S.: 800/527-0700
Canada: 800/268-8900

Thrifty
Call Tulsa collect: 918/664-8844
Metro Toronto: 416/675-3144

ALBERTA

The area code for numbers listed in Alberta is 403 unless stated otherwise.

Finding Out

The Alberta Provincial Government distributes an updated *Visitor's Accommodations Guide*, which lists approved hotels, motels, campgrounds, and resorts. Its *Adventure Guide* describes car tours and sightseeing excursions, and includes a current road map. For these and more specific information, contact : Travel Alberta 10025 Jasper Ave., Edmonton, AB CANADA T5J Or call toll-free from across Canada and continental United States at 1-800-661-8888.

Calgary

The **Calgary Tourist and Convention Association** is always eager to help. Visit, write, or call their Hospitality Center, 237 8th Ave. SE, Calgary 403-262-3866.

Edmonton

For comprehensive information about the provincial capital, contact the **Edmonton Convention and Tourism Authority**, 104, 9799 Jasper Ave, Edmonton, T5J1N9. 403/422-5505

Accommodations

Travel Alberta distributes a complete *Visitor's Accommodation Guide*, but listed below is a representative sampling of available lodgings.

Banff

Banff Springs Hotel, 762-2211 or toll-free 800/268-9411. This resort is a town unto itself. Its famous golf course is as scenic as it is challenging.

Tunnel Mountain Chalets, 234-0422. 75 Chalets designed for family accommodations; each comes with full kitchen.

Mount Royal 762-3331, Large, comfortable rooms; a downtown landmark.

Red Carpet Inn, 762-4184. 46 units comfortable.

Johnston Canyon Resort, 762-2971. Rustic units, some with fireplaces; can accomodate families and honeymooners.

Calgary

Calgary's Hospitality Center operates a free Accommodations Bureau which can make reservations from its complete list of lodgings. Call them at 263-8518, or make arrangements directly with one of the following:

Westin Hotel Calgary, 320 4th Ave. SW; 266-1611. Very large hotel located in the financial district; caters to the business set. Reputedly the finest accommodations in Calgary.

International Hotel, 220 4th Ave SW, 265-9600 or toll-free 800/567-1991. High rise hotel features over 250 gorgeous suites.

The Palliser, 133 9th Ave. SW, 266-8621 or toll-free 800/268-9411. Everything about this hotel is done on a grand scale, including the rooms. Deluxe suites are available.

Calgary Center Inn, 202 4th Ave. SW, 262-7091 or toll-free 800/661-1463. Modern rooms with all the accoutrements; part of large entertainment complex.

Holiday Inn, 4206 Macleod Tr, 287-2700. New on the scene and one of the best in the chain.

Glenmore Inn, 2720 Glenmore Tr, SE; toll-free 800/6613163. Modern rooms as well as exercise and dancing facilities.

Lord Nelson Inn, 1020 8th Ave. SW;

269-8262. 55 rooms, some with refrigerators.

York Hotel, 363 Center St. S., 262-5581. An old favorite, newly renovated.

Relax Inns, 9206 Macloed Tr., and 2750 Sunridge N.; toll-free 800/661-9563. Well-respected chain.

University of Calgary, 2500 University DR., 284-7243. Accommodations on this sprawling campus are available during the winter and summer holidays.

Edmonton

Four Seasons, 10235 101st ST., 428-7111 or toll-free 800/268-6282. Edmonton's finest accommodations; connected by walkway to Edmonton Center complex.

Edmonton Westin, 10135 100th St., 426-3636 or toll-free 800/228-3000. Large hotel; offers first class comfort, luxury touches and very helpful staff.

Chateau Lacombe, 101st Street at Bellamy Hill, 428-6611 or toll-free 800/268-9411. High-rise hotel is known for elegant, tasteful lodgings; a bargain.

Edmonton Inn, Kingsway at 119th St 454-9521 or toll-free 1-800/661-7264. The city's largest, located near the airport.

Alberta Place, 10049 103rd St.423-1565. Comfortable suites come with kitchenettes.

Continental Inn, 16625 Stony Plain Rd. 484-7751. Offers sizeable, modern rooms, and full-scale convention facilities.

Relax Inns, 10320 45th Ave., and 18320 Stony Plain Rd. 483-6031 or toll-free 800/661-9563. Well-respected chain.

Gateway Hotel, 10412 63rd Ave; 434-1461. Spartan rooms, but can't beat the prices.

Youth Hostel, 10422 91st Street., 429-0140. Bring a sleeping bag.

Jasper Area

Jasper Park Lodge, 852-3301 or toll-free 800/642-3817. Elite resort with superior amenities; perhaps the most expensive of its kind in the Rockies.

Jasper Inn, 852-4461.or toll-free 800/661-1933. Chalet offers lavish, condominium-style accommodations; indoor pool, sauna.

Tonquin Motor Inn, 852-4987. Quiet, relaxing inn; some kitchenettes.

Athabasca, 852-3386. Comfortable rooms of varying sizes and prices.

Lake Louise Area

Chateau Lake Louise, 522-3511 or toll-free 800/268-9411. This famous, castle-like resort complex, set high in the Rockies, offers all the luxury amenities. Has a social, outdoors-oriented clientéle–that's why there are no television or radios.

Lake Louise Inn, 522-3791. Large estate offers a choice of hostelry: rooms, kitchen apartments, or inn-style accommodations, some deluxe, others moderately priced.

Moraine Lake Lodge, 522-3733. Back-to-nature log cabins; write for reservations.

Paradise Lodge and Bungalows, 403/522-3595. Rustic units just a short walk from the lake.

Restaurants/Dining

Alberta has long been associated with beef, and steaks in particular are culinary specialty. Nowhere else is beef cooked in so many different ways, be it minced, grilled, barbecued, or shishkebabed with vegetables. Albertans love honey, and they'll put it in or on nearly all their breakfast foods.

Calgary

Casa D'Italia, 2820 Center St. N. Fine Italian cuisine. 277-7556.

Franzl's Gasthaus, 2417 4th St. W., 266-6882. Bavarian food and drink; lively atmosphere.

Greek Village, 1212 17th Ave. SW, 244-1144. Excellent Greek dishes.

Mandarin Chinese Food, 210 16th Ave., NE, 276-1136. Relaxing Chinese restaurant.

My Marvin's, 601 12 Ave. SW, 234-7605. Popular deli.

Sukiayaki House, 517 10th Ave. SW, 262-9153. Japanese cuisine as it was meant to be consumed: sitting on the floor.

Gourmet dining:

Caesar's, 512 4th Ave., 264-1222. Primarily steaks and ribs, reputedly the finest in town.

Lutéce, 1604 14th St. SW. 229-3330. Intimate French cuisine.

Owls Nest, Westin Calgary, 266-1611. Gourmet cooking, interesting menu; listed among the top 10 restaurants of its kind in Canada.

Panorama Restaurant, 108 17 St., NW, 276-6449. Spacious, sky-top, revolving restaurant features international fare.

Three Green-Horns, 4th St. and 4th Ave. SW, 264-6903. Top-notch steaks and seafood.

Edmonton

Bistro Praha, 1018 100 A St., 424-4218. Laid-back café dining; huge portions.

Creperie, 10220 103rd St., 420-6656. A crepelovers' delight.

Mongolian Food Experience, 12520 102 Ave., 452-7367 at 101st Ave. It's just what the name says.

Mother Tucker's Food Experience, 10184 104th St., 424-0351. Popular homestyle cooking, from the breads to the dessert.

Yeoman, 10030 107 St. 423-1511. Old world elegance in old English decor.

Avanti Ristorante, 10245 104 St., 420-0482. Large selection of fresh pastas.

Village Restuarant, Village Park Mall, 464-1200.

Banff

Banff Cafe, 129 Banff Ave., 762-2553. Popular (despite its garish décor), and for good reason: the food is filling and the service lively.

Grizzly House, 207 Banff Ave., 762-4055. Hearty dishes befit the log-cabin motif.

Ticino, 205 Wolf St., 762-3848. Swiss and Italian cuisine: steaks, cheese fondues, veal, etc.

Jasper

Iron Horse, Connaught Dr. Steak and seafood amid "old West" paraphernalia.

Tekarra Lodge, Offers a broad choice, but known for its lamb.

Villa Caruso, Connaught Dr., 852-3920. Elegant Italian dinery.

Getting Around

By Air: Calgary and Edmonton International Airports are served by a sizable number of airlines. Canada and CP Air also fly regularly into the **Rocky Mountain National Parks.** Some numbers are : **Calgary Edmonton Air Canada**: 265-955 423-1222 **CP AIR:** 234-8275 955-8276 **WARDAIR**: 261-7690 423-5533

By Train: VIA Rail services **Calgary, Edmonton, Banff, Jasper,** and **Medicine Hat.** For more information contact their toll-free number 1-800/665-8630.

By Bus: Greyhound is the region's major carrier. Their Calgary depot is at 850 16th St. SW (265-9111); in Edmonton at 103 Gopher Street. Greyhound can whisk you to its Banff depot at Street (762-2286), but **Brewster Transport** (Connaught Drive, Jasper: 852-3332) provides major bus service within the parks.

By Car: Alberta maintains a good system of paved roads. The speed limit is 100 kph (61 mph) in daylight, and 90 kph (55 mph) at night. The major car rental companies are well represented. Taxis are readily available in Calgary, Edmonton, and many of the small towns, including Banff. They're expensive though, especially in Edmonton, where a three mile jaunt can cost over $4.

Calgary

The Calgary Transit (276-7801) operates modern buses and spiffy streetcars. A ride costs, $1.25, exact fare please.

Grayline (260-0719) runs afternoon bus tours of the city and treks to the Rockies.

Edmonton

With its city buses and sleek, new **LRT** line, Edmonton Transit (421-4636) provides excellent public transport, at $1.25 a ride, exact change.

This outfit also runs a fine bus tour, covering all the main sights. Grayline (10324 103rd St.; 423-2765) and Royal Tours (425-

5342) offer several more specialized excursions around the city.

Shopping

For specialty Albertan products like furs and Hudson's Bay blankets, try The Bay in **Edmonton** or the Trading Post in **Banff.** Inundated yearly by three million visitors from around the globe, Banff, not surprisingly, is home to numerous boutiques, some cosmopolitan, others local or native.

In **Calgary**, two stores of interest are Cottage Craft Gifts (6503 Elbow Dr. SW), which offers a large collection of Indian and Inuit artifacts, and Western Outfitters (128 8th Ave. SW), which features a sizable array of cowboy outfits and accessories. Otherwise, the pedestrian mall along 8th Avenue encompasses many retail outlets.

Museums and Galleries

Calgary

Glenbow Museum, 9th Avenue and 1st Street SE; 264-8300. Primarily an art and history museum, Glenbow's impressive exhibits will often engage visitors for days at a time. One of its four floors is devoted entirely to military equipment (including one of the largest known gun collections), while another displays the history of western Canada, and still another exhibits primarily regional art and artifacts. (open Tues.-Sun., 10 a.m. - 6 p.m. $2).

Center Eye Photography Gallery, 1717 7th St., SW; 244-4816. Photographic works of an international, national and local nature are on display. Center Eye also has a resource center and museum shop: (Tues.-Sat. 12 noon - 5p.m., free).

Edmonton

Muttart Conservatory, 98th Avenue at 96A Street; 469-8190. The four pyramidical structures house one of the most extensive floral displays in North America (open daily, 11 a.m. - 9 p.m.; $2.50).

Provincial Museum, 12845 102 Ave.; 427-1730. One of Alberta newer museums, it is already among its best, featuring the human and natural history of the province(open daily, 9 a.m. - 5 p.m.).

Performing Arts

Calgary

To find out what's happening on Calgary's increasingly sophiscated performing arts scene, check local newspapers or the weekly *Action* supplement.

Calgary's cultural centerpiece is the **Jubilee Auditorium**, 14th Avenue at 14th Street NW. This beautiful modern performance hall houses the **Alberta Opera**, and the youthful **Alberta Ballet Co.**

Theaters

Calgary Center for Performing Arts is a unique facility which houses one of the most accoustically perfect halls, Jack Singer Concert Hall. Located at 205 8th Ave. SE, the complex is the home of the **Calgary Philharmonic, Max Bell Theater, Theater Calgary, Martha Cohen Theater** and **Alberta Theater Projects.**

A wide variety of performing arts groups can be found at the **Pumphouse Theater** at 2140 9th Ave. SW.

For something different, try the popular moonday performances of the Lunch box Theatre Group in Bow Valley Square, 205 5th Ave. SW., 265/4292.

Edmonton

The **Conservatoire de Ballet**, the **Edmonton Opera Society**, and the **Edmonton Symphony Orchestra** perform at the Jubiliee Auditorium, 87th Avenue, 115th Street.

Banff

The **Banff Center for Fine Arts** on St. Julien Road is becoming a significant performing arts complex. Its two theaters offer dance, drama, film, and concerts. The Festival in August highlights the summer season. Find current program information in the periodical, *Banff*, which is widely distributed throughout the area.

Nightlife

In Alberta's resort areas (and to a lesser extent, in Calgary and Edmonton), hotels generally offer the most popular hot-spots, but a little exploration can take visitors off the beaten path to watering holes which cater mainly to the locals. Some bars and "beer parlours" are laid-back, but many have a fun, free-spirited (and sometimes raucous), Western atmosphere. The provincial drinking age is 19.

Calgary

Electric Avenue, 637 11th Ave., SW. Live bands.

New York-NewYork, 131 9th Ave, SW..

Shifty's, 5940 Blackfoot Trail S. Huge, technopop disco.

The Uptown, 1117 1st St., SW. Big dance club.

Edmonton

Stop at nearly any hotel to pick up a copy of *Billy's Guide*, a comprehensive, bi-monthly guide to what's doing in Edmonton.

String Fellows, 10186 106 St. Busy pub atmosphere.

Kingsway Inn, 10812 Kingsway Ave, Choice of three rooms, each with own atmosphere, from rowdy to sedate.

Jester's, 10266 103rd St. Comedy nightclub. On Tuesday, amateurs from the audience try their luck.

Cafe Monterey/California Bar, 10130, 112 St. Only funk club in town.

The Discovery, 9929 108th St. Piano bar after dinner.

Banff

Rimrock Inn, Mountain Ave. Piano Bar.

Grizzly House, 207 Banff Ave. Slow, dinner dancing.

Cascade Inn, 124 Banff Ave. Dancing to contemporary music.

Sports, Recreation and Parks

Alberta is internationally renowned for its excellent alpine skiing. The season runs from November to May, the best (and most crowded) months being January and February. Although slopes can be found throughout the Rockies, the five major ski areas are: **Nakiska** in **Kananaskis Country, Marmot Basin** in **Jasper National Park,** and **Sunshine Village, Mt. Norquay,** and **Lake Louise** in **Banff National Park**.

Not surprisingly, water sports thrive in popularity here. Canoeing and rafting opportunities abound throughout the provincial and national parks. **Whitewater Rafting** (403/652-7238) and **Rocky Mountain Raft** Tours (762-3627) offer river excursions for those who like to "rough it."

Alberta is a fisherman's fantasyland. Pile, waleye, trout, whitefish, etc. are catchable, year-round. A proper license is of course required ($12 for non-residents). Note that the National Parks issue separate restrictions. For details, and a sport- fishing guide, contact: Fish and Wildlife Branch 99201 108 St. Edmonton T5K 2C6 427-3574.

Hunting of any kind is prohibited in Alberta's National and Provincial Parks. In other specified areas, goose, waterfowl, and some big game can be hunted, but check with the Dept. of Energy and Natural Resources about licensing and guide requirements. Travel Alberta and the Fish and Wildlife Branch can also be helpful.

Alberta has over 100 **Provincial Parks**, providing recreational outlets to suit every taste. All have cooking facilities, and many offer campsites. Camping fees range from $3-$8, depending on the services available. Contact Travel Alberta for more details.

The National Parks provide campsites. The fees range from $5-$14, depending on the services available. Camping outside of designated campgrounds is possible with a special permit from the park authorities.

For more complete information on these parks, contact Parks Canada Western Region, 520-220 4th Ave. SE, Calgary, AB T2T 3H8, 292-4440.

Banff

Many visitors choose to see this park on horseback. Trail riding outfitters offer rides by the hour or tours lasting up to a week. Visit the Stables, across from the Banff Recreation Grounds, or contact the Trail Rider Store, on Banff Avenue (762-4551).

Getting to the summits of 7000+ ft (2330+m) high mountains surrounding Banff townsite is not difficult. **Mount Norquay**, with its excellent ski slopes, can be ascended by chair-lift ($5). Enclosed gondolas offer access to **Sulphur Mountain** ($5.50; 762-6500).

Touring by helicopter is an innovative and exciting (albeit expensive) way to explore glaciers, plateaus, and hitherto inaccessible mountain peaks. For about $200 a day per person, a helicopter will lead visitors to one or more sites, where a guide can take groups hiking, or in the winter, skiing. For details, contact the Chamber of Commerce (below) or call Okanogan Helicopters in Banff at 762-4082.

For complete information about fishing, canoeing, hiking, rafting, trailriding, climbing, skiing, sightseeing, etc., contact the Banff/Lake Louise Chamber of Commerce, Box 1298, 94 Banff Ave., Banff, TOY OCO, 762-3777; or call the Park Information Center at 762-3324.

Jasper

Located just north of Banff National Park, Jasper is larger, usually less crowded, but equally as spectacular.

From April to mid-October, the sky-tram will lift tourists just short of **Whistler's Mountain Summit**, near Jasper townsite ($5; 852-3093). The panoramic view is one of the Rockies' best. Wear hiking shoes to climb the last 600 ft (200m) to the summit. 15 miles (24 km) south lies 11,000 ft high (3670 m) **Mt. Edith Cavell**, accessible by car.

The Jasper Climbing School offers lessons for beginner, experienced, and expert mountain climbers at nearby **Mt.Munro.** Contact them at 806 Connaught Dr., 852-3964.

Maligne Lake, 25 miles (40 km) southeast of Jasper, is a long narrow, ice-blue body of water set amid snow-capped mountains. It is reputedly the most photographed area in the Rockies. By all means, take the two-hour boat trip. ($10; 852-3532). For day-long fishing excursions to **Maligne**

Lake, inquire at Currie's Guiding Ltd., P.O. Box 202, Jasper; 852-565.

No trip to **Jasper National Park** would be complete without a tour of the **Athabasca Glacier**, part of the vast. Columbia Icefield. To get there, take Hwy 93 south from Jasper or north out of Banff. Mammoth "sno-coaches" and huge snowmobiles conduct 45 minute tours fo the glacier, stopping occasionally to allow passengers to get a closer glimpse ($11).

The Brewster Transport Co. (in Banff: 762-2286, in Jasper: 852-3332) offers bus tours to the icefield from Jasper. It also runs day-long tours from Banff to Jasper townsites and vice-versa.

For complete information about Jasper National Park, contact the Jasper Park Chamber of Commerce, Box 98, Jasper, TOE 1E0; 852-3858. Or call the Park Information Center at 852-6176.

Waterton Lakes

Waterton is known as the park where "the mountains meet the prairies," and indeed, it has a little of both. Along with **Glacier National Park** in Montana, Waterton forms the **International Peace Park**. Although it stays open year round, most visitors' facilities are in service only between May 24 and Sept 1. During the winter, visitors still camp, hike, ski and snowmobile, but they must register first with the park authorities.

Animal-lovers rave about this park. Despite its small size, Waterton is home to black and grizzly bear, elk, deer, fox, mink, and badger, to name just a few of the furry creatures within. Bird watchers can sight gulls, eagles, hawks, and falcons. Fishermen travel here to catch whitefish, pike, and lake trout, which are large and numerous in the higher altitude alpine lakes.

Any needed equipment is easily rented in Waterton townsite. The park wardens can be extremely helpful, and they encourage visitors to check with them when planning their stay. Contact the Superintendent, Waterton Lake National Park, Waterton Park, AB TOK2MO; 859-2262.

Attractions

See also "National Parks" in Sports, Recreation and Parks.

Calgary

The observation deck of the 625 ft high (208 m) **Calgary Tower** affords a stupendous view of the city (9th Ave at Center St., open daily, a.m-Midnight; $2; 266-7171).

The Zoo, on St. George's Island, is considered the country's finest (open daily, 9 a.m. - 8 p.m.; $5; 265-9310).

Lethbridge

The **Nikka Yuko Japanese Gardens**, laid out as a symbol of Canadian-Japanese friendship, features an elegant pavilion, set in large, graceful, Japanese garden (open daily, May-October; $2; 328-3511).

Edmonton

Fort Edmonton Park is an elaborate, on going reconstruction of the history of Edmonton's settlement. A pre-railway village, Fort Edmonton, and an adjoining nature center are completed (open daily, May-September, $4.50; 435-0755).

Vista 33 and Museum, on the 33rd Floor of the Alberta Telephone Tower, offers a panoramic view of Edmonton and its environs (10020 100th St., open daily, 10 a.m. - 8 p.m., 50¢; 425-3978).

Woe to those who miss the **West Edmonton Mall**. Its owners immodestly call this five million sq ft shopping center the "eighth wonder of the world," but they're not far off. Different sections recreate street life in New York, Miami, New Orleans, and Paris. There's a full-size Spanish galleon, miniature Pebble Beach golf course, performing dolphins, a submarine (rides $6), an indoor amusement park, an Olympic-sized ice rink (where the Edmonton Oilers practice), palm readers, a petting zoo, an arcade of fun machines and so on. Oh yes, the mall also offers over 800 stores.

Diary

Early June (Vegreville)
  Ukrainian Festival: A Ukrainian folk fair. Camp in the shadow of the world's largest easter egg, standing over 30 ft (10 m) tall in Elk Park.
Mid-July (Calgary)
  Stampede: This is deservedly the most

famous annual Canadian event: ten days of raucous western showmanship and celebration. Make hotel reservations *well* in advance for this one (by some estimates, Calgary's population doubles), and book tickets ($5-$30) for main events as soon as possible. Write the Calgary Exhibition and Stampede, P.O. Box 1860, Calgary ABT 2P 2M7.

Late July (Edmonton)
Klondike Days: For 10 festive days, the entire city reverts imaginatively to Edmonton's gold rush era. Well worth planning a trip around. Make hotel reservations far in advance.

August (Banff)
Festival of the Arts: Features professional opera, symphony, musicals and plays.

Packages

Farm and Ranch Vacations: Alberta's "country vacation" program provides the chance to experience life on an Albertan farm or ranch. Like other packages of this sort, it's fun, inexpensive, and, if you choose, hard work. Unlike other programs, you can select from a list of accommodations ranging from large cattle ranches to small family farms. Several options are available regarding camping, duration of visit, etc. To obtain more details and book reservations, write Travel Alberta, 10025 Jasper Ave., Edmonton T5J 3Z3.

Looking for a more adventurous excursion? See Sports, Recreation And Parks.

BRITISH COLUMBIA

The area code for numbers listed in British Columbia is 604 unless stated otherwise.

Finding Out

For complete information about traveling British Columbia, call or write Tourism B.C., at the Parliament Buildings, Victoria BC, V8V 1X4; toll-free 800/663-6000.

Vancouver

The highly resourceful Vancouver Travel Infocenter can be found at 562 Burrard St., 683-2000.

Victoria

The Visitor Information Centre, 812 Wharf St., 382-2127, can help with every facet of a visit to B.C.'s capital.

Accommodations

Tourism B.C. publishes the *British Columbia Accommodations Guide* which lists every accredited motel, hotel, and resort in the province. Listed below is a fair sampling of what's available.

Vancouver

Vancouver offers a wide choice of lodgings. Hotels in the "Deluxe" range stand among the very best in Canada.

Westin Bayshore: 1601 W. Georgia St., 604/682 3377. Airy rooms overlook the harbor and Stanley Parks.
Four Seasons, 791 W. Georgia St., 689-9333 or toll-free 800/268-6282. Mid-town hotel is one of Vancouver's most luxurious; the staff caters to every wish.
Hotel Vancouver, 900 W. Georgia St., 684-3131 or toll-free 800/268-9143. Spacious, old-fashioned rooms with graceful touches. Houses several fine lounges and restaurants.
Hyatt Regency, Royal Center, 655 Burrard St., 604/687-6584 or toll-free 800/228-9000. Cosmopolitan elegance, atop fashionable shopping center.

Mandarin Hotel: 645 Howe St., New Hotel, painstakingly designed and furnished; offers all the accoutrements.

Pan Pacific Vancouver Hotel, 999 Place, 662-8111. Beautiful rooms overlooking the Bayshore.

International Plaza Hotel, 1999 Marine Dr., 984-0611. Elegant resort hotel.

Sheraton-Landmark, 1400 Robson St., 687-0511. Vancouver's tallest hostelry offers all the amenities befitting a luxury hotel.

Vancouver Sandman, 180 West Georgia St., 681-2211, Downtown with convention facilities.

Sheraton Villa Inn, 4331 Dominion St., 430-2828. Quieter lodgings in Burnaby, ideal for couples or small families.

Skyline Airport Hotel, 3031 No. 3 Rd., Richmond, 278-5161 or toll-free 800/663-1106. Caters to overnight travelers, but has all the amenities, including sauna, pool, and courtesy limo to the airport.

Austin Motor Hotel, 1221 Granville St., 685-7235. Central location, rooms vary in size, décor, price.

Sylvia Hotel, 1154 Gilford St., 681-9321. Elegant old hotel overlooking English Bay, adjacent to Stanley Park. Surprising grandeur for the price, hence very popular, especially during the summer.

YWCA, 580 Burrard St., 683-2531 or toll-free 800/663-1424. Bright, comfortable rooms; accommodations available for couples.

University of B.C., 5959 Student Union Mall, 228-5441. Dormitory on gorgeous U.B.C. campus, offers cheap rooms from May through Aug. Access to campus facilities.

Victoria

Empress Hotel, 721 Government St., 384-8111. A.B.C. landmark. Tea, crumpets, and scones served every afternoon in its regal lobby. Spacious subtlely decorated rooms, with service for the discriminating traveler.

Executive House, 777 Douglas St., 388-5111. 20 storey tower features modern, relaxing accommodations.

Harbor Towers, 345 Québec St., 385-2405 or toll-free 800/663-7555. Large rooms, each designed for a unique view of the city or its inner harbor.

Olde England Inn, 429 Lampson St., 388-4353. Tudor-style mansion set on a bluff overlooking five gardened acres.

Royal Scot, 425 Québec St., 388-5463. 100 comfortable rooms and suites.

Chateau Victoria, 740 Burdett Ave., 382-4221. Pleasant, large rooms.

Chestnut Grove, 210 Gorge Rd., 385-3488.

Pacific Isle Motel, 626 Gorge Rd., E, 385-3455.

Whistler's Mountain

Delta Mountain Inn, 4050 Whistler's Way 932-1982. Resort hotel favored by skiers; much cheaper during the summer.

Kamloops Area

David Thompson Motor Inn, 650 Victoria Street., Kamloops 372-5282. Good lodgings downtown.

Lac LeJeune Resort, Lac LeJeune, 604/372-2722. Resort lodge near Tod Mountain.

Kootenay Region

Fairmont Hot Springs Resort, 345-6311. Year-round resort lodge and cabins; great for skiing, golfing.

Kelowna

Beacon Beach Resort Motel, 3766 Lakeshore Rd., 762-4225. Year-round resort complex; offers lodgings of various sizes and prices.

Eldorado Arms Resort Hotel, 764-4126. Summer resort lodge and cottages set in the mountains.

Prince George

Coast Inn of the North, 770 Brunswick Street., 563-0121. Modern lodgings, helpful staff, indoor pool.

Connaught Motor Inn., 1550 Victoria St., 562-4441. Nice motel, indoor pool.

Prince Rupert

Prince Rupert Hotel, 2nd Avenue, 624-6711. Pleasant, accomplished lodgings overlooking the harbor.

Totem Lodge Motel, 1335 Park Avenue 604/624-6761. Nice motel near ferry docks.

Fort Nelson

Coast Provincial Motel, Alaska Hwy., "Mile 300"; 744-6901. Pleasant accommodations.

Restaurants/Dining

Woe to those who leave B.C. without sampling its sumptuous fish and seafood delights! Salmon, shellfish, and king crab are restaurant favorites. English roasts, lamb in particular, are hallmarks of British Columbia cuisine. Farms in B.C.'s lush Okanagan Valley grow a myriad of vegetables and fruits, the latter producing several exceptional wines. For dessert, try Victoria's famous chocolate creams, or Vancouver Island's own loganberry pie.

Outside Vancouver and Victoria, the best bet is often a motel, hotel, or resort dining room.

Vancouver

True to its cosmopolitan reputation, Vancouver offers dining for every taste: from world-class hotel restaurants, to eclectic Robonstrasse eateries, to touristy Gastown fare, to any number of fine ethnic locales. As always, call ahead for reservations whenever possible.

La Brasserie de l'Horlage, 300 Water Street, Gastown, 685-4835. Parisian cuisine and atmosphere.

Nirvana, 2313 Main St., 682-8779. Variety of Indian curry dishes.

Viva Mexico, 1636 Broadway, 731-7717. Enjoy great Mexican food; also South American salsa for dancing.

Simpatico's, 2222 W. 4th St., 733-6824. Greek food but great pizza.

Tsunami Sushi, 238-1025 Robson St., 68-SUSHI. Featuring sushi bar with revolving sushi boats; can be pricey.

Marco Polo, 83 Chesterfield Ave., 986-1155. Chinese buffet; Canadian side-dishes also available.

Yen Lock, 67 E. Pender Street, 681-3925. Authentic Chinese cuisine.

Saigon Vancouver, 950 W. Broadway, 732-7608. Excellent Vietnamese dishes.

Ostera Napoli, 1660 Renfrew Street., 255-6441. Traditional Italian menu.

Rooster's Quarters, 836 Denman St., 689-8023. Serves up delicious French Canadian barbecued chicken; always crowded, with good reason.

Gourmet dining:

Beach House, Beach Avenue, in Standlye Park, 682-2888. Continental menu, superb wine list, unbeatable setting.

Cannery Seafood Restaurant, 2205 Commissioner St, 254-9606. Fresh seafood, excellent service; among the top restaurants in Canada.

Le Napoleon, 869 Hamilton St., 688-7436. Lavish French cuisine; owners raise their own game birds.

The Roof, Hotel Vancouver, 684-3131. *Nouvelle cuisine*; skytop view.

Le Pavillion, Four Season Hotel, 689-9333. Primarily French dishs, prepared and served perfectly.

Trader Vic's Westin, Bayshore, 682-3377. Polynesian fare; one of the best in the chain.

Victoria

Captain's Place, 309 Bellevue St., 388-9191. 90 year-old Victorian mansion, stuffed with antiques; excellent seafood, nautical atmosphere. Open for breakfast, lunch, dinner.

Chez Pierre, 512 Yates St., 388-7711. Modestly priced French cuisine; immensely popular.

Empress Room, Empress Hotel, 384-8111. Primarily Continental menu, with a few added B.C. delights. Lives up to hotel's reputation of tasteful elegance.

Japanese Village, 734 Broughton St., 382-5165. Japanese dinners, prepared at your table.

Eugene's, 1280 Broad St., 381-5456. Greek snack bar.

Genghis Khan, 809 Craigflower, 383-7822. Exotic regional Chinese Cuisine.

Pablo's, 225 Québec ST., 388-4255. Fiery Spanish cuisine; located near inner harbor.

Parrot House Rooftop Restaurant, Chateau Victoria Hotel, 382-9258. Continental menu, great view; expensive.

Kamloops

David Thompson Dining Room, 650 Victoria St., Consistent steak and seafood; pricey.

Oriental Gardens, 545 Victoria St. Chinese and Japanese dishes.

Prince George

Outrigger Restaurant, 1208 6th Ave. Menu features Polynesian and Canadian specialties.

Vienne Schnitzel Restaurant, 6th Ave. at Brunswick Street. Lively dinner specializes in Central European fare.

Getting Around

By Air: Vancouver International, located just south of the city on **Sea Island**, is B.C.'s major air hub. Most main carriers fly here. Many smaller airlines and charters also serve northern B.C. and Yukon. Some numbers are: **Vancouver Air Canada:** 688-5515, **CP Air:** 661-5192 **Wardair:** 669-3355.

By Bus: Greyhound and **Trailways** offer service into and throughout southern British Columbia Coachways is a major carrier going north. The Vancouver depot is at 150 Dunsmuit, 604/662-3222. **Pacific Coachlines** in Victoria operates throughout Vancover Island, including service to Pacific Rim National Park.

By Train: VIA Rail provides excellent service to B.C. from Alberta and the rest of Canada.

By Car: The speed limit on B.C.'s highways is 80 kph (50 mph). Wearing seatbelts is mandatory.

Several car rental agencies operate in B.C. Check the front part of the Directory for toll-free numbers.

By Ferry: The British Columbia Ferry Corporation (in **Vancouver**: 669-1211; in **Victoria**: 386-3431) is the province's major carrier, with service between **Seattle, Victoria, Vancouver,** and other points along the coast. Of note is the "Inside Passage" to **Prince Rupert**: a scenic, overnight cruise through deep fjords and narrow channels. B.C. Ferry also offers relaxing day-long tours of the east and west coasts of Vancouver Island. Write them at 1112 Fort St., Victoria, B.C. V8V 4V2, or contact Tourism B.C. for sailing times and prices. Many ferries run infrequently or not at all in the winter.

Vancouver

Taxis can usually be hailed on the streets. Otherwise, call Bel-Air Taxi (433-6666) or Yellow Cabs (681-3311).

B.C. Hydro provides a fine mass-transit system, featuring buses and trolleys which charge 75¢, and several different harbor ferries. It also runs an airport shuttle, which costs around $5, or about half the cab fare. For full transit information, call 324-3211.

Grayline (681-8687) offers several different bus tours of Vancouver and environs, including jaunts to **Capilano Canyon** and **Grouse Mountain.**

Old-fashioned sternwheelers cruise Vancouver's harbor three times daily in the summer (call 687-9558).

Victoria

The major taxi companies are Blue Bird (382-4235) and Empress (381-2222).

Vancouver Island Transit (388-8457) provides bus service to Greater Victoria, at 75¢ a ride.

Grayline (388-5248) offers several bus tours on its huge, double-decker buses, imported from Great Britain.

For slower, more romantic sightseeing, hire a horse-drawn carriage on Belleville Street, opposite the Wax Museum.

Shopping

Vancouver

For chic galleries, boutiques, and import shops, head ot **Gastown** or Robsonstrasse. Authentic-and hence pricey-native and Inuit handiwork can be found at Tempo, 1107 Robson St. Underground shopping malls proliferate downtown, offering countless specialty stores. The **Royal Center** (under the Hyatt) houses a number of classy gift shops and fashion outlets.

Victoria

Visitors will find few of the larger department stores here, the emphasis being on specialty-often import-boutiques. **The Harbor Square** and **Market Square** developments together encompass over 50 such shops. In Trounce Alley (on the 1200 block of Government St.), visit **Victoria Handloom Ltd**. to find the city's largest collection of regional handicrafts; or **Alcheringa**, which offers specialty items from Australia and New Guinea.

Museums and Galleries

Vancouver

University of British Columbia Museum of Anthropology, University Boulevard, 228-5087.

Much more than a museum, its innovative architecture is itself worth a look-see, but the equally imaginative, multimedia displays are a marvel. The exhibits are international in scope, although the Northeast Indian collection, including numerous totem poles, is particularly astounding (open daily, afternoons, except Mondays; $2).

Centennial Museum, 1110 Chestnut St., 736-4431. Aside from its military exhibits and children's displays, this is a first-rate introduction to the history of Vancouver. An admission ticket here is also good for the nearby **Maritime Museum** (1905 Ogden Ave.), which features several nautical exhibits and an interesting tour of the *St. Roch*, a WW II era, RCMP arctic patrol boat (open daily until 5 p.m.; $2).

British Columbia Museum of Mining, Britannia Beach (30 miles from Vancouver, on Howe Sound), 688-8735. The museum is set in an abandoned copper mine. The guided tour includes a demonstration of mining machinery and a short excursion to a smelting plant (open daily, mid-May-September; $5).

Victoria

British Columbia Provincial Museum, Heritage Court, 387-3701. Elaborate, sight-and sound displays feature B.C.'s natural and human history. Easily Western Canada's finest museum, well-worth the entire day that could be spent exploring it (open daily; free admission).

Miniature World, Empress Hotel, 721 Government St. These impeccably detailed miniature layouts never fail to amaze onlookers, children especially. The 100+ft (30+m) reconstruction of C.P. Railway's advance across the prairies is a striking resemblance of its real counterpart and alone is already worth the admission (open daily; adults: $4.50, children: $2.50).

Prince Rupert

Museum of Northern British Columbia, 1st Avenue, 625-3207. Coastal Indian exhibits dominate this small museum. Of note are the wood and argillite carvings.

Performing Arts

Vancouver

With the possible exception of its theater life, Vancouver's performing arts scene is not quite in step with the city's growing wealth and prominence. Nevertheless, it is worth checking the daily papers or the weekly *Vancouver Guideline* to find out what's happening and where. Tickets to most events usually cost $6-$10, but can be as high as $20.

The spacious **Queen Elizabeth Theater and Playhouse** usually hosts Vancouver's main cultural events, while providing a permanent home for the fine **Playhouse Theater Company**.

Modern Canadian drama, both light and serious, is featured at the **Arts Club Theater**, 1181 Seymour St. Several amateur (but no less talented) groups perform regularly at the multicultural **Metro Theater Center**, 1370 S.W. Marine Dr.

Victoria

Available in most hotels, the *Victoria Guideline* outlines each week's various cultural and entertainment offerings.

The Royal Theater, 805 Broughton St., and **MacPherson Playhouse**, 3 Centennial Sq., feature concerts, opera, and drama.

Professional theater can be enjoyed at the **The Belfry**, 1291 Gladstone Ave.

Nightlife

British Columbia's drinking age is 19. A complex provincial classification system mandates that taverns must close at 1 a.m., but cabarets and bars may stay open until 2 a.m.

Vancouver

Major hotels tend to operate the swankier discos, but at least five drink-and-dance locales can be found around the 600 block of Hornby Street, making it a great stretch to bar-hop, except that $3-$6 cover charges are the rule.

Folk and jazz clubs, many with a U.K. type atmosphere, line Carrall Street in Gastown. Also worth a look:

Polo Club, Royal Center Mall. Dressier disco.

Puffin's, 1277 Robson St. Piano Lounge.

Victoria

Perhaps due to the preponderance of retirees, Victoria's nightlife lacks some zip. But it's not exactly dead, either:

Old Forge, 919 Douglas St. Nightclub, dancing; part of a huge entertainment complex housing several discos and lounges.

Lord Randell Room, James Bay Inn, 270 Government St. Festive English folk music.

Buckin' Bronc, Century Inn, 603 Pandora Ave. Country and Western.

Sports, Recreation and Parks

In the summer, golf courses should not be hard to find, but Victoria's mild climate allows golfing year-round. The Canadian Rockies are a perenial challenge to mountain climbers, who should check with the national Parks to ascertain more details. Hiking is a particular favorite among visitors to B.C. The provincial and national park authorities have cleared well-marked trails.

Water sports opportunities abound in B.C., both in the interior and on the ocean. Contact the Victoria or Vancouver yacht clubs to rent boats for deep-water fishing or sailing. Canoeing is highly popular; contact Tourism B.C. for rental and route information. For the more adventurously inclined, a Vancouver outfitter, **Whitewater Adventures** (669-110) offers one-to-five-day whitewater rafting excursions. **Parksville**, a sizeable, uncrowded resort area north of Vancouver on **Vancouver Island**, lays claim to some of the best (and warmest!) swimming in Canada. More great swimming and boating can be had in the **Okanagan Valley Resort** areas.

For fishermen, British Columbia's lakes and streams offer bass, char, perch, and trout. B.C. is famous for its salmon, which can be caught on the **Fraser River**; or, book an ocean-bound charter from **Harbor Cruises** (427 Belleville St., 384-1224) in **Victoria**. The halibut fishing around **Prince Rupert** is unparalleled, while the **Kamloops** area, particularly Lake Shuswap, is home to the mammoth Kamloops Trout.

Hunters come to B.C. in search of moose, caribou, deer, cougar, mountain goat, grizzly and black bear, and waterfowl. Secluded resort camps around Prince George reward those who make the long drive with excellent fishing and hunting. Fly-in camps farther north offer still better opportunities. If planning to fish or hunt, check first with the Fish and Wildlife Branch 1019 Wharf St., Rm 400 Victoria B.C. V8W 2Z1 387-6411, about regulations and fees. A non-resident fishing permit should cost about $15, hunting about $25.

Excellent ski slopes dot B.C. from the Coast Mountains to the Rockies. The major resort areas include: **Big White,** in the **Okanagan Valley**; **Red Mountain** and **Snow Valley** in the **Kootenaya**; the

Cariboo and **Bugaboos**, in the **Rockies**; and **Forbidden Plateau** on **Vancouver Island**. **Cypress Bowl,Grouse Mountain, Hemlock Valley,** and **Mount Seymour** lie near **Vancouver**, as do the superb **Whistler's Mountain** and **Bascomb Mountain** runs in **Garibaldi Provincial Park**. By all means get a complete list of skiing opportunities and related information from Tourism B.C.

Provincial Parks

B.C. has over 300 provincial parks, large and small. For information about camping, hiking, skiing, etc., contact Tourism B.C., or call the Provincial Parks Office in Victoria 387-6696.

Mt. Seymour: Located only 20 minutes north of Vancouver, this park provides a delightful urban escape. Hiking and skiing are popular. Take the Skyride (daily; $7.50; 984-0661) to the top of Grouse Mountain for a superb view of the city and its environs; in winter, the Skyride serves as a lift. For more information about the park, call 929-1291.

Garibaldi: This one is two hours out of Vancouver, but worth the trip for outdoors enthusiasts. Skiers enjoy the Alpine runs of Whistler's and Bascomb Mountains. Glacier skiing by helicopter becomes yearly more popular.

Manning: Lying just north of the Canada-U.S. border southeast of Hope, this park is great for canoeing, hiking, and winter sports. It's also known for its rhodoendron fields, which bloom in mid-June. For more information about Manning Provincial Park, call 840-8833.

Mt. Robson: Buttressed against Jasper National Park, it is known mostly for its namesake, the tallest peak in British Columbia. Mountain climbers will find reaching its 13,000 foot (4333 m) summit a challenge.

The National Parks

For comprehensive information on B.C.'s National Parks contact: Parks Canada Western Region 520-220 4th Ave., SE, Calgary, ABT2T 3H8 403/292-4440.

Mt.Revelstoke: P.O. Box 350, Revelstoke, BC VOE 2SO; 837-1555. Though small, its mountaintops offer spectacular scenery, breathtaking passes, and great slopes for skiing.

Glacier: P.O. Box 350, Revelstoke, BC VOE 2SO: 837-1555. Located farther east in the Selkirks, this park is known for its over 100 glaciers. Its countless streams offer excellent fishing.

Yoho: P.O. Box 990 Field, BC VOA 1GO; 343-6324. Buttressed against Jasper National Park in Alberta. People come here to ski, mountain climb, hang glide, and fish.

Kootenay: P.O. Box 220, Radium Hot Springs, BC VOA 1MO; 347-9615. Located in a narrow Rocky Mountain valley south of Yoho National Park, Kootenay features warm, relaxing mineral baths in Radium Hot Springs.

Pacific Rim: P.O. Box 280, Ucluelet, BC VOR 3AO; 726-7721. This little-known strip of rocky coastline on Vancouver Island's western shore is beloved by hikers, surfers, and sailing enthusiasts.

Attractions

Vancouver

Aquarium, Stanley Park, 685-3364. The first of its kind in this part of the world, and still among the best. See performing killer whales, dolphins, and beluga whales, then tour the fascinating aquatic exhibit balls (open daily; $5).

Harbor Center, 55 Hastings St., 689-0421. The circular observation deck 40 stories up promises a stupendous view.

Queen Elizabeth Park, West 23rd Ave. at Cambie St. 873-1133. Set on Vancouver's highest point, this gorgeous park also offers an excellent view of the city, if visitors are not too busy browsing through the arboretum, Sunken Gardens, or Floral Conservatory.

Howe Sound, To view this spectacular, 40 miles long (60 km) fjord, drive north along Rte. 99; halfway to Squamish lies the B.C. Museum of Mining (see Museums and Galleries). It can also be appreciated by train: the Royal Hudson 2860 leaves every morning in the summer from the North Vancouver Station for a six-hour, round-trip trek to Squamish (978-5211).

Victoria

Sealand of the Pacific, 1327 Beach Dr., beside Oak Bay Marina, 598-3373. Octopi, eels, salmon seals, and other aquatic creatures inhabit huge tanks filled with bay water. Sealand's star performer, though, is *Haida*, a mammoth, fun-loving killer whale, who gives drenching performances hourly (open daily; adult $5).

English Village, 429 Lampson St., 388-4353. This row of dwellings harkens authentically to Tudor-era England. Its premiere attraction is a methodically detailed replica of Shakespeare's birthplace.

Buthchart Gardens, 14 miles (22 km) north by Rte. 7 or 7A; 652-4422. These are six gardens of international renown, where hedges, flowers, lawns, and statuaries combine to create a mesmerizing experience for those who make the short trip from Victoria.

Barkerville

Historic Park, 994-332. Barkerville has been entirely restored to its gold rush days, complete with stores, saloons, the courthouse (see "hanging" Judge Begbie at work), Anglican Church, Chinese Freemasons' Hall, and other such things one would find in a mining town, circa 1860. All in all, a fun summertime detour.

Skeena Valley

Accessible by overnight ferry to Prince Rupert (see Getting Around), or Hwy16 ("Yellowhead Highway") from Prince George.

Although historically an important trading route and fishing region, scenic Skeena Valley is known especially for its Northwest Coast Indian villages, inhabited by the Gitksan tribe. The best way to learn about their fascinating, ritualized culture is to visit the reconstructed village, '**Ksan**' (guided tours, May to October, $4; 842-5544), when a series of long houses details the history, lore, and art of the Gitksan.

Diary

January - February (Most alpine areas)
   Skiing Competitions: Witness expert downhill skiers showing their stuff throughout the province.

July 1 (Vancouver)
   Folk Music Fest: Multicultural dancing,

food, and exhibits, held primarily in Gastown.

First Week in July (Wiliams Lake)
   Stampede: B.C.'s premiere rodeo.

Mid-July (Vancouver)
   Sea Festival: Topped-off with famous, Nanaimo-Vancouver bathtub race.

July (Kimberley)
   Julyfest: A Bavarian celebration of folk dancing and entertainment, set in "Canada's highest city." Try the beer-filled glass boots.

August (Kelowna)
   International Regatta: Held on beautiful Okanagon Lake.

Late August-Labour Day (Vancouver)
   Pacific National Exhibition: Features parades, exhibits, sports, entertainment, and logging contests.

MANITOBA

The area code for numbers listed in Manitoba is 204 unless stated otherwise.

Finding Out

The provincial government distributes road maps and the free *Manitoba Vacation Guide*, which lists accommodations, campgrounds, sites of interest, outfitters, tours, etc. These are available from any provincial information center, or from : Travel Manitoba 7-155 Calton St. Winnipeg, MB R3C O3H or call toll-free 800/665-0040.

The Winnipeg Public Library (on Donald Street) includes in its large Canadian section an extensive collection of contemporary and historical works on Manitoba.

Accommodations

Winnipeg offers a variety of lodgings, from old and grand to slick and modern. Ask about weekend packages. In Manitoba's small towns, accommodations tend to be modest, both in décor and price. *Travel Manitoba* can provide a complete list of places to stay in the province.

Winnipeg

The Westin Hotel Winnipeg Inn, 2 Lombard Pl.,957-1350; Toll-free in Canada and U.S.: 800/228-3000. Large Westin hotel, featuring posh dining room, the *Velvet Glove*.

Hotel For Garry, 222 Broadway, 942-8251. Elegant rooms set in 75 year old French-style chateau.

Holiday Inn, 350 St. Mary's Ave., 942-0551 toll-free 800/ HOLIDAY. Service-oriented staff; indoor and outdoor pools, connected by walkway to the Convention Centre.

Marlborough Inn, 331 Smith St., 942-6411. Dignified, gothic décor, but they didn't forget any of the accoutrements.

Charterhouse, 330 York Ave. 942-0101. Good location downtown; outdoor pool.

Place Louis Riel Apartment Hotel, 190 Smith St., 947-6961 toll-free 800/665-0509. Downtown location; suites come with furnished kitchens.

Canadiana (I), 1400 Notre Dame Ave., 786-3471. Near the airport.

Assiniboine Hotel, 1975 Portage Ave., 204/888-4806. Pleasant; lounge known for Saturday afternoon jazz performances.

St. Boniface Hotel, 171 Dumoulin St., Prime location in French district for the *Festival du Voyageur* .

Brandon

Royal Oak Inn, 3130 Victoria Ave., 728-5775. Pool, sauna, nice lounge, fine dining room.

Canadian Inn, 150-5th St., 727-6404. Pool, dining room, cocktail lounge.

Thompson

Mystery Lake Motor Hotel, 778-8331. Large hotel; good service.

Riding Mountain National Park

Alk Horn Ranch, Wasagming, 848-2802. Family-oriented lodge and chalets set right in the park.

Farm Vacations are a great way to get a true sense of the prairies. Lasting from one day to a week or more, they offer a wide enough variety for different activities to suit almost any taste. For further information, write Manitoba Farm Vacation Association, 525 Kylemore Winnipeg MB R3L IB5.

If you prefer to have a similar kind of hospitality but in more urban setting, try contacting the Bed-and-Breakfast 93 Healy Cres. R2N 2S2.

Restaurants/Dining

Manitoba is known for its Selkirk whitefish, caviar, and "Winnipeg goldeye," a local delicacy often served for breakfast with champagne. Winnipeg's dining scene reflects the city's thirty-odd ethnic groups. Ukrainian cuisine-including cabbage rolls, borscht, and dumplings-stands out in particular.

Winnipeg

Bombay Palace, 598 Ellice Ave., 772-5030 Indian Cuisine.

Kum Koon Garden, 426 Main, 943-4655. Authentic Chinese dishes; specializes in dim sum.

d'8 Schtove, 1531 Pembina, 284-4339. Mennonite Cuisine.

Zorba's, 704 Sargent Ave. Greek and Canadian dishes.

Kronborg, 1875 Pembina 261-1448. Danish sandwiches.

Ichi-ban, 189 Carlton ST., 942-7493. Japanese cuisine.

La Grenoile, 150 Provencher Blvd 233-0422. Prairie dishes with French-Canadian emphasis.

Garden Créperie, 349 York Ave., 597-0221. Crépes and other light fare.

Gourmet dining:
La Vielle Gare, 630 Des Meurons St., 247-7072. Continental French cuisine; set in 1914 railway station.

Victor's, 4561 River St., 284-2339. Creative menu and décor.

Dubrovnik, 390 Assiniboine, 944-0594. Balkan specialties; located in renovated brick townhouse.

Old Swiss Inn, 207 Edmonton St., 942-7725. Consistently excellent Swiss cuisine.

Brandon

Suburban Restaurant, 2604 Victorian Ave., 728-3031. Plain good food.

Portage la Prairie

Best Western Manitoba Inn, Hwy 4, 857-9791. The hotel dining room is popular.

Flin-flon

Bakers Narrows Lodge, in Bakers Narrows. A favorite of hunters and fishermen.

Getting Around

By Air: The following airlines serve **Winnipeg International Airport**:

Northwest Airlines: 475-2730
CP Air: 783-0694
Air Canada: 943-9361
Canadian International Airlines: 632-1250
Wardair: 800/661-5678

Canadian International also flies regularly into **Churchill**, Manitoba. At the Winnipeg airport, limousines, taxis, and city buses are available for the short ride downtown.

By Train: VIA Rail operates out of the Main Street station (204949-1830) in Winnipeg. For service across Manitoba call 1-800/282-8070.

By Bus: Grey Goose and **Greyhound** serve Winnipeg through the terminal at 487 Portage Ave. (775-8301).

By Car: Manitoba's speed limit is 95 kph (58 mph), unless otherwise posted. A reliable system of paved roads extends north to **Flin Flon**. Several large car rental companies have offices in Winnipeg, both at the airport and downtown. Check the front part of the **Directory** for toll-free numbers.

Winnipeg

The Winnipeg Transit System offers two ways to get around. The free *DASH* buses shuttle people throughout the downtown between 11 a.m. and 3 p.m. Otherwise, regular city buses cost $1 (exact change required).

Taxis can usually be hailed with ease downtown. If not, call Unicity Taxi (947-661), Unicity (942-3366), or Duffy's (775-0101).

Tours

For a scenic, relaxing tour of Winnipeg during summer, try a cruise on the Red and Assiniboine Rivers. The M.S. **Lady Winnipeg** departs several times daily from Dock 312 on Nairn Avenue for a two-hour tour (669-2824). The Gray Line operates two sternwheel paddleboats, reminiscent of those which helped open the West, from their dock near Redwood Bridge (339-1696)

Shopping

If it's sold in Manitoba, chances are it can be bought in Winnipeg. Wander through **Osborne Village** (behind the Legislative Building) to find artisan and specialty shops. On weekends, a festive, open-air market springs up at Albert and Bannatyne Streets. Still more boutiques huddle in a huge old warehouse call **Townside** in the market area. **Portage Place** downtown is the most interesting of Winnipeg's more traditional shopping centers.

Museums and Galleries

Winnipeg

One of the finest museums in this part of Canada is undoubtedly the **Manitoba Museum of Man and Nature**, whose fascinating exhibits display the region's culture, history and geography (Centennial Arts Center, open daily, 10 a.m. to 9 p.m., admission: $2; 956-2830). Its Planetarium, downstairs, presents six different multimedia shows annually. Call 943-3139 for more details.

The **Winnipeg Art Gallery** boasts a large collection of Canadiana. Its Inuit art and sculpture are particularly renowned (Memorial Blvd., open daily except Monday, ll a.m. to 5 p.m., free admission; 786-6641).

The **Ukrainian Cultural Center** preserves Ukrainian artifacts and culture through its art gallery, museum, archives, and library. That this center is the largest of its kind outside of the Ukraine testifies to the substantial impact this national group has had on Manitoba (open daily except Monday, 10 a.m. to 4 p.m. free admission; 942-0218).

Churchill

Eskimo Museum, Oblate Fathers from the adjacent Catholic mission exhibit here an extensive collection of Inuit carvings. Collected over four decades, the stone, ivory, and bone sculptures depict nearly every facet of Inuit legend and culture (open daily 675-2030).

Performing Arts

Winnipeg

Consult the *Winnipeg Sun* or the *Free Press* for more information and a complete listing of performing arts events.

The Centennial Arts Center (956-1360) is the major focus of Winnipeg's cultural scene. Tickets for events here should range from $8 to $ 25. Aside from the Museum of Man and Nature, the Centennail Center houses:

-The **Royal Winnipeg Ballet**. Canada's first ballet company is also among its best. It performs from October to April.

-The **Manitoba Opera Company**, (942-7479) which gives three performances a season.

-The **Winnipeg Symphony Orchestra** (942-4576). Soon to enter its 40th year, this prestigious orchestra enjoys the benefit of the auditorium's excellent acoustics. Its season runs from November to May.

-The **Centennial Concert Hall** (956-1360), which features pop/rock groups and other contemporary artists.

From October to May, the **Manitoba Theater Center** (942-6537), reputedly the finest in the prairies, presents a series of spectacular productions in its center on Market Avenue. Its second stage, the **MTC Warehouse** , offers more experimental theater.

The **Rainbow Stage** (942-2091), set in Kildonan Park, is Canada's oldest running outdoor theater, performing classic musicals each July and August.

Nightlife

Manitoba's legal drinking age is 18.

Winnipeg

Much of Winnipeg's nightlife can be found at the downtown hotels. Even the much staid hostelries offer lively watering holes.

Top of the Inn, **The Westin Hotel** Winnipeg. Piano bar.

Swallows, 100 Osborne St., 452-6054. Jazz.

Old Bailey, Downstairs at Oliver's, 185 Lombard St., English pub.

Dancing

Stage Door, The Westin Hotel Winnipeg, 957-1350.

Uncles, Holiday Inn, 942-0551. A popular hotspot; no jeans.

Bogarts, 139 Albert St., 942-1143. Fashionable with single baby-boomers.

Marbles and **Network** are the hot spots on Rorie Street.

Sports, Recreation and Parks

Write *Travel Manitoba* for complete information on the sports and recreation activities listed below.

Golf and horseback riding are popular in the summer, as is nearly every conceivable water sport. Provincial authorities have cleared several challenging hiking trails, including the exciting "Amisk" trail in **Whiteshell Provincial Park**.

Manitoba offers both summer and winter fishing season for those in pursuit of trout, northern pike, walleye, and Hudson Bay salmon. Hunters come to Manitoba in search of black bear, caribou, deer, and moose. To obtain a license and find out about other requirements (and opportunities), contact the Game and Fisheries Branch, Dept. of Natural Resources, P.O. BOX 24, 1495 St., James St., Winnipeg, MB R3H OW9; 945-7812.

Although it cannot match neighboring Alberta, Manitoba is increasingly developing its wintertime recreational facilities. Growing numbers of resorts offer tobaggoning, snowmobiling, and of course, skiing opportunities. Cross-country enthusiasts in Manitoba take to the provincial park trails.

Manitoba's 15 provincial parks are the main focal points of outdoor recreation in the province. For details, write Travel Manitoba, 7-155 Carlton St., Winnipeg, MB R3C O3H.

Whiteshell Provincial Park, the largest and most complete in terms of outdoor opportunities, lies only 90 miles (144 km) east of Winnipeg.

Riding Mountain National Park- Located 175 miles (280 km) northwest of Winnipeg, this is a park of prairies and forested hills, lakes and streams. People come here to do it all: camp, hike, hunt, fish, play golf or tennis, ski, gaze at wildlife (including bison), sail, swim, canoe, or simply relax. For further information, contact the Superintendent, Riding Mountain National park, Wasagaming, MB, R0J 2H6; 848-2811.

The province also boasts over 10,000 campsites, which charge around $6-$10 a day, depending on the facilities. For a list of campgrounds, write Travel Manitoba at the address above.

Attractions

(See also the "Diary" and "Packages" sections)

Winnipeg

Winnipeg's Travel Manitoba Visitor Reception Center (944-3777), in the Legislative Building will detail all that the city has to offer but for the tour-minded traveler, two sites stand out:

The **Royal Canadian Mint** offers a spectacular tour of the phenomenal engineering feats required to mass-produce Canada's coinage. Mammoth cranes, furnaces, and presses convert two-ton bronze and nickel strips into over 18,000 coins per hour (open weekdays, 9 a.m.-3 p.m., free admission; 520 Lagimodiére Blvd.; 257-3359).

Visit Canada's largest **Commodity Exchange** first thing on a weekday morning to experience the unique pandemonium of 350 brokers frantically buying and selling wheat, corn, gold, bonds, and the like (opens at 9:30 a.m., free admission; 360 Main St.; 949-0495).

Diary

January (Winnipeg to St. Paul, Minnesota)
International 500 Snowmobile Race: Popular Canadian-American Event.

February (St. Boniface, Winnipeg)
Festival du Voyageur: The lively francophone community celebrates in honor of the early fur traders. Taché, St. Boniface MB RZ4 2L4; 237-76923.

Mid-July (Winnipeg)
Winnipeg Folk Festival: The internationally acclaimed folk music festival is held over four days in Birds Hill Provincial Park, and features bluegrass, gospel and good-time music of yesteryear. Contact: 8-222 Osborne St. S, Winnipeg, MB R3L 1Z3; 284-9840.

End of July (Austin)
Manitoba Threshermen's Reunion and Stampede: Antique tractor races, sheeptyping, and threshing contests draw participants from throughout the North American prairies.

July-August (Dauphin)
National Ukrainian Festival: Music, fun and games galore for the visitors.

First Week in August (Gimli)
Icelandic Festival: The towns people of Gimli take this opportunity to celebrate inhabiting the second largest Icelandic community outside of Iceland.

August (Winnipeg)
Folklorama: This four-day, city-wide festival features the food, dancing, crafts, and culture of 30 different ethnic groups. Contact the Community Folk Art Council Inc., 375 York Ave., Winnipeg, MB R3C 3J3; 944-9793.

Provincial Holiday

Civic Holiday
First Monday in August.

Packages

Leisurely, three-to five-day cruises of **Lake Winnipeg** (the continent's seventh largest) can be arranged aboard the M.S *Lord Selkirk II*. Contact Sub-Arctic Expeditions Inc., 69 Birchbark Bay, Winnipeg, MB R2P 1T2 (582-2331).

VIA Rail offers **Explorer Tours to Hudson Bay**: exciting, week-long treks to **Churchill**, via **The Pas** and **Flin Flon**. Contact the Winnipeg depot (949-1830), any other VIA Rail office, or write them at 140-123 Main St., Winnipeg, R3C 2P8 for more information. But don't delay–the waiting list can be up to a year long.

NEW BRUNSWICK

The area code for numbers listed in New Brunswick is 506 unless stated otherwise.

Finding Out
For road maps, help arranging accommodations, or suggestions for traveling New Brunswick, contact: Tourism New Brunswick P.O.Box 12345 Fredericton, N.B. E3B 5C3 453-2377 800/561-0123, toll-free in Canada and the U.S.

Accommodations

Tourism New Brunswick provides a "Dial-a-Night" service: call for information and reservations at nearly all the province's hotels and motels. New Brunswick's hostels offer very inexpensive, dorm-style lodgings. Write or call, New Brunswick Hostel Association c/o National Office 333 River Rd., Vanier, Ont. K1L 8H9 (613) 748-5638.

The list below provides a good sampling of what's available.

St. Andrews

Algonquin Hotel, 529-8823. Luxurious hotel features numerous recreation oportunities, including golf, croquet, and tennis.

Sea Garden, 469 Water St., 529-3225. Quiet, elegant rooms.

Saint John

Colonial Inn, 175 City Rd., 652-3000. Pleasant and accommodating.

Keddy's Fort Howe Hotel, 10 Portland St., 657-7320. Very modern accommodations; skytop restaurant.

Fredericton

Lord Beaverbrook Hotel, 659 Queen St., 455-3371. Luxury hotel perfectly situated downtown.

Diplomat Motor Hotel, 225 Woodstock Rd., 454-5584. A comfortable value in residential area.

Elms Tourist Home, 269 Saunders St., 454-3410. Six very quiet rooms.

Youth Hostel, 193 York St., 454-1233.

Moncton

Hotel Beauséjour, 750 Main St., 854-4344. Moncton's finest accommodations.

Colonial Inn, 42 Highfield St., 382-3395. Modern rooms in great locale; ask for a discount on weekends.

Shediac

Hotel Shediac, 532-4405, Main Street,. Dignified, old fashioned hotel.

Edmundston

Wandlyn Auberge Inn, 919 Canada Road, 735-5525. Sports, a pool and surprisingly good food.

Restaurants/Dining

Seafood, of course, is a New Brunswick staple, so Atlantic salmon, oysters, clams, chad, and lobster all find their way onto the province's menus. Other local dishes include steam brown bread, "fiddle-heads." (young fronds), and baked beans.

St Andrews

Passamaquoddy Room, Algonquin Hotel, 529-8823. Energetic students serve bountiful buffet lunches and formal dinners.

Campobello Island

Friar's Bay Restaurant, Welshpool, 752-2056. Filling, old-fashioned meals at modest prices.

Saint John

Leo's Supper Club, 2171 Ocean Westway 672- 6090. Popular Austrian and Swiss cooking.

Top of the Town, Fort Howe Hotel, 652-1157. Skytop steakhouse.

St. Hubert Bar-B-Q, 324 Rothesay Ave., 633-4945. Roasted chicken, a favorite in eastern Canada.

Putnam's, 39 King St. (located in the Delta Brunswick), 648-1981. Specializes in seafood.

Fredericton

The Victoria and Albert, 642 Queen St., 458-8810. Extensive menu includes excellent fresh seafood entrées.

Martha's Restaurant, 625 King St., 455-4773. Modes, Central European cooking.

Acadian Family Restaurant, 58 Prospect St. W (located in the Auberge Wandlyn Inn), 452-8937. Steak and seafood; homemade bread and desserts.

The Barn Restaurant, 540 Queen St., 455-2942. Specializes in chicken, ribs and seafood.

Moncton

Ming Garden, 855-5433. Excellent Cantonese-Canadian cuisine.

The Windjammer, Hotel Beauséjour, 750 Main St., 854-4344. Traditional dishes; formal décor.

Vito's Dining and Pizza Room, 726 Mountain Rd., 858-5003. Popular Italian dishes, including huge pizzas.

Cy's. 170E. Main St., 857-0032. Exceptional seafood.

Shediac

Pasturel Shore House, 532-4774. Classic seafood restaurant in port town renowned for its lobster specials.

Getting Around

By Air: Air Canada offers most of the long-distance flights into **Saint John** and **Fredericton**. In Saint John, call; 632-1500. For regional and provincial service contact **Canadian Airlines International** in Fredericton (454-4089), Saint John 657-3860) or toll-free in the Maritimes (800/565-1800). **CP Air** (857-9741) flies from Moncton.

By Train: Via Rail provides passenger service throughout New Brunswick. For details call their Moncton office at 857-9530.

By Bus: Voyageur and **Greyhound** offers routes into New Brunswick, but province-wide service is provided by the **SMT** company: Saint John (693-6500), Fredericton (455-3303), Moncton (855-2280).

By Car: The speed limit on most New Brunswick highways is 90 kph, or about 55 mph. Check the front part of the directory for toll-free numbers for car rentals.

By Ferry: There are toll-free ferries between New Brunswick and PEI, Nova Scotia and Québec. Within the province, from Blacks Harbor to Grand Manan and Deer Island to Campobello.

Fredericton

Fredericton Transport buses cost 60¢. Taxis here usually charge a flat rate.

Shopping

New Brunswick is known for its ubiquitous craft shops, which feature yarn portraits, blown glass, wood sculptures, and pottery, but before starting out, send away for a detailed guide published by the Director of New Brunswick Craftsmen and Craftshops (Department of Youth, Culture and Recreation, Handicrafts Branch, Box 6000, Fredericton, N.B.).

Saint John is New Brunswick's shopping hub with over 200 boutiques and stores downtown and in its new harborfront development. Fredericton is well-known for its string of pewter shops.

Nightlife

New Brunswick's minimum drinking age is 19.

Saint John

Entertaining pubs can be found in the Market Square area, or try:

Sullivans, Delta Hotel, 648-1981. Piano Lounge.

The Image, Holiday Inn, 657-3610. Flashy Disco.

Fredericton

River Room, 455-3371. Draws young professional crowd; often features folk singing.

Poacher's Lounge, 454-5584. Dancing to live bands.

Moncton

The Beaus and Belles, 854-6340. Lounge with 1890s motif.

Attractions

Fundy Islands

Campobello and **Deer Islands** are accessible by car from **Maine** or car ferry from **Latete**, New Brunswick. Both islands are gorgeous, and the latter features the **Roosevelt-Campobello International Park** (open daily, May to September; 752-2922), laid out in memory of the late President, who enjoyed immensely the island's beaches, lakes, and forests.

The largest and most picturesque island, **Grand Manan**, is an ornithologist's or whale watcher's delight. **The Marathon Hotel** (662-8144) organizes expeditions for the latter. Collect the unique purple seaweed, which incidentally is a local delicacy. A consistently crowded ferry leaves **Blake Harbor** several times daily in the summer (Cars: $9.00 passengers: $3.00; 662-3724).

St. Andrews

This is a charming town overlooking **Passamoquoddy Bay**, an adventurous tour of which can be taken on the *M/V Fundy Isles*

(529-8844; 10 a.m. & 2 p.m., adults: $6, children: $3).

Saint John

The **Saint John River** alternately rushes back and forth with the tides, causing the water to surge spectacularly at a bottleneck called **Reversing Falls Rapids**. For information, call 658-2990.

The **New Brunswick Museum** beautifully exhibits the province's history (open daily, 10 a.m. to 9 p.m., admission: $1; 277 Douglas Ave; 693-1196).

Several historical landmarks downtown have been strung together to form the **Loyalist Trail** in this, the "Loyalist City." For walking tours and information, contact the city's information office at 658-2990.

Moncton

The place to see in Moncton is **Magnetic Hill**, where a car in neutral will coast **uphill.** Actually, it's a very impressive, if perplexing optical illusion, and one of those few places which, though overrun by tourists, stays the same year after year. Call 853-3333 for information.

Fredericton

The **Beaverbrook Art Gallery** is a modern center internationally renowned for its collection (open daily except Monday, admission: $2; 458-8545).

The **Military Compound** displays numerous items of interest to military history buffs, and the changing of the guard (weekdays at 10 a.m. in July and August) is always fun. Call 458-3747.

Theater New Brunswick, the province's premier company, performs at the Playhouse Theater downtown (455-3222).

23 miles (37 km) west of Fredericton lies the **King's Landing Historical Settlement**, a carefully restored village which recreates life in the Saint John River Valley of 1790 (open daily, June to September, admission: $5, 363-3081).

Sports, Recreation and Parks

Tourism New Brunswick provides the most extensive and recent information on sports and recreation in the province.

In the summer, New Brunswick's 30 golf courses are rarely crowded. Boating, of course, is popular, both out on the ocean and on the gorgeous, if tame, **Saint John River. Maritime Bareboat Charters Ltd.** (Grand Bay, 454-3225) rents yachts.

In the more remote areas of northern New Brunswick, hunting for deer and small game can be arranged, with the proper licensing. **Truis Tours Ltd.** (455-8400) sponsors bear-hunting treks. Deep-sea fishing charters usually originate from **Caraquet**, while inland, the rivers of the **Miramichi** and **Restagouche** valleys are renowned for their bass and (especially) Atlantic salmon fishing.

For winter sports enthusiasts, alpine and cross-country ski trails can be found in New Brunswick's parks, both provincial and national. Snowmobiling is the rage throughout the province; **Canada East Tours** (Bathurst, 548-3449) organizes expeditions.

Parks

Most New Brunswick provincial parks have cabins and camping facilities, the latter of which cost generally $6-$12 night. Aside from the seasonal resorts, the provincial and national parks provide the best opportunities for golf, sailing, and skiing enthusiasts. Tourism New Brunswick distributes a comprehensive and handy guide to the province's parks.

Of special note is **Fundy National Park**. The tides rise and fall over 30 feet (90 m) here, leaving tidal flats abundant with exotic marine life. The park offers scenic hiking and excellent camping (chalets are available too); call the information center in Alma: 887-2000.

Diary

Last two weeks of June (Fredericton)
   The Chamber Music and All That Jazz Festival: Concerts and workshops draw top artists.

July (Saint John)
   Loyalist Days: Parades, dancing, and sidewalk festivities celebrate the landing of the Loyalists.

July (Rogersville)
   Lumberman's Festival: Lumberjack competitions.

Mid July (Shediac)
   Lobster Festival

July-August (Edmundston)
   Foire Brayonne: Perhaps the most popular New Brunswick festival, the local French population engages in boisterous celebrations.

August (Cocagne)
   Hydroplane Regatta: Scores of boats in several classes compete furiously at speeds topping 120 mph (usually held on the second weekend of the month but you can check this out with the local fans).

August (Newcastle)
   Mirimachi Folk Song Festival: Offers a fascinating introduction to the exuberent local ballads.

Provincial Holiday

New Brunswick Day
First Monday in August.

NEWFOUNDLAND

The area code for numbers listed in Newfoundland is 709 unless stated otherwise.

Finding Out

For complete information about traveling New Foundland write, the Tourism Department of Developement, Box 2016, St. John's Nfld., A1C 5R8, or call toll-free 800/563-6353 for 24-hour service.

Finding good lodgings is not difficult, and although few small-town hotels/motels are of the modern variety, travelers almost always find the rooms comfortable and the owners hospitable. As St. John's becomes yearly more cosmopolitan, so do its hotels, which are generally more modern and costlier than those of Newfoundland's interior. The Tourism Branch publishes an accommodations guide. Note that lodgings carry a 12 percent provincial tax.

Port aux Basques

Hotel Port aux Basques: Hwy, 1, 695-2171. The town's most modern lodgings.
Grand Bay Motel, 256-3956. Highly comfortable lodgings; excellent dining room.

Gander

Albatross Motel, 256-3956. Highly comfortable lodgings; excellent dining room.
Holiday Inn, 256-3981. Clean hotel boasts modern rooms.
Airport Inn, 256-3535. Modest, clean accommodations.

St. John's

Battery Inn; 722/0040. Panoramic views of the harbor and city.
Hotel Newfoundland; Cavendish Square; 726-4980. Still considered *the* downtown hotel .
Airport Inn; Airport Rd., 753-3500. Offers rooms of various sizes and prices, a few steps from the air terminal.
Best Western Traveler Inn; Kenmount Rd., 722-5540. Although located on the outskirts of St. John's, its modern rooms are a bargain.
Sea Flow Tourist Home; 53-55 William St., 2425. Small (4 units), pleasant guests house.

Restaurants/Dining

Volumes can be written about such Newfoundland dishes as: "flipper pie," "scrunchions," and "gandies." Suffice it to day that, although Newfoundlanders make imaginative use of the abundant variety of fish, meats, and vegetables available to them, their cuisine is more hearty than delicate (walking away hungry from a Newfie meal is unheard of).

Outside of St. John's, the most reliable dining with some exceptions, will be found in hotel and motel eateries and lounges. As a general rule, expect the service to be cheerful, but on the slow side.

St. John's

The Aquarium; 325 Duckworth St., 754-1392. Moderately-priced seafood; try the salmon in season.
The Galley; Harbour Drive, 753-7360. Newfoundland menu draws university students.
The Harbor View; Battery Inn, 722-0040. Romantic view of the city at night; pricey.
Act III; Arts and Culture Centre, 754-0790. Theater and gallery crowd come for light lunches and excellent dishes.
Ship Inn; 265 Duckworth St., 753-3870. Sailor's pub; inexpensive sandwiches.

Getting There

By Ferry: CN Marine's huge, oceangoing car ferries depart from North Sydney Nova Scotia four times daily during the summer to **Port aux Basques** (6-hour passage) and **Argentia** (19 hours away), Newfoundland. Argentia is about 60 miles

(96 km) from St. John's.

One-way fare to Port aux Basques should cost about $12.50 per person (kids half-price) and $38.50 for the car, and the passage to Argentia should cost a little more than twice that. Sleeping berths, meals, and cinemas are available on board for an extra charge, but the prices are reasonable.

Since the ferries almost always operate at peak capacity, reservations are usually required. Call toll-free,
• From Maine: 800/432-7344
• From the rest of Northeastern U.S.; 800/341-7981
• From Atlantic Canada: 800/565-9470
• From Ontario and Québec: 800/565-9411.

If these lines are busy, call long-distance to North Sydney, 794-7203, or write: Marine Atlantic Reservations Bureau, P.O.Box 250, North Sydney, N.S. B2A 3M3.

By Air: Canadian Airlines International serves Newfoundland from the rest of the eastern Canada region. Call them at 722-0222 in St. John's or 256-4801 in Gander. Call toll-free in the rest of the Maritimes at 800-565-1800. Car rental companies have offices at both airports. Check the front part of the Directory for toll-free numbers.

Getting Around

By Ferry: A summertime car ferry leave **Lewisport** for **Cartwright** and **Goose Bay**, Labrador. Contact the Passenger Service Supervisor at CN Marine, Box 520, Port aux Basques, Nfld. A0M 1CO.

By Air: Flying into **Labrador** requires a ski-or float equipped bush plane. Contact Labrador Travel Airways, in Conception Bay, 609/834-2195.

By Bus: Terra Transport's "roadcruisers" motor visitors from the **Argentia** and **Port aux Basques** ferry docks to **St. John's** (737-5912).

By Car: The main roads, including the **Trans-Canada Highway** (TCH) are paved, but secondary highways are generally gravel surfaced. Labrador has only one paved road outside of Goose Bay and Labrador City, a 50 mile (80 km) stretch from Blanc Sablon to Red River.

St. John's

Taxis charge $1.50 and then 90¢ per mile thereafter, but there are few on the street to hail, so call for one (Bugden taxi can be reached at 726-4400). The fare on **St. John's Metrobus System** is 75¢; call 722-9400 for route information.

Tours: **Fleetline Motorcoach** (722-2608) operate guided bus tours of St. John's and the neighboring Avalon Peninsula. **Harbor Charters** (754-1672) offers harbor and fishing tours.

Shopping

Aside from the run-of-the-mill handcrafts, Newfoundland is famous for its Labradorite jewelry, sea-skin products, and Crenfell parkas. Write the Tourism division for a complete list of shops, or browse **Duckworth St.** in **St. John's**. Note that prices for everyday goods and services will be slightly higher here than on the Canadian mainland.

Nightlife

Newfoundland's legal drinking age is 19. In general, hotels and motels are the center of nightlife in towns and villages outside of St. John's. George Street is also very popular.

St. John's

Scottish, English and (especially) Irish pubs abound, so explore and enjoy. Here are a few starting points:
Erin's Pub, 186 Water St. Wednesday is the best night for Irish folk music.
Breaker's, Hotel Newfoundland. University students and young professionals gather here on weekends.
The Majestic and **The Cornerstone** are both on George Street and are very popular. Live bands play occasionally.

Sports, Recreation and Parks

The province has laid out over twenty canoeing routes. Special tours/rentals are available, contact the Tourism Department.
Newfoundland is a *fisherman's* paradise unequaled in eastern Canada, although the

province has set stringent licensing regulations and bag limits. Pike, bass, salmon and trout roam the inland rivers and lakes, while tuna, codfish and flounder are available on the high seas. For experienced hunters, with a licenced guide, Newfoundland has moose and caribou seasons. For more information on fishing and hunting, contact the Tourism Department or better yet, The Wildlife Division, P.O.Box 4750, Building 810, Pleasantville, St. John's, Nfld A1C 5T7 (576-2815).

Most of Newfoundland's 82 provincial parks have hiking rails and swimming areas; 43 of these have camping facilities. The charge is $5 per day in addition to one-time $10 vehicle entry permit if tourists bring a car. In all likelihood, the more secluded and overgrown the campground, the greater the infestation of mosquitoes and (often peskier) black flies. Bring a strong repellent in any case.

Outdoors enthusiasts will love the two National Parks:

Gros Morne: (Rocky Harbor Information Centre: 458-2066). Deep, narrow fjords cut into the west side of the island here. The most famous is the Western Brook Pond, a spectacular gorge walled-in by 2000-foot cliffs. Getting there requires a three-mile hike inland from the coastal highway, and be sure to dress warmly, since storms can sweep in unexpectedly.

Terra Nova: (Newman Sound Information Centre: 533-2801).

Glaciers have left a rolling countryside and deep fjords, or "sounds," into which the occasional iceberg will meander in summer. Park officials have developed an innovative program of hiking, boating, and canoeing tours. Write the Superintendent, Terra Nova National Park, Gloverton, Nfld., AOG 2LO.

Other outdoor recreation possibilities are described under "Packages".

Attractions

See "Sports, Recreation, and Parks" for Newfoundland's greatest attraction: its outdoors. But here are a few others:

St. Pierre and Miquelon

These barren, rugged islands are actually part of metropolitan France. This becomes vividly apparent after strolling the narrow streets, sampling the French cuisine, and browsing through the diminutive shops. All-in-all, an intriguing diversion.

To get there, pack proper identification, then board the ferry at Fortune, Nfld. (daily in the summer, $35 round trip, call Lloyd G. Lake Ltd., 832-1955. It's often a choppy passage.) Then tell your friends back home that you vacationed in France. For more details, write St. Pierre Tourism Department, Place de General DeGaulle. P.O.Box 4274, 97500, St. Pierre and Miquelon, France or phone 41-22-22.

St. John's

St. John's most recognizable landmark is **Signal Hill**. Dominating the entrance to the harbor, it features Cabot Tower and the restored fortifications at Queen Battery. Call 772-5367 for more information.

The **Newfoundland Museum** on Duckworth St. displays the history of the province over the past seven milennia, with relics from early shipwrecks, artifacts dating to the colonial era, and exhibits on the vanished Beothuck Indians: a native culture of Newfoundland. Open daily, 576-2329.

In addition to hosting formal theater, symphony orchestra, and jazz concerts, the **Arts and Culture Center** on Prince Phillip Drive, houses the Memorial University Art Gallery, which exhibits modern Canadian artwork and sculpture. For more information and ticket reservations, call 576-3900.

Diary

June (St. John's)
   Grand Times: A traditional folk arts festival.

First Wednesday in August (St. John's)
   Regatta Day: The regatta on Quldi Vidi Lake is the oldest sporting event in North America (160 years and counting), but get up early—the rowing's over before breakfast. General festivities continue, however, for the rest of the day.

Provincial Holidays

St. Patrick's Day
   March 17

St. George Day
Around April 23
Discovery Day
Second to last Monday in June
Memorial Day
July 3
Orangemen's Day
July 12

Packages

Newfoundland is a popular destination for those seeking exciting wilderness excursions. Canoe, fishing, hunting, and even dogsled tours are available into the recently chartered depths of Labrador, but be prepared to pay upwards of $200 per person a day for these. The Tourism Branch can provide numerous relevant brochures.

Universally acclaimed as the best way to travel Newfoundland, CN Marine's coastal boats offer fascinating week-long tours of either the **South Shore** or the **East Coast** and **Labrador**. The streamers leave **Argentia, St. John's** and **Lewisport**, and call at five to six coastal villages a day, most of which are isolated form Newfoundland's road and rail network. Reservations can only be made from within Newfoundland by calling the CN Marine Reservations Bureau toll-free at 800/563-7381 or writing them at P.O.Box 520, Port aux Basques, Newfoundland, AOM 1CO.

Those with a penchant for more open waters can take week-long excursions to watch dolphins, porpoises, and whales out on the ocean. These may be arranged through **Ocean Contact Ltd.**, Box 10, Trinity, Trinity Bay, Newfoundland, AOC#2 South.

NOVA SCOTIA

The area code for numbers listed in Nova Scotia is 902 unless stated otherwise.

Finding Out

For toll-free information about Nova Scotia call the province's Department of Tourism:
From the U.S.: 800/341-6096
From the Maritimes: 800/565-7105
Newfoundland Québec: 800/565-7140

Central and Southern Ontario: 800/565-7180.

Northern Ontario, Manitoba, Saskatchewan, Alberta, British Columbia, N.W.T and Yukon: 800/565-7166, or write, Nova Scotia Dept. of Tourism 5151 Terminal Rd, 3rd Floor, Box 456. Halifax, N.S. B3J 2R5.

Accommodations

For information on hostels, contact the Nova Scotia office of the Canadian Hostelling Association P.O.Box3010 South, 5516 Spring Garden Rd., Halifax. B3J 3G6; 902/425-5450. The Dept.of Tourism also lists nearly one-hundred homes which offer bed-and-breakfast accommodations.

Hotel and Motel reservations can be made by calling the Department of Tourism's toll-free numbers, but here is a sampling:

Halifax

Delta's Barrington, 1875 Barrington St., 902/429-7410 or toll-free 800/565-7164. Features indoor pool, saunas, and modern rooms, right in the heart of Historic Properties.
Chateau Halifax, Scotia Square Complex, 425-6700. Service-oriented luxury hotel.
Nova Scotian Hotel, 1181 Hollis St., 423-

7231 or toll-free 800/565-7164. Has varying rooms for different tastes; ask about weekend specials.

Citadeln Inn, 1960 Brunswick St., 422-1391 or toll-free 800/565-7162. Large, and luxurious modern hotel across from Scotia Square.

Chebucto Inn, 6151 Lady Hammon Rd., 453-4330. Comfortable, quiet lodgings, located however, on the outskirts of Halifax.

Keddy's Halifax Hotel, 20 St. Margaret's Bay Rd., 477-5611. Large chain motel, in Armsdale.

Gerrard Hotel: 1234 Barrington St., 423-8614. Small hotel registered as an Historic Property (circa 1865), one block from the train station.

Yarmouth

Rodd's Grand Hotel, 417 Main St., 742-2446. 138 rooms and a lounge with entertainment.

Honey Hill Motel, 742-3596. Located on Middle Lake, there are 25 units, a cottage, and unsupervised lake swimming.

Antigonish

Dingle Motel, Hwy 104 east of town, 863-3730. Make early reservations for the Highland Games.

Baddeck

While Sydney is larger, most visitors to Cape Breton find Baddeck substantially more pleasant.

Inverary Inn, Hwy 205, 295-2674. Quiet tranquil atmosphere; features an excellent dining room, its own pool, and a private beach.

Telegraph House, Chebucto St., 295-9988. A Cape Breton favorite for many visitors.

Restaurants/Dining

In Nova Scotia, seafood is ubiquitous. Scallops are served in nearly every imaginable way, while clam chowder and smoked fish are popular as well. Deserts take advantage of Nova Scotia's plentiful fruit orchards—baked apple dumplings are indeed a special treat.

Halifax

Five Fishermen, 1740 Argyle St., 421-4421. Seafood lunches are popular.

Clipper Cay, Historic Properties, 423-6818. Elegant dining, great harbor view.

Fat Frank's, 5411 Spring Garden Road, 423-6618. Eclectic menu; superb entrées ensure a crowd.

The Great Wall, Granville Street in the TD Building, 422-6153. One of the city's landmark restaurant; great Chinese food.

Silver Spoon Restaurant, 422-1519. An original menu featuring items from countries around the world and specialty desserts.

Cultures, lower level of Scotia Square. Cafeteria-style cafe featuring quick, fresh salads and specialty desserts.

Newsroom, Carleton Hotel, 423-0624. Clientele of young professionals come for ribs, steak, and seafood.

The Hermitage, 1030 S. Park St., 421-1570. Swiss cuisine in casual setting.

Old Man Moria's, 1150 Barrington St., 422-7960. Magnificient Greek Dishes.

Shelburne

Hamilton House, Water St., 875-2957. Hearty seafood luncheons and dinners.

Tea Cup, King St., 875-4590. Stop in for authentic English tea and biscuits.

Yarmouth

Harris Seafood, Hwy 1, 742-5420. Excellent seafood and steaks; try the "Digby scallops".

Baddeck

The Hotel dining rooms (see "Accommodations") are popular. Try the **Bras d'Or trout.**

Sydney

Joe's Wharehouse, 424 Charlotte St., 539-6686. Standard menu; great food; lively cabaret on the lower floor.

Nightlife

Nova Scotia's watering holes stay open until midnight to 2 a.m. depending on classification, and the drinking age is 19. Most taverns in the province's small towns welcome travelers, but a word of caution: many have acquired a rough-and-tumble atmosphere unsuited to quiet drinkers.

Halifax

Most nightlife is centered in the downtown area, and the best bars, called "lounges," can be found on Argyle between Prince and George, although they are crowded on weeknights and absolutely packed on weekends.

Looking for clubs? Try the **Middle Deck Lounge** in Historic Properties offers folk music, jazz or more traditional nightclub entertainment. **Cheers** (Grafton Street,) features live rock music which draws a young crowd. And on Barrington Street lies the **Granite Brewery**, a stylish English pub that brews its own beer.

Performing Arts

Halifax

In the summertime, look for free concerts and shows on the streets of **Historic Properties**. Otherwise, daily local newspapers detail what's going on at these and other locations.

The **Kipawo Showboat Company** is a superior amateur theater group based in Wolfville, but it performs delightful musicals in the playhouse at Historic Properties (420-1840).

The **Neptune Theater**, (5216 Sackville, 429-1287) is home to Nova Scotia's only professional live repertory theater group.

The **Dalhousie Arts Center**, also known as the Rebecca Cohn Auditorium, features live concerts (424-3502).

The new **Metro Center** is a sports complex which doubles as a cultural events center. It offers top-name concert acts, but the acoustics are as yet less than spectacular.

Getting Around

By Air: Canadian Airlines International connects Halifax and Sydney with the rest of Canada (Halifax, 465-2111, Sydney, 543-4545), as does **Air Canada** (Halifax: 429-7111, Sydney: 539-6600). **CP Air** (873-4030) flies just from Halifax.

By Train: Via Rail provides service throughout Nova Scotia. For schedules and fares call the Halifax office at 329-8421.

By Bus: Acadian Lines Ltd. operates daily throughout Nova Scotia (Halifax: 454-9321, Sydney: 564-5533) while **Cabana Tours** (in Halifax: 420-1688) offers several seasonal bus tours of the province.

By Car: Nova Scotian highways are generally in very good condition, and the speed limit is 100 kph (60 mph). Cars can be rented in downtown **Halifax Yarmouth**, or **Sydney**, and at the two airports. Check the front part of the **Directory** for toll-free car rental numbers; note that there's usually a hefty return charge for dropping off the car in a city other than that in which it was rented.

By Ferry: A number of car-ferry services are available that range from one to two-hour voyages to an overnight special with accommodation and entertainment.

Bar Harbor, Maine to Yarmouth, Nova Scotia & **Port aux Basques, NFLD to North Sydney, Nova Scotia** & **Saint John, NB to Digby NS**: Write to Marine Atlantic/ Reservations, Box 250, North Sydney, NS B2A 3M3.

Or call toll-free: 800/565-9470 (Maritimes) 800/563-7701 (Newfoundland) 800/565-9411 (Ontario and Québec) 800/341-7981 (continental U.S.)

Prince Edward Island to Caribou, Nova Scotia: Contact Northumberland Ferries Ltd., Box 634, Charlottetown, PEI CIA 7L3.

Halifax

Taxis charge $1.20 and then mileage/ time, but there are few on the street to hail, so call for a pick-up. The Metropolitan Transit Commission operates a decent bus system, the fare on which is $1 (exact charge required). If driving remember that finding parking in downtown Halifax on business days can be a difficult or expensive task.

Delightful guided walking tours originate from the Old Town Clock in the summertime. Guides in period costumes take you into the night world of the 1870s; call 425-3923 for details. **Gray Line** (454-9321), the old standard, offers bus tours from the major hotels.

Shopping

Nova Scotia is known for its crafts and (especially in Cape Breton) its antiques. The Department of Tourism will gladly send its **Handicrafts Directory**, which lists crafts and antiques outlets and helps shoppers discriminate between junk and the genuine item.

Halifax

The restored **Historic Properties** district houses numerous craft shops, while nearby lies **Scotia Square**, the biggest shopping mall east of Montréal. Browse the Spring Garden Rd area to find regional goods and British imports.

Sports, Recreation and Parks

Light snowfalls in January and February allow for some skiing and snowshoeing, but Nova Scotia generally cannot match the abundant winter-time sporting opportunities usually found in the neighboring provinces.

The same cannot be said, however, for summer recreation in the province. The Department of Tourism publishes elaborate brochures on tennis, hiking, bicycle touring, scuba-diving and golfing, all popular in Nova Scotia. In good weather, visitors may join the thousands of Nova Scotians who are ocean-bound: the Department's *Sail Nova Scotia* guide provides information on rentals, charters, and marinas. Canoeing enthusiasts hold Nova Scotia's rivers, both tame and wild, in high regard; contact Sports Nova Scotia, P.O.Box 3010 South Halifax, N.S. B3J 3G8 (425-5450) for more detail information.

Fishing and hunting are highly restricted, but well worth the hassle. Salmon and trout fishermen ply the rivers, while others hunt for bigger prizes, particularly swordfish and bluefin tuna, out on the ocean. A variety of game is available to hunters, including: moose, bear, mink, pheasant, and duck. Make inquiries with the Dept. of Lands and Forests, P.O.Box 698, TD Building, Halifax, N.S. B3J 2T9 424-4467.

Parks

17 provincial parks have extensive camping facilities, open from mid-May to mid-October. Private campgrounds exist as well, but look for the 'Approved Campground" display boards issued by the Department of Tourism. In either case, camping fees should start around $5, depending on the services available.

Lovers of the great outdoors will not want to miss visiting **Cape Breton Highlands National Park**. The rough Atlantic surf here has nevertheless left several fine beaches, while inland past sloping foothills, the terrain is heavily forested and swampy. This spectacular park offers great hiking, canoeing, fishing, and even golfing. Contact the Superintendent, Cape Breton Highlands National park, Ingonish Beach, N.S. B0C 1L0 (902/285-2270)

Attractions

Spring Hill

Miner's Museum, Black River Road. Take a guided tour of an abandoned coal mine 900 feet (300 m) underground (protective gear provided). Open daily, May to October, Tour: $2, 597-3449).

Shelburne

Take an exciting canoe trip along the **Roseway River**, but don't worry about the equipment, Maritime Canoe Outfitters (R.R. 1, Shelburne, N.S. BOT 1WO; 8875-3055) rents everything needed, from around $25 per person per day.

Lunenburg

Fisheries Museum of the Atlantic, Duke St. This large museum features exhibits detailing nearly every aspect of fishing in Nova Scotia, from the boats to the commercial processing, to the fishermen's daily lives. Open daily; $2; 634-4794).

Halifax

Board the *Haligonian III* at **Privateers' Wharf** for a scenic, informative, and fun harbor cruise. A running commentary describes the shipyards, grain elevators, and Navy dockyards as they pass, then the *Haligonian* turns into the North West Arm, a channel lined with yacht clubs and beautiful mansions (daily, May to October, $9.75; 423-1271).

The Citadel is arguably Canada's most popular historic site, and not without reason. Visitors enter this imposing structure by bridge over a dry moat, but once inside are free to roam the ramparts and battlements; (open daily, 9 a.m. - 5 p.m.; 426-5080).

The **Nova Scotia Museum** features everchanging exhibits which chronicle the province's natural and social history. It's the best place to go in Halifax on a rainy day (1747 Summer St., open daily, 9 a.m. - 5 p.m., free admission; 426-4610).

Baddeck

This tranquil resort center is home to the superb **Alexander Graham Bell National Historic Park**. This large, wondrous museum, set near Alexander Graham Bell's summer home, displays numerous artifacts from the life of the brilliant inventor and humanitarian. (open daily, 9 a.m. - 5 p.m., free admission; 295-2069).

Twelve miles north lies **Gaelic College**, where young people from all over North America go to learn Highlander culture and the Gaelic language (295-3411).

Louisbourg

Louisbourg is an elaborately reconstructed French fortress, now serving as a living museum of Anglo-French rivalry and warfare in 18th Century Cape Breton. Inside, visitors can eat the same fare as did Luis XV's soldiers (from pewter and earthenware dishes), while guards periodically ask mock questions to expose spies! The stunning architecture alone makes the tour worthwhile, but be sure to bring a sweater or wrap, and don footwear appropriate for cobblestone streets. (open daily, June-September, admission: $4; 733-2280).

Diary

May-June (Annapolis Valley)
  Blossom Festival: Dancing, parades, and entertainment celebrate the blossoming apple trees.

Mid-June (Annapolis Royal)
  Annual Summer Antique Sale

July (Antigonish)
  Highland Games: This action-packed Scottish festival features caber tossing (log throwing) and continuous display of Highland dancing with hundreds of marching bagpipers.

Mid-August (Lawrencetown)
  Annapolis Valley Exhibition: Nova Scotia' largest agricultural fair.

September (Lunenburg)
  Nova Scotia Fisheries Exhibition and Fishermen's Reunion: Parades, contests, schooner races, and sumptuous seafood (including lobster specials) highlight the exhibition.

NORTHWEST TERRITORIES

Finding Out

Through TravelArctic, the Government of Northwest Territories distributes its yearly *Explorers' Guide*, a listing of hotels, lodges, restaurants, and other pertinent locales. This, and more information, is available from TravelArctic at: Yellowknife, N.W.T. XOE 1HO 403/873-7200.

Accommodations

Nearly every community has at least one inn or hotel, sometimes an Inuit cooperative. Most have dining rooms or kitchenette facilites, and meals are often included in the overnight price. The amenities will vary: private bathrooms, radios, and even TVs are not uncommon; room service is rare, bellhops unheard of. Expect to pay $50—$100 for a double, although there is no sales tax on lodgings here. Reservations for a summer stay should be made the previous spring.

For a complete listing of accommodations, ask TravelArctic for its latest *Explorers' Guide*. The list below, however, is a representative sampling.

Frobisher Inn, Box 610, Frobisher Bay XOA OHO; 819/979-5241. Two lounges, dining, convention facilities. Open all year.

Caribou Motor Inn, Box 114, Hay River, XOE ORO; 403-/874-6706. Comfortable lodgings, moderately priced.

Ptarmigan Inn, Box 1000, Hay River XOE ORO; 403/874-6781. Larger hotel open all year.

Eskimo Inn, Box 1740, Inuvik XOE OTO; 403/979-2801. Large hotel offers dining, shopping, banquet facilities.

Mackenzie Hotel, Box 1618, Inuvik XOE OTO; 403/979-2861. Comfortable lodgings; triples available.

Explorer Hotel, 48th Street, Box 7000, Yellowknife XOE 1HO; 403/873-3531. Northwest Territories' luxury hotel.

Twin Pine Motor Inn, Franklin Avenue, Box 596, Yellowknife XOE 1HO; 403/873-8511. Pleasant service with some basic housekeeping units.

Yellowknife Inn, Franklin Avenue, Box 490, Yellowknife XOE 1HO; 403/873-2601. Large (accommodates 200), comfortable hotel.

YWCA, Franklin Avenue, at 54th Street; 403/920-2777. Inexpensive lodgings for both sexes; no reservation.

Restaurants/Dining

Although food is regularly flown into NWT towns and outposts, visitors should have plenty of opportunity to sample the regional fare. Arctic char and grayling can be found on menus throughout the territories, while caribou, bear, rabbit, fowl, and even reindeer also make popular entrées. Local desserts often employ the wild berries which grow plentifully in the North. Most hotels and lodges have good dining facilities. There is no sales tax on food or restaurant meals, but prices here still are 10 percent 20 percent higher than in southern Canada.

Cabin Fever, 403/873-4046. Steaks and ribs; logcabin atmosphere.

Mike Mark's, 51st Street, 403/873-3309. Chinese food; take-out available.

Old Northwest Company, Explorer Hotel, 403/873-3531. Surprisingly cosmoplitan dining; known for fish and seafood dishes.

Polar Bear Lounge, Yellowknife Inn, 403/873-2601. Fine dining; complimentary service.

Nightlife

Northwest Territories' legal drinking age is 19, and bar time is 1 a.m. Over a dozen communities are completely dry by law (check first before flying anywhere with alcohol), but the rest of the territories more than makes up for them. In short, most watering holes are wild and wooly establishments. Licensed hotels generally sport a lounge and/or cabaret.

Getting Around

By Air: Canadian Airlines International (1-800/665-7350) flies regularly into **Yellowknife** from **Edmonton** and **Winnipeg**. From there, **Northwest Territorial Airways** (Box 9000, Yellowknife, N.W.T. XOE 1HO: 403/769-623), and numerous charter services can fly travelers to almost any destination west of Hudson's Bay. Various charter air carriers operate out of Frobisher Bay.

By Rail: Freight can be shipped to Yellowknife, but there is no passenger rail service to Northwest Territories.

By Bus: Canadian Coachways and **N.W.T. Coachlines Ltd**. ply the Mackenzie Highway Between **Edmonton** and **Yellowknife**.

By Car: N.W.T. has two major highways, both unpaved. The Dempster Hwy stretches from **Dawson, Yukon** to **Inuvik** on the Mackenzie River delta. Mackenzie Hwy runs between **Edmonton, Alberta** and **Yellowknife**.

For special precautions about driving in the north, see the Yukon Getting Around section. Note that both highways become impassable during the spring thaw and fall freeze-up (usually May and November). Call 403/873-7799 for ferry schedules and the lastest road information.Should visitors need to rent a vehicle, several agencies are available, but during the summer, make reservations as far in advance as possible.

Jiffy Quick (403/920-Taxi) operates taxis in Yellowknife.

Shopping

Dene and Inuit handicrafts and artwork are internationally coveted here. Muskrat parkas and bead mukluks are at the same time practical and aesthetically pleasing. Community cooperatives also sell soapstone sculpture, ivory carvings, delicate tapestries, and intriguing prints, all at much lower prices than elsewhere in Canada, since there are no taxes, or shipping costs.

Genuine craftwork and art can be a hefty—if lucrative—investment, so before purchasing, look for the official authenticat-

ing symbols, and inquire into the item's origins. Visitors will find most storekeepers informative and pleasant.

Sports, Recreation and Parks

Canoeing and rafting in Northwest Territories can be an adventure. Only expert canoeists should attempt such rivers as the Dubawnt or South Nahanni; nevertheless, most lakes and tamer rivers are suitable for beginner or intermediate paddlers. Remember the scourge of the north, black flies and mosquitoes, when planning a canoe trek. Bring plenty of repellent, netting, as well as warm, waterproof clothing.

Many lodges and camps offer canoe vacations and packages, usually outfitting, all the needed equipment and supplies. Otherwise, travelers can bring their own, or rent a canoe from the ubiquitous Hudson's Bay Company, which has outlets throughout the territories. For more details about the latter, contact the Hudson's Bay Company Northern Stores Department in **Edmonton**: 800 Baker Center, 10025 106th St; in **Winnipeg**: 79 Main St., R3C 2R1; 304/943-0881.

TravelArctic offers complete information about canoeing in the territories.

Although hunting here is above-average, fishing must stand as the favorite pastime in Northwest Territories.

Northern pike, Arctic grayling, trout, and the delicious Arctic char are major sport fish. Although it is possible to fish from the roadside or canoe, serious anglers stay at fishing camps or lodges (see Special Packages), or make special arrangements with an outfitter and air charter.

Hunters come to N.W.T. in search of big game: moose, caribou, black, brown, grizzly and polar bear, and wolf. Licensed guides

must accompany non-resident hunters. Checks with TravelArctic about season, limits, outfitters, and guides. Specific information is also available from The Wildlife Service, Yellowknife X1A 2Y9; 403/873-7411. Fishing licenses are available in every community.

In late spring and early fall, cold-weather sports of all kinds can be enjoyed. Ice-fishing, snowshoeing, skiing, and snowmobiling are especially popular. Equipment can often be rented from Inuit or the Hudson's Bay Company. Many lodges and resorts stay open year-round, specializing in cold-weather recreation during their off-season.

National Parks

Pangnirtung in **Auyuittuq National Park,N.W.T.**, XOA ORO; 819/437-8962. Canada's first park above the Arctic Circle, located on Baffin Island. In Inuit, Auyuittuq(oh-you-EE-tuk) means "the land that never melts," which is entirely true of the Penny Ice Cap, (one-quarter of the park) of solid ice. Auyuittuq's spectacular fjords, glacier-fed streams, and rugged highlands draw fishermen, capers, and photographers. Five- to seven-thousand feet mountain(188—233 m) peaks stud the park, making it a favorite of hikers and climbers but neither should be undertaken lightly; indeed, all visitors must register with park authorities in Pangnirtung.

Nahanni, Postal Bag 300, Fort Simpson, N.W.T., XOE ONO; 403/695-3151, 695-2443. Accessible by boats or charter aircraft only, this remote mountainous park follows the wild, South Nahanni River. At breathtaking Virginia Falls, the river cascades over 300 feet (100 m) twice the fall of the Niagara cataract. The park is also known for its hot springs and mysterious legends of hidden gold. UNESCO testified to Nahanni's beauty by making it a world heritage site in 1978.

Attractions

The isolated communites and wilderness expanse of the Northwest Territories are certainly its greatest attractions, but it is worth spending a day or two in **Yellowknife.**
Prince of Wales Northern Heritage Center, Great Mine Road, This wonderful museum overlooking **Frame Lake** is widely considered the finest in northern Canada. Most exhibits are three-dimensional or multi-media displays of the territories' history, with an emphasis on how the Inuit, Dene, and white people struggled to overcome the harsh climate (open daily, except Wednesday, 12 p.m. — 8 p.m.; free admission).

Gold Mine Tours, Frame and Perkins, 873-4892; or TravelArctic. Six tours per week leave from local hotels for the Giant Yellowknife and Cominco Mines. The excursion includes a visit to the above-ground facilities, as well as the subterranean shafts. Space is limited, so call ahead for reservations and more details.

Special Packages

Many travelers choose to stay for a week or two at one of the Northwest Territories' 70-odd wilderness/fishing camps and lodges. Packages can include meals, accommodations, transportation (usually by charter aircraft), guides, outfitting, etc., depending on what one wants and what's available. Expect to pay between $500 and $2000 per person, per week.

Another convenient way to visit N.W.T. is by package tour, most of which depart from **Edmonton, Winnipeg, Toronto,** or **Montréal**. This usually entails flying to at least one —probably several—northern outposts, stopping to sample the local food, shop, meet the resident, go canoeing, stay overnight, etc. These excursions can last anywhere from one night to one month.

For a better description of all the possiblities, contact TravelArctic. The list below, however, provides a sampling of what's available.
Arctic Adventure Tours. Horizon Holidays Ltd 160 John St., Toronto, On M5V 2X8, 416/585-9911. Comprehensive "Arctic Safaris" of Yukon and Northwest Territories.
Arctic Circler. Goliger's Tours, 214 King St., Toronto, On M5H 3N3; 416/593-6168. Jet whisks visitors to an evening above the Arctic Circle.
Consolidated Tours. Suite 480, 550 Sherbrooke St., Montréal, PQ H3A 1B9. Specializes in excursions to Baffin Island, Auyuittuq National Park.

Special InteresTours Inc. Box 37, Medina, WA USA 98039; 206/455-1960. Several tours, all above the Arctic Circle.

Voyages Marco Polo. 1117 St. Catherine St. W., Montréal, PQ H3B 1H9; 514/281-1481. Trips to Baffin Island, including Frobisher Bay, Pangnirtung.

Whitewater Adventures Limited 1616 Duranteau, Vancover, 604/669-1100. Whitewater canoeing/ rafting expeditions.

Diary

Last week in March (Yellowknife)
Caribou Canival: This week-long festival celebrates spring such as it is in the Arctic, featuring dog-sled derbies, igloo-building contests, etc. Write the Caribou Carnival Committee, Box 2005, Yellowknife, N.W.T. XOE 1HO.

June 22 (Yellowknife)
Midnight Golf Tournament: Uproarious journey at the Yellowknife Golf Club takes advantage of the midnight sun.

Mid-July (Rotates Yearly)
Northern Games: Dene and Inuit come from Yukon, N.W.T., and Alaska to compete in sport, dance, and crafts. The "good Woman" contest features Inuit women competing at seal skinning, sewing, and so on. Write the Northern Games Association, Box 1184, Inuvik, N.W.T. XOE OTO.

Territorial Holiday

Civic Holiday
First Monday in August.

ONTARIO

Finding Out

It takes a comprehensive travel bureau to describe and explain all that the province has to offer, but Ontario Travel fits the bill. It distributes booklets and brochures which explain nearly every facet of traveling the province. Among these are:
• **The Road Map.**
• **The Accommodations Guide**, which lists and rates over 4,000 hotels, motels, lodges, resorts and camps.
• **Camping**, a guide to campsites and hikes.
• Seasonal **Events Booklets**, which list the what, where and when's of special events around the province.
•**Traveler's Encyclopedia**, describing Ontario's 12 travel regions.
• **Industrial/Commercial Tours,** a delightful listing of nearly 100 tours, including tree nurseries, nuclear power plants, wineries, gold mines, and chocolate factories.

To contact Ontario Travel, call toll-free from Canada or the continental U.S.: 800/268-3735; in **Toronto**: 416/965-4008. For information in French: 800/268-3736; in **Toronto**: 965-3448. Write Ontario Travel at: Queen's Park Toronto, On M7A 2E5. Ontario Travel also operates a number of Travel Information Centers, open from mid-May to Labor Day, 8 a.m. to 8 p.m. Most have currency exchanges.

Windsor: 1235 Huron Church Rd., east of the Ambassador Bridge.

Niagara Falls: 5355 Stanley Ave., Hwy 420, west from Rainbow Bridge.

Toronto: Eaton Center, Level One.

Cornwall: 903 Brookdale Ave., at the Seaway International Bridge.

Sault Ste.Marie: 120 Huron St., at the International Bridge.

Local and Regional Travel Services

Toronto
Convention and Tourist Bureau
Eaton Center, Suite 110, Box 510
220 Yonge Street
Toronto, M5B 2H1
416/979-3143

Toll-free from Ontario, (excluding Area Code 807), Michigan, Ohio, Pennsylvania, and New York: 800/387-2999.

The Metro Library, aside from standing as an architectural masterpiece, is a storehouse of information on Toronto and Ontario history. It can be found on Yonge St., just north of Bloor.

Ottawa
National Arts Center
Information Center
18 Byward Market St.
613/230-1200

Kingston
Bureau of Tourism
209 Ontario Street
Kingston, K7L 2Z1
613/548-4415

Waterloo
Chamber of Commerce
5 Bridgeport Rd. W
Waterloo
519/886-2440

Stratford
Tourist Office
38 Albert St.
519/526-271-5140

Hamilton
Bureau of Tourism
119 King St. W, 15th floor
416/526-4222

Niagara Falls
Niagara Resorts and Tourist Association
4673 Ontario Ave
Niagara Falls, L2G 3L1
416/356-6061

Niagara Parks Commission
Queen Victoria Parkway, Box 150
Niagara Falls L2E 6T2
416/356-2241

London
Bureau of Tourism
City Hall
300 Dufferin Ave.
519/661-5000

Windsor
Tourist Information
80 Chatham St., East
519/255-6530

Georgian Bay Region
Georgian Lakelands Travel Association
Simcoe County Building
Department E
Midhurst, LOL 1Yo
705/726-9300

Sault Ste. Marie
Bureau of Tourism
616 Huron St. E
705/949-7152

Thunder Bay
Tourist Information
520 Leith St.
807/625-2149

Restaurants/Dining

Ontario does not call to mind any single style of cuisine. Early English and German settlers bequeathed a meat-and-potatoes culinary heritage, but immigrants arriving over the past several decades have left an indelibly eclectic stamp on dining in the province.

Ontario is famous for its magnificent cheese, which grace many an appetizer and sauce. Fish, not surprisingly, is also popular, especially trout and salmon. Farms on the Niagara Peninsula grow a variety of fruits, including grapes which produce some surprisingly delicate wines. Throughout Ontario, the finer resorts and hotels offer consistently good dining, and are usually licensed to serve liquor.

Ottawa (Area code: 613)

Friday's, 150 Elgin St., 237-5353. Known for steaks, ribs, Lunches are crowded, dinners on the expensive side.

The Mill, 555 Ottawa River Pkwy., 237-1311. Great seafood and steaks; overlooks the river.

Mama Theresa's, 300 Somerset St. W., 236-3023. Delightful Italian dishes; very authentic.

Hungarian Village, 164 Laurier Ave. W., 238-2827. The food and ambience of Central Europe.

The Khyber Pass, 271 Dalhousie, 235-0881. Good Afghani food at reasonable prices.

Marrakech Dining Lounge, 356 McClaren St., 234-5865. North African meals and décor, complete with the occasional belly-dancer.

Kamal's, 789 Bank St., 234-5223. Spicy Indian food.

Golden Dragon, 176 Rideau St., 237-2333. Cantonese and some Szechuan cuisine, patronized by ever-finicky civil servants.

Guadala Harry's, 18 York St., 234-8229. Mexican Lounge and Rstaurant.

Nates, 316 Rideau St., 236-9696. Deli is

an Ottawa landmark.

Brokerage, 320 Queen St., 238-5273. Light, soup and sandwich-type offering.

Marble Works, 14 Walter St., 235-6764. Features Medieval-style gluttony (including wandering minstrels) with hearty Canadian food.

Old Fish Market, 54 York St., 563-4974. Fresh fish;, consistently good.

Patty's Place Pub, 1070 Bank St., 235-1020. Rousing Irish dinery and pub in the Glebe.

First-Class Dining:

L'Echelle de Jacob, 27 Blvd. Lucerne, Aylmer; 819/684-1040. Cozy French restaurant.

Alexander's on the Island, Bate Island, 777-3828. Fine French cuisine set on the Ottawa River.

Le Restaurant, National Arts Center. 232-5713. French and International dishes.

Le Jardin, 127 York St., 238-1828. Award winning international cuisine, set in an old, Victorian home.

Japanese Village Steak House. 170 Laurier Ave. West. Japanese cuisine, prepared at your table.

Kingston (Area code: 613)

Chez Piggy, 68 Princess Street. Generally light fare, located in a courtyard off the street.

Firehall, 251 Ontario Street. Local dishes; set in an old farmhouse overlooking the harbor.

Kitchener (Area code: 519)

Bottles, 1 Market Village. Interesting menu set in renovated townhouse. Part of the Market Village complex; several other restaurants can be found nearby.

Stratford (Area Code: 519)

Stone Crock, 385 Fountain St. South. Ever popular Mennonite cooking.

The Church, Brunswick at Waterloo St., 273-3424. One of Canada's premiere dining experiences. Set in a huge church, complete with altar and organ pipes. Features unequaled lamb veal, trout, lobster, and so on. Reservations should be booked at least six months in advance.

Hamilton (Area Code: 416)

Le Papillon, 100 George Street, Créperie.

Shakespeare's Steak House, 181 Main St. East. Excellent steaks.

Niagara Falls (Area code: 416)

Victoria Park Restaurant, Varied menu in the dining room. Near the falls.

Skylon Tower Restaurant, 5200 Robinson Street. Continental menu; one pays, in part, for the phenomenal view.

Betty's One, 8911 Sodom Rd., Chippewa. Old-fashioned, home-cooked English fare.

Toronto (Area code: 416)

The influx of wealth to Toronto over the last decade has inspired hundreds of restauranteurs to try their hand. The abundance of ethnic eateries, in particular, makes Toronto an exciting city in which to dine.

South of Bloor Street

Korona, 493 Bloor St. W., 961-1824. Ukrainian specialties.

Masa, 195 Richmond St. W., 977-9519. Painstakingly authentic Japanese cuisine.

Ginsberg and Wong, 71 McCaul St., 979-3458. Deli and Chinese (!) favorites, on Village-by-the-Grange. Recommended.

Jade Court, 419 Dundas St. W., 596-8137. Dundas St. West is Toronto's Chinatown. Jade Court offers sumptuous Cantonese dishes amid Oriental setting.

The Blue Diamond, 142 Dundas St. W., 977-3388. A taste of Hong Kong. Lavish decor; excellent cuisine.

Ho Yuen,105 Elizabeth St., south of Dundas, 977-3448. Behind City Hall. Huge portions at low prices. A favorite of the Chinese community—that says enough.

Les Copains, 48 Wellington Ave. E., 869-0898. Fine French cuisine; refreshingly informal, yet tasteful.

Le Pigalle, 315 King St W., 593-0698. Features good French fare at moderate prices; this place is almost always crowded.

Maison Basque, 15 Temperance St., 368-6146. Cozy place; prix-fixe Basque meals.

Montréal, 65 Sherbourne St., 363-0179. A relaxing spot for Québecois delights.

Copenhagen Room, 101 Bloor St. W., 920-3287. Danish fare, which means mostly seafood.

Movenpick, 165 York Ave., 3663-5234. Imaginative complex of Swiss restaurants and lounges, to suit different tastes and budgets.

Vasco de Gama, 892 College St., 535-1555. Superb Portuguese specialties. West of downtown, but worth the short trip.

Sneaky Dee's, 562 Bloor St. W., 532-2052. Cheap and good Mexican food.

Noodles, 1221 Bay St. 921-3171. Mostly Italian; pricey. Successfully daring glass, tile, and chrome décor.

Old Fish Market, 12 Market St., 363-0334. Consistently good seafood, in St. Lawrence Market.

Great Canadian Soup Company, Eaton Center, 598-1590. Soup, chilli, sandwiches; branches located throughout Toronto.

Shopsy's 33 Yonge St., 365-3333. Popular deli.

Barberian's, 7 Elm St., 597-0233. Famous for excellent steaks.

Ed's Wharehouse, 270 King St. W., 593-6676. This Toronto institution serves good honest roast beef and ribs. Nickelodeon decor speaks volumes of owner Ed Mirvish. Not to be missed. Jacket and tie required.

Greg's, Bloor St. West., across from the ROM. Best ice-cream in Toronto. Open until 11 p.m.

North of Bloor Street

Shogun, 154 Cumberland Ave., 964-8665. Japanese cuisine.

Sabatino's, 1144 Eglinton Ave. W., 783-5829. Cozy restaurant, located in the heart of Little Italy.

Viva Zapata's, 2468 Yonge St., 489-8482. Great Mexican food.

Sultan's Tent, 1280 Bay St. 961-0601 North African and Middle Eastern delights.

Bregman's, 1560 Yonge St. 967-2750. Pastry, salads, grace a light menu.

Oliver's, 2433 Yonge St., 485-1051. Fine dining; just north of Eglinton Avenue.

Just Desserts, 306 Davenport Road. 922-6824. Truly sinful pies, cakes, tortes. Strong coffee for after-bar crowd. Open until 3 a.m.

First-Class Dining:

Toronto is home to at least half a dozen world-class restaurants. Dinner for two, with wine, tax and tip, should cost a minimum of $125, although lunch often runs less than half that. Proper dress usually required; call ahead for reservations.

Auberge Gavroche, 90 Avenue Road., 920-0956. Very French and elegant.

Fenton's, Gloucester, 961-8485. Choose among two elegant rooms and garden café. Imaginative menu; can be less expensive.

La Scala, 1121 Bay St., 964-7100. One of Canada's fineset Italian restaurants, with tasteful, Romanesque decorative touches.

Three Small Room, Windsor Arms Hotel, 929-2212. Internationally renowned cuisine, extensive wine list.

Royal Hunt Room, Sutton Place Hotel, 924-9221. Award-wining *nouvelle cuisine* .

Cafe de l'Auberge, Inn on the Park, 444-2561. Candlelight French dining.

Accommodations

Ontario Travel distributes an *Accommodations Guide*, which lists and describes over 4,000 hotels, motels, resorts, and fly-in camps. Ask about weekend packages—many hotels discount their rooms up to 50 percent or more if visitors stay Friday and Saturday nights.

Try to book summertime resort reservations at least three months in advance. Representing over 250 lodges and resorts, *Resorts Ontario* can provide more information and brochures. Contact them at 10 Peter St., Orillia, On L3V 6S1: 705/325-9115, or toll-free in Ontario, 800/461-0249. Or, call "Reserve-a-Resort" collect, 0-807/468-6046.

Ottawa (Area code: 613)

Chateau Laurier, Confederation Square, 232-6411. An Ottawa landmark, renowned for grandeur befitting its chateau-style appearance. Spacious rooms.

Four Seasons, 150 Albert St., 238-1500, or toll-free, in the U.S.: 800/828-1188, in Canada: 800/268-6282. Modern hotel with well-deserved reputation for comfort; excellent service.

The Skyline Ottawa, 101 Lyon St., 237-3600. Recently renovated, high-rise hotel, with all the amenities, and a rooftop lounge, *Stop 26*.

Holiday Inn (Center), 100 Kent St., 238-1122. One of the nicer hotels in the chain; revolving rooftop restaurant.

Delta Inn of the Provinces, 360 Sparks St., 238-6000. Very pleasant rooms, piano lounge, dining room; offers indoor pool, sauna, exercise room, and squash courts.

Park Lane Hotel, 111 Cooper St., 238-1331. New hotel has all the accoutrements; executive suites with kitchenettes available.

Talisman Motor Hotel, 1376 Carling Ave., at the Queensway, 722-7601. Balconied rooms overlook Japanese gardens, two pools; Suburban golf course nearby.

Lord Elgin, 100 Elgin St., 235-333. Enjoys a regal atmosphere; smallish, yet modern rooms. Great value, better location: near Parliament Hill, across from National Arts Center.

Embassy Hotel, 25 Cartier St., 237-2111. Pleasant apartments, many with kitchen.

Embassy West Motor Hotel, 1400 Carling Avenue, 729-4331 at the Queensway. Bright, comfortable motel.

Roxborough Hotel, 123 Metcalf ST., 237-5171. Small rooms, well run.

Beacon Arms Hotel, 88 Albert St., 235-1413. Family-run lodgings downtown feature large rooms with kitchenettes.

Ottawa Bed and Breakfast, P.O.Box 4848, Station F, Ottawa, ON K1S 5J1, 563-0161. This is an umbrella organization, listing and licensing the city's bed and breakfast accommodations.

For cheap, summertime lodgings, book a residence room at one of Ottawa's universities:

Carleton University, Tour and Conference Center, 1233 Colonel-By Drive, Ottawa, On K1S 5B7; 564-3610.

Ottawa University Residences, 100 Hastey Ave., 231-7055.

Kingston (Area code: 613)

Holiday Inn, 1 Princess St., 549-8400. Pool, lounge restaurant.

Prince George Hotel, 200 Ontario St., 549-5440. Charming, restored hotel on the waterfront.

Algonquin Park Area (Area code:705)

Arrowhon Pines, Little Joe Lake, 633-5661. Very popular lodge and cottages. Canoeing, swimming, hiking and other outdoor facilities.

Blue Spruce Inn, Dwight, 635-2330. Cottages and motel rooms; great for all-season recreation.

Huntsville Area (Area code: 705)

Deerhurst Inn and Country Club, 789-5543. Luxurious resort on the American Plan; caters to a youngish clientele.

Bracebridge Area (Area code: 705)

Tamwood Lodge, Lake Muskoka, 645-5172. A smaller resort, built of logs; offers all the summer and winter sports.

Elgin House, Port Carling, 765-3101. Lodges and cottages amid spacious grounds; full summertime facilities, including tennis, golf, and water sports.

Collingwood/Wasaga Beach (Area code: 705)

Blue Mountain Inn, RR 3, Collingwood, 445-0231. Lodge located at the base of its namesake; full summertime facilities, but especially popular with skiers.

Hotel Waldhorn, Mosley St., Wasaga Beach, 429-4111. Smallish (20 rooms), alpine-style beach chalet.

Beacon Low Motel and Cottages, RR 3, Collingwood, 445-1674. Comfortable efficiency units of various sizes.

Kitchener-Waterloo (Area code: 519)

Riviera Motel, 2808 King St., E., 893-66421. Large, modern hotel/motel.

Valhalla Inn, King at Benton ST., 744-4141. Pleasant hotel with popular dining room and lounge.

Desert Inn, 605 Hospeler Rd., 622-1180. Small, comfortable motel.

Stratford (Area code: 519)

Check with the Theater Box Office (see Performing Arts) about bed and breakfast accommodations during the festival.

Victoria Inn, 10 Romeo St., 271-4650. Spacious, elegant hotel. Reservations a must during the festival.

Niagara-on-the-Lake (Area code: 416)

Prince of Wales Hotel, 6 Picton St., 468-3246. Replete with the grandeur one expects in Niagara-on-the-Lake. Full indoor recreational facilities, excellent dining room, low-key disco, and exquisite lounge.

Oban Inn, 160 Front St., 468-2165. Small inn featuring old-fashioned comfort; you won't miss the T.V.

Niagara Falls (Area code: 416)

Rates vary wildly with the season, but are highest from late June to late September.

Old Stone Inn, 5425 Robinson St., 357-1234. Sizable, modern hotel retains a rustic atmosphere.

Hotel Brock, 5685 Falls Ave, 800/263-7135. An old favorite connected to Maple Leaf Village.

Inn by the Falls, 5525 Victoria Ave., 357-2011. A nice motel on an otherwise undistinguished strip.

Honeymoon City Hotel, 4943 Clifton Hill, 357-4330. Pleasant lodgings; outdoor pool.

Nelson Motel, 10655 Niagara River Parkway, 295-4754. Peaceful, family-run accommodations up the river; outdoor pool.

Windsor (Area code: 519)

Cadillac Motel, 2498 McDougal St., 519/969-9340. Large hotel with all the amenities.

Sudbury (Area Code: 705)

Peter Piper Inn 151 Larch St., 673-7801. Luxurious rooms; great dining, service.

Ambassador Motor Hotel, 225 Falconbridge Rd., 566-3601. Motel with saunas, pool.

Sault Ste. Marie (Area code: 705)

Sheraton Caswell Motor Inn, 503 Trunk Rd., 253-2327. Pleasant rooms; dining room, lounge, pool.

Thunder Bay (Area Code: 807)

Red Oak Inn, 555 Arthur St. E., 623-8189. Large, popular hotel; noted for service, dining.

Ramada Inn Prince Arthur Hotel, 17 N, Cumberland St., 345-5411. Older facade hides modern, comfortable rooms overlooking the harbor.

Toronto (Area code: 416)

Builders can't quite keep the supply of Toronto hotel rooms in step with the demand, so lodgings here tend to be expensive. The standards, though, are high. The Hotel Association of Metro Toronto offers a free summertime reservations service, weekdays, from 9 a.m. to 9 p.m. Call 961-7117.

King Edward Hotel, 37 King St. E., 863-9700. An old Toronto favorite, newly renovated. Marble columns punctuate the lobby; rooms are spacious and gracefully decorated.

Four Seasons, 21 Avenue Rd., 964-0411.

Yorkville location. Understated elegance belies jet-set clientele; spacious rooms with nice views.

Harbor Castle Westin, One Harbor Square, 416/869-1600. Plush decor; every room in the two towers offers a sparkling view of the harbor.

Sheraton Center, 123 Queen St. (across from City Hall), 361-1000, toll-free reservations, in the U.S.: 800/325-3535, in Canada: 800/216-9393. Over 1,400 rooms; atop underground shopping, restaurants, cinemas.

Hilton International Toronto, 145 Richmond St., 869-3456. Opulent lobby newly redecorated rooms have nice extras, like alarm clocks and scales.

Inn on the Park, 1100 Eglinton Ave. E., 444-2561, toll free reservations, in the U.S.: 800/828-1188, in Canada: 800/268-6682. This sprawling complex overlooks Wilket Creek Park. Resort-style recreational facilities; gorgeous landscaping. Reputedly boasts a plastic surgeon-in-residence.

Park Plaza, 4 Avenue Rd. (at Bloor), 924-5471, toll-free reservations, in the U.S.: 800/323-7500, in Canada: 800/661-1262. Older hotel presents a subdued atmosphere. Rooms of various sizes, price available; can be more expensive.

Sutton Place, 995 Bay St. (at Wellesley) 924-9221. Another elegant, low-key hotel, rising 17 stories above Bay Street. Rooms have nice touches.

Chelsea Inn, 33 Gerrard St. (between Yonge and Bay), 595-1975. Former 1000-rooms apartment house is now a luxury hotel at reasonable rates.

Constellation Hotel, 900 Dixon Rd., 677-1500. Has the class, charm, and facilities of a downtown hotel, located out near the airport. A favorite of prime ministers.

Holiday Inn (Downtown), 89 Chestnut St., 977-0707. Behind City Hall. A pleasant hotel: Holiday Inn upscaled its accommodations to compete in this location. Six restaurants and lounges on the premises.

Town Inn, 620 Church St., 964-3311. Once an apartment complex, now offers spacious suites, with kitchenettes, dining area, etc. Tennis indoor pool, sauna, lounge.

Windsor Arms, 22 St. Thomas St., 979-2341. 60 year old hotel is a sedate, dignified escape from the bustle of nearby Bloor Street. Each room is unique, although they are all decorated with Canadian antiques.

Bond Place, 65 Dundas St. E., 362-6061. Rooms are small, but the service and furnishings are commendable.

Cara Inn, 6257 Airport Rd., 678-1400. Pleasant hotel, near the airport.

Seahorse Motel, 95 Lakeshore Blvd., 255-4433. Comfortable balconied rooms overlook the lake; a cab ride to the subway, though.

Nell Wycik College Hotel, 96 Gerrard St., E., 977-2320. Spartan accommodations (it used to be a student residence); special family rooms available. Open only during the summer.

Plaza Hotel, 240 Belfield Rd. (at Hwy. 27), 241-8513. Modest, pleasant lodgings near the airport.

Victoria, 56 Yonge Street 363-1666. Old hotel downtown boasts clean, tidy rooms. Some shared bathrooms, no TVs.

Downtown Toronto Bed & Breakfast, P.O. Box 190, Station B, Toronto, ON M5T 2W1, 598-4562. Send stamped, self-addressed envelope for their brochure.

Getting Around

By Air: Pearson International Airport, just 30 minutes northwest of Toronto, is served by nearly all the major Canadian airlines and numerous international carriers as well. Some phone numbers are (area code 416):

Air Canada: 925-2311
CP Air: 869-6735
Wardair: 620-9800
American Airlines: 283-2243
US Air: 361-1560

A taxi downtown from the airport will cost around $25, but cheaper alternatives are readily available. **Gray Coach** (416/979-3511) runs buses every half-hour ($3.50) which connect to the major subway lines. It also operates an Airport Bus Service ($6), which leaves every 20 minutes for the main, downtown hotels.

American visitors to Toronto increasingly take advantage of low, domestic U.S. airfares by flying into Buffalo International Airport, and then taking a **Gray Coach** (416/979-3511) bus to Toronto. Contact Gray Coach Lines or your travel agent.

Ottawa's international **Uplands Airport** is located 20 minutes south of the city. Phone numbers:
  Air Canada: 613/237-5000
  CP Air: 613/738-2501
  Eastern Airlines: 613/733-5430
  Wardair: 1-800/387-0520
Blue Line (746-8741) runs an express bus ($4) to the downtown hotels.

Many of the province's northern hunting/fishing/resort camps can be reached only by air. Usually, chartered air fare is included in a package deal. Ask Ontario Travel for its **Fly-in-Services brochure**.

By Bus: Toronto's bus terminal is located at 610 Bay Street (416/979-3511). The major carriers include **Gray Coach, Greyhound**, and **Voyageur**. Voyageur provides bus service to and from **Ottawa**, operating out of the Central Bus Station at 265 Catherine St. (613/238-8289). In all, over 30 bus lines operate in Ontario, providing service throughout the province. For more details, pick up the *Bus Lines* brochure from Ontario Travel.

By Train: Toronto's famous Union Station on Front Street is the city's main rail terminus, with direct access to the subway as well. **VIA Rail** (1-800-268-9511) can whisk you across Canada, including to and from U.S. connections in **Windsor** and **Niagara Falls**. VIA Rail (613-238-8289) serves **Ottawa** from **Toronto** and **Montréal**. The station is located at Blvd. St.-Laurent, near the Queensway.

By Car: The speed limit on Ontario Highways is 100 kph (61 mph), unless otherwise posted. Remember that front-seat passengers can be fined for not wearing seat belts. Ontario's road network is among the best maintained in North America, so your car should leave the province in as good shape as it came. Unless of course, you travel the dirt and gravel side-roads of northern Ontario, in which case a post-vacation underbody flush is appropriate. Check the front part of the Directory for toll-free car rental numbers.

Toronto (Area code: 416)

Transport: Toronto features an excellent system of mass-transit, including clean efficient (and safe) subways, with connections to timely buses and trolley. The fare is $1.05, but cheaper if passengers buy 7 or 20 tickets in a subway station. For information, call the **Toronto Transit Commission** (TTC) at 393-4636. Route maps are often available at a hotel.

Taxis are easily hailed on the street. Otherwise, call: Diamond (366-6868), Metro (869-1871), or Yellow Cab (363-4141). A cab ride from one end of the downtown to another should cost no more than $5-$6, but longer trips can be prohibitively expensive. In any event, the TTC is always cheaper and often more convenient, although a taxi can become necessary after 1:30 am, when the subways close and bus lines thin out.

Like any large city, driving in Toronto can enervate the most patient of drivers, especially at rush hour. Parking, naturally, is expensive ($1 to $2 per hour, with daily maximums), although less so in municipal lots marked with a large, green "P." Whenever possible, walk or take the subway. When a streetcar comes to a halt, stop behind it so that its passengers can exit through the right lane to the sidewalk.

Ferries leave for **Center Island** daily every 15 minutes' from 9:45 a.m., from the foot of Bay St., ($2 return; 947-8193).

Tours: A two-hour streetcar tour is always a treat. Call the TTC at 869-1372, or **Toronto by Trolley Car Inc.**, 388-8180. **Toronto Nightlife Tours** (364-2412) makes the rounds of nightclubs and other watering holes. **The Gray Line** (979-3511) also runs a nightime dinner-and-entertainment tour (around $45), as well as several daytime excursions, which often include extended stops at the CN Tower, ROM, or Casa Loma. Moreover, Gray Line offers pleasant meandering bus tours to **Niagara Falls**, for $44 per adult.

To enjoy a harbor cruise you can call Gray Line, which offers boat tours (adults: $19) of the Islands and Port. Otherwise, wander through the Harborfront area, where smaller outfits and privately-owned yachts launch splendid tour cruises.

Ottawa (Area code: 613)

The Rideau-Carleton Regional Transit Commission (741-4390) provides a comprehensive network of bus routes though Ottawa, connecting with **Outaouais Transit** (819/770-7900) in **Hull**.

For taxis, call Blue Line (238-1111), or Diamond (235-1821).

Shopping

For **crafts** shopping, check out the superb Pillar and Post Shoppe in **Niagara-on-the-Lake**, the Canadian Craftsman in **London**, Canada's Four Corners in **Ottawa**, or the Canadian Craft Shop in **Kingston**. This last store also has an extensive collection of Inuit art and handicrafts, as does the pricier Inuit Gallery in **Toronto**.

Looking for antiques? Browse Queen St. (E. and W.), Markham Village, Yorkville, or the Harborfront in **Toronto**. Sunday flea markets in **Burlington** and **Hamilton** also offer some good finds. In Hamilton, visit the restored specialty shops in Hess Village and browse through some rare displays.

Toronto

Stories have been told of travelers who came to Toronto and actually stayed for months browsing through the city's myriad of shops, stores, boutiques, and stalls. A word to the wise: bring a good pair of walking shoes.

Yorkville Village and Bloor St. West offer the latest in European and North American fashion. The trendy cafes and chic boutiques are expensive, but surprisingly unintimidating.

Walk south from Bloor along eclectic **Yonge St**. to find gay-book stores, army surplus retailers, furriers, audio/video outlets, jewelry stores, and more. This trek leads to the famed **Eaton Center**, whose 300 stores of variety stretch from Dundas to Queen Street.

From Queen St. south lie the skyscrapers of the downtown core, underneath which winds a subterranean maze of interconnected shopping centers where you can find everything from the practical (florist, liquor and drug stores) to the stylish (hair salons, fashion boutiques). Interesting furniture stores, antique shops, cafes, and second-hand clothiers dot Queen St. W. to Bathurst.

Moving north again, you'll find **Village-by-the-Grange**, a cobblestoned, European-style complex at McCaul St. and Dundas. Venture west through bustling **Chinatown** to **Kensington Market**, which is located just north of Dundas, west of Spadina. It's a lively area, where narrow streets are lined with produce vendors, European meat markets, West Indian music shops, and second-hand dealers.

Trek north to **Honest Ed's** (Bloor St. at Bathurst), a raucous discount department store with a garish (if self-effacing) three-story, brightly-lit sign announcing its presence. Can't miss it at night! Owner Ed Mirvish has created a more sedate shopping area next door on Markham St. south of Bloor: **Mirvish Village** is a renovated Victorian mews lined with book stores, art galleries, and restaurants.

Of note outside the downtown area are two large, yet pleasant shopping malls: **Yorkdale** and **Scarborough Town Centers**. Both are accessible by mass-transit, the former by subway, the latter by subway then LRT.

Ottawa

Import shops proliferate here, catering to the Rockliffe set and the international diplomatic corps. Try **Sarah Clothes** (46 Elgin) for Asian goods, or **Puchi Mode International**, at Place de Ville.

Ottawa boasts at least three commendable shopping areas. **Sparks Street Mall** is a central, pedestrian-only stretch lined with specialty shops and assorted vendors. The new **Rideau Center** also lies downtown. Its three floors offer over 200 stores, including the major department stores. Cross the walkway to **Byward Market**, a genuine farmers' market, which also houses several fascinating artisan shops.

Highlander.

Museums and Galleries

Toronto (Area code: 416)

Royal Ontario Museum (ROM), Bloor St. at Avenue Rd., 586-5549. This famous museum houses the largest collection of Chinese artifacts outside of China. Also of note are the Egyptian Collection, European Decorative Arts department, Mineralogy section, and a spectacular Vertebrate Fossils display which features reassembled dinosaur skeletons (open daily, 10 am - 9 pm; $3).

Ontario Science Center, 770 Don Mills Rd. (at Eglinton), 429-0193. Not really a museum, its 550 exhibits emphasize a "hands-on" approach, where visitors play with computers, perform simple (though often mind-boggling) physics experiments, take part in weather forecasting demonstrations, and so on. Children love it, and everyone becomes child-like here (open daily, 10 am - 6 pm, longer hours in the summer; $5.50).

Art Gallery of Ontario (AGO), 317 Dundas St. W., 977-0414. The AGO displays a broad array of Canadian art, in addition to its fine collection of European Masters. Nonetheless, the gallery is also well-known primarily for its **Henry Moore Sculpture Center**, whose 600 pieces comprise the largest collection of that artist's work anywhere (open daily except Monday, 11 am - 5:30 pm, 9 pm, Wednesday and Thursday; $3.50).

Gardiner Museum of Ceramic Art, 111 Queen's Park Cr. (across from the ROM), 593-9300. The Gardiner exhibits a 2000-piece collection of pottery, dating from pre-columbian to modern times (open daily, except Monday; $3).

McMichael Canadian Collection, Kleinburg, 893-1121. Located in the wooded hills of the Humber Valley 25 miles (30 km) north of Toronto, the galleries are housed in a series of beautiful log and stone buildings. The collection features by far the largest display of **"Group of Seven"** paintings in existence, making this one of Canada's most important art museums. The galleries also include fine examples of intricate Inuit carvings, Woodland Indian prints, and West Coast Indian Sculpture (open daily, except Monday, Noon-5:30 pm; Free Admission).

Ottawa (Area code: 613)

Canada's capital is home to several excellent National Museums. All are open daily (except Mondays from September to April), 10 a.m. to 5 p.m. With free admission, unless otherwise indicated.

National Museum of Man, West Wing, Victoria Memorial Building, 992-3497). Its phenomenal exhibits trace the history of people in Canada. Perhaps the finest of the National Museums.

National Museum of Natural Sciences, East Wing, Victoria Memorial Building, 996-3102. Emphasizes Canadian wildlife, including a fascinating dinosaur display. Also features good geology and evolution exhibits.

National Museum of Science and Technology, 1867 Blvd. St.-Laurent, 991-3046. This museum tries to involve its visitors in its displays with do-it-yourself buttons, levers, etc. Thre are exhibits on electricity, astronomy, meteorology, and a large section featuring transportation (including a sizeable collection of antique and rare automobiles).

National Aviation Museum, Rockliffe Airport, 993-2169. Over 100 aircrafts, representing the history of aviation in Canada and worldwide, rest in three hangars. A must for aviation buffs.

National Gallery of Canada, 990-1985. The National Gallery displays the largest collection of Canadian art anywhere, along with an impressive display of European works.

National Postal Museum, 365 Laurier Ave, 995-9904. This philatelist's dreamland details the postal history of Canada, including a display of rare stamps.

Canadian War Museum, 330 Sussex Dr., 996-1420. This large museum traces the history of warfare, especially as it pertains to Canada. It boasts a life-size WW I trench, two tanks out front, and several lively displays of famous battles.

Bytown Museum, The Driveway, 234-4570. Housed in Ottawa's oldest building (near the junction of the Rideau Canal and Ottawa River), the Bytown uses historical artifacts of local interest to describe the early development of Ottawa (open daily, except Sunday, 11 am - 5 pm, May to October).

Oshawa (Area code: 416)

Canadian Automotive Museum, 99 Simcoe St. S. (1 mile north of Hwy 401), 576-1222. In addition to its historical description of the Canadian Automotive Industry, this museum displays numerous antique cars, including a rare, 75 year old Byron Carter original, the "Cartercar" (open daily; $3).

London (Area code: 519)

Regional Art Gallery, 421 Rideout St., 672-4580. A bright, new gallery, it boasts a fine collection of 18th and 19th Century Canadian works, and other temporary exhibits (open daily, except Monday afternoon; $2).

Sudbury (Area code: 705)

Science North, Ramsey Lake Rd. at Paris Street, 522-3700. This new fun museum emphasizes a "hands-on" approach to exploring science, particularly as it pertains to northern Ontario (open daily, all year).

Performing Arts

Toronto (Area code: 416)

To gather more details about what's happening in Toronto, check the daily (or better yet, weekend) editions of the *Globe* and *Mail* or *Toronto Star*, or pick up a free copy of *Now* (a weekly) or *Toronto Life* .

Ballet, Symphony, Opera

Toronto offers world-class performances year round. Tickets range $15-$50.

O'Keefe Center, One Front St. E., 393-7469, 766-3271. Aside from hosting visiting performers and companies, the O'Keefe houses the superb **Canadian Opera Company** and the internationally renowned **National Ballet of Canada**.

Roy Thomson Hall, King St. W., between Simcoe and Duncan, 593-4228. This accoustically perfect hall is designed all 2800 members of the audience sit within 110 feet (36m) of the stage. It is the winter home of the excellent **Toronto Symphony Orchestra** (368-4631), and **Mendelssohn Choir**.

Massey Hall, 178 Victoria St., at Shuter, 363-7301. Toronto's Victorian grande-dame now plays second-fiddle to the Roy Thomson, but it still attracts several international stars and musical groups to suit all tastes.

The Forum, Ontario Place. There's room for 10,000 here, 2,000 under the canopy roof. During the summer, the Forum showcases rock, jazz, and dance performances. It's also the summertime home of the **Toronto Symphony**, and hosts guest performances by the fine **Hamilton Philharmonic**.

Theaters

Toronto is one of the most exciting cities on the continent view live theater. Ticket prices usually range between $15 and $30.

Royal Alexandra Theater, 260 King St. W., Toronto, M5V 1H9: 593-4211. The "Royal Alex," with its lavish baroque decor, hosts the latest plays from Broadway and London, as well as top local productions. Try to write ahead for tickets.

St. Lawrence Center for the Arts, 27 Front St., E., 366-7723. Just east of the O'Keefe, its modern theater showcases classic and contemporary drama, with an emphasis on Canadian playwrights and local talent.

Smaller Theaters

Canadian Stage, (26 Berkeley St., 368-2856) and **Taragon Theater** (30 Bridgeman Ave., 531-1827). These theaters produce excellent works, with an emphasis on Canadian drama. The **Factory Theater Lab** (125 Bathurst St., 864-9971) and **Theater Passe Muraille** (16 Ryerson Ave., 363-2416) present innovative or experimental productions.

The Bayview Playhouse (1605 Bayview Ave., 481-6191) is a larger theater uptown, whose musicals and modern drama boast excellent talent. **Toronto Truck Theater** (94 Belmont St., 922-0084) specializes in comedy. **The Toronto Workshop Productions** (12 Alexander St., 925-8640) presents a series of international works from October to June. **Young People's Theater** (165 Front St. E., 864-9732) offers fine children drama.

Second City, the satirical comedy group, performs at the **Old Firehall** (110 Lombard St., 863-1111).

Cinemas

Toronto, particularly the downtown area, offers dozens of movie houses. Alas, some are small, ten-in-one shopping mall theaters. However, several cinemas offer foreign films, classic oldies, or the more obscure new arrivals, in very non-claustrophobic comfort. Try the **Bloor Cinema** (532-6677), **Carlton Cinemas** (598-2309), **Cumberland Four** (964-5970), or the **Uptown and Backstage** (922-3113).

Check the newspaper listings for what's playing where. Tickets cost $6.50 a piece, and lines form early on weekends. On Tuesdays Ciniplex theaters show movies for half-price.

Ottawa (Area code: 613)

The focus of Ottawa's performing arts scene is the **National Arts Center** complex (237-4400). The Center has three auditoriums: the 2300 seat **Opera House**, home to the acclaimed **National Arts Center Orchestra** and guest performers the **Theater** seats 800 for its French and English language plays; and the **Studio**, a theater for experimental works, seating 300.

The popular **Ottawa Little Theater** (400 King Edward Ave., 233-8948) has a fine resident company.

Stratford (Area code: 519)

The annual **Shakespeare Festival** (from late May to November) draws over a half-million theater-goers from around the world to this quaint, diminutive town on the banks of the Avon river. Three superb theaters perform Shakespearean, classic, and modern dramas, while hosting jazz and orchestral concerts as well.

Ticket prices range between $15 and $35, and go on sale in March. Write the Festival Theater Box Office, Box 520, Stratford, ON N5A 6V2, or call 519/273-1600 in Stratford, 416/364-8355 in Toronto.

Niagara-on-the-Lake (Area code: 416)

Set in what is surely the best preserved 19th Century hamlet in Canada (if not North America), the **Shaw Festival** is devoted to performing the works of George Bernard and his contemporaries. Expert productions with renowned actors draw large crowds to this little town and its three fine theaters, especially on weekends. Therefore, try to make prior arrangements and reservations as early as possible.

The festival runs from May through September. Tickets cost between $15 and $35. For more information, write the Shaw Festival, Box 774, Niagara-on-the-Lake, ON L0S 1J0, or call 468-2153 (468-2172 for the box office) in Niagara-on-the-Lake, or 416/690-7301 in Toronto.

Lynx.   *Beaver.*

Nightlife

Ontario possesses a set of liquor laws that are, in part, remnants from its prohibitionist past. Many restrictions are being eased but:

- several small towns (and some neighborhoods within larger cities) are still completely dry
- a brief experiment with "happy hours" has recently ended
- all carry-out alcohol is marketed through provincially owned outlets: **Brewer's Retail** for beer, and **LCBO** stores for liquor and wine. They're open until 6 or 9 p.m. (it varies), Monday—Saturday, check the phone book for the nearest one.
- You may not go out in public with an open bottle of booze or opened case of beer.
- licensed establishments can serve liquor until 1 a.m., 10.30 p.m. on Sundays.

The legal drinking age is 19, but rumoured to go up to 21 in the near future. Though the old laws remain, Ontario has long since shed its reputation for having a dull nightlife, as evidenced below.

Toronto (Area code: 416)

This entire book could be spent describing Toronto's nightlife, which is as varied as it is exciting. Yorkville and nearby Bloor St. clubs draw a younger, stylish crowd. Queen St. East, out toward the "beaches," is also trendy these days. The Yonge/St. Clair and Yonge/Ellington area bars cater to single, young professionals on the make. Yonge St. south of Bloor is home to gay bars, and heavy metal emporiums. Post new wave dancing can be had on Queen St. West. Downtown hotel lounges draw a youngish to middle aged crowd, while the increasingly gentrified Annex neighborhood (immediately north and west of the University of Toronto) has sprouted a half-dozen imported English pubs. Here are a few samplers, by category.

English-style pubs:

Dooley's, 220 King W. Lively Irish atmosphere and entertainment.

Duke of York, 39 Prince Arthur Ave., Madison Ave., just north of Bloor St., Both are plush basement lounges popular with the "after work" crowd and young singles.

The dukes, incidentally, are well represented on the Toronto pub scene:

Duke of Gloucester, Gloucester at Yonge St.

Duke of Kent, 2315 Yonge St. (just north of Eglinton).

Duke of Westminster, First Canadian Place.

Jazz:

Cafe des Copains, 50 Wellington St. E., 869-0148.

Albert's Hall, Upstairs at the Brunswick House, 964-0846.

Chick 'n' Deli, 744 Mt. Pleasant Rd., 486-1900.

Quieter Lounges:

Expect a dress code in the evenings, usually "no jeans."

Aquarius 51, Atop Manulife Center, 44 Charles St. Great mid-town view.

Club 22, Windsor Arms Hotel. Piano lounge.

Other hotel Lounges:

Magic Carpet, at the Constellation.

Dick Turpin's, at the Royal York.

SRO, at the Four Seasons.

Chelsea Bay, at the Chelsea Inn.

Not so quiet bars and clubs:

Imperial Room, Royal York Hotel. Toronto's original nightclub, books big-name entertainers.

Thank Goodness It's Friday, 204 Eglinton Ave. East.

Ryan's, St. Clair Ave. at Yonge St.

Uptown, Youngish clientele; dancing.

El Mocambo, 464 Spadina Ave., Books popular rock and blues artists.

Bemelman's, 83 Bloor St. W. Classically styled; vogue clientele.

Diamond Club, Carlton at Sherbourne. Dancing to "new music," very popular. Stiff weekend cover charge.

Disco:

Most of the major hotels have one. Many are still somewhat flashy, and most cater to a mid-20s to mid-30s crowd. A cover charge to $6 to $15 is commonplace. Try also:

Sparkles, Atop CN Tower, Unequaled view of the city at night. Kind of a singles haunt.

Drink-and-Sink:

The Morissey, Yonge St. at Davenport. Little atmosphere, but cheap beer. Draws a college crowd during the summer.

Ye Olde Brunswick House, 481 Bloor

St. W., at Brunswick Ave. Huge, famous beer hall where matronly waitresses bring cheap draught by the trayload. Raucous atmosphere, sing-alongs, contests, etc.—not to be missed!

Ottawa (Area code: 613)

Ottawa's nightlife yearly becomes more vibrant, but after 1 a.m. (bar time in Ontario), the action gravitates across to Hull, where quite literally "anything goes" until 3 a.m. A plethora of discos, singles bars, and clubs line two main strips: Promenade du Protage, and Blvd. St.-Joseph. Here are some starting points on the Ottawa side of the river.

Byward Market Area
Youngish crowd cruise and dance.
Brandy's, 126 York St.
Houlihan's, 110 York St.
Stoney Mondays, 62 York St.

Bars and Lounges:
Friday's Victorian Music Parloer, 150 Elgin St. Warm, low-key piano lounge.
Lieutenant's Pump, 361 Elgin. English Pub.
Vines, 33 William St. Wining and dining, with an emphasis on wining.
Stop 26, Skyline Hotel. Relaxing skytop lounge.

Sports, Recreation and Parks

Important Addresses

Ontario Travel
Queen's Park, Toronto
Ontario M7A 2E9
Toll-free 800/268-3735

Its *Wilderness Activities* booklet lists canoeing, whitewater, survival ports, hiking and rock-climbing expeditions and package tours.

Ministry of Natural Resources
Queen's Park, Toronto
Ontario M7A 1W3
416/965-3081

Sports Administration Center
160 Vanderhoof Dr.
Toronto M4G 2B8
416/429-7701

Resorts Ontario
10 Peter St. North
Box 2148, Orillia,
Ontario L3V 6S1
Toll-free in Ontario (except for area code 807): 800/416-0249
From elsewhere, call 705/325-9115

Hiking

Over a dozen magnificent trails slice through Ontario. The most famous is the **Bruce Trail**, which winds 430 miles (688 km) along the Niagara Escarpment from near Niagara Falls to the Bruce Peninsula (Bruce Trail Association, 33 Hardale Cr., Hamilton, L8T 1X7).

Algonquin Park offers two wilderness trails, the Uplands and Highland, both of which are relatively short and can be trekked in a day (Ministry of Natural Resources, Box 219, Whitney, K0J 2M0).

The Rideau Trail follows the Rideau Canal for 250 miles (400 km) from Kingston to Ottawa (Rideau Trail Association, P.O. Box 15, Kingston, K7L 4V6).

Trails of various length meander through most Ontario Provincial Parks. Also of note is the newly developed **Pukaskwa National Park** (see below), on the north shore of Lake Superior. Its rugged paths are not for novices.

Fishing and Hunting

A spate of regulations await anglers and hunters in Ontario, but the rewards are plentiful. Although most North American freshwater fish can be found in Ontario, the province is known particularly for its muskie, bass, walleye, pike, and trout. Hunters come in search of deer, moose, pheasant, and black bear.

Hunting and fishing are seasonal. For maps and more information about licensing and outfitters, contact the Sports Fisheries Branch or the Wildlife Branch of the Ministry of Natural Resources (see above).

True aficionados charter a plane and pilot to fly to a northern locale, where the fishing and hunting are unparalleled. Contact Ontario Travel for a list of fly-in services. Resorts Ontario (see above) also lists fishing packages.

Water Sports

With access to one-third of the world's fresh water, including over 400,000 lakes and innumerable rivers and streams, Ontario is a water sports haven. Canoeing enthusiasts can enjoy Ontario's rivers and lakes from mid-May to early November. The best known, albeit still remote, routes lay in **Algonquin** and **Quetico Provincial Parks**. The **Ottawa River** and some Provincial Parks lay claim to excellent whitewater canoeing and rafting, which grow yearly in popularity.

Canoe rentals should cost about $10-$20/day, but a full outfitting ranges $25-$45/day. For a list of outfitters, contact the Ministry of Natural Resources, or write the Outfittings Coordinator, National and Provincial Parks Association of Canada, 47 Colborne St., Suite 308, Toronto, ON, M5E 1E3.

Lake Huron's **Georgian Bay**, the **Muskoka Lakes, 1000 Islands**, and the **Trent-Severn Waterway** are all excellent boating areas. Many marinas rent motorboats, sailboats, and water skiing equipment. Ontario Travel publishes a listing of *Boat Rentals* and a *Cruise* guide.

Ontario's beaches offer excellent opportunities for swimming. Of note are the "cottage country" lakes of central Ontario, and **Georgian bay** (especially **Wasaga Beach**). Several beaches dot Toronto's shoreline, but they are sometimes closed in the summer when Lake Ontario is too polluted to swim!

Other Summer Sports and Recreation

Ontario has nearly 400 golf courses, many open to the public. Horseback riding is also

a favorite, while one of the best ways to experience Ontario is from a bicycle. Scuba divers lover **Georgian Bay**, a virtual graveyard of sunken vessels (equipment can be rented from outfitters in **Tobermory**).

For more details on everything from ping-pong to skydiving, contact the Sports Administration Center in Toronto.

Skiing

A popular downhill skiing haunt in southern Ontario is the **Blue Mountain** range near **Collingwood**. Otherwise, try the northern slopes around **Sault-Ste. Marie** and **Thunder Bay**, the latter of which is known for its titan ski jumps.

Ottawa is blessed with three alpine and cross-country skiing areas less than 20 miles (32 km) away in Québec: **Mont Cascades** (819/827-0136), **Camp Fortune** (819/827-1717) in **Gatineau Park**, and **Edelweiss Valley** (819/459-0136). More challenging slopes await at **Mont Ste.-Marie** (819/467-2812), 60 miles (96 km) north. Remember: Ottawa is but a short drive from the Laurentians (see Québec Sports, Recreation And Parks).

The Ontario Ski Resorts Association (17 Mill St., Willowdale, On M2P 1B3) can help with accommodations and packages. Ontario Travel distributes a complete listing of over 400 slopes. For the latest snow conditions, call 416/364-4722 for southern and central Ontario, or 705/726-0932 for central Ontario.

Cross-country skiers will find superb trails throughout the province. Call toll-free 800/461-7677 or 705/457-1640.

Other Winter Sports

Snowmobiling originated in this part of the world, and remains immensely popular here. Trails criss-cross the **Georgian Bay** and **Muskoka/Algonquin Park** regions, but can be found all over the rest of the province as well. For anglers who can't wait for warm weather, Ontario has an ice-fishing season. The province's hiking rails are often suitable for snow-shoeing.

Provincial Parks

Ontario boasts 128 Provincial Parks, in

addition to numerous roadside picnic areas and campgrounds. Nearly half the parks stay open all year; otherwise, the season runs from mid-May through September. Most are equipped for camping. For a complete list and more information, call Ontario Travel's toll-free number, or write Provincial Parks Information, Queen's Park, Toronto, M7A 1W3. The five largest provincial parks are:

Algonquin, Whitney, KOJ 2MO; 613/637-2780. Algonquin remains a fairly secluded park, with several access points on the perimeter, but only one through-road (Hwy 60). It is known for its excellent camping, hiking, canoeing, and fishing.

Killarney, Killarney, POM 2AO; 705/287-2368. Camp, canoe, and fish amid the white-crested La Cloche Mountains of the Canadian Shield. A gorgeous park.

Lake Superior, Wawa: 705/856-2284. This beautiful park stretches for 50 miles (80 km) along the shore of Lake Superior. Stunning cliffs rise out of the lake, giving way to forested hills. Its Indian pictographs are widely renowned.

Polar Bear, District Manager, Ministry of Natural Resources, P.O. Box 190, Moosonee, POL 1YO. This, the largest park in Ontario, lies on the southern shore of **Hudson's Bay**, and is accessible by chartered aircraft only (usually from Moosonee). A special entrance permit is required from the District Manager. Once there, visitors find a virtually untouched sub-Arctic wilderness (open June-September).

Quetico, Nym Lake, Atikokan, ON, POT 1CO; 807/597-2735. A longtime favorite of outdoors-oriented people, especially canoeists and sport fishermen. This large wilderness area lies just above the U.S. border, adjacent to Minnesota's Superior Park.

National Parks

For complete details on all the National Parks in Ontario, contact: Parks Canada— Ontario Region, P.O. Box 1359, Cornwall, K6H 5V4; 613/933-7956.

Point Pelee National Park, Leamington, N8H 3H4; 519/322-2365. This diminutive peninsula jutting into Lake Erie is the southernmost point in Canada—and an ornithologists' dreamland. Over 300 different species of birds have been sighted here, while over 100 species will congregate on any given day during spring and fall migrations.

Pukaskwa National Park, Box 550, Marathon POT 2EO; 807/229-0801. This new park is among the least developed in Canada, and has thus become a favorite of canoeing and hiking enthusiasts who truly love to "rough it."

The Trent-Severn Waterway, Box 567 Peterborough K9J 6Z6: 705/742-9267. This interconnected system of lakes, rivers, and canals, winds from Lake Ontario to Lake Huron's Georgian Bay. Perfect for houseboats.

Attractions

Morrisburg (Area code: 613)

Here travelers will find **Upper Canada Village**, the most detailed and interesting "living museum" in Canada. Inhabitants in period costumes go about their business among 35 elaborately reconstructed, early 19th Century buildings, including numerous homes, a farm, schools, store, church, sawmill, tavern, and Willard's Hall, where visitors can partake of an 1840s-style meal (Hwy 2, east of Morrisburg; open daily, May 15—October 15; Adults: $5; 543-2911).

Midland (Area code: 705)

Sainte Marie Among the Hurons is a reconstructed Jesuit mission dating to 1640. A wooden palisade encloses 22 timber buildings and an excellent museum—well worth the detour. (Hwy 12; open daily, mid-May to mid-October; $3; 705/526-7838). Nearly lies **Martyr's Shrine**, a 60 year-old stone church dedicated to eight New France Jesuits who perished at the hands of the Iroquois ($2; 526-3738).

Niagara Falls (Area code: 416)

The city of Niagara Falls is very touristy, but its major attraction remains, as always, the two massive cataracts, which can be viewed from several different locales.

Catch a ride aboard one of the **Maid of the Mist** (daily during the summer; $6; 5920 River Rd., 358-5781), which cruise right along the base of the two falls. It's a wet ride (raincoats/hoods provided), but terribly fun.

To get a view from behind the falls, take the elevator at Table Rock House down 150 feet (50 m) into the **Table Rock Tunnels**, which open out onto the back of the Canadian cataract ($3.75).

There are three towers from which to look down over the falls. They cost about $4 to $5 to ascend:

Kodak Tower, on Falls Ave. (357-3090), which is part of the impressive **Maple Leaf Village** complex, though the view is less spectacular than that from the other two.

Skylon Tower: 5200 Robinson St. (356-2651), where exterior elevators whisk tourists to its observation deck and revolving restaurant for a suberb view of both cataracts.

Panasonic Centre, 6372 Oakes Dr. (356-1501), a 325 foot-high (108 m) tower which boasts a birds' eye view of the **Horseshoe Falls.**

A great place to visit just south of the falls is the **Marineland and Game Farm**. There you'll find a delightful amusement park—complete with the world's largest steel roller coaster—and a game farm with deer, bears, and other animals. The Marine Shows make the visit worthwhile. Marineland boasts the largest sea-lion and dolphin acts anywhere; the killer whale show is unequaled. At $12-$15 per adult, admission is steep during the summer, but you'll pay half that between October and March (7657 Portage Rd. S.; 416/356-2142).

Toronto (Area code: 416)

Ontario Place, 955 Lakeshore Blvd. W., 965-7711. Ontario Place is a 100 acre recreation complex and park built on three man-made islands in Lake Ontario. The futuristic pods house somewhat dated exhibits, but don't let that discourage you—there's more to it, including: the Cinesphere (a six story movie theater), Children's Village, the Forum (see Performing Arts), paddleboats, lots of good eats, and more (open daily, until midnight, mid-May to mid-September; adults: $4, children: $2).

Harborfront. The Harborfront is home to some of the more exciting new developments in Toronto, including museums, shops, galleries, and restaurants. It's great place to hang-out in the summer. Start at the York Quay, 235 Queen's Quay W., 364-5665, home to many shops, restaurants, and artisanry, and the information center.

CN Tower, 301 Front St. W., 360-8500. The tallest structure in the world has an indoor/outdoor observation deck (complete with a revolving restaurant and Sparkles nightclub) at 1150 feet (385 m). Go up another 300 feet (100 m) to the "Space Deck," the world's highest public viewing gallery.

Center Island, The largest of the Toronto Islands, is a green, car-less park, with a spectacular view of the Toronto skyline. It's great place for a picnic, and kids will love **Centerville**, a 15 acre amusement park (362-1112). Ferries leave for Center Island daily, every fifteen minutes from 9:45 a.m., from the foot of Bay Street (adults: $1:50, children: 25¢; 947-8193).

Casa Loma, One Austin Terrace, 923-1171. This is an opulently furnished, 98 room castle built by the eccentric, if romantic, Sir Henry Pellatt betwen 1911-1914. A fascinating tour takes about an hour (open daily, 10 a.m. - 4 p.m.; $4).

Metropolitan Zoo, Hwy 401 at Meadowvale Rd, Scarborough, 284-8181. The magnificent 700 acre park features over 4000 wild animals, living in six different ecological regions. The horticulture exhibits are equally astounding. Four well-marked trails wander through the grounds; in winter, they are groomed for cross-country skiing: call 284-9781 for lessons and rental information (open daily, 9:30 a.m. to 6 p.m.; adults: $4, children: $1).

Ottawa (Area code: 613)

Parliment Hill, Free guided tours of the Parliament buildings leave every half-hour daily (992-4793). The tour meanders through the Senate, House of Commons, the Library, Confederation Hall, and the Peace Tower. If you're with Canadian friends, have them call their Member of Parliament (996-0896), who can get you into the Members' Gallery. In any event, try not to miss the outstanding "Changing of the Guard," daily in the summer at 10 a.m., in front of the Parliament Buildings.

Rideau Canal, In the summer, an hour-long boat tour leaves from the Confederation Center. But in the winter, nearly everyone in Ottawa takes to the canal—on skates! If you didn't bring any, rent a pair from the Park Lane Hotel, 111 Cooper St. (238-1331). For a daily report on the condition of the ice, call 232-1234.

Central Experimental Farm. The Driveway, 995-5287. This serene, 1200 acre farm downtown has dirt lanes, barns, and fields filled with flowers, shrubs, and trees from all over the world. They even grow marijuana here. Horse-drawn wagons conduct tours of the farm (open weekdays, May to mid-October).

Thunder Bay (Area code:807)

Old Fort William, Broadway Ave., east of town, 577-8461. Doubtlessly the finest reconstruction of a Hudson's Bay Company trading post, and an excellent introduction to 18th Century frontier and Indian life. The fort is accessible by boat from the **Port Arthur Marina** (344-2512), where, incidentally, you can take an intriguing harbor cruise among huge vessels and towering grain elevators. The fort opens daily, from mid-May to mid-September.

Diary

February (Ottawa)
Winterlude: Extravagant carnival features ice-sculpting, snowshoe races, ice-boating, and other such wintertime festivities.

May (Ottawa)
Festival of Spring: Over three million blossoming tulips highlight this festival, which also offers parades, regattas, craft shows, etcetera. For more details, contact Festival of Spring, 700-71 Bank St., Ottawa, On K1P 5N2; 613/238-6231.

May-October (Niagara-on-the-Lake)
Shaw Festival: See Performing Arts.

Last week in June (Toronto)
Metro International Caravan: Ethnic celebrations are held in pavilions all over Toronto, featuring over 60 "international cities." Call 416/977-0466 for more details.

Last Saturday in June (Toronto)
Queen's Plate: Oldest stakes race in North America, held at the Woodbine Race Track.

Early July (Oakville)
Canadian Open Golf Championship: Glen Abbey Golf Club hosts one of golf's top five tournaments.

Late July-Early August (Toronto)
Caribana: The city's West Indian community celebrates with singing, dancing, and parades, held mostly on Toronto Islands, creating a Mardi Gras atmosphere.

Early August (Maxville)
Glengarry Highland Games: North America's largest Highland Gathering.

First three weekends in August (Branford)
Six Nations Indian pagent: Iroquois tribes celebrate and exhibit their culture and history.

Mid-August (St. Catherine)
Royal Canadian Henley Regatta: The largest rowing regatta in North America draws competitors and spectators from

throughout the continent.

Mid-August-Labour Day (Toronto)

Canadian National Exhibition: The largest and oldest exhibition of its kind in the world, featuring air shows, big-name entertainment, and all sorts of exhibits. All this takes place for three weeks at Exhibition Place on Lakeshore Boulevard. For more information, write the CNE, Exhibition Place, Toronto, ON M6K 3C3.

October (Kitchener/Waterloo)

Oktoberfest: This famous Bavarian celebration attracts yearly over a half-million festive party-goers to the area's 30+ beer halls and tents. For more information and reservations, contact K-W Oktoberfest Inc., Box 1053, Kitchener, On N2G 4G1; 519/576-0571.

Provincial Holiday

Civic Holiday

First Monday in August.

Special Packages

Ontario Travel's free *Tours* and *Vacation Packages* booklet gives full information on hundreds of packages and excursion.

Bus and train tours often originate from Toronto or Ottawa, lasting anywhere from a day to a fortnight. Common destinations include: **Niagara Falls, Toronto, Ottawa, the Muskoka Lakes, 1000 Islands, Quebec, Agawa Canyon,** or **Cochrane.** Many excursions are seasonal, such as Fall Color tours, or jaunts to Ottawa for its glorious Festival of Spring.

A convenient, and often inexpensive, way to visit Toronto, Ottawa, Niagara Falls, and other cities and regions is to travel on an independent package, which usually includes transportation from the U.S. border, accommodations, and sometimes meals. The booklet also describes numerous recreation and wilderness packages, including whitewater rafting trips, snowmobiling safaris, yacht and houseboat vacations, bicycle treks, and so on.

Tours and *Vacation Packages* provides a complete list of licensed companies and operators, but below is an abridged listing of the major outfits:

Can-Am Travel Ltd.
300 Town Center
Suite 2340
Southfield, M1 USA 313/353-9740
From the US: 800/482-0629

Canadian Wilderness Trips
171 College St.
Toronto, M5T 1P7
416/977-3703
800/268-9044

Gray Coach/Sunquest Vacations
130 Merton Street
Toronto, M4S 1A4
416/482-3333
From Ontario: 800/268-8899

Key Tours
Box 1119, Station A
Windsor, N9A 6X2
Canada: 519/258-7477
US: 313/963-8787
From Michigan: 800/482-3661

VIA Rail Canada Inc
Union Station
Toronto, M5J 1E7
416/366-8411
US: 800/USA-RAIL
(Through Amtrak)

Wilderness Tours Ltd
Box 89
Beachburg, KOJ 1SO
613/582-3805
May to September: 800/267-3124

The **Polar Bear Express**, a 1-2 day train excursion from Cochrane to Moosonee on **Hudson's Bay**, has become famous for good reasons. The train travels along a historic route through a virtually untouched wilderness, offering a unique opportunity to see northern Ontario. The two-day "local" makes a few stops along the way to pick up/drop off geologists, Indians, hunters, etc., and is consequently a little less touristy. It also affords greater time to explore **Moosonee** (some bring canoes), which is the air terminus for flights into Polar Bear Provincial Park (See Sports, Recreation And Parks).

For more details, contact the Ontario Northlands Transportation Commission, 805, Bay St., Toronto, ON M5S 1Y9; 416-965-4268.

If you would like to spend all or part of your Ontario vacation on a farm, write the Ontario Vacation Farm Association, R.R. 2, Alma, ON N0B 1A0.

PRINCE EDWARD ISLAND

The area code for numbers listed in Prince Edward Island is 902 unless stated otherwise.

Finding Out

The Visitor Information Centers that dot the island are very helpful. The main branch is located at the Royalty Mall in Charlottetown; or write: Visitor Services Division, P.O. Box 940, Charlottetown PEI, C1A 7M5; or call toll-free: Maritimes: 800/565-7421; Ontario, Newfoundland and Québec: 800/656-0243: Eastern U.S.: 800/656-9060. (These numbers are in operation from mid-March to Oct. 31st. During the off season call 388-4444, not toll-free.)

Accommodations

PEI's hotels, motels, and resorts fill fast in the summer, so secure reservations as far in advance as possible. Call the PEI tourist information service toll-free from New Brunswick or Nova Scotia at 800/565-7421 for reservations or to gather lodging information. Once on the island, any Visitors Information Center can arrange accommodations, if necessary in a tourist or private home.

The center in Charlottetown also has a complete listing of farm tourist and vacation homes. For about $20 a day per person, visitors share meals, activities, and sometimes farmwork with their hosts. Those who have experienced it often claim this is the best (and cheapest) way to get to know PEI and its inhabitants.

Woods Island

Meadow Lodge Motel, 962-2022. One mile from the ferry dock.

Montague

The Sulky Inn, 4 Bink St. 838-4100. Modern rooms, ample services with housekeeping facilities.

Roseneath

Rodd's Brudenell River Resort, 652-2332. Fifty chalets rest on 1500 acres of this modern resort complex, which offers a heated pool, shuffleboard, lawn bowling, canoeing, movies, a championship golf course, tennis (bring whites), and even daycare.

Charlottetown

Charlottetown Hotel, 894-7371. Old-fashioned elegance belies modern rooms.
Dundee Arms Motel and Inn, 200 Pownal St., 892-2496. Quaint rooms vary in size and style.
Aloha Tourist Home, 234 Sydney St. 892-9947. Downtown Tourist Home; make reservations well in advance to avoid disappointment.
Islander Motro Lodge, 892-1217. Older motel near 18-hole golf course.
Gateway House, 894-9761. Small Tourist home (no credit cards.)
PEI Region Youth Hostel, 153 Mt. Edward Rd., 894-9696.

Grand Tracadie

Dalvay-By-The-Sea, 672-2048, Luxury resort; fine dining.

Summerside

Quality Inn-Garden of the Gulf, 618 Water St., 436-2295. Summerside's fanciest hotels features pool or beachfront swimming, two lounges, shuffleboard, golf, and more.
Best Western Linkletter Inn, 311 Market St., 436-2157. Has a long history, but the rooms are up-to-date, and the staff is service-oriented.
Two motels on Water St. offer comfortable rooms at low prices:
Sunny Isle Motel, 720 Water St., 436-5665.
Cairns Motel, 721 Water St., 436-5841.

Restaurants/Dining

Prince Edward Island is known for its potatoes, which find their way into local recipes. Oysters and shellfish adorn many PEI specialty dinners, and "Lobster Suppers" have become an island tradition.

Charlottetown

Colonial Dining Room, Dundee Arms Inn, 892-2496. Formal dining; acclaimed for local seafood dishes.

Claddagh Room, 131 Sydney St., 892-9661. Specializes in seafood.

King Palace Restaurant, 161 Queen St., 894-9644. Polynesian dishes.

Golden Wok, 51 Grafton, 892-0609. Chinese food at bargain prices.

Summerside

Brother Two, Water St., 436-9654. Popular seafood and steaks. Features "Governor's Feast," a pricier dinner-and-show served by talented actors, singers, and dancers in 1840s period dress; call 436-7674 for information and reservation.

Montague

Lobster Shanty North, Main St. 838-2463. Colonial style assorted seafood platter is a favorite.

Lobster Suppers: Civic groups sponsor traditional "Lobster Suppers" throughout the province in July and August. Expect to pay $14 to $18 for the evening, but they're often "all-you-can-eat" dinners. Here are several popular ones.

St. Anne's Church Suppers, Rte. 224, 964-2385 in Hope River.

New Glasgow Lobster Suppers, Rte 224 New Glasgow, 964-2870.

New London Lion's Club, Rte. 6 in New London, 886-2599.

Getting to PEI

By Air: Air Canada (892-1007 Airlines Canadian International) flies into Charlottetown daily from numerous Canadian cities, as does **CP Air** 566-3976 which serves Charlottetown from Maritime airports and also Montréal.

By Ferry: During the summer, ferries leave hourly from **Cape Tormentine,** N.B. to **Borden**, PEI, a 45 minute trip. Call 506/538-2278 in New Brunswick, or 855-2030 in PEI. From **Caribon**, N.S. to **Woods Island**, PEI is a $1^{1/4}$ hour trip, but the ferries leave daily about every 50 minutes. Call 485-6580 in Caribou, or 962-2016 in Woods Island. Both ferries are almost always crowded, with early morning and evening sailings boasting the shortest waiting lines.

Getting around PEI

By Car: The speed limit is 90 kph (69 mph). Check the front part of the **Directory** for toll-free rental car numbers. Charlottetown sports four taxi services: Art's (894-5586), City (892-6567), Ed's (892-6561), and Star (892-6581).

By Train: VIA Rail provides service throughout PEI. For details contact toll-free 800/561-3952.

By Bus: Greyhound under the auspices of SMT services the area. For information call the Charlottetown office at 894-9524. **Abegweit Sightseeing Tours** (894-9966) runs tours of **Charlottetown** and jaunts to the **North Shore** beaches on its double-decker buses. The former should cost around $4.25, the latter, $18, children half-price.

By Bicycle: Cyclists adore PEI's rural lanes. Renting a bike for a week should cost less than $5 per day. Contact **MacQueen's Bike Shop**, 430 Queen St. in Charlottetown (892-9843); **Easy Rider Cycle Rentals** on Rte. 6 in Stanley Bridge, (886-3550).

Shopping

The island offers little in the way of fashion goods, but its crafts—including leatherwork, wood carvings, weaving, and pottery—never fails to entice the province's visitors. **The Prince Edward Island Crafts Council.**, (P.O. Box 1573. Charlottetown, PEI, C1A 7N3; 892-5152) gives detailed information on PEI handicrafts and where to find them. Two of the larger outlets are worth a look:

Islands Craft Shop, 156 Richmond St. in Charlottetown.

Woods Islands Handcraft Co-op, Main St. in Murray River.

Nightlife

PEI's legal drinking age is 18.

Charlottetown

Tudor Lounge, Charlottetown Hotel, 894-7371. Quiet, elegant establishment.
Silverado, 566-4775. Club features dancing to popular music.
The Dispensary, 99 Grafton St., 892-5195. Prescribes lively fiddling on Wednesday and Saturday nights; draws a big crowd.
The Gallows Lounge, Inn on the Hill, 894-95722. Don't let the haunting décor frighten you away.

Summerside

Captain Grady's Pub, 436-9654. Boisterous Irish entertainment attracts locals and tourists alike.

Sports, Recreation and Parks

Canoeing, hiking, and cross-country skiing are all gaining in popularity here. Contact the Visitor Services Division for rental and trail information.

PEI is a summertime haven for lovers of the links, boasting at least six 18-hole courses, three of which are of championship calibre. The **Brudenell Resort's** course in **Roseneath** is perhaps the finest in the Maritimes.

Hunters will find only small game in PEI, but the fishing could hardly be much better.

After obtaining a $10 non-resident fishing license (from the Fish and Wildlife Division), find moving water and cast for fat, fresh-water brook trout and perch. Deep-sea fishing excursions can be chartered from any port on the island's eastern shore.

Prices range from $5-$40 per person, depending on how serious one is, and don't hesitate to make it a family affair, since children often go half-price. For more information, contact the Visitors Services Division, of the Fish and Wildlife Division P.O. Box 2000, Charlottetown, PEI, C1A 7N8; 892-0311.

The long, sandy beaches of Prince Edward Island National Park make for some of the best swimming in eastern Canada (Cavendish Information office:672-2211).

Private and provincial campgrounds are scattered throughout the island. The fees range from $8.50-$15 a night, depending on the services available. Note that camping anywhere other than on a designated campground is illegal.

Attractions

Charlottetown

The **Confederation Center of the Arts** on Queen St. houses a museum, library, the Charlottetown Theater (which hosts the Summer Festival), and a premiere art gallery featuring the works of Canadian and international masters. (open daily, free admission; 566-2464).

To view local and regional artwork, visit the **Great George St. Gallery** on 82 St. George St. (free admission).

Charlottetown's colorful history is exhibited at **Beaconsfield**, a century-old, sprawling Victorian Mansion on Kent St. (open weekdays, free admission; 892-9127).

Montague

Travel south of Rte. 4 to visit a small provincial park, **Buffaloland**, where roams a small herd of American bison. The beasts are ridiculously out of place on PEI, but that's half their attraction. A few miles north lies **Moore's Migratory Bird Santuary**. Well marked trails allow hikers to get close glimpses of Canadian geese, ducks, and myriad of other waterfowl. The Visitor Information Centers will gladly provide further details on both these parks.

Diary

Mid-June to Labor Day (Charlottetown)
Charlottetown Festival: The Confederation Center hosts a fine series of concerts and theater, highlighted by a musical adaptation of PEI's own *Anne of the Green Gables*. Call 892-1267 for information and reservations.

Mid-July (Summerside)
Lobster Festival: A week-long feast of Lobster.

Early August (Eldon)
Highland Games: Gathering of the Clans. Scotsmen congregate for time-honored contests and merriment.

QUÉBEC

Finding Out

Provincial Travel Bureaux:

Québec is split into 18 regional Touristic Associations, each eager to offer information and tours. Contact:

Information Tourisme Québec, Case Postale 20 000, Québec, PQ CANADA GIK 7X2; 800-361-5405(Québec);800/361-6490 (Ontario and Atlantic Provinces); 800/443-7000 (Eastern U.S.); 514/873-2015 (call collect from anywhere else).

Tourisme Québec also maintains offices in Montréal (2 Place Ville-Marie; 514/873-2015) and in Québec City (12 rue St.-Anne; 418/643-2280).

Local Travel Information:

Convention and Tourist Bureau of Greater Montréal; Place Bonaventure; 514-871-1595.

Tourist Information Office of the city's Public Relations department, which also provides the occasional free walking tour; 514/872-3561, 872-3455.

Tourist and Convention Bureau of the Québec Urban Community; 60 rue d'Auteuil; 418/692-2471.

Accommodations

As a rule, try to book lodgings as far in advance as possible. Large hotels often offer discounts on Friday, Saturday, and Sunday nights, but resort areas will be crowded and therefore more expensive on weekends. If you reserve rooms with two double-beds, your child can usually stay free of charge; if need be, rent extra roll-away beds at small extra cost.

Montréal (Area code: 514)

Most hotels fall in the Expensive to Deluxe range, especially those downtown, which, incidentally, rarely have swimming pools. Yet, a full range of accommodations are available, and as an added bonus, most hotels have excellent restaurants.

The Ritz Carlton, 1228 Sherbrooke St. W., 842-4212. Located amid the downtown shopping area. The Ritz caters to an élite clientele.

Montréal Meridien, 4 Complexe Desjardins. 285-1450. Integral part of stunning Desjardin Center, with its infinite variety of attractions nearby; two pools.

Queen Elizabeth, 900 René-Lévesque St. W., 861-3511. Dependable comfort in prime location.

Les Quatres Saisons (Four Seasons), 1050 Sherbrooke St. W., 284-1110. Excellent hotel adjacent to McGill University; less business/convention oriented.

Holiday Inn, Richelieu, 455 Sherbrooke St. W., 842-8581. One of five Montréal Holiday Inns which vary in size and price.

Ramada Renaissance du Parc, 3625 Parc Ave., 288-6666. One of four Ramadas, all providing good service.

Hotel Roussillion Royal, 1610 St. Hubert, 849-3214. Modern accommodations in Latin Quarter.

Crescent Apartment Hotel, 1214 Crescent St., 878-2711. Save money by cooking own meals in furnished kitchenettes.

These tend to cater to the young, and prices are often negotiable:

Auberge Internationale Montréal, 3541, Alymer, 843-3317.

Concordia University Residences, 1455 Maissoneuve Blvd. W., 848-3830.

McGill University Residences, 3935 University St., 398-6367. Summer is best time for these.

Youth Hostel, 3541 Aylmer Rd., 843-3317. Clean rooms draw young, international crowd.

Tourist Homes:

Alpes Tourists, 1245 St. André St., 845-9803. Modern rooms set in Gallic neighborhood.

Castel St. Denis, 2099 Saint-Denis Blvd., 8428719. Good value in Latin Quarter.

Québec City (Area code: 418)

Although a wide variety of accommodations can be found within the walls of the old city, Québec is renowned for its grand old hotels and modest. European-style guest homes. Visitors looking for larger or more modern lodgings may have to stay in the new city.

Chateau Frontenac, 1 rue des Carriéres, 692-3861. 500 room castle set atop a cliff overlooking the St. Lawrence river—worth seeing even if one doesn't stay overnight.

Auberge des Gouveneurs, 609 rue St. Cyrille., 647-1717. Modern, yet tasteful accommodations in ideal location.

Hilton International Québec, 3 Place Québec, 647-2411. Consistent quality; kids often stay free.

Holiday Inn, 395 rue de la Couronne, 647-2611. 235 rooms; indoor pool and sauna.

Hótel Clarendon, 57 Ste-Anne, 692-2480. Centrally located, good value.

Manoir Ste.-Geneviéve, 13 Ave. Ste-Geneviéve, 694-1666. Like most small Québec hotels, the Ste.-Geneviéve offers a variety of charming, comfortable rooms.

Chateau Bellevue, 16-18 rue Laporte, 692-2573. Antique facade conceals ultra-modern accommodations.

Chateau Fleurs-de-Lys, 15 Ave. Ste.-Geneviéve, 694-1884. Wide selection of rooms, all of which include continental breakfast.

Hotel de la Place d'Armes, 24 rue Ste.-Anne, 694-9485. Simple but elegant rooms; excellent locale near city hall.

Hotel Chateau Laurier, 695 Grand-Allée E., 522-8108. Old, but well-maintained; perfect location for Winter Carnival.

Hotel Doyon, 109- rue Ste.-Anne, 694-1720. Informal guest house.

Maison Acadienne, 43 ru St.-Ursule, 694-0280. Quiet rooms just outside city walls.

Auberge de Jeunesse, 19 St. Ursula St., 694-0755. Sizable youth hostel featuring bed and breakfast lodgings.

Ste.-Adéle (Area code: 514)

Le Chantecler, 229-3555.

Sun Valley, 229-3511. These sprawling, luxurious resorts have their own ski trails.

Hotel/Motel Chatel Boisé, 1997 Blvd. Ste.-Adéle, 229-6616. Located right in town, near Mont Alouette ski area.

Val David (Area code: 819)

Hotel la Sapiniere, 322-2020. La Sapiniere is perhaps the finest luxury resort in Québec. Prices are steep (doubles can run up to $200 a night), but they include three sumptuous meals daily. Cottages are also available.

Aubergrge de Vieux Foyer, 322-2686. Swiss-style inn is small but comfortable.

Ste.-Agathe des Monts (Area code: 819)

Motel Ste. Agathe, 100 rue Principale, 326-2622. Modern lodgings near town.

Mont Tremblant (Area code: 819)

Chateau Beauvallon, 425-7575. One of the area's many small, cozy, New England-style resorts. Ask about ski packages.

Gray Rocks, 425-2771. Famous, year-round resort, where they've thought of nearly everything, including a private airport for those flying in.

Mont Orford

See "skiing" under **Sports, Recreation and Parks** for lodging information.

Hull (Area code: 819)

Hotel Plaza de la Chaudiere, 2 rue Montcalm; 778-3880. Luxury accommodation with extra touches.

Sherbrooke (Area code: 819)

Auberge des Gouveneurs, 3131 King St. W., 565-0464. High-quality Québec chain.
Holiday Inn, 3535 King St. W., 563-2941. Tends to be business-oriented.

Chicoutimi (Area code: 418)

Hotel Chicoutimi, 549-7111. Known for its fine Québecois cuisine.

Gaspé (Area code: 418)

Adams Motel-Hôtel, 368-2244. Small and comfortable.

Percé (Area code: 418)

Hôtel-Motel La Normandie, 782-2112. Modern accommodations overlooking the sea.

Getting Around

Montréal (Area code: 514)

The **Montréal Urban Community Transport Commission** (MUCTC) services the city with buses and its excellent *Metro* . The cost is $1 and you can use a bus transfer for admission to the subway and vice-versa. Bus service downtown from **Mirabel** and **Dorval** airports will cost about $5.00 per adult. The ubiquitous taxis charge $1.20 base price and 70¢ per kilometer thereafter.

If you drive, try to make overnight parking arrangements in advance with a hotel. Be prepared to pay $6-$10 per day to park around the city.

Guided Tours: The city occasionally sponsors free walking tours—check with the Tourism Information Office at 872-3561; 872-3455.

The romantically inclined can hire a horse-drawn caléche for $20-$30 (try to negotiate) per hour at Dominion Square, Place Jacques-Cartier, or at Beaver Lake atop Mount Royal. (844-1313).

Bus tours are offered by the Murray Hill Co. (1380 Barre, 937-5311) and the Gray Line (1241 Peel 'St., 280-5327). These should cost about $10 per person, children ride half-price.

For something different during the summer, sample a river/harbor boat cruise available from Montréal Harbor Cruises (842-3871) at prices comparable to the bus tours.

Québec (Area code: 418)

In the old city, walking is by far the easiest and most convenient way to get around. Woe to those who drive: parking is scarce and expensive (check with your hotel). Cabs charge $1.20 plus 70¢ per kilometer, and riding the bus costs 85¢.

You can avoid four-wheeled traffic snarls by renting a bicycle from Location des Bicyclettes (641 Grand-Allée East. 522-2040).

Guided Tours: Call 828-2275 for information on walking tours.

A caléche can be hired year-round at the Place d'Armes or on the rue d'Ateuil. The driver will charge $25-$30/hour to serve as your guide.

Various bus tours originate from the Place d'Armes, call 662-7420., the Gray Line.

The Province

By Air: Dorval International Airport is on the outskirts of the city. Driving into the airport can be an adventure in itself. It is served by all major Canadian lines and numerous international carriers as well. Some numbers are:
Air Canada: 514/393-3333
CP Air: 414/286-8532
Wardair: 514/288-9231
Visitors piloting private aircraft should check first with the **Montréal Flying Club** (514/861-5878) or **Transport Canada** in

Ottawa. **Canadian Airlines International** (418/694-0281) in **Québec City**) will fly you to northern Québec.

By Rail: CN and **CP Rail** have tracks into, out of, and throughout the province. In **Montréal**, call 514/871-1331, in **Québec City**, 819/692-3940. **Le P'tit train du Nord** will whisk passengers to the Laurentians in style from **Montréal**.

By Bus: Greyhound and Voyageur Lines serve Québec. In Montréal, call 514/842-2281; in Québec City, 418-/524-4621.

By Car: Perhaps the best way to travel Québec is by automobile, which gives you the flexibility to explore obscure villages, the freedom to stop and sample the local cuisine, and the ability to meander through the exceptional provincial parks. While good maps are available from most service stations, remember that as one is driving north of the major population or resort areas, the road may become increasingly unpaved and perhaps impassable in winter.

Restaurants/Dining

Due perhaps to the traditional French passion for fine cuisine, dining out is taken very seriously in Québec. Patrons of Québec's restaurants will find the service kind, polite, and energetic. Diners generally return the favor by phoning in advance to make reservations and then arriving on time. Be sure to check the dress code—they can be surprisingly flexible—and ask about credit cards if necessary.

Although wine with meals can be expensive, food is often of exceptional value, since even small or modest restaurants will prepare the simplest dishes with professional care. When figuring prices add a 10 percent provincial meals tax and an appropriate tip (15 percent is customary).

Montréal (Area code: 514)

Over 5,000 restaurants feature a variety of French and international cuisine. Here is a small sampling:

La Chamade, 1453 Belager, 727-7040. Fine nouvelle cuisine; as is often the case in Québec, delightful lunches can be had here at bargain prices.

Chez Delmo, 211 Notre-Dame Quest, 849-4061. Consistently excellent seafood.

Elysée Mandarin, 1221 Mackay St., 866-5975. One of the few Parisian style Szechuan restaurants in North America.

Kam Fung, 1008 Clark St., 866-4016. A "dianhsin" house serving faddish Chinese brunches.

Schwartz, 3895 St. Lawrence Blvd., 842-4813. New York-style smoked beef (no credit cards).

Chez Magnani, 9245 Lajeunesse, 387-6438. A long travel, well worth the meticulously prepared Italian dishes.

Ben's Delicatessan, 1475 Metcalfe, 844-1000. Late night deli spot, Pierre Trudeau has been known to stop by.

Québec City (Area code: 418)

Québec is internationally renowned for its haute cuisine, and even the more modest restaurants reflect this dedication to culinary excellence.

Le St. Amour, 48 rue Ste. Ursule, 694-0667. French cooking in quiet romantic setting.

Café Le Grek, 99 Chemin St.-Foy, 525-7525. Great Greek Food.

Kyoto, 560 Grand-Allée, 529-6141. Japanese steak house.

L'Anse aux Barques, 28 Champlain,

692-4674. Specializes in French cuisine and seafood.

Au Petit Coin Breton, 1029 rue St. Jean, 481/694-0758. Crepe-lovers' haven.

The Province

The *habitant* cooking of rural Québec takes hearty advantage of the fresh herbs, vegetables, fish, rabbit, mutton, and other meats found bountifully throughout the province.

Ste. Agathe-des-Monts

Restaurant La Petite Bourgeoise, 626 2 Morin Val-Morin, 322-2211. Fine French food; you can bring your own wine.

St. Adéle (Area code: 514)

Le St. Trop, 229-3298. Classic French cuisine in rustic setting; can be expensive.
TJ's, 179 rue Morin. 229-4417. Fine, varied menu; informal.

Val David (Area code: 819)

La Sapiniére, 322-2020. Prize-winning entrées (rarely under $30) join exquisite wine list for sumptuous dining.

Hull (Area code: 819)
(See also 'Ottawa' in "Ontario")

Café aux Quatre Jeudis, 44 Laval, 819/ 1771-9957. Café set in unlikely neighborhood.

Troise Riviéres (Area code: 819)

Chez Claude, 375-4921. Excellent cuisine features subtle, French seasonings.

Sherbrooke (Area code: 819)

Restaurant Le Provencal, 864-9124. 5156 Blvd. Bourque. Offers a variety of Canadian dishes.

Ile d'Orléans (Area code: 418)

I'Atre, 4403 rue Royale, 829-2474. 300 year old farmhouse serves good old habitant cuisine; cozy setting.

Chicoutimi (Area code: 418)

Chez Georges, 433 rue Racine, 543-2875. Intimate if modes restaurant known for its filet mignon and chicken entrées.

Bale St.-Paul (Area code: 418)

Maison Otis, 21 Rue ST., 435-2255. Simple lunches, followed by unique, habitant dinners.

Gaspé (Area code: 418)

Auberge Fort-Prevel, 368-2281. Seafood lovers' delight set in hotel complex converted from historic military installations (open June 10-Labour Day).

Shopping

Quebecois crafts such as patchwork quilts and Inuit carvings and drawings are traditionally popular items, but shop around and ask questions, be sure that what you buy is genuine. Price is often a good indicator: authentic crafts tend to cost more than the mass-produced variety.

The major department stores of cosmopolitan **Montréal and Québec City** will carry the latest Continental fashions, and the smaller shops and boutiques will offer an intriguing range of styles and merchandise to the persistent browser.

Although shopping hours can vary with season or locale, the following is fairly typical:

Monday-Wednesday 10 a.m. - 6 p.m.
Thursday, Friday 10 a.m. - 9 p.m.
Saturdays 10 a.m. - 5 p.m.
Sundays, Holidays Closed

Montréal

The Underground City, a sprawling system of subterranean passages linking business complexes, offers theaters, cinemas, hotels, restaurants, and shops, all underground and connected to the Métro. In Center Town, St Catherine St. is home to the major department stores, while Sherbrooke St. features high fashion outlets. Smaller or more specialized boutiques dot the downtown area, both above ground and below.

Visitors in search of crafts should visit the

Centrale d'Artisanat de Québec (541/849-6091), or **The Canadian Guild of Crafts** (both at 2025 Peel St.), which displays a smaller though more select collection.

Québec City

Although Montréal offers substantially more shopping opportunities, a sizable antiques district has formed around St. Paul St. in the recently restored **Lower Town**. For the right price, dealers will part with Victorian furnishings, Québec furniture, and various colonial objects.

Museums and Galleries

Several of the most extensive museum and art exhibits in Canada can be found in Montréal, while Québec city is world renowned for its carefully restored and preserved battlements, houses, and landmarks. Quaint museums and fascinating historical sites await those who explore the province's smaller towns as well.

Museums and galleries generally stay open to the public from late morning to late afternoon on weekdays, and may offer viewing hours on Thursday evenings, but most are closed on Sundays and sometimes Mondays as well.

Montréal (Area code: 514)

McCord Museum, 690 Sherbrooke Ave., 398-7100. Objects displays, and photographs develop a social history of Canada with special emphasis on Québec. Admission: $1.

Canadian Historical Museum, 3715 Chemin de la Reine-Marie, 738-5959. This misnamed gem is actually one of the finest wax museums in the world, and its exquisitely costumed figures display a variety of non-Canadian historical events as well. Adults: $5.50, Children: $3.00.

Montréal Museum of Fine Arts, 1379 Sherbrooke St.W., 285-1600. Eclectic, large, and evergrowing collection of art. Admission $4.

Canadian Rail Museum, 122A rue Saint-Pierre, 632-2410. Features over 100 cars and engines. Open May to September; admission: $3.50.

Museum of Hunting and Nature, 1260 Voie Camillien Houde, Mount Royal, 843-6942. Exhibits rotate monthly in this 100 year-old farmhouse. Admission: $3.

Bank of Montréal Museum, 129 Saint-Jacques St, on the Place d'Armes, 877-6892. Features historical coinage and banking displays. Free admission.

Québec City (Area code: 418)

Quebec Museum, Southern reaches of Plains of Abraham, 643-2150. Features Québecois crafts and artwork. Free admission.

Musée du Fort, 10 Ste.-Anne St., 692-2175. Reenactments of local military history. Adults: $3, chilren, 75¢.

Chevalier House, Place Champlain, 643-9689. Widely acclaimed displays trace evolution of Québecoise furniture. Free admission.

Historical Wax Museum, 22 St.-Anne, 692-2289. Full of surprises, including Iroquois warriors torturing Jesuits—all in wax, of course. Adults: $2.50, children: $1.25.

Huron Village Museum, Village-des-Hurons, 842-4303. Features artifacts of Huron life, past to present. Free admission, by appointment only.

Performing Arts

Québec offers nearly limitless opportunities for cultural diversions and entertainment. The best way to find out where to see what there is available is to contact local travel bureau, but newspapers can be a helpful resource as well. Ballet, symphony, and opera tickets range from $5 to $30 and up, theater tickets can be more expensive; (although some productions are free), and cinema houses will charge $6.50 per person for admission. As a general rule, call ahead for program information, especially concerning movies and plays, the majority of which will be in French.

Montréal (Area code: 514)

The "Week-end" editions of *Gazette* and *La Presse* update Montréalers on what's happening around town.

The Place des Arts, 842-2112. Holds three halls, offering the finest in performing arts: **Salle Wilfred Pelletier,** home to the acclaimed **Montréal Symphony Orchestra**, **Montréal Opera company** and **Les Grandes Ballets Canadiens. Maissoneuve Theater**, featuring chamber music and plays. **Royal Theater**, housing the **John Duceppe Company**, a famous Québec drama group.

Centaur Theater, 453 St.-Francois-Xavier, 288-3161. Performances in English from October to June only.

National Theater School of Canada, Monument National 5030 St. Denis., 842-7954. Features plays in English and French.

Québec City (Area code: 418)

Théater du Petit Champlain, 68 rue Petit Champlain, 692-2631. a unique theater where patrons pay a cover charge ot view French language productions in a licensed café.

Institute Canadien, 37 rue Sainte-Angéle, 692-2135. Mostly French language plays.

The Québec Conservatory of "Dramatic Arts, 30 rue St.-Denis, 643-2139. Mostly English language productions.

The Laurentians

In the summertime, this ski resort area hosts a number of theater productions, many outdoors. For more information, write: Association Touristque des Launrentides, 100 rue Labelle, Bureau 200, St.-Jérome, Quebec, J7Z 5N6, or call: 514/436-8532.

Nightlife

The drinking age in Québec is 18. Cocktail lounges stay open until 2 a.m., bars and cabarets until 3 a.m.. Use discretion when tipping—15 percent is standard—but be forewarned: servers in Québec tend to become vocally hostile when they feel a gratuity has been inadequate.

Montréal (Area code: 514)

The major hotels house lavish nightclubs which feature discos, cabaret shows, comics, and other entertainment. Cover charges generally range from $25 up. One club of special note is the Caf-Conc' at the Chateau Champlain, which will transport patrons for an evening to the Moulin-Rouge district of Toulouse Lautrec. Drinks are $6 in addition to the cover admission (878-1688).

Most clubs and bars are located in the downtown area, where explorers can sample the chic Crescent St. scene, St. Catherine St.'s red-light district, or trendy Bishop St. Here are a few starting points:

Thursday's, 1449 Crescent St., 849-5635. Make the Yuppie connection.

Deja-Vu, 1224 Bishop St., 866-0512.

Woody's, 1234 Bishop St., 861-5130.

The Cock'n Bull, 1944 Ste.-Catherine St., 933-4556.

Metropolis, 59 St. Catherines St. E., 288-5559. A large, popular disco.

The Passport, 4156 St. Denis St., 842-6063. Popular drinking spot.

Old Munich, 1170 St.-Denis St., 288-8011. Sing along sportingly to German oompah bands.

Several skytop lounges will provide dinner, drinks and dancing, all with a panoramic view, for just a few extra dollars. Try **Chateau Champlain's** rooftop bar for the experience.

Québec City (Area Code: 418)

The city sports few clubs, but many small cafés and bars. Stroll rue St. Jean to find sidewalk cafés. while rue Ste.-Anne offers more expensive fare. Cavort with the bohemian Latin Quarter crowd at **l'Ostradamus**, 29 rue Couillard.

Le Bistro, 1053 rue St.-Jean. Disco.

Eden, Atop Québec Hilton, 647-2411. Like most Québec City discos, there is no cover charge, but drinks will cost moderately, between $4 and $5.

Attractions

Québec is divided into 18 touristic regions. Each region's Touristic Association eagerly provides travel information, and perhaps more importantly, they offer a variety of tours, many of which will take the adventurous visitor "off the path" normally beaten by tourists in Québec. The system is sponsored by Information Tourisme Québec. Call toll free; 361-5405, or write: Tourisme Québec, Case Postale 20 000, Québec, G1K 7X2.

Montréal (Area code: 514)

Mount Royal

This 750-foot (250-m) mountain and its immediate environs make up a 530 acre park where Montréalers stroll, relax, and otherwise enjoy the excellent view. Winter recreation in the park includes tobogganing, skiing, and ice skating. **The University of Montréal**—the largest French University outside of France—sits on the mountain's west flanks, as does **St. Joseph's Oratory**, where millions of pilgrims have flocked to be cured (733-8211).

Downtown

Aside from **Place Ville-Marie** and the **Underground City** (see Shopping), Sherbrooke St. offers numerous art galleries and boutiques for the fashionable set.

In the **Latin Quarter**, sidewalk cafés patronized by local college students can be found on St. Denis Street. Specialty shops, small restaurants, and a youthful nightlife can be found on Prince Arthur St.

Old City

Place Jacques Cartier and **Place d'Youville** are popular meeting places,

especially during the summer. The former is known for its artists and artisans, while the latter has been the recent subject of major restoration projects.

The Place d'Armes is home to the beautiful stone church, **Notre-Dame de Bou-Secours**, (845-9991). Nearby runs St. James St., one-time financial capital of Canada (and still lively). Just north is rue Lagauchetiére, Montréal's Chinatown.

St. Helen's Island

Expo '67 pavilions have been transformed into annual summer show called Man and His World (admission: $6: 7872-6222). Nearby lies **The Old Fort**, which houses a museum of Canadian military history and features reenactments of Scottish Highlander regimental maneuvers during the summer (daily except Monday, 10 a.m. to 5 p.m., admission, $3: 861-6701).

Ile Notre-Dame

Watch huge vessels pass through the St. Lawrence Seaway's **St. Lambert's Lock** at the east end of Victoria Bridge (April-November, 8 a.m. to 6 p.m., 672-4110).

Olympic Park Area

The facilities built for the 1976 Summer Olympics now comprise Olympic Park, which includes **Olympic Stadium**, home to several Montréal sports teams (Sherbrooke St. at Pie IX; guided tours, $5. 252-4737).

The nearby **Botanical Gardens** is a horticultural wonderland where over 20,000 species of plants are displayed (4101 Sherbrooke St. E., open 9 a.m. to 6 p.m. daily, 872-1400).

Québec City (Area code: 418)

The Old City

The best way to take in the Old City is to explore it on foot. Here are a few starting points:
• Rue de Trésor, where artists display their works.
• Rue St.-Louis, where some of the oldest houses in Canada are open for public viewing.
• The **Basilica Notre-Dame de Québec**, and its famous, 320 year old seminary, set in the city's nostalgic Latin quarter (tours: Free admission, June to August; 692-2533).

- The **Ursuline Convent**, near the Place d'Armes, dates to a similar period. It includes among its interesting displays the skull of the French General, La Marquis de Montcalm (tours: free admission, open daily except Monday; 694-0694).
- Stroll the **Dufferin Terrace**, which runs 750 yards along the city's cliffs and affords a spectacular view of the Lower Town and the St. Lawrence River.

Fortifications

The Citadelle: This tremendous fortress traditionally housed Québec own 22nd Regiment. A ceremonial changing of the guard takes place daily at 10 a.m. (weekday tours: $3, 648-3563).

Artillery Park: These restored military barracks are located on the northwest corner of the city walls (open daily, 648-4205).

Outside the Walls

The Québec Provincial Parliament legislates from the **Assemblée Nationale**, a sprawling and elegantly decorated Renaissance-style edifice off Avenue Dufferins (weekday tours, 643-7239).

Recently restored, the **Lower Town** lies beneath the cliffs of the Old City (guided tours leave daily in the summertime from 29 rue Nortre-Dame, 643-6631). Be sure to see the **Royal Battery**, Québec's oldest defence structure. The nearby ferry to **Levi** oldest provides an excellent view of the city from the St. Lawrence River (pedestrians: $1, car: $1.50; sails every half-hour, weather permitting 6 a.m. to midnight).

Ile d' Orléans

This island in the St. Lawrence between Québec City and St.-Anne de Beaupré is known for its rustic farmhouses and quaint restaurants. It is a two-hour tour by car.

St.-Anne de Beaupré

Nearly 1 million Catholics make a pilgrimage every year to the basilica which houses a shrine reputed to have curative powers.

Percé

The **Gasp** peninsula rewards its visitors with breathtaking scenery, particularly around the resort village of **Percé**, perhaps the only place in North America where a huge limestone coastal rock (accessible by sandbridge at low tide, otherwise by ferry) does not seem out of place. The local information office can help (782-5448).

The Saguenay Fjord

To acquire the best view of the majestic cliffs which tower above the Saguenay River, reserve a tour by boat (June—September; excursions of various lengths leave Chicoutimi: 543-7630, or Tadoussac: 235-4421). Try to schedule an August tour, when the river's deep waters are a breeding ground for beluga whales.

Magdalen Islands

Located in the Gulf of St. Lawrence, les **Iles de la Madeleine** form an exotic, 60 mile (96-km) archipelago featuring stunning red sandstone cliffs sculpted by the fierce winds and sea. By car ferry, it is a five-hour trip from **Souris**, P.E.I. (daily in the summer; contact Coopérative des Transport Maritime: 902/687-2181, or a two-day cruise from **Montréal** (weekly, April to December; call 514/527-8361 in Montréal). The islands' Tourist Association can be reached at 418-2245.

Ste.-Agathe-des-Monts

This Laurentian community offers tremendous wintertime skiing (see Sports, Recreation, and Parks). but in the summer, a cruise amid the beautiful islands of **Lac des Sables** on an "alouette boat" can prove both relaxing and scenic. For those with loftier ambitions, **Air St.,-Agathe** will take visitors for a quick spin on the lake in an amphibious plane (boat trips, adults: $7, children; $3, call 819/326-3656; air tour, twenty minutes to an hour, $20 to $35 per person, call 819/326-5366).

Ste.-Adéle

This Laurentian resort area cum artist and writers' colony is a joy to explore. When taking a break from skiing, golfing, or other recreation, visit the **Village de Seraphin**, a reconstructed 19th Century Laurentian community (open daily, May to mid-October, admission: $5. Call 514/229-4777 for tour information—most are in French).

Hemmingford

The **Richelieu Valley** is known for its

decidedly North American fruit orchards, but visitors to **Safari Park** drive their cars, through an African Savannah setting, complete with lions, elephants, giraffes, and other wild beasts (lock your doors). It's touristy but fun (west of Route 15, just north of the New York state border. Open daily, May though Labor Day; $34.95 per carload, 514/247-2727).

Sports, Recreation and Parks

The Provincial Government has printed an excellent series of brochures detailing sports and recreation activities, including skiing, boating, hunting and fishing. Write:
Tourisme Québec
150 Blvd. St.-Cyrille E.
15th Floor
Québec, P.O. Box G1R 4Y3
418/643-2280

Canoeing and hiking are popular in the summertime, particularly in the lake-strewn forests of the Canadian shield. Canoers will find that Provincial Parks offer the best excursions. Quebeckers have also cleared over 1200 trails for cross-country skiing, snow-shoeing, and snowmobiling.

Québec's rivers and lakes are renowned for their excellent fishing. In fact, provincial officials claim that there are more fish in Québec than in any other foreign country! Deep-sea excursions and trips to northern fly-in camps are popular with the afficionados. Details of fishing, and hunting licensing, seasons, limits, and packages can be obtained from Tourisme Québec.

Downhill Skiing: An average of 130 inches of snow falls on Québec downhill slopes between October and April, making the province a skiers' paradise. Lift ticket prices vary with the time of year and day of the week (Saturday and Sunday are more expensive), but they average $15 to $20/day. Enquire at resorts about weekend or week-long packages which often include lodgings, meals, lift tickets, lessons, and more.

The Laurentians

Just northwest of Montréal, this region offers a plethora of superb hotels and resorts, which, incidentally, are the favorite of the golf and tennis set during the summer.

Ste.-Adele

Le Chanticler Resort, 514/229-3555.
Center Municipale, 514/229-2727.

Mont Tremblant

Station Touristique de Mont Tremblant, 819/425-8711.
Gray Rocks, 819/425-2771.

The Eastern Townships

Mont Orford is the place to ski. Call or write Mont Orford Reservations, (819/843-6548; C.P. 248, Magog, P.Q., J1X 3W8) to plug into a highly-organized network of facilities which can arrange transportation, as necessary, and variety of different accommodations and packages.

From Québec City, skiing 2625 foot (875 m) high **Mont Ste-Anne** can be a one-day excursion by bus or car. Call the Parc du Mont Ste.-Anne (418/827-4561) for details of the extensive and well-groomed downhill and cross-country trails only 25 miles (40 km) from the Old City walls.

Parks

Québec government parks and reserves are well-equipped to serve outdoor enthusiasts. Facilities include free camping units, reception areas, and equipment rental/repair stations at key locations. For information, reservations, and a Calendar of Events, write Tourisme Québec (see above).

Diary

January (Québec City)
International Bonspeil.
World-class curling.

Late February (Québec City)
Carnival: Normally staid Québeckers engage in eleven days of revelry, heightened somewhat by the ubiquitous "Cariboo," a concoction of whiskey, sweet red wine, and other surprises. There's a parade, ice-sculpture contests, and even a canoe race on the frozen St. Lawrence!

February (Chicoutimi)
Carnival-Souvenir: Winter carnival.

February (Lachute to Hull)
Canadian Ski Marathon: Cross-country skiing marathon.

Early April (Province-wide)
Sugaring-off Parties: General festivities accompany collection of maple tree sap.

Late May to Early June (Sherbrooke)
Festival des Cantons: Hayrides, dancing, contests, all-around boisterous good fun.

Mid-June (Matane)
Shrimp Festival: This is a great time to feast on excellent shrimp and salmon.

Late June (Mont St.-Pierre)
Féte du Vol Libre: Hang-gliding festival.

June to August (Mont Orford)
Festival Orford: Performances of the Jeunesses Musicales du Canada draw international talent and are given throughout the summer in Mont Orford park's music center (call, 819/843-398. or write: C.P. 280, Magog, P.Q., J1X 3W8).

Early July (Québec City)
Summer Festival: Features free concerts and lively shows throughout the city.

July (Peribonka to Roberval)
Swimming Marathon: International marathon across Lake St.Jean, followed by a three-day, 265 mile bike race along the lake.

July (Montréal)
Grand Prix Molson: Auto racing.

August (Latuque to Trois-Riviéres)
International Canoe Race.

Provincial Holiday

St.-Jean Baptiste Day
June 24

Packages

Tourisme Québec and the regional Tourist Associations offer literally thousands of tours, excursions and packages.
Farm Vacations: The Agritour Federation and the Québec ministry of Agriculture co-sponsor an inexpensive bed-and-breakfast farm vacation program which offers several possibilities for every season. It's also an interesting alternative for campers. Contact: Fédération des Agritours du Québec, 4545 Piewrre de-Coubbrtin, Montréal, P.Q., H1V 3R2, 514/252-3138.

Excursion to Hydro-electric Developments: Fly into the largest construction site in the world, taking place on rivers emptying into James Bay. This is one of the best ways to get a good look at northern Québec's spectacular landscape (contact: Voyages Marco Polo, 117 rue Ste.-Catherine o, Montréal, P.Q. H3B 1H9, 514/281-1481; or 1430 rue Ste.-Denis, Montréal, P.Q., H2X 3J8, 514/842-3381).

The three most northern Tourist Association can arrange any number of similar excursions for travelers with a penchant for adventure but a distaste for crowds.

North-West Québec: Association touristique Abitibi-Témiscamingue, 212 Ave., du Lac, Rouyn, P.Q.. J9X 4N7; 819-762-8181.

North Shore-Duplessis: Association touristique régionale de Duplessis, Boulevard Laure, Sept-Iles. P.Q., G4R 2X2; 418/962-0808.

New Québec James Bay: Ministere du Tourisme, 710 Place d'you Ville 3rd Floor, Québec, P.Q. G1R 4Y4., 643-2230.

SASKATCHEWAN

The area code for numbers listed in Saskatchewan is 306 unless stated otherwise.

Finding Out

The provinicial government's *Sask Travel* can be very helpful. Its Saskatchewan Travel Guide not only lists and rates accommodations, but also provides additional information concerning campgrounds, parks, resorts, outfitters, and auto tours. Contact Sask Travel at:1919 Saskatchewan Dr.,Regina , SK S4P 4V7. Call 565-2300 or 800/667-7191, toll-free during the summer.

Regina

Sheraton Center, 1818 Victoria Ave., 569-1666. Full-service, luxury hotel; its solarium dome covers indoor pool.

Regina Inn, Broad Street at Victoria Avenue., 306/525-6767. Comparable to the Sheraton; houses a piano bar, comfortable lounge, and excellent steakhouse.

Regina's Westwater Inn, 1717 Victoria Ave., 757-0663. Part of Best Western chain.

Hotel Saskatchewan, Victoria Avenue at Scarth Street, 522-7691. Old-fashioned hotel offers modern accoutrements.

Landmark Inn, 4150 Albert St., 586-5363. Accommodations match those downtown, but rooms are cheaper here.

Relax Inn, 1110 E. Victoria Ave., 565-0455. Modern rooms, indoor pool, but limited food service.

Saskatoon

Sheraton Cavalier, 612 Spadina Crescent East, 652-6770. Ultra-modern rooms and facilities; skytop lounge.

Bessborough Hotel, 601 Spadina Cr. E., 244-5521. Elegant chateau-style hotel, where each room (there are 225) is different.

Holiday Inn, 90 22nd St. E., 244-2311. Dependable service; great location across from Centennial Auditorium.

King George Hotel, 157 2nd Ave, N., 244-6133. Although 80 years old, the lodgings are modern and imaginative.

Travelodge, 106 Circle Dr. 242-8881. Large rooms, set in Saskatoon's north end.

The Senator, 21st St. and 3rd Ave. 244-6141. Old-fashioned hostelry downtown.

Prince Albert

Marlboro Motor Inn, 67 13th St. 763-2643.

Best Western Inn On the Park, 602 36th St., 922-9595.

Swift Current

Travel Lodge Motel, Hwy 1 East. 800/255-3050.

Restaurants/Dining

Saskatchewan's bountiful wheat makes for good homemade breads, while its grain-fed steers provide cuts of beef choice enough for any steak-lover's fantasy. For dessert, blueberry-like "saskatoons," which are native to Saskatchewan.

Regina

L'Habitant, 1711 Victoria Ave., 525-1551. Fine steakhouse with Québecois atmosphere.

Golf's Steakhouse, 1945 Victoria Ave., 525-5808. The menu is ordinary, but the food and sevice are excellent.

Harvest Restaurant, 379 Albert St. North, 543-3777. Canadian prairie dishes; lavish exterior decorations belie relaxing ambience inside.

Geno's, 545 Albert St. N., 949-5455. Regina's best Italian food, including award-winning lasagne.

Mieka's Kitchen,1810 Smith St., 522-6700. Highly-imaginative lean vegetarian fare.

W.K. Chop Suey House, 1717 Saskatchewan Dr., 522-1433. Chinese restaurant is a consistent favorite in Regina.

Saskatoon

Aerial's Cove, Bessborough Hotel, 244-5686. Regina's best seafood, flown in from the Maritimes.

St. Tropez Bistro, 243 3rd Ave. S., 642-1250. Artsy atmosphere; interesting food.

China Inn, 403 33rd St. W., 242-3322. Chinese smorgasbord.

Cousine Nik's, 110 Grosvenor Ave., 274-2020. Greek and Saskatchewan dishes.

Artful Dodger, 119 4th Ave. S., 653-2577. English fare; set in Dickens motif.

John's Prime Ribs, 401 21st. St. E., 244-6384. Ribs, steaks, and other prairie dishes.

Getting Around

By Air: Saskatchewan's two major airports, in Regina and Saskatoon, are served by the following airlines:

Regina Saskatoon
Air Canada 525-4711 625-4181
CP Air 757-2670 664-1179
Norcanair 552-8711 652-7741
Canadian Airlines International 569-2307 665-7688
Frontier Airlines — 244-4488

By Train: For passenger rail service, contact **VIA Rail** or toll-free at 1-800/665-8630.

By Bus: The Saskatchewan Transportation Co. (STC) and **Greyhound Bus Lines** serve the province from the Regina terminal at 2041 Hamilton St., and the Saskatoon station at 50 23rd St. For more information, try calling them in Regina at: 787-3340.

By Car: The speed limit in Saskatchewan is 80 kph (50 mph). Free maps are available from Sask Travel or any other travel bureau in the province. Remember that wearing seatbelts is compulsory in Saskatchewan, under penalty of fines.

Regina

Taxis are readily available downtown; otherwise, Capital Cab (522-6621) is a popular choice to call for a pick-up. Regina Transit (569-7777) runs several bus routes through the city.

Saskatoon

For a taxi, call United at 652-2222, but at $1.20 a mile, they're expensive.

Museums and Galleries

Regina

Royal Canadian Mounted Police Barracks and Museum, Dewdney Avenue, 780-5838. There's no better way to learn about "Mounties" and their fascinating history than to visit this museum and barracks (open weekdays, 8 a.m. — 5 p.m.).

Museum of Natural History, Corner of College Avenue and Albert Street, 565-565-2815). Considered one of the finest museums of its kind in Canada, its exhibits provide a fascinating introduction to the province (open daily 9 a.m. - 6 p.m.).

Saskatoon

Mendel Art Gallery, 950 Spadina Crescent, 664-9610. Aside from its collection of European and Canadian (including *Group of Seven*) artwork, the gallery arranges exhibits featuring Saskatchewan and prairie art (open daily, 10 a.m. - 10 p.m.).

Western Development Museum, 2610 Lorne Ave., in Saskatchimo Exhibition Grounds, 931-1910. The museum's big draw is its "Boomtown Saskatchewan" exhibit, an intriguing reconstruction of a Saskatoon neighborhood circa 1910, complete with authentic smells and sounds, as well as sights. Sizable collection of vintage car and tractors is also noteworthy (open daily, 9 a.m. — 9 p.m.; admission: $2.50).

Performing Arts

Regina

Regina's major dance, theater, and symphony performances are held at the **Saskatchewan Center of the Arts**, on 200 Lakeshore Dr. Call the box office (584-5555) for more information.

The small, intimate **Globe Theater** at 1801 Scarth St. (525-9553) offers theater-in-the-round.

Saskatoon

The Centennial Center on Auditorium Avenue at 22nd Street (975-7777) hosts Saskatoon's main concert and entertainment events.

The Twenty-fifth Street Theater is a professional dance company performing at the Saskatoon Theater Center on 20th Street and Avenue H (343-9966).

Nightlife

The nightlife here suffers from Saskatchewan's teetotalling past (dancing in establishments which sold liquor was illegal until 1979), but visitors with a penchant for stepping-out find yearly more hot-spots, particularly in **Regina** and **Saskatoon**. In smaller towns, the nightlife tends to center around the hotels and resorts. Saskatchewan's drinking age is 19.

Regina

China Doll, Northgate Shopping Center 352-122. Laid back piano bar.

WH Shooters, 2075 Broad St. Country and Western.

Saskatoon

Fast Freddie's, Park Town Hotel, 942

Spadina Cr. E. Younger singles come here to dance and meet the opposite sex.

Top of the Inn, Sheraton Hotel, 612 Spadina Cr. E. Dancing to lighter music.

Artful Dodger, 119 4th Ave. S. English Pub.

Samurai Lounge, Bessborough Hotel, 601 Spadina Cr. E. Pleasant spot for relaxed conversation.

For foot-stomping country and western music, try **Bar K Ranch House**, 2415, 22nd St. W.

Sports, Recreation and Parks

For information on sports and recreation in Saskatchewan, contact the Dept. of Parks, Recreation and Culture, 3211 Albert St., Regina, SK S4S 5W6; 787-2700.

The people of Saskatchewan love curling, and nearly every small town has a bonspiel in January or February. Hiking and cross-country skiing are popular, especially through the national and provincial parks. Saskatchewan has lots of surface water—over 30,000 sq. mi. of it, to be exact—so water sports are a favorite. Among them, canoeing is probably the best. The province has laid out nearly 60 routes, for amateur and veteran alike. Canoe outfitters can put together a package to suit any need by arranging lodgings, food, and equipment rentals as necessary. Contact SaskTravel for more information about canoe vacations and a list of tours and outfitters.

Hunters will find large game as well as several species of birds available in Saskatchewan. For fishermen, the province's northern lakes and streams offer an abundance of catch, including: trout, northern pike, and Arctic grayling. For information about fly-or drive-in camps, outfitters, licenses, etc., contact the Dept. of Tourism and Renewable Resources.

Saskatchewan has 17 provincial parks, scattered throughout its southern prairies and northern forests. They stay open from mid-May to early September, or slightly later in some cases. Cabins can be rented, but camping-out gives a visitor more flexibility. Camping fees range from $6-$10. As a general rule, it's best to contact *SaskTravel* in advance to reserve a campsite.

Prince Albert National Park: The area around **Waskesiu** is a favorite of the recrea-tion-minded who come regularly to lawn bowl, play tennis and golf, or sail. However, this national park is more than big enough to accommodate those looking for a more secluded wilderness escape. Bear, moose, and elk roam freely within its 1500 square miles enclosure. The park is also home to Canada's largest colony of white pelicans. For further information, Prince Albert National Park, Waskesiu Lake, Box 100, 'Saskatchewan SOJ 21O; 663-5322.

Attractions

Saskatoon

Saskatoon (along with Manitoba) may be Canada's breadbasket, but one of its most important resources, potash, lies 3500 feet below the fertile topsoil. If visitors are not claustropobic, and can make reservations at least a month in advance, then try to take a mine tour. It's a great way to get a feel for Saskatchewan, since potash mining, refining, and distribution is a principal source of livelihood in the province. Besides, the tour is both fun and educational. Contact Tours, Industrial Relations, Potash Corporation of Saskatchewan, Sedo Center, Saskatoon, SK S7K 3Y5; 935-8500.

Diary

Second Week of July (Saskatoon)
   Pioneer Days: This is a popular, week-long fair featuring contests, historical displays, horseracing, and livestock exhibitions. For more information, contact Pioneer Days, Box 407, Saskatoon, SK; 665-8344.

July (Battleford)
   Saskatchewan Crafts Festival: Attracts handicraft enthusiasts from throughout the region.

First week in August (Regina)
   Buffalo Days: This 10-day celebration harks back to the "pioneer days," when bison roamed the prairies. Beard-growing contest, livestock judging, horseracing, and grandstand entertainment are just some of the events on the itinerary. Contact Buffalo Days, Box 1533, Regina. SK: 527-4658, for more details.

Packages

Farm Vacations: There are farm vacations and then there are Saskatchewan farm vacations. Time and again, travelers return home with glowing accounts of their stay on a Saskatchewan farm: the hearty home-cooking, the fresh air, even sharing the chores, are often raved about. Camping on a farm can also be arranged. *SaskTravel* had a list of participating farms, but Mrs Irene Lightbody (Secretary, Saskatchewan Farm Vacations Association, Box 24, Bateman, SK SOH OEO; 648-3530) can provide more details.

Canoe Trips/Vacations: See "Sports, Recreation, and Parks."

YUKON

Finding Out

Tourism Yukon provides a wealth of information for visitors to the territory. Its *Come on in to Canada's Yukon* booklet lists lodgings, restaurants, service stations,and comes with a road map. This, and other brochures, can be obtained by contacting Tourism Yukon at Box 2703, Whitehorse, Yukon, Y1A 2C6, 403/667-5340

Accommodations

Yukon offers a good variety of lodgings. Make reservations early in the year for the crowded summer months. As a general rule, the territory's hotels and motels equal those in southern Canada, except in price: rooms in Yukon are more expensive. *Tourism Yukon* provides a complete list of accommodations, but a representative sampling is offered below.

Whitehorse

Westmark Klondike Inn, 9288 Second Ave., 403/668-474. Modern hotel with nice touches, great view of the mountains. Cocktail lounge, cabaret on the premises.

Airline Inn, 16 Burns Rd., 403/668-4400. Newer, alpinish hotel, steps from the airport.

Regina Hotel, 102 Wood St., 403/667-7801. Though remodeled, hostelry dates to early days of territory. Large, tasteful rooms.

Yukon Inn, 4220 Fourth Ave., 403/667-2527. Modern, spacious rooms. Two lounges: a cabaret and a singles' haunt.

Whitehorse Center Motor Inn, 206 Jarvis St., 403/668-4567. 30 rooms, some with kitchenettes. Licensed lounge, parking available.

Haines Junction

Kluane Park Inn, 403/643-2261. Open all year; licensed lounge.

Dawson City

Downtown Hotel, Box 780, 403/993-5076.

Restaurants/Dining

Yukon meals still reflect the influence of hunters and trappers. Sheep, bear, rabbit, and squirrel find their way onto menus in this territory, but an old favorite is moose. Salmon and Arctic grayling add a little variety. Sourdough biscuits, made simply with flour, water, and nautral yeast, are a Yukon staple.

Most restaurants also offer traditional dishes, be they hamburgers, pizzas, or omelettes. Outside Whitehorse, the best bet is usually your hotel or resort dining room.

Whitehorse

Sam and Andy's 506 Main St., 668-6994. Mexican food.

Golden Garter, 212 Main St., 403/667-2626. French entrees; emphasizes seafood. Closed Sunday.

Golden Horse Restaurant, 38 Lewes Blvd, 668-7878, Peking Style Chinese food.

Getting Around

By Air: CP Air (403/668-3633) flies from **Edmonton** and **Vancouver** to **Whitehorse**, where smaller carriers and charters offer service to the rest of the North. A limousine ($6) shuttles between Whitehorse and the airport.

By Rail: There's a rail line between **Whitehorse** and **Skagway Alaska**. An exciting all-day excursion, the train travels through breathtaking mountain passes and alongside gorgeous Lake Bennett. Skagway boasts ferry connections to **Prince Rupert** and **Vancouver**; see B.C.'s Getting Around section.

For more details, contact White Pass and Yukon Railroad, P.O. Box 2147, Seattle, WA USA 98111; 206/623-2512.

By Bus: Greyhound and **Coachways** travel from **Edmonton** to **Whitehorse**, then along the Alaska and Klondike Highways through Yukon.

By Car: The speed limit is 80 kph (50 mph). Yukon roads are well maintained, but all unpaved. The Alaska Hwy runs from **Dawson Creek**, Alberta through **Whitehorse** and **Haines Junction**, Yukon, and on into Alaska. The Klondike Hwy cuts north from **Whitehorse** to **Dawson**, where it splits into the Dempster Hwy which runs due north to **Inuvik**, N.W.T. and The Top of the World Hwy which drops west into Alaska. A new road (Hwy 2) is now open between **Skagway** and **Whitehorse**.

These are gravel roads, open year-round, but travel is recommended only between June and October. Service stations can be found at regular intervals, but frequent fill-ups are advised. Any trek should be planned and undertaken with great care, following these recommendations:

Gravel is thrown up constantly, so expect some nicks. Cover headlights with plastic covers and protect the bottom of your gas tank with a rubber mat. Most travelers cover their radiator grills tank with wire mesh. Slow down when passing or approaching other vehicles.

Headlights must remain on at all times.

In the summer, dust can be a problem. Open the vents, but shut your windows.

When journeying between October and April, make sure that the vehicle is properly winterized.

Before starting, ensure that the vehicle is in good working order. Bring at least two spare tires.

Enjoy the magnificent scenery.

Whitehorse

For taxi bookings, call the Yellow Cab at 403/668-4811.

Nightlife

Yukon's drinking age is 19; bar-time is 2 a.m. Most hotels sport licensed restaurants and lounges, and in the summer, when Yukon swells with visitors, the nightlife resembles that of southern Canada. One locale of special note is in Dawson City.

Named after a gold rush belle of (ill-) repute. **Diamond Tooth Gertie's** on Queen Street is Canada's only legal gambling casino. The action starts at 8 p.m. sharp, but the stakes stay pretty low most of the time. The decorations and entertainment, however, are pure Klondike. Closed Sundays and Tuesdays.

Sports, Recreation and Parks

Yukon is a haven for canoeists of intermediate level or better. The Stewart and Yukon Rivers are fairly tame. The Klondike and Big Salmon, conversely, can be challenging and treacherous. In any event, non-residents must register with the RCMP, while all canoeists should remember to bring emergency supplies.

Hiking is popular, though Yukon's jagged terrain means that this often entails rock or mountain climbing as well. **Kluane National Park** is a favorite for this, but Tourism Yukon can give details about hiking and climbing throughout the territory.

Essentially a wilderness, Yukon is perfect for fishing and hunting. Obtain a license from Tourism Yukon ($5-$20), then cast for trout, Arctic grayling, salmon, and northern pike. Some of the best fishing spots lie just off the main roads although some prefer the more obscure fly-in camps and lodges.

The **Hospitality Yukon** booklet describes fishing opportunities and lists fishing lodges.

Big game and bird hunting is possible during the prescribed season (usually in fall). Non-resident hunters must be accompanied by a licensed guide. For more information on regulations, seasons, limits, and outfitters, write the Director of Game, Box 2703, Whitehorse, Y1A 2C6.

For more details about wilderness or adventure tours and packages, see the Special Packages section.

Numerous camp grounds, many with modern facilities and hook-ups, dot Yukon, especially along the highways. bring a tent, camper, or trailer. Contact Tourism Yukon for more details.

Kluane National Park

Mile 1019, Alaska Hwy., Haines Junction, Yukon, YOB 1LO; 403/634-2251. This large park occupies the entire southwest corner of Yukon Territory. The terrain consists largely of ice-fields, glaciered plateaus, and rugged hills, punctuated by the stupendous St. Elias Mountains, including Mount Logan (19,500 ft—6,500 m) and Mount St. Elias (18,000 ft—6,000 m). It is also known for its lakes, streams, marshlands, and coastal sand dunes. People come here to mountain climb, hike, canoe, camp, and marvel at the abundant wildlife. The park's interior is accessible by plane only usually chartered in **Haines Junction**. Visitors are strongly encouraged to bring guides.

Attractions

Whitehorse

The MacBride Museum, First Avenue. This log cabin structure is filled with artifacts dating to the gold-rush, alongside commendable Yukon wildlife displays (open daily, May—September; $2.50).

S.S.Klondike, Second Avenue. This restored sternwheeler is now open to the public (guided tours daily until 5:30 p.m., June—September; 403/667-4511).

Miles Canyon Boat Trip, Atlas Travel, 208 Steele St., 403/668-3161. Twice daily, the *M.V. Schwatka* departs for a two-mile (3 km) tour rapids, lined by towering basalt walls. Hydroelectirc projects downstream have slowed the current, but the cruise remains exciting (June—mid-September; $14, including transportation).

Dawson

Dawson City Museum, Museum exhibits the region human history, including over 25,000 gold rush artifacts (open daily, June—September; $3).

Palace Grand Theater, King Street. This ancient pinewood theater now sponsors a variety of performances, including drama and opera. It's famed, however, for its vaudevillan "Gaslight Follies," performed nightly (except Tuesday) at 8 p.m. during the summer.

S.S.Keno, King at Front Street. Known as the last of the sternwheelers, the 65 year old *Keno* has not fired up her boilers since 1960 (daily guided tours, June — mid-September).

Special Packages

Wilderness, adventure, and sightseeing tours abound in Yukon. They can last from two hours to two weeks. A few examples are noted below, but for complete details, contact Tourism Yukon.

Marvel Travel Service, Box 220, Cassiar, B.C. VOC 1EO; 604778-7720. Arranges cruises and ferries.

Klondike Travel Ltd., P.O. Box 417, Dawson City, Yukon YOB 1GO; 403/993-5200. Delightlful adventure and sightseeing charters.

The Marlin Advantage, 204C Main St., Whitehorse, Yukon; 403/668-2867. Tour packages and cruises. They have a toll-free number 800/661-0417.

Diary

June 21 (Dawson)
   Night of the Midnight Sun: The night when locals can boast that the "sun never sets on Dawson." Well, almost.

Third weekend in August (Dawson)
   Discovery Day: Parades, dancing, races, and general merriment to celebrate the anniversary of the discovery of gold near Dawson City.

Last week in February (Whitehorse)
   Sourdough Rendezvous: Native born Yukoners call themselves "sourdoughs," after those famous biscuits. Their rendezvous is a week-long bash celebrating the Klondike days. It includes such local traditions as dog-sled races, dressing up in '98 costumes, and drinking heavily at the nightly cabarets.

Territorial Holiday

Civic Holiday
First Monday in August.

ART/PHOTO CREDITS

Cover	Joe Viesti	41	Joe Viesti	83	Joe Viesti
3	Harry M. Walker	42	Joe Viesti	84L	M. Hetier
5	Joe Viesti	43	Joe Viesti	84R	Joe Viesti
6/7	D. Wilkins	44	Joe Viesti	85L	Joe Viesti
8/9	Charles Shugart	45	By Courtesy of Archives Canada, C W Jefferys	85R	Joe Viesti
10/11	Joe Viesti	46	D. L. Aubry	86L	Joe Viesti
12/13	Joe Viesti	47	By Courtesy of Archives Canada, L'Iris 1863	86R	Joe Viesti
14	Joe Terbasket	48/49	By Courtesy of Archives Canada, Robert Harris	87L	Joe Viesti
16/17	Pat Canova	50	By Courtesy of Ontario Archives	87R	Joe Viesti
18/19	Joe Viesti	51	By Courtesy of Ontario Archives	88L	Joe Viesti
20	Joe Viesti	52	By Courtesy of Ontario Archives	88R	Joe Viesti
22	By Courtesy of Archives Canada	54	By Courtesy of Archives Canada, C W Jefferys	89L	Joe Viesti
23	Maxine Cass	55	By Courtesy of Ontario Archives	89R	Joe Viesti
24	By Courtesy of Ontario Archives	56/57	Joe Viesti	90	Tony Stone Worldwide
25	By Courtesy of Ontario Archives	58/59	Sue Fleishman	91	Harry M. Walker
26	Joe Viesti	60	Joe Viesti	92	By Courtesy of Ontario Archives
27	Joe Viesti	61	D. L. Aubry	93	By Courtesy of Archives Canada
28/29	Joe Viesti	62	Joe Viesti	94	Harry M. Walker
30	By Courtesy of Archives Canada	63	Joe Viesti	95	Harry M. Walker
31	Terence Barrow	64	Joe Viesti	96	Harry M. Walker
32	By Courtesy of Archives Canada, C W Jefferys	65	Joe Viesti	97	Tony Stone Worldwide
33	By Courtesy of Archives Canada	66/67	D. Richard	98/99	M. Hetier
34	Joe Viesti	68/69	By Courtesy of Ontario Archives	100/101	Joe Viesti
35	Joe Viesti	70	Joe Viesti	102/103	Joe Viesti
36	By Courtesy of Archives Canada	71	By Courtesy of Ontario Archives	104/105	Tony Stone Worldwide
37	By Courtesy of Archives Canada, C W Jefferys	72	By Courtesy of Ontario Archives	106	Joe Viesti
38	By Courtesy of Archives Canada, C Kreignoff	73	By Courtesy of Ontario Archives	110/111	Joe Viesti
39	By Courtesy of Archives Canada, C Kreignoff	74L	By Courtesy of Ontario Archives	112	Joe Viesti
40	By Courtesy of Archives Canada, C Kreignoff	74R	By Courtesy of Ontario Archives	113	Joe Viesti
		76	Maxine Cass	115	Joe Viesti
		78	Joe Viesti	116	Joe Viesti
		79	By Courtesy of Archives Canada	117L	Joe Viesti
		80	Joe Viesti	117R	Joe Viesti
		81	Joe Viesti	118	Joe Viesti
		82	Pat Canova	119	Joe Viesti
				120	M. Hetier
				122	Joe Viesti
				123L	Joe Viesti
				123R	Joe Viesti
				124	Joe Viesti
				125	Joe Viesti
				126	Joe Viesti
				127	Joe Viesti
				128	Joe Viesti
				129	By Courtesy of Ontario Archives
				130	D. Wilkins
				131	Joe Viesti

INDEX